THE
MODERN
TEXT-BOOK
OF
ASTROLOGY

By William Lilly. As penned by him in 1647. Inscribed and presented to **The Faculty of Astrological Studies**, 1951.

' My Friend, whoever thou art, that with so much ease shalt receive the benefits of my hard studies, and doest intend to proceed in this heavenly knowledge of the starres ; In the first place, consider and admire thy Creator, be thankfull unto him, and be humble, and let no naturall knowledge, how profound or transcendant soever it be, elate thy mind to neglect that Divine Providence, by whose al-seeing order and appointment all things heavenly and earthly have their constant motion : the more thy knowledge is enlarged, the more doe thou magnify the power and wisdome of Almighty God, the purer judgement thou shalt give.'

By Francis Thompson
' All things, by Immortal Power,
Near and far,
Hiddenly,
To each other linkéd are.'

By Lincoln Barnett
' Einstein's objective in the broadest sense is to show that all forms of nature—stars, planets, light, electricity and possibly even the tiny particles inside the atom—obey the same basic universal laws.'

By Carl G. Jung
' Whatever is born or done this moment of time, has the qualities of this moment of time.'

THE
MODERN
TEXT-BOOK
OF
ASTROLOGY

by

MARGARET E. HONE
D.F.Astrol.S.

Principal of the Faculty of Astrological Studies
1954–1969

L. N. FOWLER & CO. LTD.
1201/3 HIGH ROAD, CHADWELL HEATH
ROMFORD, ESSEX RM6 4DH

This book is dedicated to

CHARLES E. O. CARTER

B.A., D.F.Astrol.S.

President Emeritus of the Astrological Lodge of London
Principal Emeritus of the Faculty of Astrological Studies
Author of many books on Astrology

His work has followed that of the late Alan Leo (1860–1917). Through his careful and scholarly writings, and his Libran chairmanship of the Astrological Lodge of London, the Headquarters of Astrology in Great Britain, the " Royal Art " has flourished in this century, has been purged of many of its superstitions and has gained the respect of all who give time to its study.

First edition December, 1951

Revised and Enlarged July, 1955

First Impression January, 1958

Second Impression January, 1962

Third Impression December, 1964

Revised Edition July, 1967

Fourth Edition (Revised) July, 1968

Reprinted May, 1969

Reprinted September, 1969

Reprinted May, 1970

Reprinted August, 1971

Revised Edition April, 1972

Reprinted October, 1973

Reprinted January, 1975

Revised Edition January, 1978

Reprinted November, 1980

Reprinted September, 1986

Printed and bound in Great Britain at The Camelot Press Ltd, Southampton

S.B.N. 85243 357-3

CONTENTS

CONTENTS

DIAGRAMS, CHARTS AND TABLES

Diagrams by William G. Kingswell
Picture on page 45 by Miss Phyllis Dolton

PREFACE

It gives me great pleasure to send a few introductory words to this notable work, for such it is.

It is a considerable time since a new text-book on astrology has appeared in Great Britain. On examination the reader will appreciate that this is, in the best sense, an ambitious work, designed to set a fresh and higher standard of astrological achievement in text-books. I can bear personal witness that neither trouble nor expense has been spared to produce completeness ; but I believe equally that padding has been rigorously excluded. Thus, if the price is, necessarily in these days, high, the purchaser may know that he is paying for substance and not for mere verbiage, of which there is none.

The diagrams merit special mention for their clarity and beautiful workmanship.

A glance at the Index will serve to show that much is included that is highly interesting to anyone studying astrology with the background of a wide general culture, but which has never before appeared, to my knowledge, in an English work of this kind. Chapter XVII, ' The Historical Background,' is a case in point.

Naturally, in a subject such as astrology, there are many differences of opinion even on fundamentals, and differences, too, as to how the art should be taught. As for this latter, much must depend on the intelligence of the pupil, and his or her previous studies. Hitherto most students, it is to be feared, have learnt their methods largely by rote, with only a limited understanding of the reasons for what they did. In this book the authoress has sought to correct this common defect and to lead the student to technical proficiency in a manner that will enable him to understand not only what he is doing, but also why.

Another feature that merits commendation is the lack of dogmatism that characterises the work. Varying opinions are given fair play, and Mrs. Hone does not force her own views down the reader's throat in the somewhat arrogant manner employed by less fair-minded writers, especially in the old days.

Yet another point to be applauded is the inclusion of carefully worded definitions; and similarly the key-word system is used in a way that is both practical and theoretically sound.

One may in fact assert that a student will need no other library than this book for some considerable time ; and he might indeed be wise if he confines his reading to it for several months, thus gaining a comprehensive basis for his astrological investigations before adding to his library. When he feels ready to take this step, he will find guidance in the Appendix.

The authoress has generously acknowledged the help she has received in compiling this work, a matter which, it has been said, natives of Leo are sometimes prone to overlook. But the book bears throughout the stamp of her own vivid and comprehensive mentality. It will unquestionably be a guide and help to many— and not only to beginners.

CHARLES E. O. CARTER

ADDENDA:

Summer Time in Great Britain

1956	22 April to 7 Oct.			1963	31 March to 27 Oct.			
1957	14 , to 6 ,,			1964	22 ,, to 25 ,,			
1958	20 ,, to 5 ,,			1965	21 ,, to 24 ,,			
1959	19 ,, to 4 ,,			1966	20 ,, to 23 ,,			
1960	10 ,, to 2 ,,			1967	19 ,, to 29 ,,			
1961	26 March to 29 ,,			1968	18 Feb. to 31 Oct. 1971			
1962	25 ,, to 28 ,,			1972	19 March to 29 ,,			

(One hour advanced of G.M.T.)

ERRATA

p. 20 (4th line from bottom, small type) *for* The student is asked by buy . . . , *read* The student is asked to buy. . . .

p. 87 (3rd line from bottom) *for* those of the planet ruling them, *read* those of the sign ruling them. . . .

p. 102 1945 *for* Dec. 31st *read* Oct. 7th.

p. 117 (6th line from bottom) *for* 20ʰ 58ᵐ 04ˢ, *read* 20ʰ 58ᵐ 02ˢ.

p. 129 (Bracketed explanation under Fig. 15) *for* (As for Fig. 10 . . .) *read* (As for Fig. 13 . . .).

p. 130 (Bracketed explanation under Fig. 16) *for* (As for Fig. 11 . . .) *read* (As for Fig. 14 . . .).

p. 139 Fig. 21 : 4°53 ♀,♒ has been omitted from 8th house; Mercury should be Aquarius 21°28 (not 21°48); Saturn should be Virgo 16°25 ret. (not 16°55 ret.).

p. 140 Fig. 22: Venus should be Aquarius 4°53 (not 4°33); Saturn should be Virgo 16°25 ret. (not 16°55 ret.); Mercury should be Aquarius 21°28 (not 21°48).

p. 181 (Line 24) *for* Fig. 3 *read* Fig. 4; *for* element *read* quality;
(Line 27) *for* 4° Leo, *read* 26° Leo.
(Line 28) *for* 26° Gemini, *read* 4° Gemini.

pp. 200–201 John Smith chart: Venus should be retrograde; the result of the sidereal time noon G.M.T. added to interval reads 8.52.37, but this should read 8.32.37; Mars should be trine Ascendant; Saturn BQ Uranus; Venus □ Mars. ☽ 's Declination should be 11°57S.

Facing p. 222 John Smith chart: Venus should be retrograde; *for* Mars 28°50, *read* 28°56; Moon's Declination should read 11.57 S; Mars should be trine Ascendant; Venus should be □ Mars, Saturn BQ Uranus.

Between pp. 222–3 John Smith prog. chart: Progressed Moon should be quincunx Venus progressed in December 1949, and opposition Mercury progressed in March 1950; Mutual aspects: for *Mercury quincunx Mars 49*, read Mercury quincunx Mars. p. 49. Venus should be retrograde.

p. 319 *for* Primary system, 224, *read* Primary system, 225.

p. 319 *for* Pole, of equator, 109, 183; of ecliptic, 125, 183 . . . *read* Pole, of equator, 109, 182; of ecliptic, 125, 182.

INTRODUCTION

This book is written after many years of astrological practice, during which a system of teaching has been built up.

The experience of contact with successive classes of students who have tried to teach themselves from books has shown that, while all can theorise on the planets, the signs and the houses, few can be systematic in their lay-out of work preparatory to a lucid and comprehensive interpretation of a natal chart, or arrange for an over-all survey of several years of a life, so as to indicate its trends.

With the aim of improving and facilitating the work of those who wish to use astrology either as their main or their subsidiaı y profession, or to use it as an interesting spare-time occupation, more detailed teaching and more examples of work done in actual practice have been given than has been customary in text-books of the past.

Experience of partly-taught students has also brought to light the fact that few have any understanding of either the astronomical or historical backgrounds of their study. Therefore a change in presentation has been made in that much information about both of these has been included in chapters on working methods to which they are relative.

It has been found that a teaching period should be divided into an informatory and theoretical part, and a practical part, the student thus remembering the unaccustomed facts more easily because they are relevant to the work done.

By such tuition, taken either in class or in home study, it is hoped that the notion that " learning astrology " consists of the immediate acquisition of a fragmentary idea of chart construction and an unrelated series of delineations of factors will be completely eradicated from the minds of modern students.

Such knowledge is only part of a great whole, which should be the steadily accumulated store of the properly grounded and informed student.

I should like to express my grateful thanks for the help and friendly criticism which has been given by those who have read this book for me, Mr. Charles E. O. Carter, B.A., Brigadier R. C. Firebrace, C.B.E. and Mr. R. M. Trotter; also to Mr. J. M. Filbey for the checking of computations and planetary significators.

MARGARET E. HONE

LONDON, 1950

INTRODUCTION TO SECOND EDITION

In this second edition, no major changes have been made. Figures 2, 9 and 11 in which there were errors have been re-drawn. Additions which have been thought advisable have been added at the ends of chapters 8, 9 and 10. The formation of the houses by the Placidean system has been more clearly explained.

The main changes are in Chapter 15 which has been brought up to date by the recommendation of Mr. Carter's new book on Political Astrology instead of the earlier one mentioned : by leaving the new edition of the *Encyclopaedia of Psychological Astrology* by the same author as the only book suggested under the heading of Degree Meanings (with some alteration of text) ; by changing the section on the Pre-natal Epoch in the light of research recently completed ; lastly, by adding a note on the constellations to Section 7, naming recently written informative books.

Much has happened since the writing of the first edition of this book. To my gratification, it was adopted as the official text-book for the use of students of the Faculty of Astrological Studies. Based upon it as text-book, I was able to construct the three graded *Courses for External Students,* and then to write *Applied Astrology,* in which book the system of interpretation of astrological charts, as put forward in the text-book, could be demonstrated in its application to the analyses of the birth charts of various people, thus repeating in different ways chapters 11 and 12 of the present book. These have perhaps brought more letters of appreciation than any other chapters.

The circulation of the books and of the Courses for External Students has changed the field of my work beyond any expectation. The world seems to have become a small and friendly place, lessening in size because of the apparent closeness of the many writers of air-mail letters from far-away countries with whom correspondence is carried on.

The system of interpretation has proved its worth by the excellence of the examination work done by those trained on it from their start as students.

By founding a Research Section in connection with the Faculty and opening a Research Fund, a beginning has been made towards meeting the modern necessity of controlling the banks of the growing river of astrology. As was pointed out at the beginning of Chapter 17, this must be done by students who will work to provide proof and reasoning.

It has been suggested that the serious work of astrology should be given the more modern name of *The Cosmic Correlation Theory.* The advisability of changing old names is debatable but the profound idea embodied in the new name is one for which all thoughtful astrologers wish to bring supporting evidence. It is hoped to do this in modern statistical manner, the time having gone by in which arbitrary statements can be put forward with any hope of acceptance.

If my work helps in any way to achieve this great aim, I shall feel richly rewarded.

MARGARET E. HONE

LONDON, 1954

CHAPTER I

INTRODUCTION TO THE MODERN SITUATION IN ASTROLOGICAL THOUGHT

THIS book starts with no intention of attempting to include all the vastness of astrological knowledge within its pages. It is written with the idea of giving all *necessary* knowledge to a student who wishes to study and experiment for about a year, followed by a summary of more advanced work for a second year.

The first-year student should read as widely as he can and attend lectures if possible. By the end of such a year, he should be able to discuss general astrological topics with an informed mind ; he should be capable of listening to advanced discussion with reasonable understanding and be able to make and interpret an astrological chart. These charts are simply a method of listing certain factors.

Constant practice with these factors familiarises the student with the principles which he must understand.

Present Situation of the Art of Astrology

Though the earliest knowledge of astrology dates back to the mists of antiquity, it lives and grows and needs constant re-presentation in the light of current research. Its development may well be compared with that of medical knowledge. From time to time, certain treatments have been believed to be the most effective possible. Further experience changes these ideas and differences of opinion are then acknowledged.

One of the greatest handicaps of modern astrology is that work has been done mainly by isolated researchers, thus affording little opportunity for building their work into a solid body of opinion.

1900-49

A great recrudescence of the popular interest in astrology took place in the earlier years of this period, because of the energetic writing of certain authors in books and technical magazines. These were careful to put forward varying points of view.

Over-Simplification

These writings were followed in the later period by many which have been excellent, but which have often made an understandable attempt to carve a clear line through such points of controversy, in the interest of simplification. A result of this has been to give an impression of settled opinion on many points which are by no means settled, and which indeed may be beyond the finiteness of man to settle.

Newspaper " Astrology "

During this time the popular press began to realise that members of the public were interested in forecasts and in trying to understand themselves by means of descriptions of persons born in certain months. The war brought about an added keenness to know what might be expected of the future in the sphere of political activity.

The work necessary for this is highly technical and needs wide knowledge of world conditions before astrological deductions can be made. These were not always correct any more than the diagnoses of doctors are infallible. The efforts of the very few astrologers who specialised in this way were copied by others less well informed, with the result that the wide publicity given their failures led readers to discredit what they imagined to be the whole of ' astrology'.

Journalists now began to publish character descriptions and personal forecasts based on the one and only factor known to the public, the month of the birth-day. As the student will soon learn, this is but one of *many* factors. The discerning reader soon saw that such descriptions might fit one acquaintance born in the month mentioned, but were totally inadequate for others.

These writers did not hesitate to bestow upon their remarks such technical names as ' Astrology ', ' Horoscope ', etc. The depths of over-simplification were now reached, and, since the average educated person has never read a sound book on the subject but has formed his ideas from its travesty thus publicised, the art has been further discredited.

The Swing of Public Opinion

The ending of the war has freed astrological workers from tasks of national importance and has reopened channels of communication with workers in other countries. These are writing and lecturing and there is now no excuse for the un-informed attitude of the critics of the art. Until he has learnt enough to enable him to meet such arguments properly, the student is advised to ask his critic whether he has ever read a serious book on the subject and whether he has ever attended an informative lecture ? If the answer is in the usual negative, he can then point out that argument with the ignorant is hardly worth while.

General education enables a person to be critical. The average educated adult is now aware that he must not be misled either by fallacies of over-simplification or by the biased opinions of those who have academic status in other fields of learning and use this to induce their hearers or readers to believe that their ideas on astrology must therefore have validity. To quote one instance, such methods were made very obvious when it became known, by his own admission, that the writer of a book which by its title purported to be about Astrology, did not even know how to cast and interpret a horoscope. He therefore had no practical knowledge of the working of this art, which he attempted to discredit in his book.

Such public awareness to the pitfalls of lack of information has naturally led to a desire to know more of the truth.

Present Legality of Astrological Practice

The Witchcraft Act of 1735 and the Vagrancy Act of 1829 include those who practice astrology as ' charlatans, rogues and vagabonds ', and imply that ' fortune-telling ' is illegal.

The entire basis of astrology rests on the premise that the ' pattern ' of a person correlates with the planetary pattern of his birth-moment. The pattern will, at times, exteriorise as ' events'. The accuracy of these, which can be checked in earlier life, gives the astrologer the belief that tendencies deduced from calculations of future dates may be expected to eventuate as certain types of happenings in later life.

Until these Acts are altered, the astrologer is advised to preface all his remarks with a statement which shows that he realises the position, and conforms with the law of his country in making it plain that he is not dogmatically stating that events *will* happen, but that, from *his point of view*, the likelihood is that tendencies of a certain nature may bring about results of that nature.

The Status of the Astrologer

If the above Act is altered, then astrologers must protect themselves against pseudo-astrologers, as the medical profession has had to protect itself against ' quacks '. As in any other profession, proficiency can only be assessed by examination. To this end, a teaching school has been founded under well-known responsible leadership. Its diploma may be gained by those prepared for examination by its own tutors or by external teachers or correspondence courses. As in medicine, the passing of the examination does not imply that the successful candidate is an expert in his subject. But it does show that he has successfully assimilated that which he has studied and is now fit to do work which will give him the experience by which he may eventually become expert. (See p. 315.)

Modern Presentation of Astrology

What, then, is to be the student's attitude to this subject ? Before he has had time to read widely, he will be pressed to explain what it is all about and why he thinks there is truth in what he is learning. Undoubtedly, he will be asked such questions as ' How can such far-off planets influence the actions of ourselves ? '

At this stage, his best reply is that he believes in no such thing, but that he observes that certain traits of character and certain *types* of events appear to *correlate* with certain planetary relationships. He will be wise to drop the word ' influence ', which implies direct action, but at the same time he must point out that an astrologer uses many words colloquially, knowing full well what they mean to him. He may quote the parallel case of the customary ' How do you do ? ' No one using this expects in return a factual statement of how his friend ' does ' in every detail.

Astrology is NOT A SCIENCE, in the modern meaning of the term, which implies that knowledge is built up through the proving of theories by the repetition of experiments which have the same results, from which certain laws may be formed. The ' results ' of astrology are often *not* ' the same ' in outwardly assessable meaning, but to one used to its symbolism, are ' the same ' in their nature.

Science proves by statistics.   While broad principles of astrology can be proved in this way, the more the student learns, the more he will realise that statistics may be misleading in the assessment of an intricate interlacing of planetary cycles, which are constantly changing in relation to each other, and at varying rates of speed.

Astrology is NOT an innate ABILITY, such as clairvoyance or psychometry or telepathy.   (It must here be stated that many practitioners who have such abilities cannot help but use them as is their natural manner, thus adding intuitively gained detail to their work, which they themselves would explain to be ' extra ' to astrological deduction.   Comparison with medicine again brings to mind the many doctors who ' know ' what is the matter with a patient before they have begun to apply routine clinical tests.)

Definition of Astrology

Since there are as many angles of approach to astrology as to religion or to art, it is not easy to formulate a definition to suit all, but few will find any disagreement with the following :—

ASTROLOGY IS A UNIQUE SYSTEM OF INTERPRETATION OF THE CORRELATION OF PLANETARY ACTION IN HUMAN EXPERIENCE.

This may be expanded by the explanation that astrologers think of the Universe as a *whole*.   This implies that there is a constantly moving relationship between the very large moving objects in it such as the Sun, Moon and planets, and the small moving objects such as human beings and animals.   Furthermore, science has shown us that what we used to call inanimate objects are, in fact, in a constant state of movement, non-observable to us by reason of our limited senses.

Correlation

Astrologers postulate that the movements of *everything* in the universe are *correlated*.   The use of this word conveys a truer meaning than does the older term of ' influence '.

In this vastness, an unproportionate view has been taken of humanity, since it is within the limits of observation of the human senses.

The comparison with medicine again helps to understand astrological method. If a doctor wishes to assess the state of heart or stomach, he does not cut the entire body open to examine these.   He feels the pulse or looks at the tongue, and from his learning and experience makes certain deductions.   Similarly, the astrologer has found out that by determining the positions of Sun, Moon and planets at any time, he can ' chart ' these positions, and, from his learning and experience, can make certain deductions.

Time

A great phrase was moulded by C. G. Jung*, the psychologist, when he wrote : ' Whatever is born, or done, in this moment of time, has the qualities of this moment of time '.

Here is the secret of astrology. It lies in the understanding of TIME, and time guards its secrets.

Psychology of Astrology

Whereas, in even more material days than the present, astrology was used in relation to purely physical happenings, it is now realised that many happenings in a man's life are concurrent with certain psychological states, which in turn spring from an inner motivation. It is the study of man, from this point of view, which is perhaps the strongest trend in MODERN ASTROLOGY.

Freewill

The student will find that no discussion of astrology will ever end without the raising of the subject of freewill. Without experience, he will find it difficult to take his part.

Modern thought on this topic is changing. With the cataclysms that have fallen on the last two generations, it is obvious that man is only free within limits. Synchronisation with a planetary pattern *apparently* denies freewill entirely. An answer to this problem takes the student into the realms of philosophy and religion. Perhaps a true understanding of the latter in its widest sense will provide the only answer.

Inasmuch as a man identifies himself with his physical self and the physical world about him, so he is indissolubly part of it and subject to its changing pattern as formed by the planets in their orbits.

Only by the recognition of that which he senses as greater than himself can he attune himself to what is beyond the terrestrial pattern. In this way, though he may not escape terrestrial happenings, by the doctrine of free and willing ' acceptance ', he can ' will ' that his real self is free in its reaction to them.

* *The Secret of the Golden Flower*, page 143. By C. G. Jung.

CHAPTER 2

HOW TO BEGIN TO LEARN

A SERIOUS student should NOT have omitted the first chapter, thinking it only introductory. It is *necessary* for his information.

It is now essential that he should go through each chapter, *in order*, as the book is so planned that each chapter is explanatory of what comes later. Skipping will only cause confusion, unless under the direction of a competent teacher. (In this case, a separate study could be made of Chapters 6–11.)

First Things

The multiplicity of first things will not dismay the beginner if he will remember that the same trouble arises in learning to drive a car. It does not really matter which of several necessities is learnt first. Before a learner takes his first corner, he has to make it reasonably habitual to change gears, use his accelerator, use his brake, put out his indicator, control his steering, look in the direction in which he intends to go and yet watch for careless pedestrians and possible sudden change in the driving of other cars. To combine all this seems impossible and yet he knows by observation that all his driver friends not only do all at once but at the same time carry on a conversation about completely different mattèrs.

Similarly, before a beginner starts his first attempt at a personal astro-analysis (or ' horoscope ' to use the traditional word) he must list all the factors that he finds in the chart before him, and he cannot do this until he has understood each, if only partially. Fuller understanding comes with practice and he will soon see at a glance, what he has to ponder over at first.

Personal Charts

Why must the beginning be by the study of these ? Because the application of the theory in its working in charts of himself and his intimate friends and relations is the quickest way for him to experience the meaning of the *principles* of the planets, which is the basis of astrological work.

The Pattern of the Moment of Beginning

It appears that the changing planetary pattern is indicative of a changing cosmic pattern. There is constant change in all substances at all moments. Creation never stops.

When anything changes its ' mode ', it may be said to make a new ' beginning '. The postulate of astrology is that, at such a moment, there is a correlation between the characteristics of what is begun, and of the planetary pattern of the moment of beginning.

The Potentialities of the Pattern

This pattern is not static. Just as a baby begins to grow ' old ' from the moment of its birth, so the potentialities of its pattern develop from that moment.

It is the *potentialities for development* which it is the job of the astrologer to assess.

He then evaluates *future trends*. He makes his **deductions** from these. Such deductions depend on the acumen and experience of the astrologer. The very common mistake which has brought contumely on to astrology is to confuse the human deduction which may be right or wrong, with the assessment of the *trend* which can be technically ascertained.

Planetary Principles

As explained when discussing the term influence, astrologers use many colloquialisms which sound wrong to the public but are understood by their users. The Sun and the Moon are customarily included in the term planets, meaning the heavenly bodies. The first task, then, is to realise that each planet embodies, or stands for, what may be termed a *Principle*.

Astronomers suggest that, at one time, the Sun, Moon and planets were enclosed in one body which eventually split, leaving the planets in their order from the Sun as they now are. This may or may not be so, but the idea remains that the principles of the planets seem to be the subdivision of one main principle or driving force behind everything.

Astrological books will be found to state that a planet is benefic, expansive, adaptable, etc. ; that it ' makes ' its natives faithful, original, etc. ; that it ' rules ' old age, churches, love, deceit, etc. An accustomed astrologer knows exactly what this means, and in fact has a great affection for the old terminology of his chosen study.

' Native ' is the term often used for the person whose chart is under scrutiny.

' Rules ' is the term used to decide that the planet has an affinity with certain attributes, traits, behaviours, objects, and people.

It will be found that under the headings of the names of the different planets, signs and houses (explanation Chapters 3, 4, and 5) comes everything which life contains, as if all were placed into their correct compartments in an enormous filing cabinet.

Indeed it may be true that the planets do have this direct effect on human beings, or perhaps that one main unknown power is passed on by each planet with varied results. These are nature's secrets, as yet undiscovered. Astrology does not pretend to explain the *modus operandi*. It only studies the results as it can assess them.

Drives or Urges

From the point of view of psychology, a more modern expression of the same truth is that each planet seems to represent in the person, a certain drive or urge in the unconscious. He is subject to its compulsion but the more he becomes consciously aware of it, the better he can deal with it, for the sake of attaining his own self-understanding and his resultant ability to become a happy member of society. He is also the recipient of the effects of the principles of each planet, through other people and through outer circumstances.

Signs of the Zodiac

These are the traditional divisions of the zodiac which have been handed down to us. Each planet manifests its nature differently when found in each of these signs. They may be termed its MODES of action.

Houses of the Chart

These are divisions of the astrological map which is made by the charting of details, arrived at by calculation from the birth-data. Each one, traditionally, carries a significance of correlation with certain *spheres of life-activity*

Hence the task of the student is to learn how each PRINCIPLE or URGE will manifest in each MODE. Then how the interpretation of each SPHERE of life will be different, according to its connection with PRINCIPLE and MODE.

This triple activity will be modified by many other considerations, to be described later, one of the most important being the angular relationships which each planet may make to the others. The technical word for these is ASPECTS.

Note on the Use of Ephemerides

The student is asked by buy a Raphael's Ephemeris either for the current year or for the year of his birth so that he may see the words and symbols used in the following chapters.

It is more convenient to use one of these for each year as required (see Chapters 6 and 12) but it is more economical, when calculation is understood, to buy a condensed ephemeris for many years.

CHAPTER 3

BASIC CONCEPTS

EVERY text-book repeats one sound piece of advice, which is that the student can never hope to be a quick and practised astrologer if he relies on copying descriptions from his text-book. This may seem a disheartening difficulty at the beginning, but the way out of it is easy.

The student must get an understanding of the *meaning* of each *planet, sign* and *house,* must understand their *strength* in the chart under consideration, and make a *synthesis* of his findings. A text-book has to cover the full meaning of each, but the student is confused if he has to try to pick out from this what may apply in each particular case.

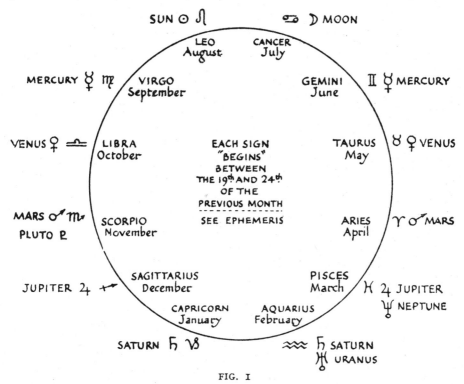

FIG. I

THE PLANETS AND THEIR SYMBOLS, PLACED BESIDE THE SIGNS WHICH THEY RULE, WITH THEIR SYMBOLS AND THE CALENDAR MONTH TO WHICH THEY MAINLY REFER.

The student is asked to copy the diagram again and again, to try to memorise it, but he will find that as soon as he comes to *use* the symbols in it, he will automatically remember it.

A new method of teaching is now used in which the simplest of meanings in one or two words will be given for each and the student can easily learn these and combine them, replacing the obviously stilted phrases which will result by his own characteristic way of speaking.

After this, lists of words will be given which expand the central idea. Later again, more explanatory books on each special detail must be read and lectures heard.

In the northern hemisphere, in which lie most of the countries where astrology has been developed, the temperature is at its greatest in July–August. This is probably the reason why the ancients connected the Sun with the zodiacal sign of Leo, in which it was seen in those months. The body which reflects its light, the Moon, was connected by them with Cancer, the June–July sign, because it could be seen at its highest point in the heavens when entering that sign ; it was particularly noticeable for its brightness around the winter solstice when full in that sign.

The Lights

This term refers to these greater and lesser Lights, i.e., the Sun and Moon. The interpretation of these two in characterology will be found to be highly important. The student can now understand the phrase generally used without any idea of its meaning, ' He acted according to his lights '.

In Fig. 1, the important Lights and their signs are placed at the top, for it is then easy to see that the rest of the planets follow round in the same order, either to the left or to the right. This is, in fact, their order in the heavens, from the central Sun, outwards ; the Moon, of course, pursuing its path round the Earth. This is not so obvious if they are first learnt as a list. It will be noted that each planet rules two signs, but that in three cases, an extra planet is placed below. These are the three which have been discovered in modern times. They are not placed in their order from the Sun but beside the signs which they are now thought to rule.

Rulership

This is the term used to describe the connection between planet and correlative sign or house.

It will also be noted that though each sign corresponds, in the main, with a calendar month, it does not do so exactly, but begins from between the 19th–24th of the previous month. A glance at the Ephemeris shows it to be arranged after the fashion of an almanac, and it will be seen that the date of the sign-change is earliest in the winter months, altering gradually to its latest in the summer months.

The Symbols of the Planets

These may be seen to be composed of different combinations of three parts, ◖ the circle, ◡ or ◗ the half circle, + the cross.

This will have more meaning to the modern student if he understands that they date from the earliest days of mankind before reading was known, when an idea had to be taught to the people in pictorial form.

- ○ The circle is said to symbolise eternity, the never-ending ; hence spirit or primal power.
- ⊙ When a dot is put inside the circle it signifies the beginning of the emergence of that power.
-) ∪ The half-circle signifies soul.
- + The cross signifies the material world.

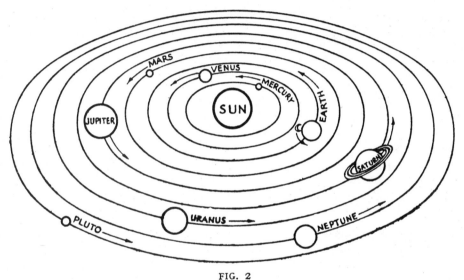

FIG. 2

THE SOLAR SYSTEM. PLANETS AND THEIR ORBITS.
(Diagrammatic. Not to scale.)

THE PLANETS AND THEIR PRINCIPLES : CENTRAL IDEAS

The planets are bodies in the solar system, which revolve in elliptical orbits round the Sun. (They must not be confused with the stars, which shine by their own light, and keep the same relative positions in the heavens. The apparent movement of these is very small but it can be measured over a long period of time.)

Fig. 2 gives an idea of the relative sizes of the planets and their orbits.

An orrery, or working model to illustrate this, can be seen in science museums.

It is named after the fourth Earl of Orrery, in whose day they were first made (1676–1731). An excellent picture of one of these, and also one of a simplified orrery for use by hand, can be seen in a small hand-book.*

* *The Planets and Us.* By D. and K. Bartlett.

Further astronomical information will be required by the keen student or one who is working for examination, but it is better to learn this from books on that subject,* or the Astronomical Supplement to this text-book. (See p. 315.)

The planets are to be studied first of all, because they are the centre and core of astrological tradition. From them comes that which we are to try to interpret as we recognise it in the everyday life of the world.

THE PLANETS AND THEIR PRINCIPLES IN KEYWORD FORM

Sun	Power ; Vitality ; Self-expression.
Moon	Response ; Fluctuation.
Mercury	Communication (mentally and by transport).
Venus	Harmony ; Unison ; Relatedness.
Mars	Energy ; Heat ; Activation.
Jupiter	Expansion ; Preservation.
Saturn	Limitation ; Cold.
Uranus	Change (Revolutionary ; Disruptive ; Dictatorial).
Neptune	Nebulousness ; Impressionability.
Pluto	Elimination ; Renewal ; Regeneration.

Important Note

The above table is given in the attempt to place a *central idea* or keyword in the mind of the student about each planet. He is to clothe this with a wealth of meaning as time goes on, and must not imagine that the above word is by any means all that is to be said.

Introductory Descriptions

To avoid repetition, descriptions will be short and will be expanded and clarified when they can be referred to later in connection with their appropriate signs and houses.

It will be seen later that, in a chart, a planet may be found to be in one or other of the signs or houses, not necessarily its own. It will always show its essential self in the *mode* of that sign and in the *sphere of activity* of that house. It will also bring to that sphere something of the meaning of the sign which it ' naturally ' rules.

Strength of planet in sign. This will be explained later. (p. 148.)

SUN

KEYWORDS :—POWER, VITALITY, SELF-EXPRESSION

This is the most powerful of all the horoscopic factors. When considering a personal chart, the judgment of the *type of person* will depend largely on his *solar* characteristics.

Solar traits are very much those of the sign Leo (p. 59), which is ruled by the

* *The Solar System.* By D. and K. Bartlett.

Sun. They are expressed also in the activities of the 5th house, which is the natural house of this planet and sign.

The real underlying *self* will be largely shown by the placing of the Sun in sign and house and by its strength in the chart. (Chapter 9.) Without the actual Sun, nothing would grow or flourish, hence in astrological interpretation it is understood as the creative principle, the power-giving body, the personal self-expression.

☉   Its symbol is that of Eternity, and of the power of spirit of primal motion, from whence all else issued and was created. It stands for the masculine principle of fatherhood.

SOLAR WORDS

TRUE MEANING	OVERSTRESS OR MISUSE
Dignified	Arrogant
Dominant	Autocratic
Faithful	Averse to any change
Gay	Childishly playful
Good Organiser	Condescending
Magnanimous	Despotic
Open-handed	Domineering
Powerful	Extravagant
Proud	Gushing
Regal	Overbearing
Truly affectionate	Pompous
Vital	Profligate

MOON

KEYWORDS :—RESPONSE, FLUCTUATION

The Moon has no light of her own. She reflects the powerful light of the Sun. But she has movement of her own and her constantly changing phases are reflected on earth by the tides, and in human life by the feminine rhythms.

When considering a personal chart, the judgment of the *outward mannerisms and general behaviour* of the person will depend largely on his *lunar* characteristics.

Lunar traits are very much those of the sign Cancer which is ruled by the Moon. They are expressed also in the activities of the 4th house, which is the natural house of this planet and sign.

A key to the understanding of the 'ability to respond to conditions' of the person will be given by the placing of the Moon by sign and house and by its strength in the chart. It may be understood in this way. The power to respond begins in babyhood, which is the period of life governed by the Moon. At this period, the person is nothing but a bundle of instinctive responses to feelings, such as hunger, discomfort and so on. The adults in charge begin to condition these responses, till the child forms habits and manners, partly by education, partly by copying those around him. These become the adult's outward traits, usually the first to be observed on meeting him. The Moon then will show him in his habitual response to life in general.

☽ Its symbol is that of two semi-circles—part reflections of the power of ' Spirit'. It stands for the feminine principle of motherhood.

LUNAR WORDS

TRUE MEANING	OVERSTRESS OR MISUSE
Changeable	Faulty in reasoning
Good memory	Fussy
Imaginative	Holding to the self
Indrawn	Inverted
Maternal	Over-absorbent of influence
Protective	Over-accumulative
Receptive	Remembering slights
Sensitive	Touchy
Tenacious	Unreliable

MERCURY

KEYWORDS :—COMMUNICATION (MENTALLY, AND BY TRANSPORT)

Much can be learnt of the nature of each planet by thinking of the nature of the god named after it in the old myths, which were the stories of the planets. Mercury was the swift messenger of the gods.

When considering a chart, the judgment of the *mentality* of the person and of his *type of nervous reactions* will depend largely on his *Mercurian* characteristics. Mercurian traits are very much those of the signs Gemini and Virgo, which are ruled by Mercury. They are also expressed in the activities of the 3rd and 6th houses, which are the natural houses of this planet and these signs.

A key to estimate the ability to communicate, or the urge to do so, will be given by the placing of Mercury in sign and house and by its strength in the chart.

It may be understood in this way. The child begins to communicate in early years, the period of which is governed by Mercury. At this period, he begins to talk, to use his hands to bring things to him, to make responses through his nervous system and then to learn and use his mind and to form communications, i.e., contacts, in all ways. He begins to go about and contact other people and other places. Mercury will show his mental and educational ability and general tendency to motion, in action or in getting from place to place.

☿ Its symbol contains all the three basic symbols. The circle of spirit is overpowered by that which is only a part reflection. Below it is combined the symbol of earthly material matters.

It is considered ' neutral ', in that it takes colour from any planet aspecting it, rather than giving to them.

MERCURIAN WORDS

TRUE MEANING	OVERSTRESS OR MISUSE
Adroit	Artful
Apt	Chattering
Clever	Critical
Cool in affection	Diffuse
Expressive	Hair-splitter
Good at detail	Inquisitive
Intelligent	Loquacious
Logical	Nervous
Quickly perceptive	Never heart-felt
Talkative	Slick
Versatile	Sly

VENUS

KEYWORDS :—HARMONY, UNISON, RELATEDNESS

Venus was the goddess of beauty and love. Both forms and colours, people and nations must be united in harmonious relationships in order to achieve the happiness brought by these.

When considering a chart, the power of the person to make close *relationship with others* and his ability to *attract* others into ties of *partnership*, either for business or through affection, will largely depend on his *Venusian* characteristics.

Venusian traits are very much those of the signs Taurus and Libra, which are ruled by Venus. They are expressed also in the activities of the 2nd and 7th houses, which are the natural houses of that planet and these signs.

It may seem strange that the 7th house is sometimes called ' the house of war ' and ' the house of open enmity ', but a relationship has to be formed even before a quarrel can take place and each participant may be impelled by the urge or drive to give shape to his idea of harmony with which the other entirely disagrees.

A key to the understanding of the ability to achieve harmony, or the urge to do so by all forms of affection, beauty, art and partnership, and the possession of lovely things and the money to buy them, will be given by the placing of Venus in sign and house, and by its strength in the chart.

It may be understood in this way. In adolescent years, the period of which is governed by Venus, the person begins to attract and to be attracted to others, to make close ties, to have his own possessions. Venus will show his general ability to attract, to love, to express beauty and harmony in every way.

♀   Its symbol contains the circle of Spirit, having precedence over the cross of matter. In medicine and in all the biological sciences it is still the symbol for the feminine.

VENUSIAN WORDS

TRUE MEANING	OVERSTRESS OR MISUSE
Adaptable	Arty-crafty
Artistic	Indecisive
Companionable	Indefinite
Gentle	In love with love
Graceful	Languid
Harmonious	Lazy
Loving	Never satisfied
Peace-loving	Peace at any price
Placid	Unreliant
Tactful	Weak

MARS

KEYWORDS :—ENERGY, HEAT, ACTIVATION

Again the mythological name helps to show the nature of the planet. Mars is known as the god of war. Hence Mars denotes the drive to display energy. It is primitive initiatory force, hotly, incisively expressed.

When considering a chart, the urge in the person to take courageous, *pioneering action*, the drive to be *energetic* in every way, to become *heated* either in feeling or by illness, will largely depend on his *Martian* characteristics.

Martian traits are very much those of the signs Aries and Scorpio, which are ruled by Mars and are expressed in the activities of the 1st and 8th houses which are the natural houses of that planet and these signs.

A key to the understanding of the ability to be energetic, or the urge to be so by all forms of personal effort either in business or profession, or in personal life, will be given by the placing of Mars in sign and house and by its strength in the chart.

It may be understood in this way. In the years of manhood and womanhood, the period of which is governed by Mars, the person has to exert himself to make his way in life. This may often demand initiative, pugnacity, courage, while a woman's life often requires in addition the use of energy in the bearing and rearing of children. Mars will show the general ability to assert the personality, to fight the way through life.

♂ Its symbol contains the circle of spirit, the older form having the cross of matter exactly above, ♂, signifying that this planet has more to do with material things than Venus, the oppositely shaped symbol.

The way in which it is now written pictorially shows its initiatory meaning. In biology, it is still the sign for the masculine.

MARTIAN WORDS

TRUE MEANING	OVERSTRESS OR MISUSE
Active pioneer	Aggressive
Combative	Angry
Constructive	Cruel
Courageous	Destructive
Direct in speech	Foolhardy
Energetic	Impatient
Forceful	Must be first
Good leader	Pugnacious
Impulsive	Rampageous
Indignant (justly)	Restless
Passionate	Rude
Quick	Sensual
Strongly sexed	Thoughtless

JUPITER

KEYWORDS :—EXPANSION, PRESERVATION

The urge or drive to expand cannot very well be satisfied without the opportunity to do so. Hence, this is the planet of opportunity.

When considering a chart, the tendency of the person towards *cheerful*, jovial optimistic *expansive* ways will largely depend on his *Jupiterian* characteristics.

Jupiterian traits are especially those of the sign Sagittarius which it rules and are also expressed in the activities of the 9th house, which is the natural house of this planet and sign.

They are also expressed in the mode of the sign Pisces and in the sphere of 12th house matters, since Jupiter was the traditional ruler of these until the discovery of Neptune, under the rulership (or part-rulership) of which they are now considered to be (see pp. 34 and 83).

A key to the understanding of the ability to prosper, often through the taking of opportunities and of the general aptitude for well-being of a person, will be given by the placing of Jupiter in sign and house and by its strength in the chart.

It may be understood in this way. In the years when life should expand to some fruition of earlier effort, which period is governed by Jupiter, the person has usually passed the time of preparation for life and can begin to " spread himself " with more ability. It must not be forgotten that the " fair, fat and forty " period is also often the beginning of the " middle-aged spread "

Jupiter will show the person's general ability to grow in physical, mental and moral ways, his urge to expand his knowledge of the world and its wisdom and to gain success, and his opportunities for doing so.

♃ Its symbol contains the half-circle of soul, slightly to the side of, and above the cross of matter.

JUPITERIAN WORDS

TRUE MEANING	OVERSTRESS OR MISUSE
Expansive	Extremist
Fond of sport	Improvident
Fortunate	Jocose
Generous	No sense of detail
Good conversationalist	Over-trusting to luck
Jovial	Provocative
Large in outlook	' Sporty '
Optimistic	Wasteful

SATURN

KEYWORDS :—LIMITATION, COLD

The urge towards limitation may be expressed by the desire to keep within bounds, to be cautious and to work to achieve security.

When considering a personal chart, the judgment of a person's power of *control* will largely depend on his *Saturnian* characteristics. However, the placing of *limitations* also implies the narrowness of the bounds so drawn, so the ability of the person to feel *insufficiency in life* will also be shown. Also his tendency to become *chilled* either emotionally, or physically by illness, will be indicated.

Saturnian traits are very much those of the sign Capricorn which it rules. They are expressed also in the activities of the 10th house, which is the natural house of this planet and sign.

They are also expressed in the sign Aquarius and in the sphere of 11th house matters, since Saturn was the traditional ruler of these until the discovery of Uranus, under the rulership (or part-rulership) of which they are now considered to be (see pp. 33 and 78). Authorities differ, especially on the Continent.

A key to the understanding of the ability to endure difficulties patiently (but nevertheless to feel them keenly), the urge to rise by overcoming such difficulties, and the ability to bear the weight of responsibility entailed, will be given by the placing of Saturn in sign and house and by its strength in the chart.

It may be understood in this way. In older years, the period of which is governed by Saturn, the person begins to settle down to the responsibilities of life and to grow old.

Saturn will show his general need to accept the ties of necessity in life and his ability to deal with them.

♄ Its symbol is the semi-circle of soul ; again, as in Mars, with the cross of matter taking precedence, though a little to the side, as in Jupiter. Again, the affairs of the material world predominate. It will be noticed that as Saturn is now written, the cross is hardly more than a ' tick '.

SATURNIAN WORDS

TRUE MEANING	OVERSTRESS OR MISUSE
Aspiring	Depressive
Careful in speech	Dogmatic
Cautious	Dull
Controlled	Fearful
Just	Grasping
Patient	Limited
Practical	Mean
Responsible	Severe
Serious	Unappreciative of beauty
Thrifty	Uninspired

NOTE ON " OLD " AND " NEW " PLANETS

The student will now see that Shakespeare's *Seven Ages of Man* were in part the seven periods of life of the nature of these planets, so much more generally understood in his day than in ours.

'All the world's a stage,*
And all the men and women merely players.
They have their exits and their entrances
And one man in his time plays many parts,
☽ *His acts being seven ages.* At first the infant
Mewling and puking in the nurses' arms ;
☿ And then the whining schoolboy with his satchel
And shining morning face, creeping, like a snail,
♀ Unwillingly to school. And then the lover
Sighing like furnace, with a woeful ballad
♂ Made to his mistress' eyebrow. Then a soldier
Full of strange oaths, and bearded like the pard,
Jealous in honour, sudden and quick in quarrel,
Seeking the bubble reputation
♃ Even in the cannon's mouth. And then the justice
In fair round belly with good capon lined
With eyes severe and beard of formal cut,
Full of wise saws and modern instances
♄ And so he plays his part. The sixth age shifts
Into the lean and slippered pantaloon
With spectacles on nose and pouch on side
His youthful hose, well sav'd a world too wide
For his shrunk shank ; and his big manly voice
Turning again toward childish treble, pipes
And whistles in his sound. Last scene of all

* *As You Like It.* Act 2, Scene 7.

> That ends this strange eventful history,
> Is second childishness, and mere oblivion
> Sans teeth, sans eyes, sans taste, sans everything.'

He leaves out the creativity of the Sun, but gives us the accurate descriptions of the babe, the schoolboy, the lover, the soldier, the justice and the older man. The description of the attributes of Mars, as applied to the soldier, is most striking when thought of in connection with the two signs ruled by that planet. There is first the physical signature of Mars, the strongly growing hair on the face, then the jealousy (♏), the sudden quarrelsomeness (♂), the desire for the bubble reputation (the 'me-first-ness' of ♂), but even so, the courage and the bravery to display this 'even at the cannon's mouth'.

His seventh stage would seem to be the change to the Neptunian dissolution, as described from purely material observation, without comment on the spiritual awakening to come.

The diagram on page 21 must now be studied again. It will be seen that whichever way is taken round the circle, the end is Saturn, the planet of *limits*. The seven planets were those which the ancients could see with the naked eye and which were spoken of in myth and in history.

The many 'sevens' of the Bible relate to this category of principles of the One. The seven Spirits before the Throne of God symbolised them, the seven branches of the candlestick show them again, the seven Archangels represent them. The seven days of the week, the seven primary colours, and the notes of music all have their correlation with them.

The Sun and Moon ruled one sign each, the rest ruled two. The scheme was a tidy one from the dawn of recorded history until Herschel's discovery of Uranus, in 1781. Since then two other major planets have been discovered, the orbits of all three being outside that of Saturn (i.e., further from the Sun). Esoterically, his limits have been passed, and as each new planet comes into the conscious knowledge of mankind' there seems to arise an ability to respond to its nature. This is strange, since the three planets were always there, but the reading of history seems to prove that it is so. The symmetry of the scheme is upset, since three signs now have double rulerships. It would be satisfying to a sense of fitness of things, if two more planets were discovered so that each sign might now have its 'new' as well as its 'old' ruler. Astronomers have no news of them yet. Perhaps the manufacture of yet larger telescopes will help in their discovery.

The Rulerships of the " New " Planets

Astrologers had to work by trial and error to find out which signs seemed to be the ones most likely to be ruled by the new planets. No *definite* decision has yet been made, but the ideas which are now coming to be accepted will be given. It may be that these new planets embody principles which are wide in their meaning and that they should not be confined to any one rulership, as in the traditional manner.

One way of speaking of them is that each is a ' higher octave ' of one of the earlier known planets. It is as if they raise the thoughts and widen the outlook of humanity.

THE EXTRA-SATURNIAN PLANETS

(Their orbits are outside that of Saturn)

URANUS

KEYWORDS :—CHANGE (REVOLUTIONARY, DISRUPTIVE, DICTATORIAL)

This planet was discovered in 1781 by Herschel. It was formerly named after him and that name will be seen in the older Ephemerides.

From the time of its discovery much has gone on which is changeful and revolutionary. The urge towards freedom has been marked in both nations and people.

When considering a chart, the judgment of the urge towards wilful or rebellious *freedom* will depend largely on Uranian characteristics. Changes so made can rarely take place without a break with the past.

Uranian traits have something in common with those of the sign Aquarius, which is thought to be now more under the rulership of Uranus and less Saturnian than before. In fact, many astrologers state that Uranus does rule Aquarius,* but some authorities disagree. These traits are expressed also in the activities of the 11th house, which is the natural house of this planet and sign.

A key to the understanding of the ability to make and suffer changes, to act unconventionally, often crudely, to act under a flash of intuition rather than by slow reasoning, to incline to all that has to do with modern invention, especially that which uses ' rays ' or ' waves ', will be given by the placing of Uranus in sign and house, and by its strength in the chart.

Saturn was the old god Chronos. The only one older was Ouranos. It may then be that the period of this planet is extreme old age with its transition to another state of life.

♅ Its symbol is said by some to be the H of its discoverer, Herschel, and by others to be the two curves of soul with the cross in between. If this esoteric idea is of interest, then it will be observed that, concurrently with the notion of a new and revolutionary attitude of mankind at this time, especially caused by the scientific redescription of what was solid matter and now is thought of as electricity in motion, the cross bar of the cross of matter has changed its position and is a rung higher up the vertical bar. There is a tiny circle below.†

Other symbols are used in many countries abroad. In England, the shape of the symbol is to be seen on the roof of many houses in which there is the Uranian invention, a television set.

---

* The beginner is advised to take Uranus as the main ruler of Aquarius.
† As with the symbol for Saturn, the manner of writing varies (See Figure 1), and is different from the printed symbol.

URANIAN WORDS

TRUE MEANING	OVERSTRESS OR MISUSE
Autocratic	Abnormal
Friendly	Attracted to dubious forms of occultism.
Inventive	Changeful
Magnetic	Compulsively attractive
Original	Dangerous
Outspoken	Detached
Positive occultism	Eccentric
Progressive	Fascinating
Reformative	Perverse
Strong willed	Rebellious
Unconventional	Rough
Unusual	Wilful

NEPTUNE

KEYWORDS :—NEBULOUSNESS, IMPRESSIONABILITY

This planet has to do with what hides itself from view, hence it is the most difficult for which to find a suitable one-word description.

It was discovered in 1846, and, true to its nature, this was done by indirect means. The planet itself was not at first seen, but its position was postulated because its pull altered the regular path of Uranus. From the time of its discovery, much has happened which implies veiled strength from behind the scenes, often in a vicarious or substitute way. This may be subversive or kindly, but the main characteristic will be its formless, boundless, non-material nature.

Ether was first used for surgery in 1846. Gas began to be used for lighting. These things escape if not confined in containers or pipes. Like all Neptunian things, they are elusive. The non-materiality leads to connection with intangibility, hence ideas of spirituality come under this rulership. The depths of confusion may be reached, or the heights of mysticism which seem nebulous to those who are not themselves on that plane of thought.

When considering a personal chart, the judgment of the urge towards the *non-material*, the *non-confined*, the spiritual or the merely vague will depend largely on Neptunian characteristics.

Neptunian traits are very much those of the sign Pisces, which is thought to be now more under the rulership of Neptune and less Jupiterian than before. In fact, many astrologers state that Neptune* does rule Pisces. They are expressed also in the activities of the 12th house which is the natural house of this planet and sign.

A key to the understanding of the ability to dissolve the bounds of the material world and to act under the inspiring urges from the intangible, which seem to come through the unconscious, giving contact with the world of inspiration in art, in

* The beginner is advised to use Neptune as the main ruler of Pisces.

dreams, in trance, in hypnosis and kindred states, will be given by the placing of Neptune in sign and house and by its strength in the chart.

Neptune was the god of the sea, which is the least material part of the earth. It may be that the period of this planet is that which is past earthly life.

Ψ   Its symbol is said by some to be the trident of Neptune—by others to be the two curves with the cross in between, the circles now raised so that their ends are level with the cross-bar. There is a small circle below.*

If this esoteric idea is of interest, then it will be observed that, concurrently with the notion of the hidden but subtle strength of Neptune, this was the time when the movement of Spiritualism began in its modern form. Interest developed in man as a less material being, able to ' dissolve his bounds ' by the use of telepathy, etc. The study of psychic matters developed. Science began to explain ' matter ' in non-solid ways.

In 1942, the Greek letter Ψ, the nearest approach to the symbol Ψ, was adopted by certain psychical researchers to imply psychic function. In 1949, they adopted the Hebrew letter ‫ש‬, again like Neptune, to mean spirit.†

NEPTUNIAN WORDS

TRUE MEANING	OVERSTRESS OR MISUSE
Artistic	Careless
Can play a part	Castles are in the air
Dreamy	Deceptive
Emotional	Head in the clouds
Idealistic	Hypersensitive
Imaginative	Irritated by discord
Inspirational	Sentimental
Mediumistic	Subversive
Rhythmic	Unstable
Sensitive	Wandering
Spiritual	Woolly
Subtle	

PLUTO

Keywords :—Elimination, Renewal, Regeneration

This planet was discovered in 1930 by the Lowell Observatory and was first called Pluto-Lowell.

From the time of its discovery, much has gone on which is eruptive. That which was in the dark or bound or enclosed is violently ejected or vice versa. One instance is the development of the atom bomb. At about the same time, that of the beginning of the 1939 war, homes were plunged into the darkness of the blackout.

---

* As with the symbol for Saturn, the manner of writing varies (See Figure 1), and is different from the printed symbol.
† ' Proceedings ' of Society for Psychical Research, Part 166, page 5.

This planet has been connected with the underground activity of gangsterism, from which came violent outbreaks.

There has been the growth of psychology, which, by means of psycho-analysis, helps the patient to eliminate from his unconscious self much that is repressed there.

Pluto seems to have relation to the working of the life force itself in its stages as the sexual act (which is also Martian, being initiatory) and birth, and death (regarded as new life). In all these, what has been bound is eliminated and there is a significance of a transmutation. Hence this planet is also said to be connected with beginnings and endings.

When considering a personal chart, the judgment of the ability for quick eliminative *getting-rid-of* action will depend largely on *Plutonian* characteristics. This planet, less understood than any other at the time of writing (1950), has been known to astrologers for only twenty years. Also, it is so far from the earth and can have such wide latitude that it may be that its meaning cannot be taken too personally (unless prominent in a chart) but has more of a *mass* effect.

Plutonian traits are very much those of the signs of Mars, i.e. Aries and Scorpio. Opinion inclines to give it the rulership of the latter. This is not settled. These traits may be said to be expressed also in the activities of the 8th house, which is the natural house of this sign.

A key to the understanding of the ability of a person to free himself, perhaps violently, from what has bound him, may be given by the placing of Pluto in sign and house and by its strength in the chart. As Pluto stays on an average about twenty-one years in a sign, not too much personal emphasis must be put on to sign position.

Pluto was the god of the underworld, so the connection with what is submerged is seen.

♇ Its symbol is the PL of Pluto Lowell combined. In the U.S.A., the symbol used is like Neptune with the upper part of the central line replaced by a small circle.

PLUTONIAN WORDS

TRUE MEANING	OVERSTRESS OR MISUSE
Beginnings and endings	Cataclysms
Deep-working	Eruptive
Eliminative	Forcefully re-forming
Out-bringing	Underground activity
Regenerative	Violent
Revealing	

CHAPTER 4

THE ZODIACAL SIGNS

(a) THEIR NATURES THROUGH THEIR GROUPS

In the first chapter, it was stated that the principles of the planets manifested themselves in different ' modes ' according to the sign of the Zodiac in which they might be. It is impossible to affirm with assurance *why* these twelfths of the Zodiac seem to be like twelve different coloured windows through which a shining white light is unmistakably varied. The astrological hypothesis is that each sign is of a different *nature*. People born with one or other of these signs prominent in their charts will be very much of the ' nature ' of these signs. It is therefore simpler to explain their characteristics by reference to people in whose charts they are strong. The manner in which each planet ' works ' in each sign can then be stated by change of descriptive adjective to adverb. (See section *f* of this chapter.)

Traditionally, the twelve are subdivided into groups in various ways. Instead of immediately trying to differentiate between the natures of the twelve, it will be easier to know them first as members of such groups, whose customary names are conveniently self-descriptive. In this way, the knowledge of many astrological terms will be acquired and further description will be simplified. A thorough learning of the differences between these groups will be of the greatest help later, as the details cannot be repeated when each sign of that group is described. It is this groundwork knowledge which aids quick interpretation later on.

(b) Group 1.—THE TRIPLICITIES (or Elements)

KEYWORDS :—

FIRE	... ...	Ardent ; Keen
EARTH	... ...	Practical ; Cautious
AIR	... ...	Intellectual ; Communicative
WATER	... ...	Emotional ; Unstable ; Sensitive

It will be seen that the signs are united by triangles in groups of three. Those so grouped have something in common in their natures. (See Fig. 3.)

Aries, Leo and Sagittarius are of the Fire Triplicity

KEYWORDS :—ARDENT, KEEN

All three have something in common. All three have something of the nature of fire which actively burns, crackles, consumes, warms, delights or annoys according to whether it is suitably placed or not. It is delightful in the hearth, obnoxious if causing damage in places where it should not be burning.

Hence all people with one or more of these signs strong in their charts are *active*, ardent, enthusiastic, aspiring, emotionally able to *burn* with excitement or **feeling** of any kind, to become noisy actually or metaphorically, to have strong

37

appetities for life, to be too overpowering in consuming their less forceful companions, to be inflamed with the warmth which they bring to any interest, to delight others when such somewhat exuberant traits are in place, but to tire and annoy when not in congenial company. They tend to be impatient of more sensitive or gentler people, thinking them slow or damping. 'Fire' feels that 'Water' will extinguish it and 'Earth' will smother it, but that 'Air' will fan its flames.

They are cheerful, gay, fond of sport and the joy of eager pulsating life. Their possible faults are those of being *too* lively, often rushing rashly into over-excitable, over-vivid, unthoughtful, hence harmful or destructive ways. But no one is all Fire and such tendencies may be balanced elsewhere in a chart.

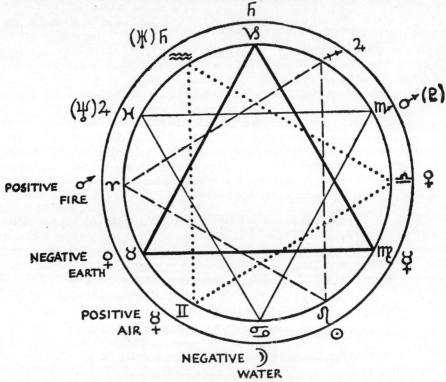

FIG. 3 THE TRIPLICITIES

Taurus, Virgo and Capricorn are of the Earth Triplicity

KEYWORDS :—PRACTICAL, CAUTIOUS

Again they are as the traditional old name implies. From this comes the phrase 'He is of the earth, earthy'. The phrase 'down to earth' is explanatory—also 'down to bedrock'.

Earth is solid, dependable for support, motionless, dry, in modern idiom 'functional' and rather uninteresting. No one is all 'earth', but those in whose charts one or more of these signs are prominent have these traits of solid, dependable *practicality*. They are capable and hard working in sensible ways, either in actual building, or the building of careers and organisations.

They are careful and trustworthy with possessions or finance and will look after the small matters which make the complete whole. They tend to be suspicious or dubious about more lively agile-minded people, thinking them disturbing and trivial.

Earth feels that 'Air' will dry it, 'Fire' will parch it, but that 'Water' will refresh it.

Their faults are liable to be that in their customary application to material ends, they lack knowledge of the more abstract and inspirational things of life and may be thought dull by livelier people. Their faults can be narrowness of outlook, and too close addiction to order and to routine. Certain expressions are indicative—'He's rather a clod.' No one is all Earth and such tendencies may be balanced elsewhere in the chart.

Gemini, Libra and Aquarius are of the Air Triplicity

KEYWORDS :—INTELLECTUAL, COMMUNICATIVE

Again these are much as their name implies. Air is the medium in which living things breathe, it is the medium for the carrying of sound ; no speech could happen without it ; it *connects* all things ; it blows to and fro.

Hence those in whose charts one or more of these are prominent tend to stress communication in some way. They are inclined to reasoning, intelligent pursuits, working in the realm of ideas. They like to bring into connection thoughts, people or places. They tend to be unimpressed by extreme prudence or sensitivity in others. 'Air' does not wish to be confined in underground caverns, nor to have its light freedom saturated by 'Water'. It enjoys the leaping response of 'Fire'.

Their faults can be lack of deep emotion and a tendency to occupy themselves too much with schemes and theories. Certain expressions are indicative—'Ideas all in the air'. 'Talking hot air.' 'Too airy-fairy.' 'Blowing in and out.' No one is all Air and the less desirable tendencies may be balanced elsewhere in the map.

Cancer, Scorpio and Pisces are of the Water Triplicity

KEYWORDS :—EMOTIONAL, UNSTABLE, SENSITIVE

As with the others, these are much as their name implies.

Water reflects, dissolves, washes away, helps growth. The sea has unplumbable depths and holds much within it. It can have a calm exterior which can be deceptive, since sudden storms blow up, and hidden undercurrents can drag down.

Water has no shape of its own. It takes the shape of its container. Once contained, it can be calm and useful, but often damping. As a rushing torrent, it can be overwhelming and destructive. It has great carrying power and force if properly contained or canalised. This is best exemplified in the fixed sign Scorpio.

Those with one or more of these signs prominent in their charts have a certain distrust of self. They need someone to ' reflect '. They are happier when their fluidity is given shape by someone else. They are naturally sensitive and are the carriers of intuition and inspiration which they can express in such ways as the rhythms of art or poetry, music, dancing, or in the exercise of the psychic faculties. They are deep, emotional, secretive, protective.

They tend to dislike people who are boisterous or who have strong personalities, finding them tiring. ' Water ' feels that ' Fire ' will make it boil and ' Air ' will make it evaporate, but ' Earth ' will contain it.

Their faults can be that they are literally ' unstable as water ', too easily being a reflection of the last person they were with, too inclined to emotional storms, too ready to be a drag on others by subversive action, too sensitive to influence. Slang words are aptly descriptive of this side of the Water nature : ' sloppy ', ' wet ', ' a wet blanket ', ' a drip '. No one is *all* water and the less desirable tendencies may be balanced elsewhere in the map.

(c) Group 1.—THE QUADRUPLICITIES (or Qualities)

KEYWORDS :—

CARDINAL	...	Outgoing
FIXED ...	...	Resistant to change
MUTABLE	...	Adaptable

It will now be seen that the signs may be said to be united by squares in groups of four, and also by crosses from the angles of the squares. Those so grouped have something in common in their natures. (Fig. 4.)

There is more in common between the two opposites, than between the others. This will be explained further under *Polarity* (see page 182 under ' Opposition ').

Aries and Libra, Cancer and Capricorn are of the Cardinal Quadruplicity

KEYWORD :—OUTGOING

All four have something in common. The dictionary gives the meaning of cardinal as something principal, denoting that on which a thing hinges or depends. The cardinal points of the compass are those occupied by the first degrees of these signs at the time of the beginning point of the vernal equinox (page 276). There is something fundamental about these four. Each in its way takes definite *action*.

Hence, those people in whose charts these signs are prominent are *outgoing* in their natures. They will set things going, lead others and work to an end. Their faults may be those of restlessness. To aid easy memory by visual impression in Fig. 4, their cross is drawn in lines *outgoing* from the circle.

Taurus and Scorpio, Leo and Aquarius are of the Fixed Quadruplicity

KEYWORDS :—RESISTANT TO CHANGE

All four have something in common. Fixity implies stability, steadfastness, but lack of volatility. These four signs are represented in old literature (see Ezekiel, Chapter I) by their animal symbols. They were known to be corner-stones of support.

Each has its way of determined fixation. Hence, people in whose charts these signs are prominent are *stable* in their ways. They will not be so good at getting things going but will guard and conserve that which is started, and may be depended upon to see that what they think is to be done, truly *is* done.

Their faults may be those of inertia, of lack of imagination, a lack of quick adaptability to circumstances.

To aid easy memory by visual impression in Fig. 4, their cross is drawn in heavy, solid lines within the circle.

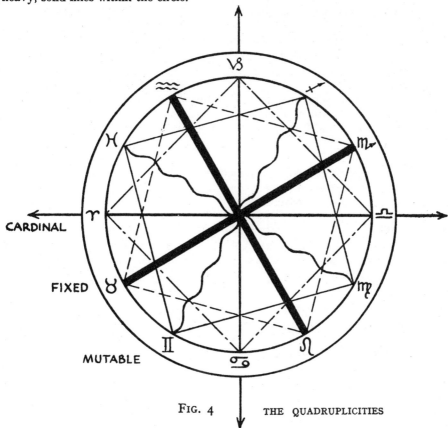

FIG. 4   THE QUADRUPLICITIES

Gemini and Sagittarius, Virgo and Pisces are of the Mutable Quadruplicity
KEYWORD :—ADAPTABLE

All four have something in common. Mutability is described by the dictionary as tendency to change, or inconstancy. These signs are also called the 'Common' signs. The derivation of the word helps in its understanding (Latin *con*—together, and *munis*—serving, obliging).

The ' common ' people are the people in general, hence the word has come to mean those who are usual or ordinary and ' those who serve '. From this it must not be gathered that there are no distinguished people in whose maps mutability predominates. Nevertheless, there is a *desire to serve* in many of these. An admiral is a distinguished man but he serves his country.

The outstanding characteristic of the four is their versatile adaptability. Each has its way of expressing this changefulness. To them it is normal, to the other two groups it may appear slack or inconstant. Such people tend to act for others either in self-seeking or in selfless ways. They are more varied than the other two types. Their faults are over-diffuseness and lack of stability.

To aid easy memory by visual impression in Fig. 4, their cross is drawn in wavering lines within the circle.

Double Signs

The three Common signs Gemini, Sagittarius and Pisces are so called because their exceptional versatility often gives them a duality of nature. This is most noticeable in Gemini and Pisces, the pictorial symbols of which are dual (♊ and ♓.)

Overstrength

Just as no one person can have a chart in which only one triplicity or element is emphasised, so it is a very rare, though possible thing for a person to have all important points in one quadruplicity.

Lack of Strength

Such lack in triplicity or quadruplicity may be made up for by strength of planet ruling a sign of the weakly represented subdivision, or by strength in the corresponding houses.

(d) POSITIVITY and NEGATIVITY

(Sometimes referred to as Masculinity and Femininity)

KEYWORDS :—
POSITIVE   ...   Self-expressive
NEGATIVE   ...   Self-repressive, receptive

The signs are alternately positive and negative (starting from Aries). Reference to Fig. 3 will show that the Fire and Air signs are positive, while the Earth and Water signs are negative.

While the word positive, used astrologically, carries its normal conversational meaning of definite assurance, the word negative, used astrologically, does not carry the somewhat derogatory meaning now given to it conversationally. People with more strength of Earth and Water in their charts have a receptivity from which they can again give out. They may therefore gain what the self-expressive person is too busy to notice.

Combination of Triplicity and Quadruplicity

Diagrams 3 and 4 can be superimposed and drawn as one, but this is confusing. If the student will now look at the two together, he will see that, of the *three* signs in every triplicity, each belongs to one of the quadruplicities, while similarly, of the *four* signs in every quadruplicity, each belongs to one triplicity.

Each sign will now be described. It must be remembered that the traits mentioned will be those of anyone in whose chart such a sign is *prominent* in any way and that a planet will ' work ', in the astrological meaning of the word, in the ' mode ' of those traits if found in that sign (see later chapters).

(e) THEIR LOCATION and CORRESPONDENCES*

The Ecliptic

This is the apparent path of the Sun in the heavens. It has been established since the sixteenth century that it is really the Earth which revolves round the Sun, taking a year to do so. (Kepler, 1572–1636, confirmed the theories of Copernicus, 1473–1543.)

The Zodiac

Astronomically this is described as *a band* extending about 8° on each side of the Ecliptic. It is sometimes described in theosophical language as ' the Earth's aura ', or, more scientifically as ' the Earth's magnetic field '. These attempts are inadvisable as it is impossible to be exact in description about what is essentially a conception.

However it may be described or explained, the band referred to is the width on each side of the Ecliptic through which the Earth receives that which is given to it by the Sun and planets.

Since its various divisions and names have been found in all countries of the world, from time immemorial, no precise information can be given as to the beginning of this system.

The ancients who first began to study the movements of the heavenly bodies, connected happenings on Earth with them. This was the earliest ' astronomy-astrology '. With the invention of precise instruments for weighing, measuring and observing, the study of everything material in the world came to be known as science, and henceforward the great scientists of the succeeding centuries have given us more and more information about that which can be observed, weighed and measured.

The study of the heavens, with the greatest accuracy possible, is now called *Astronomy* ; while the attempt to correlate the factors used in this with a meaning in human life is called *Astrology*.

When it was thought that the path seen was the actual path of the Sun, the astronomer-astrologers divided it into segments for measurement and reference. The present form of the system which we use appears to have started in Chaldea and

* See Fig. 2 and notes on page 46.

Babylonia and is the well-known division into the twelve zodiacal signs. The only reasonable explanation proffered for this is that, in ancient days, the times for examination of the heavens were shortly after sunset, and again shortly before sunrise. These two inspections would cover all visible stars with the exception of those within the beams of the Sun, for the time being. After sunset and before sunrise, there was a short period of twilight, so that brighter stars remained visible only when they were over 12° from the Sun, and fainter stars only *when 15° or more* distant from it.

On a certain evening, an observer would be able to see a star for a few moments after sunset, then on the following evening it would be seen no more. (Such a star remained invisible for a certain time each year and was spoken of as combust.) After a period of twenty-four to thirty days, according to its brilliance, it would appear again before sunrise. This disappearance in the west and reappearance in the east was termed heliacal (Greek, *helios*—sun) setting and rising. The time when each of these ' twelfths ' of the ecliptic which were successively combust coincided roughly with the time the Moon required for a complete revolution.* Hence, the twelve zodiacal signs and the beginning of the calendar month.

Astronomers nowadays attempt to deride the naming of the signs, which, they say, were named after the constellations and were given because men foolishly imagined that the groups of stars forming them did look like the animals and so on, by whose names they are known. As these are quite palpably *not* all in these shapes, the idea does not seem sound.

It is more probable that some of the names were given because these ancients learnt by observation that the people born when the Sun was in those signs, did in fact have such characteristics. Some were possibly given in relation to the type of weather in the countries in question in those months.

It is just as reasonable to suppose that the constellations (groups of *stars*), when recognised as such, were named *after* the signs with which they once coincided. The truth of this can never be known. Available information shows that in early times men had no idea of the phenomenon known as *the precession of the equinoxes* which is responsible for the slow but continuous shift of the signs (which follow each other in sequence from the point of the vernal equinox, which astrologers term 0° Aries), against the constellations which are groups of stars (p. 276).

Even when this was discovered, it was not realised as a permanent motion.

Fuller explanation is given in Chapter 15, section 7.

The names of the signs should have been learnt from Fig. 1, page 21. Something of the *nature* of the signs can now be learnt from their symbols, which pictorialise either the representative animal or object, the traits of which are, to a certain extent, those of the people in whose charts such signs are strong (p. 47, 1st para.). Some pictorialise the part of the body with which they correlate. The human body may be seen to fit the circle of the signs as in the following diagram.

* For full description, see "Sun, Moon and Stars" by F. von Oefele, page 48, Vol. 12, *Encylopedia of Religion and Ethics*. Edited by James Hastings.

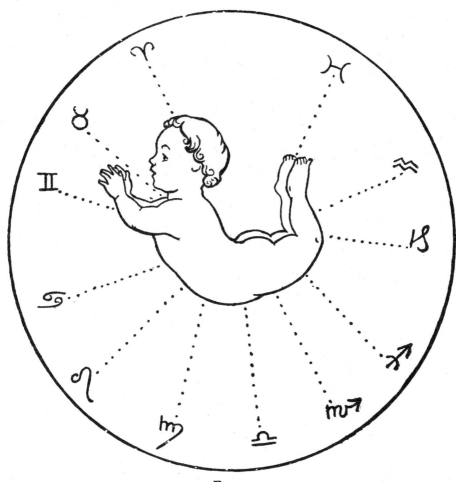

FIG. 5

THE SIGNS IN RELATION TO THE BODY

Note on Connection with the Glands

There is no traditional teaching on the connection of the signs with the endocrine glands as these were comparatively recently discovered, but the attempt to correlate them will help the student to understand the psychology of a person whose glands are not in healthy order. Conversely, by deducing the astrological correlatives from his observed behaviour, he may help such a person to understand himself and make the effort to control himself and such reactions.*

* Generalities with regard to glands gathered from *Diagnosis of Man*, Chapter 3. Kenneth Walker.

Note on Medical Astrology

The student is *strongly cautioned* against attempting to use astrological deduction in anything more than *broad outline*, in application to medicine. Modern work by fully trained doctors who have knowledge of astrology, has shown that much more painstaking research by experts must be done before precision can be reached, and that rules cannot be dogmatically laid down, as in the past.

SUMMARY

TABLE OF SUGGESTED CORRESPONDENCES

Sign	Symbol	Ruler	Symbol	Name	Month	Shape Suggests	Part of Body	Bodily System
1. Aries	♈	Mars	♂	The Ram	April	Ram's horns	Head	
2. Taurus	♉	Venus	♀	The Bull	May	Bull's head and horns	Throat	
3. Gemini	♊	Mercury	☿	The Twins	June	Two children	Hands, arms, lungs	Nervous
4. Cancer	♋	Moon	☽	The Crab	July	The breasts	Breasts, stomach	Alimentary
5. Leo	♌	Sun	☉	The Lion	Aug.	The heart	Heart, back	Cardiac
6. Virgo	♍	Mercury	☿	The Virgin	Sept.	Feminine sexual parts	Intestines	Alimentary
7. Libra	♎	Venus	♀	The Balance	Oct.	Scales	Kidneys	
8. Scorpio	♏	Mars	♂	The Scorpion and	Nov.	Masculine sexual parts	Sexual organs	Generative
		Pluto	♇	The Eagle				
9. Sagittarius	♐	Jupiter	♃	The Archer	Dec.	Arrow	Hips, thighs, liver	Hepatic
10. Capricorn	♑	Saturn	♄	The Goat	Jan.	Bended knee	Knee	Bony
11. Aquarius	♒	Saturn Uranus	♄ ♅	The Waterbearer	Feb.	Waves of water or air	Calf, ankle	Circulatory
12. Pisces	♓	Jupiter Neptune	♃ ♆	The Fishes	March	Two fishes	Feet	Lymphatic

When the signs are described, the correspondences will be seen in their application.

(f) DESCRIPTION OF THEIR ATTRIBUTES

In these days, most people have a very good idea of the characteristics of each zodiacal sign since good descriptions are in many books and are constantly repeated in astrological sections of magazines.

They will now be given with special reference to rulerships, classification by groups and other natural correlatives so that the student may realise *why* these characteristics should be so clearly understood to relate to each sign.

They are not intended to refer *solely* to the ascending sign, *or* to the Sun sign, *but to be indicative of the mode of the sign in question, wherever it is emphasised in a chart.*

When ascending, each will have a purely personal significance, since it is then on the cusp of the most personal of all the houses (see Chapter 5).

When containing the Sun, it will still have a very personal significance since its mode will modify the principle of the Sun, which of all planets is the most representative of the person, but it will combine this added connection with the house it rules in the chart.

A sign is also emphasised in a chart when it contains three or more planets—such a group is called a *satellitium*.

Planet in Sign

A planet in a sign will show its own principle, urge or drive, but it will do so *in the mode of* the sign.

In interpretation, descriptive adjectives can be changed to adverbs or adverbial phrases for suitable expressions. Examples will be found at the end of the description of each sign.

THE SIGNS AND THEIR MODES IN KEYWORD FORM

A planet will show its nature in the signs as follows :—

In Aries	Assertively.
Taurus	Possessively.
Gemini	Communicatively, with alert versatility.
Cancer	Sensitively, protectively.
Leo	Creatively, joyfully.
Virgo	Critically, detailedly.
Libra	Harmoniously, unitedly.
Scorpio	Passionately, secretively, penetratingly.
Sagittarius	Widely, deeply, free-ranging.
Capricorn	Prudently, coolly, aspiringly.
Aquarius	Detachedly, scientifically.
Pisces	With appreciation of the intangibles, often confusedly.

Important Note

As with the planets, the above table is given in the attempt to place a *central idea* or keyword in the mind of the student. Naturally, no one word could wholly describe a sign but its use is helpful until wider experience brings fuller knowledge.

THE FIRST SIX SIGNS

These are, in the main, expressive of *personal* activities, while the last six are more concerned with activities entered into with other people or further afield than the narrow personal surroundings.

Of these, *the first four* have what has been described as a certain primitivity. In the lower types, this may indeed mean that they have something in common with the primitive races.

In the more cultured types, in spite of upbringing and education in its widest sense, they will still have an extremely personal attitude to life.

ARIES

Ruler	...	...	Mars
Natural House	...	...	1st (see Chapter 5)
Classification	...	...	Cardinal—Fire.　Positive
Symbol	...	...	The Ram
Glyph	...	...	♈
Part of Body	...	...	The Head
Metal (of Mars)	...	...	Iron
Colours Liked	...	...	Red

Cardinal—Fire.　Positive

The rushing, burning, noisy, inflammatory fire is accentuated by the go-ahead activity of Cardinality, and the self-expressiveness of Positivity.

Mars

♂　This rulership adds energy and initiatory force to what is already there in plenty.

The Ram

He is to be thought of as the leader of the flock, the bell-wether. This term is indeed figuratively used to describe the turbulent, agitator type.

Glyph

♈　This represents the horns of the Ram again showing the insistent pushfulness of the sign.

The Head

The correlation indicates the impulsive, head-first-ness and the head-strong-ness.

Iron

This gives the idea of the cutting tools and the machines so natural to the Martian.

Red

The colour of blood, so often shed by Martian action. It is improved by its metal iron, in medicinal form.

The Suprarenals

So far as can be observed these glands, which have been called " the glands of emergency," should be Arien. They lie at the upper pole of the two kidneys. (Aries–Libra polarity, p. 182, under " opposition".)

Their secretion, adrenalin, is poured into the blood-stream under stress of anger or fear, helping a person to the energetic action necessary to meet an emergency. The glands also have the pugnacity of Aries, helping the body to fight against disease.

A strongly Martian person who cannot control the swift rush of anger, may do so if he knows it to be " only extra adrenalin."

The Predominantly ARIES Person

He is very much of a firebrand or battering-ram. He will forge his way through life with courage, daring, energy and initiative and enterprise. He is the true pioneer. His one-pointedness of aim makes him direct and unable to use subtlety. He is incisive and often satirical in speech, cutting in invective.

He goes ahead by assertive aggressiveness, caring little for the feelings of others. His attitude has been described as " Me first."

In love, he is passionate, with strong sexual feelings.

Overstress or misuse of these traits will mean selfishness, crudeness, egotism, pugnacity, bad temper, foolhardiness, churlish behaviour.

Inhibition of his natural traits will be caused if subjected to deadening routine and a sedentary life, bringing violent reaction.

As a child, the Aries will be tough, rampageous, noisy, very full of beans, using a lie sometimes if it puts him foremost. Though he must be disciplined, he should be allowed plenty of outdoor life and games to work off his spirits. He cannot be over-tamed.

Physical Characteristics (unmodified)

If unmodified by other factors, various features may be evident.

A longish stringy neck like a sheep.

A look of the symbol ♈ in the formation of eyebrows and nose. Well marked eyebrows.

Ruddy complexion.

Red hair.

Active walk.

Illnesses

The head may be injured. Cuts and burns and scalds are frequent. Headaches occur. Their cause is often from the kidneys. (From Libra, the opposite sign, see p. 65.)

Manner of Life

The Aries is at his best in any sphere where his natural urges can be reasonably expressed. He is therefore better as boss, even if only in a small way ; better where noise and dash are not objected to ; better where initiative is needed, better where cutting tools are used.

He would be well placed in any business which deals with metals or machinery, as an employé in crowded noisy " Works," as a soldier (so long as activity and not routine predominates), or as a surgeon, butcher, or writer of satirical works.

Spare-time Activities

These should be all that are active and competitive and even hazardous. All those which need the use of cutting tools—wood carving—grafting.

Example in keywords.—Venus, *harmony, unison*, will express its principle in Aries *assertively, energetically*.

Suggested Interpretation to a person in whose chart this placing is found :—

" You have an intense, innate desire for harmony in life which you will try to satisfy by every possible way. You will not rest till your house, your clothes, your possessions, conform to your idea of beauty, even if at the expense of the feelings of others.

" You will strive to make your friends and family as you want them to be, in order to attain happiness.

" You will fall in love quickly, violently and want the loved one all for yourself. You would be wise to stop sometimes and give yourself time to think whether anyone else's idea may be first rate too, and whether your loved one may also like to express individuality at times."

(The interpretations which are given for each sign should be carefully considered, as they will help the student to get the idea of fuller interpretation when he reaches that stage.)

Significator

This term is used of a planet in its relation to everything possible, abstract or concrete, which may be put into its compartment of the " card-index " of the universe. In referring both to planet and corresponding sign, the expression used is that such things " come under " them.

Matters and occupations which come under Aries and of which Mars is the significator :—

Anger	Active soldier
Caustic words or acids	Butcher
Courage	Metal worker
Energy	Surgeon
Impulsiveness	
Iron	
Leadership	
Pioneers	
Pugnacity	
Redness	
Satire	
Sharp instruments	

TAURUS

Ruler	... ...	Venus
Natural House	... ...	2nd
Classification	... ...	Fixed—Earth. Negative
Symbol	... ...	The Bull
Glyph	... ...	♉
Part of Body	... ...	The Neck
Metal (of Venus) ...	...	Copper
Colours liked	... ...	Blues and pinks, sometimes green

Fixed—Earth. Negative

The solid, worthwhile, practicality of earth is made even more static by the mixture of the steadfastness of Fixity and the indrawnness of Negativity.

Venus

♀ This rulership brings charm and love of beauty to the Taurean. He will delight in beauty in the home, in the good things of the earth for his food and drink and flowers in garden and house to please his eye.

In art, he will often prefer heavy sculpture to lighter forms of expression.

The Bull

He is often extremely representative of Taureans.

Applicable expressions are :—" Bull-necked "—" Boys of the bulldog breed "— " a bull in a china shop." These are descriptive of the stubbornness of resistance, the refusal to let go of any possessions, the rage when the naturally placid type is goaded to anger.

Glyph

♉ In eastern countries, where astrology began, the cattle have large, curved horns, which this represents.

The Neck

This correlation gives a key to the endurance and stability of the Taurean. It bears the head, the most important part of the body. It will be noticed that when this is weak mentally, the neck usually fails to support it stably.

Copper

This is the metal of Venus.

Blues and Pinks

These are the usual Venusian colours, though green is often liked by the Taurean.

The Thyroid

This gland, being situated in the neck, should be Taurean. Lack of thyroid causes an exaggeration of "Earth" traits. The person becomes inert, sluggish in body and mind. The scars of operation on glands in the neck may often be seen on a Taurean. Slow development by a Taurean child is sometimes due to this deficiency and can be dealt with by a doctor.

The Predominantly TAUREAN Person

He is essentially to be trusted as a reliable, careful, steadfast person, of pleasant hospitable ways. He loves the country and his garden and is contented with his possessions which mean a great deal to him. He has real feeling for such things. He is not enterprising, preferring to conserve and to prosper in well-tried ways. He can become a little boring, as he is so fixed in his opinions.

In love he is charmingly affectionate, but over-possessive.

Overstress or misuse of these traits will mean inertia, stodginess, obstinacy and a tendency to suspicion of more lively people. Love of good things and possessions may turn to greedy and grasping ways.

Inhibition of his natural traits will be caused if he is subjected to overmuch rush and excitement, bringing overtiredness.

As a child, the Taurean will be charming, biddable, enjoying nursery rules and school routine. He will be a great success when at the top of the school, because of such good ways. He is apt to take some time to get over this, failing to adapt himself to the emergencies of the bigger world. His mind does not work swiftly, so he should be given time to achieve his results. He may be what is called a slow developer.

Physical Characteristics (unmodified)

The neck will be emphasised. It is usually heavy, especially in later life. Sometimes it is unusually beautiful. Just as the bull has curls on the front of the head, so the Taurean often has a particularly curly lock of hair which will not lie down. He is generally thick set and gives an impression of being solidly and weightily "earthed." The "John Bull" type. Movements will be deliberate.

Illnesses

Parts affected may be throat, glands, generative organs.

Manner of Life

The Taurean is at his best in any sphere where his natural urges can be reasonably expressed. He is therefore better in a position of trusted responsibility, rather than as a "go-getter," better in country pursuits than in town, better where he can deal with art and beauty and nature rather than where he is upset by too much movement. The physical emphasis is on his throat, hence he will often be a naturally good singer.

Since he is practical and likes solid possessions, he will like to invest his money in house property or interest himself in building.

Spare-time Activities

Gardening, painting, sculpture, music—hobbies which mean sitting still for a long time, embroidery and so on.

Example in keywords.—Mercury, *communication*, will express its principle in Taurus *possessively, conservatively*.

Suggested Interpretation to a person in whose chart this placing is found :—

" Your thoughts and conversation tend to be somewhat limited in their expression. You might with advantage try to enlarge your scope by reading. On the other hand, your friends will know that they can always depend on what you say and will rely on you. Your letters and conversation need a little more ' sparkle.'

" In dealing with those near you, you will stick to established ways and like to feel that your neighbours and relations are *yours* to enjoy."

Matters and occupations which come under Taurus and of which Venus is the significator :—

Beauty in art
Earth and all that is grown from it
Modelling
Money
Patience
Possessions of all kinds
Property
Sculpture
Throat

Art dealer
Farmer
Financier
Singer

GEMINI

Ruler	Mercury
Natural House	3rd
Classification	Mutable—Air. Positive
Symbol	The Twins
Glyph	♊
Parts of Body	Hands, arms, nerves, lungs and respiratory system
Metal (of Mercury) ...	Quicksilver
Colours liked	A variety

Mutable—Air. Positive

The constantly moving, communicative intelligence of Air is combined with the adaptability of Mutability and the self-expression of Positivity.

Mercury

☿ This rulership emphasises the communicatory faculty.

The Twins

♊ From this symbol can be deduced the quite extraordinary duality of the Geminian. " Quick-change artist " is a suitable phrase and for some less desirable types " two-faced " is descriptive.

Glyph

♊ This is like the Roman numeral for 2 and shows the essential duality of the sign.

Hands, Arms, Nerves, Lungs

Note that there are two hands, two arms, two lungs and two nervous systems. The Geminian uses all of them, and two at once if he can ! He is prone to gesticulation with his hands, and to easy use of them in writing and in manual occupations. His nervous reactions are quick.

Quicksilver

This gives the idea of the agility of the type and the quick changes of mood, now up, now down, which they exhibit. They change with the conversational and social temperature around them.

Colours

With his usual versatility, the Geminian seems to like all colours and feel none inharmonious.

The Thymus

This gland lies inside the chest, beneath the breast-bone, a Geminian area. It is well developed in youth, the Mercury period, but shrinks in adult life. It may be surmised that it is of importance to a Geminian.

The Predominantly GEMINIAN Person

He is intelligent, quick-witted, lively and intensely versatile. He is " Jack-of-all-trades," but especially the trades or professions which mean plenty of movement both of mind and body. He is chatty, intelligent, witty, inquisitive, somewhat nervously " on-the-go " most of the time.

It has been suggested that, if he had an animal symbol, it should be the monkey with its chattering, imitative nature and its constant jumping from place to place.

In love he is coolly affectionate, very expressive but rarely deeply held. He is too versatile to enjoy only one chosen love and will go true to type by running after two at a time. He frequently marries twice.

Overstress or misuse of these traits will mean diffuseness, lack of continuity, heartlessness, undependability, lack of perseverance, failure through divided objectives. Mental agility without sound education may produce the slick, " smart-Aleck " type. The phrase, " fingers in too many pies " is applicable.

Inhibition of his natural traits will be caused if subjected to lack of change, bringing boredom.

As a child the Geminian will be intensely lively, amusing in his talk, quickly picking up any new ideas, easy to teach if only his attention can be held. Though he must be kept quiet sometimes, it will not do to be over-insistent that he should stop fidgeting or that one thing at a time should be patiently done.

Physical Characteristics (unmodified)

Long arms ; sloping shoulders ; quickly darting, restless eyes ; slender build ; springing walk ; alert expression ; youthful appearance all through life.

Illnesses

Nervous complaints. Diseases of the respiratory system. Psychological troubles, such as general debility through circumstances which are too confining—*air must move*.

Manner of Life

The Geminian is at his best in any sphere where his natural urges can be expressed. He is therefore better in a non-static job where he can " blow in and out " at a moment's notice. He is better at doing mental rather than *heavy* manual work, but good at *lighter* manual work where dexterity of touch is required, especially if this requires thought as well. He is the typical Fleet Street reporter, off to another assignment as soon as one is dealt with, or the commercial traveller. His communicatory ways have full scope either in learning, teaching or lecturing.

In adult life, he will go on studying new subjects for the enjoyment of using his brain. Any literary work suits him. He can usually draw or paint, often using both hands for it. Communicatory again are the go-between, the agent, the middleman and the spiv.

Spare-time Activities

These should be widely varied and mentally interesting. Games should be dexterous rather than boisterous. The agility of foot, hand, eye and brain which combine in the fencer is very Geminian.

The Geminian will like to drop in on his friends for a chat, phone them or write them, or go for walks with them.

Example in keywords.—Jupiter, *expansion*, will express its principle in Gemini *communicatively, with alert versatility.*

Suggested interpretation to a person in whose chart this placing is found :—

" You are one of the most versatile of people, with your fingers in many pies.

" You are usually to be found ' just off ' to a next visit, having ' just read ' the last new book, and off to see the newest film. Chatty, busy, ready to argue and debate with anyone and even to take both sides if necessary.

" Bored by inaction, you go from one interest to another. Stop and look at yourself sometimes and check up on your multitudinous activities. Surface cleverness may be improved by more ' depth '."

Matters and occupations which come under Gemini, and of which Mercury is the significator :—

Brothers	Commercial Traveller
Learning	Journalist
Letters and all other means of communication	Lecturer
	Linguist
Magazine work	Messenger
Reporting	Pupil
School work and education	Secretary
	Teacher
Story telling	Writer
Teaching	
Travel Agencies	
Translating	

Travel between two
places
Twins and anything else
always in pairs

CANCER

Ruler	...	...	Moon
Natural House	...	...	4th
Classification	...	...	Cardinal—Water. Negative
Symbol	...	...	The Crab
Glyph	...	...	♋
Part of Body	...	...	The breasts, the stomach and alimentary system
Metal (of Moon)	...	...	Silver
Colours liked	...	...	Silver and soft shades

Cardinal—Water. Negative

The emotionality and instability of Water becomes active and restless when combined with the outgoing-ness of Cardinality ; but, it is a negative sign. Hence, unlike the self-expressive Cardinality of Aries, the activity of those in whose charts this sign is strong is less on the surface.

Moon

☽ This rulership brings a changeability to the Cancerian. Using its power of absorbing and reflecting that which it receives, the Cancerian very quickly picks up ways, habits and mannerisms of others in whose company he has been. Opinions heard will be brought out as if his own.

The Crab

It is often extremely representative of Cancerians. It appears hard-shelled, but is soft and easily hurt beneath its cover. Similarly, the Cancerian will put up a show of sophistication and hard-shell, but underneath is very sensitive, in both meanings of the word. They are " touchy " and easily offended, but also are sensitive to finer shades of meaning, to art, to intuitively understood things, to psychic contacts.

Like the crab, when hurt or apprehensive they go off sideways, they take evasive action. Like the crab again, they suddenly snap unnecessarily.

Glyph

♋ Is sometimes said to represent the breasts, giving the idea of nourishment and motherhood.

The Breasts, the Stomach, and the Alimentary System

All are to do with feeding and nourishment.

Silver

This is the metal of the moon, and shows the reflective, responsive character of Cancer.

The Mammary Glands

These are in the breasts. Cancer is the " mother " sign. The correlation is shown with the desire to nourish, and to care for and protect others. This is based on emotional feelings.

The Predominantly CANCERIAN Person

He reacts to his emotions rather than his reason, though he will seek to rationalise his instinctively obtained ideas. Even so, he will say, " I feel that," rather than, " I think that." Towards people he likes, he will be sympathetic, protective and guarding, while as regards things, he will have a natural instinct towards collecting. This may lead to the collection of any rare and interesting things, or may be no more than the urge to let things collect, so that clutter never gets thrown away. He is a great home-lover. Like the crab, he needs the shelter of his own shell. He is patriotic about his own country, and devoted to his own family. It is the " me and mine " sign. " He " is good in business and " she " in the home because the innate protectiveness makes both of them cautious and economical. Memory will be good. This Water sign is like a calm deep lake with its sudden storms.

In love he is emotional and tender; maternal if a woman, protective if a man, easily offended, becoming moody and even sullen, but eager to make it up again.

Overstress or misuse of these traits will mean fussiness and restlessness, the " clucking-hen " type. Morbid touchiness and over-sensationalism can occur.

Inhibition of his natural traits will be caused by being subjected to an over-rational life without anyone to " have and to hold." Lack of " nippers " in the slang term will mean that the crabby nippers will snap at the nearest victim.

As a child, the Cancerian is lovable because usually devoted to home and parents. When naughty, the appeal should be made to his feelings rather than to his reason. " It makes Mummy unhappy if you do so and so." Though he may have moods of snappiness, those in charge should think twice before they " snap " back. Hurts go deep and are remembered and brooded over. The frequent request of " Tell me a story " should be complied with as often as possible, as the Cancerian's vivid imagination needs paths in which to wander.

Physical characteristics (unmodified)

The whiteness of the Moon seems to show in the whiteness of skin of Cancerians, especially in the clear white forehead. The traditional description is of a soft-fleshed, not very muscular person, with a round " moon " face. Experience seems to show that this is not always so, the reflective ability of the sign showing so often in that the appearance will be more like that of the sign in which the Moon is found. " Crab-faced " means a peevish look and the more " touchy " often adopt this slightly annoyed glance.

Illnesses

Digestive troubles are frequent, also gastric ulcers. The strength or weakness of the feminine reproductive organs may be judged partly from the condition of this sign.

Manner of Life

The Cancerian is at his best in any sphere where his natural urges can reasonably be expressed. He is therefore better where he is busily looking after something or someone. The busy housewife is typically Cancerian. Even the men often enjoy cooking. Any business to do with catering to the public is congenial. He or she is better in a safe occupation. Though Cardinal, the busy ways are better when used for the home or for an organisation than for the too worrying needs of a personal business.

Spare-time Activities

Cancerian women are often essentially feminine and will occupy themselves with the usual sewing and knitting. Men enjoy the happy domestic evenings at home. Collecting is often a hobby, whether it is antique furniture or stamps. Everything to do with the sea, such as sailing and bathing will be enjoyed.

Example in keywords.—Uranus, *sudden change* (*disruptive*) will express its principle in Cancer *sensitively, protectively.*

Suggested Interpretation* to a person in whose chart this placing is found :—

" You are a ' live wire ' in the home, often making changes and introducing new ideas and ways.

" You will be unconventional in your ideas of bringing up your family, but everything you do will be for the better care of those in your charge. You will like to stock the house with the latest electrical devices for cooking and cleaning.

" Your independence and changeability will cause you to move house more often than most people. Your feelings are likely to be sensitive and it is not unlikely that such sensitivity will bring you into touch with occult or psychic matters."

Matters and occupations which come under Cancer and of which the Moon is the significator :—

All places of retirement and rest	Caterer
Antiques	Collector
Boats	Housewife
Cradles	Mother
Food	Nurse
Graves	Sailor
Homes	
Stalls	
The Sea	
The Masses	
The Womb	
Tides	
Women in general	

* As Uranus remains in each sign for 7 years, and so is general for all born during that time, it is not likely that its effects by sign position will be marked in the character, *unless* it is prominent as ruler, by house-position, or by aspects.

It is used here as an example of the working of its principle.

LEO

Ruler	...	...	Sun
Natural House	...	...	5th
Classification	...	...	Fixed—Fire. Positive
Symbol	...	...	The Lion
Glyph	...	...	♌
Part of Body	...	...	The Heart. The Back
Metal (of Sun)	...	...	Gold
Colours liked	...	...	Gold and scarlet

Fixed—Fire. Positive

The burning enthusiasm of Fire is less wild than in its expression in the first sign, Aries. There is still the self-expression of Positivity. The combination with Fixity brings a resistance to change, a desire for the enthusiasms to exhaust themselves continually in the same ways.

Sun

☉ This rulership adds a shining, gay, strong, powerful, sunny quality.

The Lion

He is thought of as the King of beasts. This symbol shows the regal nature of the sign, its dignity, its courage, its affection and its power. Applicable expressions are :—" lion-hearted "—and " The lion's share."

Glyph

♌ It is usually stated that this slightly inclined shape represents the heart ; others say it is the curl of the lion's tail, but another possibility is that gained from the study of the source of the most ancient of symbols, the carved stones of such places as Easter Island, and ancient engraved tablets found in India.

 On the former has been found this shape representing the Royal Escutcheon of the fabled lost continent of the Pacific with its civilisation, sometimes called " The Empire of the Sun."* It is said to mean " The Ruler," a typically Leonian phrase. It seems to be the origin of the letter M and contains the Solar circle.

The Heart

This correlation indicates the vital power of the sign. The heart is the dominating organ of the body and the Leonine person is most frequently the dominating person who takes the lead most naturally and organises others to follow, and who generously gives in a " heart-felt " way. Indicative phrases are :—" He puts his heart into what he does," " He said that from his heart."

The Back

This gives the idea of the stable uprightness of the sign. Conversely " He has no backbone."

* *The Lost Continent of Mu*, page 122. James Churchward.

Gold

This metal is shining like the Sun and is that generally used for a king's crown. Indeed this too is regarded as a Leo symbol, showing rulership.

Gold and Scarlet

These regal and sunset colours are applicable.

The Predominantly LEONIAN Person

He is dignified, proud, regal, commanding, powerful, magnanimous, large-hearted, generous, strong-willed, reliable, fixed in his opinions and principles, a good leader, a good " creator " both of a family and of ideas for organisations. He is faithful and trusting. He is usually cheerful, fond of games and amusement and the theatre (preferring the stalls to the gallery !).

His abounding vitality makes him very able in many ways, quick at work or play. He goes ahead by unconsciously banking on his innate self-assurance that the top must be the place for him. Such a naïve attitude of expectation often has something almost childish in it, but is this not consonant with the phrase " His Majesty, the baby " ? He often feels unappreciated, since he looks to others for the same open-handed trust which he himself gives. He fails to find it and is hurt when he finds his trust misplaced. He tends to do everything in a rather " big " way. His handwriting will be large.

In love he is whole-heartedly and sincerely affectionate, wanting to bring sunshine and happiness to the loved one.

Overstress or misuse of these traits will mean domineering insistence on being " top-dog," refusal to be content with second place, a conceited, self-appraising, snobbish attitude, a desire to keep the reins of power and make no changes. A " power-complex " will develop. Affection may become too patronising and the feeling of personal regality may lead to the treating of others as subjects. Speed may become impatience. A blithe enjoyment of taking risks may become recklessness, and overspending may take the place of generosity.

Inhibition of his natural traits will be caused if subjected to too much snubbing and too ignoble an existence. It is likely to produce broken-heartedness and dejection. The light of the Sun is covered by clouds.

As a child the Leonian will be sunny, happy, strong, playful, affectionate. He should not be too constantly " squashed," even if he does become too pleased with himself, as it hurts him to damp his natural high spirits and enthusiasms. The tendency to be " bossy " with other children should be gently restrained, not by refusal to let his natural leadership come out, but by showing him that he must play fair and others must have their turn, even though he does think he can do it best. He must be made to realise that it is undignified to show off.

Physical Characteristics (unmodified)

Good strong, well-formed back. Red lips and good colour. Generally a sunny look. Nose straight and short giving appearance of up-tilted nostrils. Dignified poise. Quick manner and walk.

Illnesses

Those which affect heart and back.

Manner of Life

The Leonian is at his best in any sphere where his natural urges can be reasonably expressed. He is therefore better as a leader than a follower, better where a broad sweep is required rather than too close an application to detail, and where he can feel himself the king-pin, rather than a common rafter, and where his organising ability is appreciated and not resented. He should be where a little showing-off and publicity will be appropriate.

Spare-time Activities

These should be gay and cheerful, including games and amateur acting. The Leo likes to spend money on his amusements and to entertain his friends. The theatre is much enjoyed.

Example in keywords.—Mars, *energy*—will express its principle in Leo— *creatively, joyfully*.

Suggested Interpretation to a person in whose chart this placing is found :—

" You have a most powerfully expressed energy with which you can set schemes going and organise affairs.

" You will use it to create whatever is your choice, whether in art, business, or hobbies.

" You will be ardent in your affections and will pour out your heart in your desire to make life gay and happy for your family. You will be liable to much disappointment, as such an overstrong personality is frequently too much for others and you will never get the same enthusiasm out of them, which you can give from yourself."

Matters and occupations which come under Leo, and of which the Sun is the significator :—

Circles	Actor
Crowns	Commissionaire
Fatherhood	Chairman
Fires	Film star
Positions of prominence	Games professional
Shining gay places	Goldsmith
Ornamentation	Jeweller
Sun bathing	Manager
Theatres	Monarch
Thrones	Organiser
Warmth	Overseer

VIRGO

Ruler	...	Mercury
Natural House ...	...	6th
Classification ...	...	Mutable—Earth. Negative
Symbol	...	The Virgin
Glyph	...	♍
Part of Body ...	...	The hands, the nervous system, the intestines
Metal (of Mercury)	...	Quicksilver
Colours liked ...	...	Grey and navy. Spotted patterns

Mutable—Earth. Negative

Earth, which the student began to understand in Taurus, is now looser and freer than in that sign since it is combined with Mutability. Like the other Earth signs, there is the indrawnness of Negativity, but the change is to the greater adaptability given by Mutability.

There is the same addiction to practical material things, not now possessively but more in a desire to serve others.

Mercury

☿ This rulership, as in Gemini, emphasises the communicative faculty, but it now expresses itself in concrete ways and in practical mental interests rather than abstract ones, and in manual occupations that are definitely useful. There is usually an endless running to and fro on countless errands and chores.

The Virgin

In the old pictures, she is shown with an ear of corn in her hand and a child in her lap. Hers is the symbol of fertility, so from this can be deduced the connection between Virgo and all crops such as corn and all which feeds, and the work necessary to produce them. From the figure of the virgin herself, we get the idea of purity, of inviolability, but the child shows the potentiality for motherhood.

Glyph

♍ See Scorpio.

The Intestines

These are necessary for the digestive process, again emphasising the connection with food. They are small and consist of many convolutions. It will be found that Virgo is interested in many small details.

Quicksilver

Though this is the Mercury metal, it does not seem so correlative with Virgo.

Grey, Navy Blue and Brown

Clothes, ties and fabrics of these colours and with spots or small patterns appeal to the quiet taste of Virgo.

The Predominantly VIRGO Person

He is essentially a worker, and often as a server of others. He does not want to take the lead, preferring to play the rôle of Martha, even if it is wearisome. The constant attention to detail makes a most careful worker where observation and exactitude matter. It brings personal neatness and precision. With the practicality of Earth, sensible necessary tasks are enjoyed and not shirked, and with the adaptability of Mutability, the constant change of detail in work is enjoyed. The desire for purity leads to an interest in hygiene and cleanliness while the correlation with inviolability leads to a desire to be happy within the home or the work-place, so long as others do not intrude too casually and without invitation. Many Virgos intensely dislike too close a proximity with others or to be touched too much. There is the same mental emphasis as in Gemini but the Earthiness makes it have a less light and airy touch. Virgo tends to neatness in everything. His handwriting will be precise and his letters tidily written.

In love he will be cool and retiring and " virginal." This can mean a charming modesty of behaviour or an over-sensitive untouchability. Sexually, he is interested and inquisitive and yet not eager to lose the virginal attitude and to partake fully of life.

Overstress or misuse of these traits can alter the pleasant reserve to a stand-offish attitude, which friends cannot break through, and from which they get little response, so they tend to go to more entertaining companions and the Virgo is then likely to complain of solitariness. An exaggerated attention to detail means that no detail is ever overlooked, so a pernickety, fault-finding attitude ensues and a constant interference with the less tidy and less strictly hygienic ways of others, often very well meant but highly irritating. Too much " keeping-oneself-to-oneself " can seem inhospitable.

Inhibition of his natural traits will be caused by inattention to his wishes and by a demand for impossible emotional response, resulting in nerviness, irritability and resentfulness.

As a child the Virgo will be dainty, lively, busy, ready to do little tasks. A little shy and not pushful. At school, he will work well and with tidy, neat ways. At home, he should be given opportunities of using his hands, such as in carving, gardening and general making of things. He will be more popular in adult life if he can be taught not to be *too* tidy and *too* fussy.

Physical Characteristics (unmodified)

Sometimes a widow's peak. Sometimes a limp (Vulcan, the lame god, is connected with this sign). Quiet eyes. Like Gemini, keeps youthful appearance.

Illnesses

These are liable to be intestinal and are often caused by worry, this being *over-concern* with matters of detail. Faulty intestinal action can bring rheumatism and gout.

Manner of Life

The Virgo is at his best in any sphere where his natural urges can be expressed. He likes to see that many tiresome details are meticulously attended to, especially in the sphere of cleanliness. He likes productive, practical work, however detailed it is and he is better as the " power behind the throne " than on the throne itself. Hence, he is excellent as the trusted secretary looking after every detail, or as a public health officer seeing to the many hygienic necessities of towns, schools, etc. As a craftsman he excels in making small objects and working out detailed plans of manufacture.

Spare-time Activities

These should be busy, practical, intelligent, varied. All hobbies that mean detailed constructive work, writing, gardening, careful collection of arrangement of data about any chosen interest. Quiet reading. Activities in clubs or societies which meet for study or criticism. The better type of Virgo will rarely live without including in his scheme, some way of being of service to others in a quiet, unassuming way.

Example in keywords.—Sun, *power*, *vitality*, will express its principle in Virgo *critically and in detail.*

Suggested interpretation to a person in whose chart this placing is found :—
" Your best expression of your real self is shown when you are able to exert your critical faculties. Whether this is applied to music, literature, or technical work, you will excel in your careful attention to the matter in hand. The use of your power in so many detailed ways is tiring and worrying, so rest in quiet surroundings is most recuperative."

Matters and occupations which come under Virgo, and of which Mercury is the significator :—

Actual work of an industry, rather than writing or talking about it	Accountant
	Agent
	Craftsman
Charitable societies	Critic
Cornfields	Dietician
Diet	Doctor
Fault-finding	Grower of Crops
Harvesting	Health Officer
Industry	Inspector
Literary criticism rather than light story telling	Teacher
	Masseur
Sanitation	Naturopath
Small animals	Secretary
The Services	

THE LAST SIX SIGNS

It will be noticed that each sign has something in common with the nature of that one to which it is opposite in the Zodiac.

If an orange is peeled so that the sections can be seen, and an elastic band is placed around it, passing through the top and bottom, it will go over one section on one side and another on the other side. This would apply to all and each of the opposing sections. They are then seen to be connected by this encircling. This will be explained more technically when a simple astronomical lesson will be given (p. 182).

In each of the second six signs, something relative to the nature of its opposite will recur, but will function less personally and in a wider field.

LIBRA

Ruler	... ...	Venus
Natural House	... ...	7th
Classification	... ...	Cardinal—Air. Positive
Symbol	... ...	The Balance
Glyph	... ...,	♎
Part of Body	... ...	The kidneys
Metal (of Venus) ...	...	Copper
Colours liked	... ...	Blues and pinks

This is opposite to the first sign of the original six, Aries.

The **Aries** person was described as the very *personal*—the " me-first."

Libra is the expression of the person in his relatedness to others or one special " other." He may attempt this amicably or otherwise, but though he may fail, his desire is for unison and partnership.

Cardinal—Air. Positive

Like its opposite (Aries), this is a Cardinal and Positive sign, so it has the outgoing activity and self-expressiveness which would be expected of this quadruplicity. It is also the second of the Air signs, so this now combines with the moving communicativeness, and the intelligence connected with that triplicity. Air is the medium of connection between all people, and on it are carried the words of speech. The special communicativeness of the Libran is with other people. He likes to bring himself into companionship with others and also to be the one who brings others together.

Venus

♀ Just as this rulership brings love of beauty and charm to the Taurean, so it does the same to the Libran. But in this sign it brings personal beauty and a love of harmony which means good taste and a desire for happy conditions and relationships.

The Balance

♎ From this symbol can be deduced the main feature of the character of the Libran, in that he is constantly bringing two things or people together, opposing the one to the other and " weighing them in the balance." In general it results as a strong desire for " another " in the life, who will keep the scales in balance. A husband or wife, or a business partner may be this person. If in disharmony, that person will be " the enemy." Through this ability the person shows his success or otherwise in achieving relatedness to others in life. Unfortunately, it also typifies the constant balancing by the Libran, in that he weighs the pro's and con's of a situation so long that he often cannot make up his mind or makes it up too late. Also, though he loves a mate, he rarely achieves a truly soul-satisfying partnership as he is too prone to notice small faults and weighs these up against the virtues of the chosen one.

Glyph
≏   This seems to portray the beam of a balance, or a yoke.

The Kidneys
These are excretory organs. The Libran is apt to get rid of things and people in his life, who are " weighed and found wanting " in his scales.

Copper
Again the Venusian metal.

Blue
This is a favourite colour except in darker shades, also pinks and soft rose.

The Endocrine System
This as a whole would seem to be Libran, since its equilibrium is reached by adaptation to new surroundings if these glands respond successfully.

The Predominantly LIBRAN Person
He is companionable and easy to be with, because he himself *wants* company and wants to create an atmosphere of pleasant delight. " He " will have a pleasantly furnished home and " she " will wear pretty clothes and usually be " easy on the eye " and be welcoming and happy. His love of the other is more as a complement to himself than to satisfy any deep emotion and his marriages are not always successful for this reason. " The other " is a necessary part of the furnishings to complete the harmony which *must* be obtained. The Libran is unhappy and nervous if in ugly or dirty or inadequate or uncongenial surroundings. He is usually tactful in his dealings with others and likes to bring people together for some desirable end. Unless of the completely vapid " chocolate-box " type, he is usually intelligent and says, " I think " rather than " I feel." He has been called " Lazy Libra." Another phrase which has stuck is " Lazy Libra loathes a duster," but this Cardinal sign is not really lazy, being far too interested in getting what it wants, especially if this can be through " the other " or with a partner. The customary *pose* is that of languor, but it is only the beauty of calm restfulness till the next occupation begins.

In love he is charming, longing to attract ; in love with love itself, rarely quarrelling, since that would " upset the balance."

Overstress or misuse of these traits can mean a discontent with real life which, in its very nature, can never be completely harmonious. Also a fatal tendency to " sit on the fence." The constant " seeing both sides " leads to indecisiveness and vacillations. The Libran finds it very hard to say " No " and then suffers regret. He tries too hard to please too many people, and fails.

Inhibition of his natural traits will be caused if subjected to loneliness or to ugly depressing surroundings. Resentful " Air " becomes inactive.

As a child the Libran attracts because he is so pretty and yielding and easy to train to charming manners. He is rarely rough or rude. He is perhaps the most popular of all children since he is so naturally sweet and lovable. He is very ready to be friendly and is thought a credit to his parents because of his good looks.

Physical Characteristics (unmodified)

There is usually a regularity of the features that is pleasing and beautiful. The figure will be well proportioned, the colour good, the eyes gentle. The most characteristic feature is the spontaneous smile which comes so readily to eyes and mouth. " She " may be of the extremely feminine dimpled type ; " he " may be so good-looking that he is almost effeminate. The voice is usually softly modulated and often a little drawling.

Illnesses

Usually healthy, but inclined to headaches and kidney trouble.

Manner of Life

The Libran is at his best in any sphere where his natural urges can be reasonably expressed. He is therefore better in clean, beautiful surroundings which satisfy his idea of harmony. He is better at the learned professions than at anything rough, or at artistic pursuits. If in trade, the objects made or sold should be beautiful or for the obtaining of beauty. His tactfulness makes him a good diplomat or " contact " man of any kind. He is better with a partner than by himself.

Spare-time Activities

Any lazy happy occupation, sunbathing, chatting with a friend from the armchair, reading in comfort, having beauty treatments. Painting, writing, making lovely clothes, dancing.

Example in keywords.—Moon, *response*, will express its principle in Libra *harmoniously, unitingly*.

Suggested Interpretation to a person in whose chart this placing is found :—

" On first meeting, you would be a delight to see, to hear and to be with. Your mannerisms and ways are all calculated to please and charm. Your ready sympathy and kindly ways make you a true " good companion."

Matters and occupations which come under Libra, and of which Venus is the significator :—

Affection	Artist
Beauty in form or shape	Beauty specialist
Art or literature	Diplomat
Marriage	General
Partnerships	Juggler (balance)
	Staff officer
	Valuer

SCORPIO

Ruler	... ...	Mars (and possibly Pluto)
Natural House	... ...	8th
Classification	... ...	Fixed—Water. Negative
Symbols	... ...	The Scorpion and the Eagle
Glyph	... ...	♏
Parts of Body	... ...	The generative organs
Metal (of Mars and Pluto)		Iron—Plutonium (possibly)
Colour liked	... ...	Deep red

This is opposite to the second sign of the first six, Taurus.

The **Taurean** was described as steadfast and determined. His feelings mattered very much to him, especially in practical matters.

In the case of **Scorpio** the feelings are intensified and are directed towards people rather than things, towards the feelings engendered by others and shared with others.

Fixed—Water. Negative

Like its opposite, this is a Fixed and Negative sign, so in it may be seen the same desire to remain firm in conviction and set ways. But, this is the second of the Water signs, so the combination of such Fixity is with the emotionality of this triplicity. Water has been described as unstable, hence the Scorpionic person is often at war with himself in this utterly contrary mixing of two trends in his very deep nature. His Negativity appears as depth of character and reserve of force.

Mars

♂ Just as this rulership brought energy and initiatory force to Aries, so it brings it to Scorpio, and emphasises the " war within himself," which is often a most unavoidable matter in the life of a person in whom Scorpio traits are strong.

Pluto

♇ It would not be correct to state that this newly-discovered planet has been decidedly adjudged to this sign, but opinion seems to be trending in that direction. The deep-working forcefulness of Pluto seems to accord with Scorpio, and the eliminative, ejectory action of the planet seems to fit with the connection with the life processes which come under Scorpio. This applies to birth, the sexual act, and death, at all of which times there is, to the thoughtful, a mystical depth of emotion as well as the actual physical happening. From the bound and the hidden, a new life can begin. There is a transformation at work.

The Scorpion and the Eagle

From this dual symbolism can be deduced much of the true meaning of the Scorpionic character in that the fight within the self may result in one of two ends. *The Scorpion* crawls on the ground, secretes itself in hidden places, then ejects its Martian sting with venomous power when least expected.

The Eagle takes wings and rises above all earthly considerations and enters a new sphere of expression in the heights he gains. While on earth he too can be cruel, seizing the unsuspecting lamb in his talons, but he *has the power* to rise above this if he wishes.

Glyphs
♍ Of Virgo.
♏ Of Scorpio.

It will be seen that these are the same except for their endings,* and that between them comes Libra. It must be remembered that these old symbols probably preceded any known writing, being displayed to the people to show the ideas inherent in them. This seems to be the picture of the oldest of racially remembered stories, that of the Creation of man and woman, and of the Fall. Tradition tells that there were once only ten signs, Virgo and Scorpio being one. Then came the division into two and the insertion of Libra. The woman was said to be made from the man, and the downfall of their happiness was caused by the Serpent. These signs are made of the customary serpent coil, but each ends in a characteristically male and female form. The Serpent (Hydra) is seen on the old celestial charts, lying beside them.

The Generative Organs
This correlation shows the connection with the deeper emotions, and also the privacy and secretiveness of the sign. It shows the connection with the life-force itself. The mystery of this is forever unexplainable.

Iron
The metal of Mars, denoting strength and energy, but *Plutonium* is the new metal of which we know very little.

Deep Red
The colour of the stronger Martian impulse.

The Gonads
The sex glands have great effect on the voice and on singing. Again the effect on the opposite sign is seen.

The Predominantly SCORPIONIC Person
He is deep in his feelings, passionately and devotedly attached to the person or the cause that is his, but equally passionately unchanging in his detestation of what is disliked. Such strength of feeling naturally drives to extremes of behaviour, but the entire chart must be studied before an idea can be gained as to the way in which such strength may be used. Even so, there is a note of regeneration in this sign. The aim and the expression may change completely. It is the drive and the depth and the passion that endure. The working from the hidden depths may produce the underground activity of the criminal with his cruel " sting," or the devoted work for a loved person, work or cause. The true feelings are often kept very secret. If for a cause, the hiddenness which is common to all the Water signs may be related

* The written symbol is more indicative than the printed one. See Fig. 1.

to that oneness to which mysticism in its highest sense forever points. This " Water " sign has the force of a mountain torrent and the unfathomableness of the depths of the sea.

In love he is passionate and with strong sexual feelings. Whereas the Martian Aries was ardent and forceful in his fiery nature, this Martian is deeply emotional, often with a mystical intensity in his love.

Overstress or misuse of these traits will mean passions which will not be deflected in their aim. Deep smouldering resentments against another, jealousy in love, hatred of fellow-man, can lead to danger and disaster. Over-secretiveness may cause bitter misunderstandings. The hidden sting may lead to death, which in Plutonian manner ends one chapter of life and begins another.

Inhibition of his natural traits will be caused by subjection to too " pedestrian " an existence.

As a child the Scorpian will be affectionate but liable to sudden rages and storms. Like the Arien, he should be given something to *do* so that this energy is used. It must be remembered that this is emotional energy, hence the outlets should be through emotional channels, through people to love, pictures to paint, poetry to be written, leading the child to " love the highest when he sees it."

Physical Characteristics (unmodified)

The eyes tend to be deep-set and steady in their gaze, often so markedly that the look appears hypnotic. Even if not to this extent, the Scorpian often appears to be watching and waiting for something or someone. He has an eagle-eyed look. The bone above the eyes seems prominent and is very frequently made more so by an exaggeration of the Martian eyebrows. This denotes strength of character for good or ill. Of late years, the feminine habit of thinning such eyebrows or removing them altogether and replacing them with an attempt to copy the delicate Venusian curve, shows that without knowing the cause, femininity realises that it is the truly feminine look which attracts!

Illnesses

All fixed signs have a tendency to rheumatism. The connection with the opposite sign indicates possible trouble. Difficulties with generative organs occur. Ruptures and abscesses may also be mentioned.

Manner of Life

The Scorpian is at his best in any sphere where his natural urges can be reasonably expressed. He is therefore better when he can deal with real life and not with trivialities.

The Mars rulership is very evident in the desire to cut, to penetrate and to probe. In real life the Scorpian wishes to do so for healing purposes. His desire is to transform, to give wings to those who are bound by illness, physical or mental.

He will be well placed as a doctor or preferably a surgeon who cuts into the body, or a psychologist who probes into the mental states of the unconscious self, endeavouring to bring to the surface and get rid of (Pluto) what was hidden. His ability to search for what is hidden and his persistence in tracking it down make him a good detective. Hence he inclines to research, whether in industry, science, or in more abstract ways, such as psychical research, occultism or mysticism.

Like Cancer, the first water sign, he will love art, music, poetry, and romantic literature and will put strength and depth into any creative work which he does. Again like Cancer, he will love the sea and often goes to sea by way of profession.

Spare-time Activities

These should be varied so that both the energy of Mars and the intuition of Water can be used. Hence, active sports such as boxing, also the arts and the occult studies. All water sports are enjoyed.

Example of keywords.—Mars, *energy*, will express its principle in Scorpio, *passionately, secretively and penetratingly.*

Suggested Interpretation to a person in whose chart this placing is found :—

" You have it in your own hands to be a power for good or ill in the world. You can draw from hidden depths of reserve energy and can exert an almost hypnotic power over others.

" It is necessary that you should know yourself and realise this so that you can train yourself to direct this strength towards ethical, therapeutic and mystical ends. Failure to do this will be destructive to yourself and others."

Matters and occupations which come under Scorpio and of which Mars is the significator :—

Army and Navy	Butcher
Passion	Coroner
Research	Detective
Sexuality	Pharmacist
The Procreative Act	Psychologist
	Public Analyst

Those more connected with Pluto are :—

Birth	Sanitary Inspector
Considerations of life after death	Surgeon
Death	Undertaker
Mediumship	
Secret matters	
Sewage disposal	

SAGITTARIUS

Ruler	... ...	Jupiter
Natural House	... ...	9th
Classification	... ...	Mutable—Fire. Positive
Symbols	... ...	The Centaur with Bow and Arrow
Glyph	... ...	♐
Parts of Body	... ...	The hip and thighs. Liver and hepatic system
Metal	... ...	Tin
Colour liked	... ...	Purple and deep blue

This is the opposite to the third sign of the first six, Gemini.

The Geminian was described as intelligent, active, versatile and interested in mental pursuits.

The Sagittarian goes further with these interests. The scope of his journeys, indeed all his activities will be wider and his studies more profound.

Mutable—Fire.　Positive

Like its opposite (Gemini) it is Mutable and Positive, so it has the adaptability of Mutability and the self-expression of Positivity, but this is the third of the Fire signs, so the enthusiasm and burning ardour of Fire is now combined with these.

Jupiter

This rulership emphasises the *expansive* ability. The Sagittarian is jovial and ready at any time to widen his scope to include more and more experiences.

The Centaur with Bow and Arrow

From this symbol can be deduced the main feature of the Sagittarian character. Of him it must have been written,* " I shot an arrow into the air, it fell to earth, I know not where." His objective in life seems to be to cover distance and it is curious that he so often cares little for what he attains at the end of the journey. Another fitting quotation would be, " It is better to travel than to arrive."

The Sagittarian will start off in a car without making any decision as to the place to be reached ; he will almost let that decide itself. He will shoot off conversational arrows in a provocative way, but often without real interest in the replies they call out. The arrows of Sagittarius are often wounding—he has not noticed that he hurts.

Glyph

♐　This is the arrow which shoots afar.

The Hips and Thighs.　The Hepatic System

The power of the thigh in the hip joint is correlative with many of the activities of the Sagittarian, who is a walker, a bicycler and a rider. Expansion is the keynote of this sign and one of the functions of the liver has to do with the metabolism of the body.

Tin

The metal connected with Jupiter, hence Sagittarian.

Purple

The colour always connected with the formal and dignified side of Jupiter but as it is not a fashionable colour for ordinary wear, its connection is not fully seen, deep blue being more usual for clothes.

The Pituitary Gland

This gland seems to control growth, hence its connection with the Jupiterian Sagittarius. Jupiter is part-ruler of Pisces and will be further referred to under that sign.

* *The Arrow.*　Song by Longfellow.

The Predominantly SAGITTARIAN Person

He is not only intelligent but intellectual. His mind interests itself in deeper profundities than does that of the Geminian. His tendency to constant movement urges him to take many journeys. He, like the arrow, must be free to find a mark. He wants to go far to explore, both physically and mentally. He loves all sport and games, and especially if in the greater freedom of the out-of-doors. In the earlier days of astrology, he was always connected with the horse. The Archer is often depicted as having the body of a horse. Undoubtedly he is often the " horsey " type or the man who loves to ride freely across wide spaces of country.

In love he is difficult to understand. The Fire side of him is ardent and enthusiastic, but he is Mutable, and can change, and above all he wants to be free. He often puts off marriage till a late date. A wise partner will let him have " plenty of rein."

Overstress or mis-use of these traits will mean an over-jovial, over-expansive type who becomes boisterous, slangy, sporty, and whose insistence on freedom means that he must be a law unto himself. The hell-for-leather type becomes too careless, too extravagant, too extreme. Joking can become " horse-play."

Inhibition of his natural traits will be caused by subjection to a life too sedentary or too narrow in activity and outlook. He will react by fits of temper or sulkiness.

As a child the Sagittarian will be alert, clever, good at games, lucky in most ways. Like a young colt, he must be taught to be controlled or he will get out of hand. Like all the Fire signs, he should be given the means of letting off his spirits and exuberance especially in out-of-doors activities.

Physical Characteristics (Unmodified)

Usually tall, athletic looking. The Jupiter rulership shows in a dignity of carriage, though the behaviour is often casual. There is often a high, dome-shaped forehead. The less developed and the young frequently adopt a free carelessness of dress. The tie flies out, the collar is soft and the corners are untidy. A lock of hair will drop over the face and be continuously flung back. With training, the true dignity of Jupiter arrives in middle age. The nervousness can result in restless manner and much talkativeness.

Illnesses

Nervous and respiratory complaints. Accidents. Psychological upsets. Mental overstrain. Liver troubles.

Manner of Life

The Sagittarian is at his best in any sphere where his natural urges can be expressed. He is therefore better when both body and mind have equal freedom for development. The natural fields for his mind are the profundities of the law, religion and philosophy. He is sufficiently versatile to study more than one of these, without neglecting the constant exercise without which he cannot feel healthy. If under-exercised, his liver suffers. Like Gemini, he is apt to have too many interests and to be very enthusiastic over each in turn.

Spare-time Activities

Like his usual occupation, these should be both mental and physical. Games, sport, walking, hiking, riding should be combined with going to lectures on the topic of interest of the time and with study of a serious nature. Any form of travel is a relief and a pleasure.

Example in keywords.—Saturn, *limitation*, will express its principle in Sagittarius in conflict with its *free-ranging manner.**

Suggested Interpretation to a person in whose chart this placing is found :—

" Whenever you wish to exercise either your mind or your body, the one by the study of your chosen subjects, and the other by travel or sport, you will find that you are subject to limitations and delays in your projects. Disappointments will be less upsetting to you if you realise this as part of your life pattern, and you will find that you will learn to concentrate on single-minded aims rather than to try to achieve too much."

Matters and occupations which come under Sagittarius and of which Jupiter is the significator :—

Archery
Foreign travel
Horses, riding, horse training and trading
Law
Philosophical thought
Prophecy
Religion
Roaming, hiking, tramping

Barrister
Horse trainer
Huntsman
Jockey
Lawyer
Metaphysician
Minister
Philosopher
Publisher
Sportsman

CAPRICORN

Ruler	Saturn
Natural House	10th
Classification	Cardinal—Earth. Negative
Symbols	The Goat
Glyph	♑
Parts of Body	The bony system and the knee in particular and the skin (the " limits " of the body)
Metal	Lead
Colours liked	Dark hues

This is opposite to the fourth sign of the first six, Cancer.

The **Cancerian** seeks to satisfy his need for security through safety and happiness in the basic things of life, in particular through his home surroundings, where he also provides shelter for others.

The **Capricornian** widens the field for this, striving to achieve security by his activities in the outer world.

* Saturn remains in each sign for 2½ years, so is general to *all* maps.

Cardinal—Earth. Negative

In Cancer, the Cardinality was combined with Water, but now it is combined with Earth, hence, as with Taurus and Virgo, there is a practical application to the concrete, everyday necessities of life. Negativity shows itself as an ability to withdraw from the rush of life and wait for the right time.

Saturn

♄ This rulership brings a caution and sense of limitation to the Capricornian. In mythology, Saturn was Chronos, the god of Time, hence timing is important to the Capricornian. His Cardinality keeps him on the go but he orders his actions, keeps to his time-table, and looks ahead cautiously for contingencies. The acceptance of responsibility is a Saturnian trait, so the person in whose chart Capricorn is strong will not hesitate to undertake this.

The Goat (Often depicted as a mythical sea-goat)

As there are two types of goat, so there are two types of Capricornian. In the countries where astrology must have begun, the goat is a domestic animal, a sad-looking creature kept to provide milk. It is seen limited to the sphere of activity by the rope to which it is tied. If free, it is stopped from making its way through the surrounding hedges of its field by the wooden cross bars on its neck. It has nothing to do but eat what it can find and give its milk. Many a Capricornian has this sad, long face and seems to spend his life in a very limited sphere, debarred from wider enjoyments, strictly keeping to the main point in life, which is provision of sustenance for the family by practical sensible work. He never ceases his efforts to " get somewhere," but actually goes round the same stake on the same rope for ever.

However, the mountain goat or antelope is a very different animal. Gaily leaping from crag to crag, he mounts higher and higher in his search for what is good. The phrase " to play the giddy goat " is now applicable. This other type of Capricornian has a delightful sense of humour and yet is never trivial. His common-sense and practised ability never desert him. He constantly aspires to higher and higher positions, ambitious to get to the top in whatever sphere of activity is his.

Glyph

♑ There is no explanation of this, unless some early type of goat had a twisted horn.

The Bony System and the Knee and the Skin

The bones are the scaffolding of the body. They keep it in proper order and shape. This is typical of the Capricornian and the key to his success in organisation. However, to mount the stairs, the knee must bend and the Capricornian will unbend when it suits him and if to his advantage. The skin is the final limit of the physical body, a most Capricornian matter.

Lead

This metal has always been connected with Saturn. Even in the dictionary, saturnine is given the meaning of " pertaining to lead." Capricornians are liable to " make heavy weather " of life and to live seriously.

Dark Colours

These in general and black in particular are usually connected with Saturn.

The Predominantly CAPRICORNIAN Person

He is practical, cautious, responsible and ambitious. He will work hard if it is going to get him somewhere. He will bear with limitations and frustrations since his very nature is conditioned to them. It is through the realisation that success is achieved through the willing acceptance of necessity, that he wins through in spite of all obstacles. " Saturnine " is well understood as meaning gloomy or grave, but the Saturnalia, the festival of Saturn, was a time of gaiety and fun.

In love as in everything else, he is cautious. Before taking on the responsibility of marriage, he will want to be very sure that he is safe in his choice. Once satisfactorily married " he " is likely to be happy, as he is a natural " good provider," and knows how to " husband " his resources. " She " will be economical and will run her house well, and will aid her husband in the social side of any " climbing."

Overstress or misuse of these traits will mean too utilitarian an attitude to life, too stern a behaviour to younger people. Economy can become mean and miserly. Love of punctuality and orderliness can become a reason for fussy nagging. Cautious looking ahead can become a selfish counting the cost before any action is taken.

Inhibition of his natural traits will be caused by being subjected to a careless, disorderly type of life with no possibility for advancement. Reaction will be the seeking of " place " by mean ways.

As a child the Capricornian is sometimes a " slow developer," like the Earthy Taurean. The Saturnian period is that of older life and he may be expected to come into his own all in good time. He should be made to share his toys and not hoard them for himself only.

Physical Characteristics (unmodified)

The darkness of Saturn is usually in evidence, both in skin, hair and eyes. There is a bony look, especially about the knees and knuckles. A typical signature is the presence of long deep creases at the sides of the mouth. The face is often long. Usually a grave, serious bearing.

Illnesses

Diseases which limit, such as rheumatism. Orthopaedic troubles.

Embryologists show that the endocrine glands and the central nervous system are formed from an infolding of the outer layers of the developing embryo, so they may be said to be related to the skin. Skin eruptions often follow a nervous shock. This may explain some of the skin troubles of this sign.

Manner of Life

The Capricornian is at his best in any sphere where his natural urges can be reasonably expressed. He is therefore better in routine work or in the organising of work on such lines. Hence, any business or government or political organisation suits him, or the church and the army from the point of view of an organised body. In such placing, he can look ahead and feel safe, since he will have steady advancement and a pension at the end. His sense of order makes him a good servant or official since he will carry out orders from above faithfully and will see that those below do their duty.

Spare-time Activities

The Capricornian is generally happy alone and in the enjoyment of serious reading and music, and in practical hobbies.

Example of key words.—Venus, the urge towards *harmony and unison* will express its principle in Capricorn, *prudently, coolly, aspiringly*.

Suggested interpretation to a person in whose chart this placing is found :—

" Even in love, the old proverb ' look before you leap ' will show your attitude. You will never rush thoughtlessly into too close a relationship with anyone, but will assess the situation and wait your time before showing your feelings. In your business or profession, you will show the same care before making any relationship which will involve close working together. You will incline to think of the practical value that such a relationship will bring you."

Matters and occupations which come under Capricorn and of which Saturn is the significator :—

Cold

Concentration

Crystallography

Discontent

Gates and doors

Old age

Orderliness

Responsibility

Civil servant

Mathematician

Osteopath

Politician

AQUARIUS

Ruler	Uranus (Probably)
	Saturn (Traditionally)
Natural House	11th
Classification	Fixed—Air. Positive
Symbols	The man with the urn of water
Glyph	♒
Parts of the Body ...	Shin and ankle. Circulatory system
Metal (of Saturn and Uranus)	Lead (possibly uranium)
Colours liked	Electric blue

This is the opposite to the fifth sign of the original six, Leo.

The **Leonian** person was described as regal, dominating, fixed in his own ways and opinions, whole-hearted in his feelings, and creative.

The **Aquarian** is just as fixed but his mixture is with Air instead of Fire, so he is mentally inventive. His objectives are more widespread.

Fixed—Air. Positive

Fixity, as before, betokens a firm resolute nature, insistent on keeping to its own way of decided self-expression (Positivity). As with the other fixed signs, it is hard to move from its preconceived ideas. A person with this predominance will be faithful to his commitments and to his friends. This is now the third of the Air triplicity, so the communicativeness of Air is evident. The special communicativeness of the Aquarian is by way of being a *carrier* of information and ideas, and *a disseminator* of such ideas through groups of people rather than mainly through writing and teaching, as with Gemini, or through personal contact, as with Libra.

Uranus (Probably) : Saturn (Traditionally)

♅ ♄ As stated before, though opinion in England tends to think of Uranus as the new principle, correlated often with Aquarius, opinions on the Continent vary. It does seem that the three new planets may not be so closely attached to any one sign. On the other hand, it may be that, just as they themselves are beyond the orbit of Saturn, the wakening of human consciousness to the acceptance of their inherent principles is taking mankind forward to a superconsciousness, only dimly realised at the present time. The expression is often used that Uranus is " taking over " the rulership of this sign from Saturn.

The traditional associations of *Saturn* with the sign indicate its caution and limitation and sense of timing and of responsibility, as it did to Capricorn, but the modern rulership of *Uranus*, the awakener and the rebel, brings a fight within the self, as did Pluto to the Fixity of Scorpio. Uranian independence and unconventionality seem completely at variance with Saturnian caution and sedateness, but, on closer examination, who is more set in his ideas and determined that no one shall deflect him from his purpose than the typical revolutionary?

The Man with the Urn of Water

The man is sometimes depicted in old illustrations as an angel, thus hinting at the super-conscious source of the " living water " which he pours out freely for all humanity, without thought or care for any idea of relative merit or need among the recipients.

Though this is an Air sign (reasoning intelligence), it is water which the man pours. Water represents that which is past reason, the intuitive or inspirational ability. Hence, it seems that the strongly Uranian person may add the flash of genius to the reasoning faculty. The water is poured out indiscriminately, an obvious indication that the Uranian will be interested in humanity as a whole, and be no " respecter of persons."

The Glyph

♒ This is especially noticeable in the light of modern knowledge. In the earliest of records on carved stones of antiquity, its wave-like form represented water. But also, the knowledge has come down through the ages that the two matching, undulating curves originally represented two serpents. The serpent represents wisdom (either truly wise or merely crafty). The lower was supposed to reflect the light under-belly of the upper. These ideas are centuries old. It is therefore extraordinary that, in modern times, they so accurately portray the Uranian-Aquarian, with his predilection for science, which is the use of the intuitive idea worked out by the reasoning mind and disseminated by every modern form of broadcast, cinematograph, radar, wireless, etc., for all of which " waves " are necessary, as we now know they are for the carrying of light.

The Circulatory System

Leo's bodily representative is the heart, the engine of the blood supply, while that of Aquarius is the complement of it, the supply to " all men " (the cells) of the bodily whole. This is a confirmatory testimony to the " broadcasting " tendency of Aquarians. What they have in either sensible ideas or wild revolutionary notions, is to be, or must perforce be, for everyone.

Shin and Ankles

These parts of the leg, necessary for walking, assist in the communicatory getting about, so usual for Air.

Lead

This metal was connected with this sign through the Saturn rulership, but we now know of *Uranium*, though little can be said about it at present.

Vivid, Bright Colours

These, such as electric blue, seem to be liked.

The Pineal Gland

This is often referred to as " a third eye." The ancients thought of it as the seat of the soul. It is a surmise that the extension of consciousness by Aquarian invention may give a clue to this relationship.

The Predominantly AQUARIAN Person

He is freedom-loving and perverse and original and independent, as compared with the so-called normal individual, but he is limited in that he often stresses his ideas to the neglect of all else, and fixed in that he finds it difficult to adapt himself to other ways, or even to see that there are other points of view besides his own. It is then obvious that the Aquarian will have something of the Saturnian gravity but, as with all the latter six signs, he will not apply it mainly in a self-seeking way, but will have objectives for his fellow men, and will seek to circulate his ideas through groups and in widespread ways. Since the Saturnian principle is now expressed through Air and not Earth, it will take a less severely practical form.

The demand for personal freedom is insistent, but the allegiance to those who will accept a friendly association with the limits of such a condition, is faithful and sincere. The objectives will be out of the ordinary, studies will be of the unusual, frequently of the very old or the very new.

Membership of clubs, lodges and societies will be more congenial than personal bonds. Human contacts are thus made in an impersonal, detached manner, rather than with the ardour of the Fire signs or the emotion of the Water triplicity.

Others must learn to be tactful and self-effacing if they are to live in harmony with the typical Aquarian, fixed in his ways and ideas, even if they are a complete *volte-face* from those he held a few years before.

In love he is as paradoxical as ever, having all the faithfulness of Fixity (to the loved one of the moment), but the detachment and lack of emotionality of Air. A happy partnership can be maintained if " the other " realises that the Aquarian does want to be free to pursue his mental interests and must circulate amongst his club or society friends.

Overstress or misuse of these traits will produce a rebel from everything, a person whose fixed idea is that the customary is wrong and that his ideas for drastic alteration are what all the world should accept. He is the fanatical reformer or the agitator type. Outspokenness will become rude tactlessness. Originality will be mere crankiness. The Saturnian side will then manifest as depression and isolation since there will be disappointment that the objectives cannot be reached.

Inhibition of his natural instincts will be caused by being subjected to an over-conventional, dull, hidebound life. He will become a malcontent.

As a child the Aquarian is healthy and happy, since he has something of the sunniness of his opposite sign. His good circulation keeps him warm and fit. He is usually good-looking, so his elders are proud of him. He will have original and inventive ideas which should be encouraged in every way possible, training being given which will be a foundation on which to build his edifice of thought. Without training, his tendency to originality is apt to become a rebellious insistence that he knows best and that all customary ways and ideas are old-fashioned, and he will become perverse and eccentric.

It is no use making an emotional appeal to an unemotional, aloof child, but once his *heart* is gained, which is different from mere emotion, he will be a sincere friend. He is likely to be a brilliant, galvanic type, quick at lessons and it may be necessary as with the Leo, to teach him not to show off.

Physical Characteristics (unmodified)

The bodily system being the circulatory, the complexion is usually fresh and well coloured. Next to Libra, this is probably the best looking of the signs. The Saturnine rulership gives a good bony framework but shows as a difference from the Leo opposite by the longer shape of the face. Often like a Leo, but with less polish and often with a deliberate and intentional oddness in the clothes or way of doing the hair. Ankles noticeable.

Illnesses

Those of the circulatory system, varicose veins, hardening of the arteries. Injuries are likely to be to the shin and ankle and it is confirmatory of the traditional bodily connection, that these bones and the joint they form are those most frequently broken or sprained. For Uranus, ruler of Aquarius, is also the significator of fractures.

Manner of Life

The Aquarian is at his best in any sphere where his natural urges can be reasonably expressed. He is therefore better away from mental, scholastic or personal restrictions of a too hide-bound or conventional nature. Being naturally a rebel, his temperament will be ruined by too conventional a life but he is one of the most trainable of people, having brain to train and the swift flash of genius to bring ideas for the trained brain to use. He is, then, the inventor of the new, whereas his opposite number, the Leonian, was the creator, the source of the new in life. Since the time of the discovery of his planet, Uranus, he can express himself best through science in its many inventions, new ideas, and readiness to change its decisions if new light is thrown on any question.

The understanding of the wave theory, and of everything to do with light, makes him ready to engage in any study which uses these. Photography, electrical work, radio, radiography, radiology, science in all its branches, study of unusual subjects such as archaeology and astrology are his best occupations. As one of the most revolutionary inventions since the discovery of Uranus is that of the aeroplane, the Aquarian naturally tends to its use, and to the study of everything necessary for its manufacture and improvement. Communication has thus been given an entirely new meaning as a correlative of Air.

Spare-time Activities

These are usually connected with his work or in some other expression of Aquarianism as indicated above. He is Fixed and he likes to go on in his chosen ways. Politically, he is likely to have advanced ideas, different from whatever is the usual manner of his day.

Example of keywords.—Neptune, *nebulousness, impressionability*, will express its principle in Aquarius, *detachedly and scientifically*.

Suggested Interpretation to a person in whose chart this placing is found :—

" In all matters in which the concrete and the material are forgotten and the intangible, the idealistic or the visionary are of more importance, your ability to tune yourself with these will be in interesting and inventive in ideas. Such ideas are indeed likely to react in material ways as new thoughts, of use in scientific fields and for the benefit of humanity.

" It would be as well for you to subject such ideas to careful scrutiny, so that muddled thinking is prevented."

Note.—The Neptune-in-sign position is general for all people for fourteen years (p. 169). Not too much importance must be read into it, *unless it is prominent* in the chart. It will not re-enter Aquarius until the end of this century. It is used here only as an example of the working of its principles.

Matters and occupations coming under Aquarius and of which Uranus is the significator (though the traditional connection with Saturn remains) :—

Aeronautics
Ankles
Astrology
Clubs
Co-operative Societies
Detached acquaintance
Eccentricity
Free-thinking
Humanitarianism
Light
Paradoxes
Positive occultism
Radar
Radiesthesia
Radio
Radionics
Rays
Revolutions and rebellions
　reforms
Science in general
Telepathy
Television
Waves

Airman
Broadcaster
Inventor
Photographer
Radiologist
Scientist

PISCES

Ruler	...	...	Neptune (Probably)
			Jupiter (Traditionally)
Natural House	...	...	12th
Classification	...	...	Mutable—Water. Negative
Symbol	...	...	The Fishes
Glyph	...	...	♓
Part of Body	...	...	The feet. The Lymphatic system
Metal	...	...	Tin (possibly neptunium)
Colour	...	...	Sea-green

This is opposite to the last sign of the original six, Virgo.

The **Virgo** was described as a practical worker with a desire to serve others and accustomed to the need for adaptability in conditions.

The **Piscean** has the same adaptability which is from the Mutability which they share, but his sign is the third of the Water signs, so in place of the intense practicality there is the emotion and intuition of Water.

His " service " is more from the desire to attain to a distant ideal, than for the meeting of the practical needs of which the *Virgo* is so aware.

Mutable—Water. Negative

Mutability, as before, indicates an ability to make changes without feeling annoyance, to adapt to circumstances. The mixture with Water, with its instability, makes this the most fluid of all signs. The negativity gives an indrawnness which is more marked than in the others. It leads to a hiddenness and a depth which are hard to fathom. This Water is the water of the sea, boundless, infinitely deep, calm at times on the surface, yet capable of sudden change to the wildest of storms. It is inoffensive at first sight, but with undercurrents which can be subversive and dangerous.

Neptune (probably) : Jupiter (traditionally)

Ψ, ♃ As stated before, though opinion in England tends to think of Neptune as the new principle, correlated mainly with Pisces, as well as the traditional Jupiter, opinions on the Continent vary.

As with Uranus, it does seem as if the finding of this extra-Saturnian planet is co-incident with a step forward in a new development of men in the direction of super-consciousness, as if the development of mind were now to be enhanced by the wider use of the intuitive faculties.

The traditional *Jupiter* rulership brings its expansion and its joviality as it did to Sagittarius, but the modern rulership of *Neptune*, the dreamer and the reacher for the intangible brings an emotional and idealistic side to the nature. The expansion is noticeable as an extremism, a bountifulness, a lack of putting limits to anything. The clouds and mists of Neptune are as a veil, hence the joviality of Jupiter is often as a veil to hide the ready tears of Pisces.

The Fishes

These are traditionally drawn swimming in opposite directions, but linked by a ribbon. They are representative of man's dual nature, his physical visible self and his hidden reality behind that self. The " silver cord " holds them together but each has its own goal to reach and they are in different directions. The Piscean almost invariably finds difficulty in life. He is pulled two ways and especially in his innermost, unconscious self. It is the unseen undercurrent which pulls and for a person without knowledge of modern psychology that is very confusing. The dual pull on the Piscean is responded to in a multiplicity of ways (Jupiter expansion), therefore the sign confuses and hides its true meaning, which is consonant with its nature. Confronted with danger, the fish hides.

The inadequacy and shifting weakness of this mutable sign when not at its best are shown in the instinctive shrewdness of slang, which dubs such a person as a " poor fish." The dubious nature of much that is Piscean is reflected in the expression that the possibility of treachery or deceit is termed " something fishy."

The Watery multiplicity of the sign will be shown by the floods of tears which spring easily to Piscean eyes and the torrent of words with which such a one will tell his dreams or experiences. This sign is intimately connected with the whole of the story of Jesus who was the Saviour of the cosmic period of time during which the vernal equinox has occurred in the constellation Pisces. This story can be told later, but the polarity (p. 182) between Virgo with its sheaf of corn and Pisces with its multiplicity and its fishes, will be obvious to the student if he remembers the parable of the loaves and the fishes and attendant multitudes and the limitless way in which the crumbs multiplied. Such astrological symbolism was common knowledge in those days and understandable by the people.

Glyph

♓ Again duality is shown. Pisceans can play a part and can dissemble, while the psychic can take on another personality. As well as being the two fishes with their link, it is also representative of man's physical and spiritual sides, joined yet separate.

The Feet

These are the last and most lowly parts of the body. They bear the weight of the whole. It will be found that the Piscean is often ready to put himself last, to sacrifice position and advantage to help others. He often bears a burden for others, unobtrusively and patiently. This was shown in the Christian symbolism when Jesus abased Himself to wash the *feet* of His disciples. These were men whose work was to catch *fish*.

Tin

This Jupiterean metal was originally connected with Pisces, but we now know of Neptunium.

Sea-green

This is the Neptunian colour, but in connection with the traditional Jupiterean rulership, violet or *purple* applies.

Pituitary Gland

If there is one glandular connection which seems obvious, it is this one. It is hidden deeply in the brain, and closely connected with the *Thalamus*, regarded as the seat of emotional life. It controls certain *rhythmic* activities in the body, such as the rhythm of sleeping and walking. These are Piscean activities. It is also supposed to be well developed in those who have artistic ability. It may therefore be found to be connected with psychic manifestations in which rhythmic ebb and flow, sleep or trance, are evident.

The Predominantly PISCEAN Person

He is essentially emotional, intuitional and expansive, going to extremes of elation and depression. He is the most sensitive of all the Water signs, reflecting what he sees, taking the shape into which he is poured. This is noticeable in the way he depends on others for " shaping " or support. It can now be seen that such impressionability is very dangerous. At its best, it gives an ability to receive from unknown sources and without rational thought, though little use can be made of such gifts if the mind has not been trained to use them. Every great painter, poet, musician or artist of any sort knows that his best work has been done in moments of inspiration. The sign Pisces will be found to be prominent in the charts of such people. This applies also to workers in material ways such as scientists who, in a dream or in waking moments will get the solution of a problem which has eluded them.

A further extension of this power to take an impression, to take the shape of the containing vessel, to hide the self behind a veil will be seen in the power of the medium to become controlled, to surrender her personality, to talk with another voice. It is also seen when the clever actor hides his own self to take the character of the part he plays.

The further sacrifice of self leads to devoted selfless service for others. This is especially so in the " behind-the-scenes " healing work of true nursing of the sick, when taken as a vocation.

The call of the intangible brings the Piscean into touch with all that is mystical, beautiful, not of this earth. About such things, more practical people may use Neptunian and Watery phrases as " up in the clouds," " smoke dreams," "unattainable Utopia," " muddled vagueness," " ideas of sloppy sentimentality," " bubble schemes," but the Piscean must be allowed to make heaven on earth in his own way and no other.

In love he will be intensely emotional, lost in an ecstatic dream (and so not very clear-minded about it). He will be a poetical, lyrical lover but not very practical about the financial necessities of marriage.

Overstress or misuse of these traits brings a great change in the impressionable Pisceans.

Clouds may obscure the vision as a fog does, and much confusion of thought and muddled behaviour may occur. Such cloudiness is deceptive, hence treachery or underhanded dealing may result. The desire to rise from material trammels may result in nothing but an escapism from responsibilities. " Fishes " can develop slippery ways. An old phrase is that this is the sign of " one's own undoing " and it is true that hiddenness and seclusion can come to the Piscean as imprisonment in actual fact, or as a withdrawal into the prison of self through pitying self rather than others or through the escapism of drugs or drink. He is caught in a net of his own weaving.

Inhibition of his natural traits will be caused by subjection to a material outlook, and an over-orderly existence. Reaction will be worry, and a complex of inadequacy.

As a child the Piscean will be gentle, soft, cuddlesome, dainty. Being over-emotional and over-sensitive, allowance should be made for this. He is not the type for rough games, but should swim early and like to handle a boat. He should not be reproved if he tells long stories of his dreams. On the other hand, since he has to live in a hard world, he should be encouraged to write these down in the hope that his vivid imagination may be trained to be of use later on if he wishes to be a writer.

Physical Characteristics (unmodified)

Feet noticeable—either very dainty and beautiful or the " sloppy " feet of the washer-woman type. Eyes slightly protuberant, like a fish, but often with a liquid beauty. Mouth often like a cod's mouth. In the very slack type, it often is open. The figure loses its shape early and in women there is much glandular development. The chin is sometimes indeterminate and weak, but in those whose artistic development is strong, it is particularly long and the nose is large.

Illnesses

The sensitiveness of the sign causes many of the diseases, digestive and nervous, which are due to this over-impressionability. Poisons and drugs affect easily.

Manner of Life

The Piscean is at his best in any sphere where his natural urges can be expressed. He is therefore happy when he has a " stronger vessel " in which to pour himself, such as an understanding partner or member of the family, who will look after the material worries of life while he can devote himself to art, music, poetry, imaginative writing. The connection with feet is shown in the love of dancing. This may be developed as a profession. So close is the connection that more practical Pisceans have been known to invent flooring materials for the feet to walk on, and to become chiropodists and bootmakers, repairers or sellers. The sea has a constant rhythm and this is a characteristic of poetry, music and dancing, which are all Piscean.

Mediumship as a profession is truly Piscean, using every characteristic of impressionability and non-materiality ; and with the less worthy, the ability to pretend.

Ministers of religion are often strongly Piscean, using the kindly sympathetic side of the sign and the strong desire to " help the under-dog."

Nursing the sick is again deeply sympathetic, connected with healing and carried on in the seclusion of hospital life.

All occupations to do with the sea attract the Piscean, whether to do with shipping or fish. All trades to do with liquids, from the wine trade to that of a laundry, are congenial to him, also businesses to do with oil.

On the stage, he excels as a character actor, so easily taking the shape of the one who he impersonates.

He is at his best when he follows his instincts. In a modern way of expression, it is to be realised that he is deeply in touch with his own unconscious, and with the whole wide realm of the vaster unconscious from which he gains his inspirations. He easily contacts the unconscious of another, hence his success in telepathy, clairvoyance, psychometry, and kindred abilities.

His fluidity allows him to change his ways frequently and his multiplicity gives him a wide choice in his manner of life.

Spare-time Activities

These should be rhythmic, artistic, by water, not too energetic, changing from gay to reflective. They should appeal to the emotions rather than the reason.

Example in key words.—Venus, *harmony, unison,* will express its principle in Pisces *nebulously and with impressionability.*

Suggested Interpretation to a person in whose chart this placing is found :—

" You have a keen sense of the harmony to be found in the less concrete things of life. You prefer to find beauty in the intangibles and to look for your closest companions amongst those who have similar ideas.

" In your affections, you will be sympathetic, tender and emotional and overflowing with feeling."

Matters and occupations coming under Pisces and of which Neptune is the significator (though the traditional connection with Jupiter remains) :—

The Abstract
Anaesthetics
Boats
Cheating
Clouds
Escape
Falsity
Fish
Fogs
Gas
The Intangibles
Intuition
Mazes
The Mystical
Plastics
Pretence
Psychism in all its branches
Retirement
Sacrifice
Schemes
The Sea
Simulation
Sleep
The Spiritual
Substitution
Veils

Artist
Character actor
Medium
Poet
Professions to do with the sea
Psychic
Spy
Wine merchant

(g) DIVISIONS OF THE SIGNS

As the Ecliptic has been divided into 360°, so each sign, being one-twelfth consists of 30°.

Decanates or Decans

These are divisions of each sign into three. They have no names other than those of the planet ruling them. Thus :—The Leo Decanate of Aries.

The first 10° of each sign are said to be most emphatically of its own nature and are ruled by its own ruling planet. The next 10° are sub-ruled by the planet ruling the next sign in the same triplicity. The final 10° are sub-ruled by the next in order in that triplicity.

By reference to Fig. 3, it will be seen, as an example, that the decans of the sign Capricorn would be ruled and sub-ruled as follows :—

> 1st decanate (1–10°) by Saturn.
> 2nd decanate (11–20°) by Venus.
> 3rd decanate (21–30°) by Mercury.

Navamsas and Dwadasamas

These should be mentioned as subdivisions of one-ninth and one-twelfth of a sign respectively. They come to us from Hindu astrology. They are rarely used by Western astrologers and further consideration of them can be left till that system is studied.

Lunar Mansions and Critical Degrees

This division comes to us from the Chaldeans and consists of a division of the 360° into twenty-eight parts of 12⅘° each. Each is a " Mansion " of the Moon in her daily motion. Not counting fractions, the degrees which mark the beginnings of these are known as " critical degrees." It is not necessary for a beginner to commit these to memory, but they must be mentioned in their place, so that reference can be made to them when required.

It is thought that planets found on these degrees are likely to express their principles with greater strength than otherwise.

TABLE OF CRITICAL DEGREES

	Signs				Degrees		
Cardinal	♈	♋	♎	♑	0°	13°	26°
Fixed	♉	♌	♏	♒	9°	21°	
Mutable	♊	♍	♐	♓	4°	17°	

THE HOUSES

REFERENCE to the early part of Chapter 2 will remind the student that he has to understand several " first things " before he can begin to set up and interpret a chart of the heavens for any given moment.

The name " house " has come down to us from early astrological usage. In earlier writings (see Ptolemy's *Tetrabiblos* and other early books), the meaning was merely the " place " of a planet, and apparently referred to the sign which it ruled. We read in Ptolemy's works " when Saturn is in its house of Capricorn " and so forth.

However, from earliest times the attempt has been made by astrologer-mathematicians to repeat the twelvefold division of the signs, using as a starting point that degree of the ecliptic which is rising over the horizon at any given time. For a personal chart, this will be determined by the *moment of birth*. This is because one of the main postulates of astrology is that the nature of anything in the universe can be judged from an understanding of the interpretation of the cosmic pattern of *the moment when it began.*

Hence, the first *house*, as counted from that degree, will correspond in meaning to that of the first *sign*, but, whereas the *sign-meaning* will give an understanding of a MODE of action or behaviour, the *house-meaning* will give an understanding of the SPHERE OF LIFE to which this may be expected to relate.

This is so in general terms, though there is an overlapping of meaning between the two.

Fig. 6 is a representation of the houses, as seen in a circular chart. The method of arriving at their placing will be found in Chapter 6 on " Computation " and a full example is given in Chapter 11.

In a chart, the houses are always arranged in approximately the position shown, even though this may not be astronomically correct. For quick inspection it is easier that the visual impression should always be, as nearly as possible, the same.

Rotation of the Earth

As the earth rotates once in every twenty-four hours, consequently the twelve signs appear to pass through the twelve houses in that period. The arrangement of the birth chart shows the alignment for the birth moment.

Naming of the Houses

These are commonly referred to by their numbers. But, each in its basic correspondence with its *natural* sign denotes something of the *element* of that sign. The names of the elements are placed in the houses *to remind the student of this important classification.*

Hence, the 1st, 5th and 9th houses are Fire houses, 2nd, 6th and 10th are Earth houses, 3rd, 7th and 11th are Air houses, and 4th, 8th and 12th are Water houses.

The Angles

The four points on the ecliptic defined by the degrees ascending over the horizon and culminating at the meridian and their opposites, are known as the Angles. Full description of the astronomical meaning of these terms will be given in the chapter on " Computation," p. III–II2.

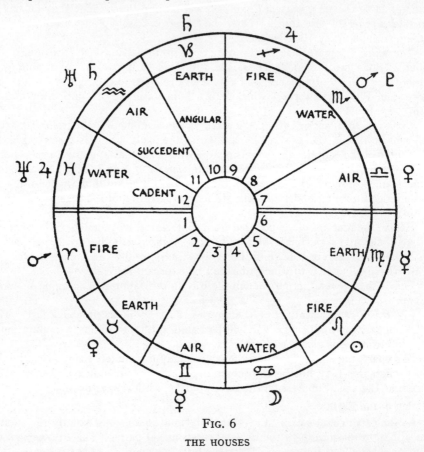

FIG. 6

THE HOUSES

Early astrological books were written in Latin, or translated into Latin from Greek or Arabic. Hence, the houses after the Angles (in the order of their numbers, Fig. 6) were called the Angular houses. The Latin verb *succedere*, meaning " to follow," gave the name to those which followed the angular ones. The Latin verb *cadere*, meaning " to fall," gave the name to those which " fell " furthest from the angles. This classification applies to houses by Quadrant systems only (see p. 131).

Meaning of the Terms Angular, Succedent and Cadent (In Quadrant Systems)

KEYWORDS

Angular	...	Powerful ; initiatory
Succedent	...	Resultant status
Cadent	...	Dispersion of ideas and energies

It will be seen that these words give much the same meaning as those given for the correlative quadruplicities.

In the *Angular* houses, in the ways of their differing natural triplicities, each is indicative of power and newness ; 1st, the person ; 4th, the home ; 7th, the partner ; and 10th, the outer life of the world, are all sources of power and life.

In the *Succedent* houses, in the way of their differing natural triplicities, each is indicative of a state which results and which it is hoped to keep steady ; 2nd, the possessions, 5th, the children, etc., 8th, partner's possessions and strong feelings, 11th, the friends and objectives. To a great extent these are the results of self effort, home training, partner's effort and outer activities.

In the *Cadent* houses, in the way of their differing triplicities, each signifies a dispersal, a more spread-out activity ; 3rd, the mental interests, 6th, the work, 9th the travel and study, 12th, the many *hidden* matters, all signify a spreading or dispersion. These meanings are not so concise and clear as some others, neither is the traditional idea of the strength of the houses so true.

When the houses are equal, that is, each containing the same number of degrees of ecliptic as in the Equal House system (see Chapter 7), the terms *Cardinal, Fixed* and *Mutable* are more applicable to the 1st, 2nd and 3rd and so on sequentially, since the cusps of the 4th and 10th are not necessarily coincident with the angles, nor are there always three houses between angles.

It used to be said that planets in the angular houses were the strongest, in the succedent were weaker, and in the cadent were weakest of all.

It would now seem more true to experience to state that *each house is as strong as every other in its own right*, and that Cadency has been mistaken for weakness because its strength has not been apparent in worldly affairs and has therefore not been appreciated from a materialist point of view.

The strength of Angularity is better expressed by saying that planets are undoubtedly strong when they are close to one of the angles, especially to the Ascendant or Midheaven, irrespective of which side of these they may be. This is then seen to be NOT primarily so in relation to house position by any system, but by reason of nearness to the degrees of ecliptic brought into prominence because rising or culminating, these being highly important points of mundane significance.

Cusps

The points of division between the houses are known as the cusps.

Connection Between the First Six and the Last Six of the Houses

Just as the first six *signs* were said to express a personal application, while the last six were said to be more concerned with activities entered into with others or further afield, so the *houses* correlate in meaning. Similarly, as each *sign* was said to have something in common with that one to which it is opposite, the same is true of *each house.*

THE HOUSES AND THEIR MEANINGS IN KEYWORD FORM

1–6—PERSONAL

1. The person
2. Possessions and feelings of the person

3. Short communications. Mental interests.   Nearest   relations   such   as brothers and sisters. Neighbours
4. Home (Base)

5. Creativity,   risks,   pleasures,   love, children
6. Service ; in work, in health

7–12—WIDER EXPRESSION

7. Others in close connection
8. Possessions   of   or   from   others. Legacies,   shared   feelings.   The life-force in birth, sex, death and after-life
9. Longer   communications.   More profound mental interests

10. Matters outside the home. Public standing.   Attainment
11. More detached contacts such as friendships. Objectives
12. More   secluded   service.   Retirement ; escape ; sacrifice ; hidden life of the unconscious

Important Note

As with the keywords given for the planets and signs, these must be taken as an attempt to give a *central idea* only. This must be understood and amplified.

HOUSE MEANINGS

To each will be given its classification with reference to natural sign, natural ruler, corresponding element, and position in relation to the angles.

THE FIRST SIX HOUSES

The First House

As *Aries* was described as an intensely personal sign, so the first house refers to the matters about which the chart is set up, thus in a personal chart, it will refer to *the person.* His type and to a great extent his physical characteristics, may be inferred from the planets in the first house and the sign on its cusp.

Mars, Fire, Angularity and Cardinality all show the initiatory purposefulness of the person.

Note on the First House as the Ascendant

The cusp of this house, and sometimes the entire house, is spoken of as the Ascendant, since it is the house beginning from the Ascending degree. It is therefore of the greatest importance, because when delineating a chart, every trait of character deduced from any other part of the chart, must be considered in relation to the *type of person* evincing it, as shown by the Ascending sign.

The Second House

As *Taurus* was described as a possessive sign, but with strong feelings for that which is his, so the second house refers to the *possessions* and *feelings* of the person. Hence, it has to do with *money*, particularly that earned by the person.

Venus, and *Earth* show the affections, the resources, the property of the person, while Succedency and Fixity show the desire to keep these.

The Third House

As *Gemini* was described as a communicatory and mental sign, so the third house refers particularly to all sorts of communications, whether by speech, letter, telephone, lecturing, teaching, learning, signalling, etc. Also to all sorts of communicatory *activity* such as walking, bicycling, motoring, visiting. All *mental activities*, such as those above and such work as reporting, clerking, story writing. The *mental quality* is also shown by this house. Also those relations closely connected, generally *brothers and sisters* and those living within easy communication as neighbours.

Mercury and *Air* will be seen to correlate with these meanings, while Cadency and Mutability show their dispersion.

The Fourth House

As *Cancer* was described as a protective, material sign, so the fourth house refers particularly to anything enclosed which surrounds and protects. Chiefly *the home*, also the womb and the grave. From its position in the chart comes its meaning as the *base*, as a home is the base from which one starts out in life. This house generally refers to the mother, though the connection is not as infallible as older books imply. The mother does not always connect herself solely with the home as in days of large families and little outer life for women.

Moon and *Water* correlate with these meanings, while Angularity and Cardinality show the busy liveliness of the home. In particular, the Water houses seem to be connected with the private and the hidden, as also understood in the occult, the mystical, and the unconscious.

The Fifth House

As *Leo* was described as a creative, sunny, happy sign, so the fifth house refers to the *creativity* of a person. This does not refer to the sexual impulse so much as to the principle of fatherhood, the desire to express the self happily. There is often a risk taken in so doing. From the above may be understood the link between creativity as expressed in children or any of the creations of the artist, the author or the actor, also pleasures, making love, engagements, lovers, children, games, racing, gambling and speculation.

The *Sun* and *Fire* correlate with these meanings. while Succedency and Fixity imply the desire to keep such things.

The Sixth House

As *Virgo* was said to be a critical sign and addicted to detail, so the sixth house refers to detailed *work*, usually of a practical nature, as its Earth connection shows

Virgo also signified *service* and the sixth house refers to this especially. Its connection with *health* and *hygiene* can be seen, partly through the Virgo love of purity and cleanliness ; but there is another link. In any organisation, group, or even in the home, it is the combined *work* of each concerned, the *service* given by each, which makes the whole a properly functioning unit. Similarly, it is the efficient functioning, or *service* given by each cell of the body which combines to make a healthy whole.

Mercury and *Earth* correlate with these meanings, while Cadency and Mutability point to the detailed nature of the above.

THE LAST SIX HOUSES

The Seventh House

As *Libra* was described as uniting and harmonising, so the seventh house, the opposite to the first (*the person*), refers to any *others* with which the person seeks to unite himself. These can be *partners* in marriage or in business or very close friendships. As there must be a bringing together, even to effect a disharmony, so this house also refers to the enmity of others.

Venus and *Air* correlate with these meanings, while Angularity and Cardinality show the outreaching nature.

The Eighth House

As *Scorpio* was described as a strongly passionate sign and deeply mystical as regards the feelings and their transmutation, so the eighth house, the opposite to the second (possessions), refers to *feelings* and *possessions* gained through *others*. It has been called " the house of death," but this is an over-emphasis on but one stage of life. Possessions from others include money from partner or person closely connected. Hence legacies, left by another.

A re-reading of the Scorpio meaning will recall the connection with the life force as at work in birth, in the sexual act and at death as the beginning of a new life. These are times of the arousing of deep and strong feelings, such as passionate love or hate, jealousy or revenge. As with the other Water houses, the eighth is especially connected with the mysteries of occultism and psychism and with research into the problems of the after-life.

Mars, Pluto and *Water* correlate with these meanings while Succedency and Fixity point to the need to settle matters.

The Ninth House

As *Sagittarius* was described as a sign of longer communications and of deeper mentality, so the ninth house, the opposite to the third, refers to longer communications, hence *foreign travel and foreign lands* and *more profound mental activity*. In this may be included higher education, the universities, deeper studies, such as philosophy, the law, religion and, more serious writings of more enduring literature, hence publishing and all people to do with such things. It has been called " the house of dreams " and has been connected with prophecy. The latter seems more allied to the Water houses, but certainly there is travel into realms unknown when in dreamland.

Jupiter and *Fire* correlate with these meanings, while Cadency and Mutability show the more scattered or widened tendencies.

The Tenth House

As *Capricorn* was described as an ambitious, practical, cautious sign, so the tenth house, which is opposite to the fourth, refers to all practical, ambitious, security-making matters outside the narrow protective circle of the home. It used to be called " the house of the career and the father."

It must be remembered that in the very early days of astrology, people tended to live where they were born and to stay in the same stratum of society from which they sprang. As there were few means of getting about and trying other ways of living, it was natural that a man should learn a trade or profession from his father and should carry on in the shop, the farm or the practice, which had been built up for him. To judge by the old books, a woman was not considered worth a horoscope unless she was of great importance, since we only find them for such as a queen. Needless to say, every woman has a tenth house to interpret just as a man, but many women have no career other than that of home keeping. Hence it would seem that the essential meaning of the tenth house is the *expression of self in the outer world*, especially as regards *attainment* in life.

This house often does NOT describe the career but rather the way in which the person tackles his or her outward expression. Naturally, in a world where most people have to earn a living, this is usually expressed in the daily work, done to achieve *security* for self and family and usually with *ambition* to succeed. Its connection with the father is by no means infallible, though the fourth and tenth houses may show the parents from the angle of vision of the child in question.

Saturn and *Earth* correlate with these meanings, while Angularity and Cardinality emphasise the outward expression.

The Eleventh House

As *Aquarius* was said to be a detached, intelligent sign, so the eleventh house, which is opposite to the fifth, refers to *connections, interests and objectives* which are more detached than those of the fifth (Air instead of Fire).

People referred to will be friends (not *close* friends who are to be considered more as partners) and acquaintances made in social groups or especially in clubs or societies which meet for a certain cause, 'ism or objective. Hence, all objectives come into this category. It used to be called " the house of hopes and wishes." These are subject to change and have not the personal, heartfelt meaning of those of the fifth house.

Uranus and *Air* correlate with these meanings, while Succedency and Fixity show the resultant as such activities will result from out-of-home contacts.

The Twelfth House

As *Pisces* was described as a hidden, emotional, sacrificial, intuitive and psychic sign, so the twelfth house, which is opposite to the sixth, refers to the *hidden*, the *service which is sacrificial*, the *psychic* and the *unconscious*. It also refers to the more serious states of ill-health and to incarceration in hospital, prison or asylum. It used to be called " the house of one's own undoing " and " the house of sorrows." Old-time astrology seemed to dwell on catastrophes and troubles more than does its modern equivalent. It must be said that, with the advance of medicine and with a greater personal freedom in life, many sorrows are not as drastic as they used to be. Even so, the deepest sorrows and the hardest sacrifices are often concealed, and the willing unselfish service for others is often behind four walls. The séance takes place in a quiet and secluded room.

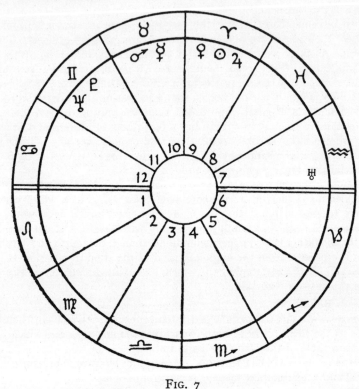

FIG. 7

PLANETS, SIGNS AND HOUSES

Visits to hospitals, prisons and asylums are sometimes the results of a person's own mistaken ways. Perhaps the most modern conception of the twelfth house is its relationship to the unconscious of the person, lying as it does behind the first house, the person himself. Here indeed are the results which are of our own undoing, if we thrust into the unconscious that which we are not brave enough to accept and face as part of ourselves. Here too is the channel for intuition, inspiration, and the most mystical spirituality, if we will allow it to bring these from its hiddenness.

In a more factual way, since this house has to do with the less tangible and graspable, it includes all that *escapes* if not well guarded, such as gases, anaesthetics, vapours, prisoners, would-be suicides. Other matters are those which are boundless, hence the sea and imagination. Also that which is not what it seems to be, hence cheats, forgers, deceivers, impersonators, character actors, plastics.

As with Pisces, everything to do with trades of the sea and with fish must be included, also all kindly and truly sympathetic vocations, also oil which not only is slippery but actually begins its life by being made by tiny creatures under the sea.

Neptune and *Water* correlate with these meanings, while Cadency and Mutability imply the dispersion inherent in the interpretation of the symbolism.

PLANETS, SIGNS AND HOUSES

These rarely correspond precisely as in Fig. 7. A sign usually extends partly over one house and partly over another.

The figure is given (as yet without computation) so that the student may begin to practise *Interpretation* in a simple form.

Interpretation of Planet in Sign and House

Refer to keywords on pages 24, 47 and 92, and put their meanings together, first in what will be the stilted keyword language and then in conversational words.

Example 1.—Sun in Aries in ninth house.

By keywords :—" Your *power* and *vitality* are used *assertively* in matters of *travel* and *deeper study*."

By interpretation :—" You are a busy, forceful, energetic person, keen to get about, see other countries and use your brain for serious study."

Example 2.—Uranus in Aquarius in seventh house.

By keywords :—" Your urge to be *disruptive* is used *detachedly* when dealing with others in *close connection*."

By interpretation :—" You have a strong tendency to split from anyone with whom you have placed yourself intimately, either in marriage or in business. You will do this coolly and in an independent spirit."

The student should practise with other combinations of planets, signs and house.

Only in this way can he learn to be a true astrologer, giving his own interpretation in the light of his knowledge of the true meaning of the various factors.

The use of ready-made interpretations from text-books can NEVER take the place of this.

Exercise

Re-read Chapters 3, 4 and 5, but in a different way.

The method is to read *as a whole* that which has been read separately about each *planet*, the *sign* it rules and the natural *house* of that sign. If the planet is connected with two signs and houses, the description of the planet and its principles should again be read in connection with these. In this manner, a further understanding can be gained of the intertwined meaning of planets, signs and houses.

Interpretation of Sign on House-Cusp

The affairs correlative with any house are affected not only by a planet in it (and there may be none) but by the sign on the cusp.   It will be helpful to think of the sign *as taking the place of* the natural sign of that house, which therefore has to show itself in this adopted manner.

Thus in the interpretation of any sign on the first cusp, the natural energetic self-seeking forcefulness of Aries is modified by the sign in question.

Further Examples.—Capricorn on fifth cusp—the natural joyousness of Leo now manifests in a more cautious, controlled way.

Aries on third cusp—the natural communicativeness of Gemini now manifests in a more active, forceful manner.

Interpretation of Planet as Ruler of House

The way in which the sign will affect a house on the cusp of which it is placed in a chart, will be according to the conditioning of the planet ruling that sign.   This will be understood better after reading the chapter on Aspects (Chapter 10).

CHAPTER 6

COMPUTATION

IN this chapter, the reasons for the calculations to be made are explained and definitions are given of all terms used. As the same understanding is required of a student of astronomy, surveying, aerial or marine navigation, fuller explanation of the principles involved will be found in text books on these subjects.* As much of it is of interest to the general public, the same explanations will be found in a necessarily restricted astronomical section of *Whitaker's Almanack.*

However, there may be readers whose interest in astrology has led them to wish to learn to erect a chart, but who have no desire for explanations of the steps taken to do this. For them, it will be enough to read the explanations and then follow the summaries of the instructions (pp. 108 and 118). Consideration must also be given to those whose mature understanding of human nature can be of great worth in the helpful interpretation of a chart to the person concerned, but who feel disinclined towards calculatory work of any kind. These are recommended to use an automatic calculator in the form of a circular slide-rule,† or to have correct charts cast for them by an astrological practitioner.

Checking the Birth Moment

Inquiries as to the accuracy of the time given for the birth moment should be made.

The time usually given is that of the child's first cry, it being understood to be almost coincident with its first independent intake of air into its lungs. Opinions differ. It may be thought that the time of extrusion from the mother should be taken, or the time of severance from the mother.

If the time is not known exactly, the attempt may be made to work backwards to the birth time if events in the life are known. This is called " rectification " (see p. 259), but is by no means as infallible as its name implies.

Casting the Horoscope

This is the phrase technically used to cover the process of finding the positions of the signs and planets for any given time and place and then charting them. (Certain other details are also added.)

" Putting up a chart " and " doing a map " are the more informal and customary modern expressions used.

The work necessary for a chart should not take more than ten minutes when once understood, though the complete assessment of details and careful entering on to a chart-form will take another twenty minutes.

This falls into two parts :—

Part 1

The calculation to find the zodiacal longitude of each planet for the given *time*.

* See *Astronomy for Surveyors*, Rice-Oxley and Shearer. Methuen & Co. Ltd.
† Made by John Gay and obtainable from L. N. Fowler & Co., Ltd.

Part 2

The calculation to find the Sidereal Time for the given moment of the meridian of the given *place*, known as *local* Sidereal Time and hence to find, by reference to " Tables of Houses," the degree rising over the horizon (Ascendant) and the degree culminating at the meridian (Midheaven—see p. 112), from which the house cusps remaining will then be found.

Forms for Calculations

Until the student is familiar with the work, he will find it helpful to use the forms on which the explanation of these two parts is summarised (pp. 108 and 118). He can buy these for use (see p. 315) or copy if preferred. Good presentation on chart-form will be made easier by these means. For full examples see Chapter 11.

Part 1.—*TO FIND THE ZODIACAL LONGITUDE OF THE PLANETS FOR ANY GIVEN TIME*

Explanation of various " Times " Commonly Used and Conversion of Birth Time to Greenwich Mean Time if Not so Given

Examine the birth moment to see in what category of " time " it has been given.

Clock Time

This will be the time *generally* used. The clock registers the division of the day into twenty-four hours, which is approximately the time taken for the earth to rotate once on its axis.

Zone or Standard Time*

This is the " clock time " used in most countries, clocks being synchronised so that they all show the same time throughout the whole of the country ; or, in the case of a very large country (or ocean) divisions are made into zones, each of which keeps its own zone or standard time. If such an arrangement were not made in each country, it would be impossible to co-ordinate arrivals and departures of trains, radio programmes, and so on, as time would be measured in *local time* ; noon at any place being that instant when the Sun transits the local meridian. At local noon at any given place, those places eastward from it will have already experienced their local noon, whilst those places to the westward will not yet have experienced local noon. Thus the necessity for a uniform standard of time throughout a territory is obvious. Consequently standard or zone time, as this synchronised time is called, has come to be used in practically every country throughout the world, and in order that the various zone times can be conveniently related to one another, the various countries have agreed to base their times on Greenwich Time, but to vary it in multiples of 1 hour (or ½ hour). Thus, Berlin, whose Local Mean Noon occurs 54 minutes before that of Greenwich Mean Noon, uses zone time of + 1 hour, and clocks there will show exactly one o'clock when the Greenwich clock shows noon.

* See Appendix.

Greenwich Mean Time (G.M.T.)

As the days (by solar time) are not exactly equal, a " mean " or average is taken. The letters G.M.T. are customarily used to denote this mean time for Greenwich. It is the zone or standard time used in Great Britain and some other countries. These expressions are unfamiliar in the British Isles as the arrangement to use Greenwich Time throughout the country had been made before the other countries adopted the system of zones. In former times, each country kept its own standard time, usually that of its capital.

Birth Time

It will now be realised that this will be usually given in the *standard time* of any country (or zone of country), the British *standard* being referred to as G.M.T.

Exceptions

(1) In 1916, an Act of Parliament was passed in England, to authorise what was known as Daylight Saving. This decreed that, on a certain day in spring of each year, the clocks should be put forward one hour, in order to make better use of the long summer evenings. On a specified date in the autumn the clocks revert to G.M.T.

(2) In 1941, a further Act was passed in England, ordering that Summer Time, as it was then called, should be kept all the year round, with a second advancement of the clocks in the summer months. This was for the better use of the daylight hours for war emergencies. It continued until 1945, and was used again in 1947 for the purpose of saving electricity. These times are referred to as :—

British Summer Time (B.S.T.) and British Double Summer Time (B.D.S.T.).
IT IS OF THE GREATEST IMPORTANCE THAT THE ADJUSTMENT FOR THIS SHOULD NOT BE OVERLOOKED.

Before the emergencies of the war years, the time of alteration to and from B.S.T. was printed on the first page of each Ephemeris. To make sure that the adjustment will NOT be forgotten, the student may find it a useful hint to attach a piece of adhesive paper across the front of the Ephemeris of each year for which it must be remembered. In this way, he cannot take up one so marked without being reminded.

Summer Time in Great Britain

(Changing at 2 a.m. G.M.T.)

1916	May	21	to	Oct.	1	1927	Apr.	10	to	Oct.	2
1917	Apr.	8	to	Sep.	17	1928	Apr.	22	to	Oct.	7
1918	Mar.	24	to	Sep.	30	1929	Apr.	21	to	Oct.	6
1919	Mar.	30	to	Sep.	29	1930	Apr.	13	to	Oct.	5
1920	Mar.	28	to	Oct.	25	1931	Apr.	19	to	Oct.	4
1921	Apr.	3	to	Oct.	3	1932	Apr.	17	to	Oct.	2
1922	Mar.	26	to	Oct.	8	1933	Apr.	9	to	Oct.	8
1923	Apr.	22	to	Sep.	16	1934	Apr.	22	to	Oct.	7
1924	Apr.	13	to	Sep.	21	1935	Apr.	14	to	Oct.	6
1925	Apr.	19	to	Oct.	4	1936	Apr.	19	to	Oct.	4
1926	Apr.	18	to	Oct.	3	1937	Apr.	18	to	Oct.	3

1938	Apr.	10	to	Oct.	2		*1947	Mar.	16	to	Nov.	2
1939	Apr.	16	to	Nov.	19		1948	Mar.	14	to	Oct.	31
1940	Feb.	25	to	Dec.	31		1949	Apr.	3	to	Oct.	30
*1941	Jan.	1	to	Dec.	31		1950	Apr.	16	to	Oct.	22
*1942	Jan.	1	to	Dec.	31		1951	Apr.	15	to	Oct.	21
*1943	Jan.	1	to	Dec.	31		1952	Apr.	20	to	Oct.	26
*1944	Jan.	1	to	Dec.	31		1953	Apr.	19	to	Oct.	4
*1945	Jan.	1	to	Dec.	31		1954	Apr.	11	to	Oct.	3
1946	Apr.	14	to	Oct.	6		1955	Apr.	17	to	Oct.	2

(See Addenda 1956-1967, on Page x.)

*Double Summer Time

1941	May	4	to	Aug.	10		1944	Apr.	2	to	Sep.	17
1942	Apr.	5	to	Aug.	9		†1945	Apr.	2	to	July	15
1943	Apr.	4	to	Aug.	15		1946	No double summer time				
							1947	Apr.	13	to	Aug.	10

Most countries adopted the summer time arrangement at about the same year as Great Britain but with varying dates and there must be considerable confuson concerning the war years until official records are published. As an example, in India, certain towns where war necessities were manufactured, adopted this change early in the war, while near-by places did not.

If it is required to cast a map for a place in any country for which details are not given in Whitaker or similar reference book, a request for information about the *time* used, on the *date* given, at the *place* stated, may be made by letter to the Secretary of the Embassy or Legation of the country in question, if it has one in England. The addresses of these can be found in the *London Telephone Directory* or in *Whitaker's Almanack*. Particular care is necessary in dealing with places in the U.S.A. as the dates for beginning and ending summer time are by no means uniform throughout the country.

Obviously, what information is given in earlier text-books or in earlier editions of those now current, must be taken as applicable *to the years before writing only*. At the present moment (1950) there is insufficient information available on which to compile a correct list of all changes in the war years.

Other exceptions are :—

(3) Births in years before the passing of the laws ordering Standard Time. In England, Standard Time came into operation in 1880.

(4) Births in countries where no such laws exist, or in a few parts of countries where such laws have not been adopted because of remote location or because of religious scruples.

In the last two exceptions (3 and 4), the birth-time will be according to the local noon and will be called *Local Mean Time*.‡

Time Used in Raphael's Ephemeris

The positions of the planets are given in the *Nautical Almanac* in " Right

† Not Sunday, as customary, out of consideration for early attendance at church, it being the Sunday of Easter.

‡ See *The New Waite's Compendium*, pp. 228-34. Colin Evans, 1953.

Ascension and Declination " and are then converted into zodiacal longitude.* These longitudes are given in Raphael's Ephemeris for each day at noon, Greenwich Mean Time—G.M.T. There are other Ephemerides in which the positions of the planets are given for midnight (o hours) G.M.T. When G.M.T. is reckoned from midnight, it is sometimes referred to as Universal Time and is shortened to U.T.

As the necessary calculation for birth moment depends on the G.M.T. noon position as given in this Ephemeris, it is obvious that, whatever time is used for the recording of the birth moment, this MUST be converted into G.M.T. before the adjustment of planetary position for birth-time after or before noon can be made, or the Local Sidereal Time for birth can be found.

RULES FOR CONVERSION OF GIVEN TIME TO G.M.T.

(1) For the British Isles, the birth moment *will be in G.M.T.* (unless before 1880, when Rule 5 must be applied). If the chart form used gives space for zone or standard time, write this as o hours.

(2) If the birth time is given in *the zone or standard time of any other country*, refer to a list of standard times (see Appendix p. 307). If the standard is fast of Greenwich (example : 4 hours fast it would be written + 4 hours), subtract the hours given and the result will be G.M.T. If the standard is slow of Greenwich (example : 4 hours slow would be written −4 hours), add the hours given and the result will be G.M.T.

(3) If in a period of *Summer Time*, subtract 1 hour. If chart form has no space given for this, enter it as Standard Time, adding the letters B.S.T. Enter the reduction as G.M.T.

(4) If in a period of *Double Summer Time*, subtract 2 hours. If chart form has no space given for this, enter it as Standard Time, adding the letters B.D.S.T. Enter the reduction as G.M.T.

(5) If (and this will be rare), *in the time of a country which has never used a Standard Time*, or before such a time was legalised (as in England before 1880), the time used will be *Local Mean Time* (L.M.T.). Find the longitude of the birth place by reference to an atlas. The difference in time between this and G.M.T. can then be calculated very simply. Each degree of longitude equals four minutes of time.† Call the degrees of longitude minutes of time and the minutes of longitude seconds of time and multiply them by 4. If the birth place is WEST of Greenwich, ADD your result to the given time. If the birthplace is EAST of Greenwich, SUBTRACT your result from the given time. The result will give the equivalent G.M.T.

Examples :—

1. For Zone or Standard Time

(a) Birth time 6 a.m. New York City (after 1883).

This will be Zone Time (i.e., Eastern Standard Time or E.S.T.). Reference to Appendix gives this as −5 hours. G.M.T. is then 11 a.m.

---

* Terrestrial longitude is the distance east or west from a given meridian. Celestial or zodiacal longitude is measured along the ecliptic from o° Aries.

† The explanation of this is that the earth takes 1,440 minutes (i.e., 24 hours reduced to minutes) to rotate its 360 degrees. Therefore it takes 4 minutes to rotate through 1 degree (1,440 ÷ 360 = 4).

The G.M.T. of the birth time may occur *on a date before or after* that of the given date of birth. This *date* and *time* must be used for every subsequent calculation.

(*b*) Birth time 10 p.m. E.S.T. 1st April, 1950, New York City.   Hence :—

New York Time	10 p.m.	1st April, 1950
Zone Time difference	+5 hours	
G.M.T. of birth	3 a.m.	2nd April, 1950

2. For Local Mean Time

Birth time 6 a.m. Pembroke (before 1880).   Longitude of Pembroke 4° 53' West. Call this minutes and seconds of time and multiply by 4.

$$4' \, 53'' \times 4 = 19' \, 32''$$

Refer to Rule 5.   Pembroke is *West* of Greenwich.   G.M.T. is then 6 h. 19 m. 32 s. a.m.

CALCULATION TO FIND THE ZODIACAL LONGITUDE OF EACH PLANET FOR GIVEN TIME

Interval TO or FROM Noon

Having made sure that the birth time *is* in G.M.T. or that it has been converted to G.M.T., find out how many hours and minutes it is *after* or *before* noon G.M.T. It is simple to note that 5 p.m. is 5 hours after noon, and it is equally simple to make the mistake of noting 5 a.m. as 5 hours *before* noon. Such slips can easily be made if care is not taken : 5 a.m. is, of course, 7 hours before noon. These times should be written as + 5 hours and − 7 hours respectively.

1.—For Birth at Noon in London

No adjustment is necessary. The planets' places (degrees of zodiacal longitude) are given in the Ephemeris *for noon*. They can be entered on to the chart form if the student has had some practice. If not, it is better for him to list them in their numerical order in their signs first, so that charts are not spoilt by the making of alterations. The position of Pluto will be found separately on p. 39 of Ephemerides since 1940. For its position in earlier years, see special Ephemeris.*

2.—For Birth at any Exact Hour of Day from which the Hours to or from Noon Divide without Remainder into the Twenty-four Hours

Adjustment can be made by proportion.

Example.—8 a.m. is 4 hours from noon. This is *one-sixth* of the twenty-four hours.

Turn to p. 26 in the Raphael's Ephemerides published since 1906, and refer to the lists which give the motions of the faster moving planets for each day. Those of the slower ones can be easily seen in the Ephemeris. (For p.m. times use the motions of the day given. For a.m. times use those of the previous day.)

* Several can be bought at special booksellers. See page 315.

When using earlier Ephemerides, the motions must be found by subtraction of the noon degree from that of the day before, or after, as required. By simple division find out what is a sixth of each of these daily motions. Since this particular birth was *a.m.* it was, of course, short of noon, so *subtract* each sixth from the noon position of the planet dealt with. Note that the difference in time for 4 *p.m.* would be exactly the same but, being later than noon, the sixth would be *added* to the noon position If the planet is retrograde, this is reversed (see p. 107).

Moon's longitude at noon 3rd September (taking nearest minute)	25° 58′ ♑
Subtract longitude noon 2nd September	−13° 05′
Moon's motion noon 2nd to noon 3rd (p. 26 later Ephemerides)	12° 53′

By proportion, one-sixth of this is approximately 2° 9′

Position of Moon at noon 3rd September is	25° 58′
Subtract Moon's motion for 4 hours *before* noon	− 2° 09′
Moon's longitude at 8 a.m. 3rd September is	23° 49′ ♑

3.—For Birth at any Time of Day from which the Interval to or from Noon will not Divide without Remainder into the Twenty-four Hours

Adjustment must be made by the use of diurnal proportional logarithms.

The above method is very simple for even hours and divisible times, and is usable for rough work if only an approximation is needed to get a good idea of the chart in an approximate way or for imprecise birth-moments. The student who is applying himself seriously to the subject must be more accurate if the birth moment is accurately given. Those who do not understand the use of logarithms are apt to think of them as something very difficult in the way of " mathematics." Actually, the use of the simple addition and subtraction required is much less trouble than the complicated buying of 6¾ yards of material at 19s 6d. per yard, which any non-mathematician could work out.

Refer to table of diurn. prop. logarithms on the last page of every Ephemeris or to the much larger print of *The Enlarged Table of D.P. Logarithms* (see p. 315). The figures along the top row refer to either hours or degrees, and (since both are sub-divided into 60 minutes) the figures down the side refer to minutes.

Example by Logarithms :—

Moon's motion (as above) is found to be	12° 52′ 46″
Discarding seconds (as above) call this	12° 53′
By reference to hour and minute columns :—	
D.P. Log. of Moon's motion	.2702
D.P. Log. of time between birth and noon (4 hours)	+ .7781
By addition	1.0483

Find this (or nearest to it) in the main columns;
Read the number of degrees at the *head* of the column
  and the number of minutes from the *side* column.
This is called the anti-log.
So—anti-log. of 1.0483 (nearest), is 2° 09'
  As before :—

Position of Moon at noon 3rd September is	25° 58′ ♑
Subtract Moon's motion for 4 hours before noon	2° 09′
Moon's longitude at 8 a.m. 3rd September is	23° 49′ ♑

For a time lapse which will not divide into twenty-four (such as 3 hours 25 minutes) this is much the easier method and is customarily used.

Cautions.—A rough calculation should be made mentally in order to check the result. The date must be that on which the G.M.T. occurs.

Listing of Planets' Zodiacal Longitudes†

Use Form A,* (or copy it on to rough paper) and keep for reference in case mistakes may have been made. Calculate the positions of Sun, Mercury, Venus and Mars exactly as shown in the example for the Moon. The movements of Jupiter, Saturn, Uranus, Neptune and Pluto are so slow that their positions at the given time can easily be calculated mentally by proportion. Tabulate all in their numerical order under the heading of the sign in which they are. They will thus be arranged for tidy charting later. See Summary, p. 108 which gives working for full example in Chapter 11; also reference pages from Ephemeris, p. 228–9.

Retrograde

This is the term used to denote *apparent* backward motion of planets. In the Ephemeris changes of motion are denoted thus :— Retrograde, ℞ ; Direct, D. Care must be taken to notice these. A retrograde planet is *always* listed as such.

Example.—♃ ℞

Each planet continues to move forward in its orbit. What varies is the angle from which it is seen, from the moving earth, as against a background of stars.

A planet appears to be stationary before it changes its apparent motion. This is abbreviated for listing as Sta:Dir: or Sta:R. (See p. 179).

Declination

The distance of a planet from the celestial equator. This may be north or south.

* See pages 108 and 118.

† Terrestrial longitude is the distance east or west from a given meridian. Celestial or zodiacal longitude is measured along the ecliptic from 0° Aries.

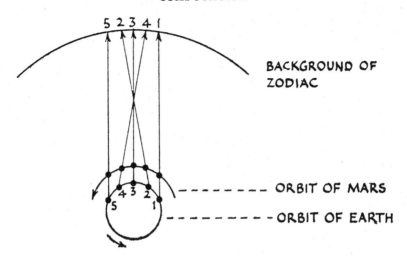

Fig. 8

RETROGRADE MOTION

The small circle shows the Earth in five different positions from which lines are drawn through Mars, also in five positions. By following the lines drawn, the apparent positions in celestial longitude appear as numbered.

Listing of Declinations of Planets

The daily variation is so small that it can be calculated mentally with ease. That of the Moon is the only exception. It is therefore given with the planetary motions on p. 26 of Raphael's Ephemerides and should be calculated at the same time and in the same way as the planetary positions in zodiacal longitude and entered on chart-form later (see example Chapter 11). The anti-log must be added to the noon declination if its distance from the equator is increasing either to north or south and subtracted if it is decreasing. The daily increase or decrease can be observed in the columns headed " Moon's Dec " in the Ephemeris.

Part 2.—TO FIND LOCAL SIDEREAL TIME FOR ANY GIVEN TIME AND PLACE, HENCE THE DEGREES OF ECLIPTIC RISING AND CULMINATING (Asc. and M.C.)

(a) Explanation and Definitions of Terms to be Used

As in Part 1, these terms MUST be understood before they can be used. Later on, the keen student must learn them accurately. They should be applied to actuality by the help of a Celestial Globe. The student should examine one in a science museum if possible. The drawing on page 109 will be only a substitute.

CALCULATION OF ZODIACAL POSITIONS OF PLANETS FOR GIVEN TIME

1. Enter birth date and time as given.
2. **CONVERT TO G.M.T.** by adding or subtracting Zone Standard. E —, W +.
3. If standard is G.M.T., state as 0 hours.
   If summer time, subtract 1 hour ; if double summer time, subtract 2 hours.
4. **Result** is G.M.T.
5. If result has altered date, enter.
6. Enter hours and minutes TO or FROM **noon G.M.T.** (before or after noon).
7. Fill in remainder of form as indicated.

		D	M	Y
Birth date		21	6	1924
		h	m	s
Birth time as given		3	35	00 a.m., p
Zone Standard	*E —. W +	0		
*Summer- (double-) time		—1		
G.M.T.		2	35	00 a.m., p

G.M.T. date   21 : 6 : 1924
Interval TO or FROM noon   2   35
Log. of interval ... ...   0·9680

PLANET	☉	☽	☿	♀	♂	Moon Dec
Daily Motion	0° 57′	13° 24′	1° 52′	0° 28′	0° 21′	3° 4
Diurn. prop. log of Motion	1·4025	0·2531	1·1091	1·7112	1·8361	0·80
Diurn. prop. log of interval ...	0·9680	0·9680	0·9680	0·9680	0·9680	0·96
Addition of diurn. prop. logs... ...	2·3705	1·2211	2·0771	2·6792	2·8041	1·76

	☉	☽	☿	♀	♂	Moon
Sign containing planet	♊	♒	♊	♋	♒	—N. S.
Noon position of planet	29° 48′	28° 22′	13° 53′	14° 59′℞	28° 54′	12° 22
Anti-log. of addition, a.m. —, p.m. +* (Reverse if retrograde)	0·06	1.26	0·12	0·03	0·02	0·25
Position at given time	29·54	29·48	14·5	14·56℞	28·56	11·57

TABULATION OF PLANETS IN NUMERICAL ORDER

♈	♉	♊	♋	♌	♍	♎	♏	♐	♑	♒	♓
° ′	° ′	☿ 14 5	♇ 11 34	♆ 18 21	° ′	♄ 25 40℞	° ′	♃ 13 6℞	° ′	♂ 28 56	♅ 21 3
		☉ 29 54	♀ 14 56℞							☽ 29 48	

*Strike out whichever is not required.

Calculation Form A.   Designed by M. E. Hon

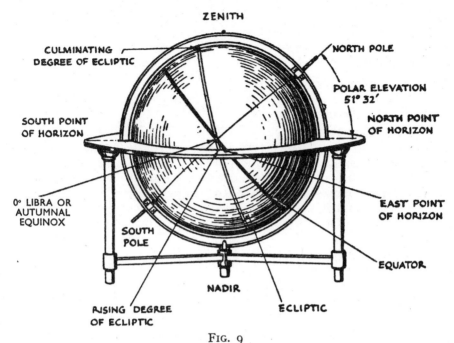

ZENITH

CULMINATING
DEGREE OF ECLIPTIC

NORTH POLE

POLAR ELEVATION
51° 32'

SOUTH POINT
OF HORIZON

NORTH POINT
OF HORIZON

0° LIBRA OR
AUTUMNAL
EQUINOX

EAST POINT
OF HORIZON

SOUTH
POLE

EQUATOR

NADIR

RISING DEGREE
OF ECLIPTIC

ECLIPTIC

FIG. 9

CELESTIAL GLOBE SET FOR LAT. 51° 32' N.

The heavy lines are the framework which holds a metal ring (the outer) which, at the points marked North and South Pole, supports a globe which rotates at these points.

On it are marked all the fixed stars and, showing the joining of these into constellations, the figures of strange humans, animals, birds, and so on, by which the ancients named them. Students of modern astronomy think this slightly absurd and prefer the more accurate methods of numerical positioning used to-day. It must be remembered that their forebears had not the means for such accurate charting and used whatever methods of locating were possible. The comparison can be made with house-naming. In country districts, scattered houses have similarly been given fanciful names to identify them. It is only the relatively modern growth of towns with straight streets of houses which has led to the sequential numbering of them.

The observer is understood to be looking, from the outside, at what he is accustomed to seeing as " the sky " from the inside. When inside, he is to be thought of as being on a tiny terrestrial globe (earth) inside the celestial one (heavens).

The horizontal circle, which is part of the holding frame work, represents the horizon of the place for which the globe is set. This must not be confused with the tiny horizon customarily seen.

Great Circle

Any circle, the plane (level) of which passes through the centre of the Earth. (Imagine a circle drawn round the middle of an apple. The level of a cut straight through, on this circle, would go through the centre of the apple.)

Visible Horizon (that customarily seen)

The circular line formed by the apparent meeting of the earth and sky (this is referred to as a " small circle ").

Rational Horizon

A great circle, parallel to the visible horizon and produced to meet the heavens.

As the framework cannot be tilted about, it is kept stationary to form the *rational horizon*, while the globe is adjusted for any locality.

On the metal ring are engraved the 360°. In the drawing, the Northern Hemisphere (celestial) is shown uppermost. The globe is set so that 51° 32' are between the North Pole and the north point of the horizon (latitude of London).

Polar Elevation

The height of the Pole above the horizon. Measurement in degrees equals latitude of place.

As London is about $\frac{1}{2}$° above the 51st parallel of latitude (terrestrial),* the celestial globe in Fig. 9 is set with the Pole elevated at $51\frac{1}{2}$° as for that latitude.

Zenith

A point in the heavens immediately overhead at any place.

The topmost spot marked Zenith is then immediately over the head of a Londoner, imagined to be on the small Earth inside. A line from any place to its Zenith would always be at right angles to the plane of its horizon.

Nadir

A point in the heavens immediately opposite to the Zenith (not to be confused with I.C., p. 112).

The Celestial Equator

This is the terrestrial equator projected to the heavens.

The Ecliptic (marked as double line)

The great circle around which the Sun *appears* to travel in a year. In actuality, the Earth so travels and views the Sun.

Plane of the Ecliptic

The level on which that circle lies, it being projected to infinity.

The Obliquity of the Ecliptic

The angle between the plane of the ecliptic and the plane of the equator. At the present time, this is nearly $23\frac{1}{2}$°. (Fig. 10.)

The Constellations

Groups of stars in all parts of the heavens. (See p. 277.)

*Terrestrial latitude is the distance, in degrees, of any place north or south of the Earth's equator. Celestial latitude is the measurement of any planet or star north or south of the ecliptic.

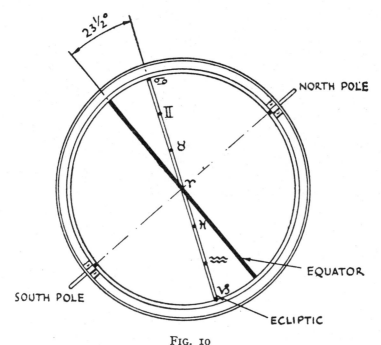

FIG. 10

THE OBLIQUITY OF THE ECLIPTIC

Zodiacal Constellations

Those more nearly in the plane of the Ecliptic.

Rising and Culminating Degrees (" Ascendant " and " Midheaven ")

It is difficult to have a model which shows the Earth in its daily rotation *inside* the celestial sphere, so this sphere is made to rotate instead, as if the sky were rotating around a stationary earth. In this rotation, it can be seen that, at any moment, a certain degree of one of the signs of the Zodiac will be *rising* over the eastern horizon, while another arrives at its greatest height, when it is said to *culminate* at the upper meridian of the place in question. The two which rise and culminate at any moment of birth *are highly important in the making of a chart* and must be properly understood. They are customarily called the Ascendant and the Midheaven (see p. 112). The point opposite to the Ascendant (i.e., 180° from it) is called the Descendant, because it is descending on the western horizon at the moment when the Ascendant is rising on the eastern horizon.

Nonagesimal

The point 90° from the Ascending point; *the highest point of the ecliptic* above the horizon.

Meridian of Longitude (Terrestrial)

An imaginary great circle passing through the Poles of the equator (north and south) and any given place.

" The " Meridian

An imaginary great circle passing through the Poles of the heavens (celestial) and *the Zenith and Nadir of the observer*. The sun crosses this at midday.

Midheaven

(Latin, *Medium Coeli*—M.C. initials very frequently used. The opposite point is the *Imum Coeli*—it is customary to use the initials I.C. (See Nadir, p. 110.)

As remarked before, astrologers use many old terms because they are customary. No harm is done if the incorrect implication is understood. Unfortunately, this is not always the case.

The degree of ecliptic which reaches *its highest point* at the meridian of any place is said to be *culminating*. (Note difference from Nonagesimal, p. 111.)

In the northern latitudes of the temperate zones including the British Isles, most of Europe and of the U.S.A., the Sun can be seen at its greatest height at apparent noon due south. It is then culminating. Its height is greater in summer than in winter. Therefore the slope of the ecliptic above the horizon will be less in winter than in summer.

At *no* time is the Sun seen overhead, or nearly so, except when seen *from localities on or near the equator*. When exactly at the equator, the terrestrial equator is underfoot and the projected circle of the celestial equator is overhead. The North and South Poles are then in a line with the north and south points of the horizon.

At the spring and autumn equinoxes, the Sun is then seen *directly* overhead at noon, coincident with the celestial equator, the ecliptic path being as the two dotted lines (Fig. 11), the central line shows the equator while the two lighter lines show its position in midwinter and in midsummer, its culminating point at noon being marked with a dot.

To the equatorial observer, the three points would *appear* very close to each other, and to be actually " *in the middle of the heavens*," near the Zenith.

In the very early days of astrology, the countries which were the centres of knowledge lay near the equator, hence, presumably, this expression came about. Until the Middle Ages, books used by European astrologers were chiefly written in Latin, hence this survival of usage has come down to us.

When a student hears experienced astrologers saying that a chart for the medium latitudes has planets " in the Midheaven " or " at the M.C." he must understand that this is not meant in the colloquial sense, *but in the astronomical sense*. Both meanings are given in good dictionaries. *The correct statement would be that such planets are in degrees of the ecliptic which are culminating at the meridian, or nearly so.*

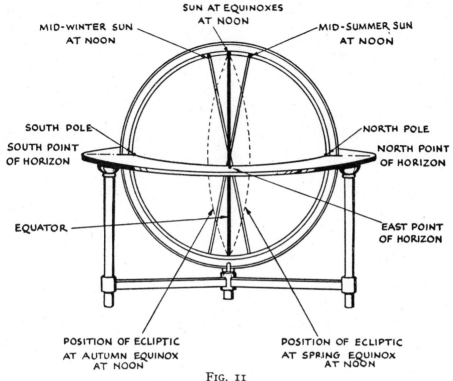

SUN AT EQUINOXES
AT NOON

MID-WINTER SUN
AT NOON

MID-SUMMER SUN
AT NOON

SOUTH POLE

SOUTH POINT
OF HORIZON

NORTH POLE

NORTH POINT
OF HORIZON

EQUATOR

EAST POINT
OF HORIZON

POSITION OF ECLIPTIC
AT AUTUMN EQUINOX
AT NOON

POSITION OF ECLIPTIC
AT SPRING EQUINOX
AT NOON

FIG. II
CELESTIAL GLOBE SET FOR LAT 0°

DIFFERENT KINDS OF "DAY"

One Day

This is a complete rotation of the earth, but there are various ways of measuring the exact time taken for this.

Solar Day

The time between two successive passages of the Sun over a fixed point of observation. As the Earth moves at a variable speed according to its place in its orbit, the Sun *appears* to move either more or less than 1° per day, so the Solar Day is variable.

Mean Day

Because of the above variation, the mean, or average, is taken. (See G.M.T., p. 101.)

Equation of Time

The addition or subtraction to be made daily if required to convert Solar Time into Mean Time.

Sidereal Day

In order to register a complete rotation *exactly*, the time is taken between the moment when a certain fixed star is exactly due south (as seen by precision instruments), and the moment when it is again in the same position. This " day " is nearly 4 minutes shorter than the day measured by the clock. A sidereal clock is in every observatory and is set at o hours o minutes o seconds when o° Aries is culminating on the meridian of that place. Thus the *Sidereal Time* at noon, on any day, shows *what degree of ecliptic is culminating* (degree of M.C., p. 119), from which can be calculated *the degree ascending*.

(b) Calculation to Find Local Sidereal Time at Birth for any Given Place in Order to Obtain Ascendant and Midheaven

Note.—When the student has become familiar with this calculation and the previous one, he will find that in practice it is more straightforward to begin by finding the Ascendant and Midheaven, entering them straight on to a *chart-form* with the remaining house cusps, according to the system of house division used (Chapter 7). The form will then be prepared for the recording of the planets' positions.

For the purpose of learning, the calculation for the planets' places has been given first, so that the student may have understood the conversion of *given time* into *Greenwich Mean Time* without which he cannot proceed with this section.

Conversion of Mean Time to Sidereal Time

This is necessary for the finding of the LOCAL SIDEREAL TIME at birth for any given place in order to obtain the degrees of ecliptic culminating (" Midheaven " see p. 119), and ascending (" Ascendant " see p. 117), at a given time.

Having converted the *birth time* into *Greenwich Mean Time* if necessary, the next step is to find *the Sidereal Time at Greenwich at birth* and then to adjust this for the *longitude* of the locality in question. The method of *conversion from Mean to Sidereal Time* is given in text-books and almanacs as referred to in the preceding section (p. 99).

Important Note on the Use of the Direct Method

Students already familiar with astrological technique, will have been taught, or will have read in text-books* that two *necessities* for the erection of a horoscopic chart are *firstly* the conversion of Greenwich Mean Time into Local Mean Time† (or " True Local Mean " an expression never used by astronomers) and *secondly*, the confusing return to the noon of the date before the birth date if the birth occurred before noon. *Both these unnecessary habits will be discontinued in the much simpler and more accurate " DIRECT METHOD " to be given in this modern book.*

---

* But see 4th edition of *Principles of Astrology*, by Charles E. O. Carter, 1952
† Local Mean Time is obtained by the addition or subtraction of Longitude equivalent in time to Greenwich Mean Time (see p. 103).

These customs did not start without reasons. The reason for the extra process of the conversion to L.M.T. (or T.L.M.) was because astrologers of the last fifty years had continued the methods of the text-books written around the turn of the century when many countries, not having adopted a standard time, were still using Local Mean Time. Astrologers then adult in the British Isles were frequently doing charts for those born before British Standard Time (G.M.T.) had been adopted. . The use of L.M.T. involved the making of *a correction for longitude for all places other than those on the Greenwich meridian.** As the correction is small, it has usually been omitted when casting maps for localities near Greenwich. One result of this is that these maps are slightly incorrect, which can be seen by comparing the two example charts in Chapter 11. This mattered very little since few birth times are accurately given.

A worse consequence was the causing of a feeling in the minds of beginners that the erection of a foreign chart was harder than that of an English one. By discontinuing the former practice, *the special correction necessary for maps for places distant from the Greenwich meridian can also be discontinued as it is covered by the calculation as now given.*

By the use of THE DIRECT METHOD, exactly the same calculation is used for charts for *all localities* in the world. See examples, pp. 121 and 122. *By any method, there is a final simple adjustment for localities in the Southern hemisphere* (p. 123), but this is merely to avoid the unnecessary printing of separate Tables of Houses for southern latitudes (p. 120).

The reason for the return to *previous noon* was that it was thought that fewer mistakes would be made if the interval of time from noon to birth was always found by addition.

Example.—3 p.m. = + 3 hours from noon of same day.
3 a.m. = + 15 hours from noon of the day before.

Experience of teaching has proved that *the opposite is the case* as the addition for the 12 hours is so often forgotten. By the present system of teaching in which the calculation of the positions of the planets is taken first, *the interval from a pre-noon birth TO noon G.M.T. has already been understood as a minus quantity, so there is no need to confuse the issue by using the noon of an earlier day for the next step in calculation.*

THE DIRECT METHOD

Beginners will find it helpful to use Form B† given as a summary on p. 118, showing the working for the example chart in chapter 11. The calculatory section is again shown in the examples on pp. 121 to 123, and on the completed chart forms in Chapter 11. It should be noted that the examples for Liverpool ; for Kingston, Jamaica ; and for Melbourne, Australia, *are all calculated in exactly the same manner.*

* See earlier editions of *Principles of Astrology*, Chapter 2, Correction 1. C. E. O. Carter.
† See page 115.

Information Already Used in Part 1

Enter on to Form B :—
Birth date.
Birth time as given.
Zone Standard.
Summer or double summer time if necessary.
G.M.T.
G.M.T. date if altered by conversion.

Birth Place.   Latitude and Longitude

Find these by reference to an atlas.   Enter.

Sidereal Time at Noon G.M.T.

This will be found in the Ephemeris of the year in question, by reference to the G.M.T. date. Enter on form.

Interval TO or FROM Noon G.M.T.

Find this as in Part 1.

Example.—3 a.m. G.M.T. will be entered as − 9 hours.
3 p.m. G.M.T. will be entered as + 3 hours.

For birth before noon, *subtract* this from Sidereal Time.
For birth after noon, *add* this to Sidereal Time.

Conversion of Mean Time to Sidereal Time

As Sidereal Time is short of Mean Time by nearly 10 seconds for each hour (p. 114), multiply interval TO or FROM noon by 10, calling the results minutes and seconds (ignore fractions). The precise correction is 9·86^s but such exactitude is not necessary except for a birth timed to seconds.*

Example.—Acceleration for − 9 hours = − 1^m 30^s.
Acceleration for + 3 hours = + 0^m 30^s.

As before, for birth before noon, *subtract* this from Sidereal Time.
For birth after noon, *add* this to Sidereal Time.

(As the use of double subtraction has been considered to be a possible cause of mistakes, two lines have been placed on Form B so that each step of the double subtraction may be performed separately. This will soon become habitual and can be done in one step as with a double addition.)

It should be noted that all calculation is in G.M.T., therefore it is the *interval in G.M.T.* which is multiplied. (When L.M.T. was used, the interval was in L.M.T. and was referred to as " Correction for Sidereal Time " or " S.T. Corr.")

Acceleration on Interval

The word " acceleration " is unfamiliar to many astrologers. It is the correct word, as can be seen in contemporary text-books on other subjects for which this conversion of time is needed. It will therefore be used.

* If precision is required, use Acceleration Table Appendix p. 313.

Sidereal Time at Greenwich at Birth

This is the result of the conversion from Mean to Sidereal Time and *the calculation is then FINISHED for a map for London, or any other place on the Greenwich meridian.*

Longitude Equivalent in Time

For any place other than those on the Greenwich meridian, an adjustment must be made for the difference in longitude. The earth rotates 360° in 24 hours (1,440 minutes) ; it therefore rotates 1° in 4 minutes. To obtain the longitude equivalent in time, multiply the degrees and minutes of longitude by 4. Call these hours, minutes and seconds of time, or refer to table, p. 314.

If birth is east of Greenwich, *add* to Sidereal Time at Greenwich.

If birth is west of Greenwich, *subtract* from Sidereal Time at Greenwich.

Caution.—A very frequent mistake is to enter minutes in column for hours and vice versa. This can be checked by seeing that the entry for longitude equivalent in time does not greatly differ from the standard for the zone. Note this in the four examples which follow.

Local Sidereal Time of Birth

This is the result of the addition or subtraction of the longitude equivalent in time to the Greenwich Sidereal Time. It is the Sidereal Time for the meridian for *the locality* of birth *at the time* of birth.

Charting of Results

Charting is explained in Chapter 7. At present, only the calculation of Local Sidereal Time can be transferred to the chart form to be used.* The use of " Tables of Houses " for finding the Ascendant and Midheaven is explained on page 119.

Note.—This method for calculation is used in exactly the same way when using Ephemerides calculated for *midnight* (such as the *Deutsche Ephemeride* 1931–50, or the similar *Aries Press Ephemeris* 1931–50). In this case, the Sidereal Time used will be that of the previous *midnight* and the interval to G.M.T. time of birth will be that from previous *midnight*, G.M.T.

METHOD FOR FINDING THE DEGREE OF ECLIPTIC ASCENDING OVER HORIZON

This is termed " THE ASCENDANT " and is generally shortened to Asc. At the end of each modern Raphael's Ephemeris will be found Tables calculated for the three latitudes of London (lat. 51° 32′ N.), Liverpool (lat. 53° 25′ N.), and New York (lat. 40° 43′ N.). These Tables can be used for any places in the world on the same parallels of latitude. Tables for other latitudes can be obtained.

In the first example (p. 121) the birth place is Liverpool, so the appropriate Table must be used.

Under the column marked " Sidereal Time," find the one which is *nearest* to the Local Sidereal Time arrived at by calculation. This was 20ʰ 58ᵐ 04ˢ. The nearest to it is 20ʰ 57ᵐ 52ˢ. In a line with this and in the column which is headed "Ascen," followed by the sign ♊ are the figures 20° 25′. Thus the Ascendant is found to be 20° 25′ Gemini. It is better to use the nearest degree, i.e., 20° ♊, than to record this as 20° 25′ ♊, which would imply that precise calculation had been made.

* See full examples of charts and working in chapter 11.

CALCULATION FOR LOCAL SIDEREAL TIME FOR GIVEN TIME IN ORDER TO OBTAIN ASCENDANT AND MIDHEAVEN

FOR NORTHERN HEMISPHERE

1. Enter birth-date and place on form.
2. Find latitude and longitude from atlas.
3. Enter birth-time as given.
4. Convert to **G.M.T.** by adding or subtracting Zone standard. E −, W +.
5. If standard is G.M.T. enter as o hours.
   If summer time, subtract 1 hour, if double summer time, subtract 2 hours.
6. **Result** is G.M.T.
7. If conversion to G.M.T. has altered date, enter.
8. From ephemeris, take Sidereal Time at **Noon G.M.T.**, enter.
9. Enter hours and minutes TO or FROM **Noon G.M.T.**
   For a.m. birth, **subtract**, for p.m. **add** interval to S.T.
10. Calculate acceleration on interval (10 seconds for each hour).
    For a.m. birth **subtract**, for p.m. **add** to above result (No. 9).
11. **Result** is Sidereal Time at Greenwich at birth.
12. Find longitude equivalent in **time** by multiplying longitude by 4 and calling result minutes seconds of time. Long W −. Long E +.
13. **Result** is LOCAL SIDEREAL TIME AT BIRTH.
14. Find Local Sidereal Time in Tables of Houses for given latitude to obtain degrees of Ascendant Midheaven (M.C.).
    Chart according to system of house division used.

FOR SOUTHERN HEMISPHERE
(a) Add 12 hours to Local Sidereal Time of birth.
(b) Reverse signs. Example : For Cancer, read Capricorn.

										D	M	
1.	Birth-date ...	...	...	...	...	...	...	...	21	6	1	
	Birth-place	...	..	...	...	...	...	...		Swindon	
									o	,	,	
2.	Latitude ...	...	...	...	...	...	...	...	51	34	0(
	Longitude ...	...	...	...	...	...	...	... ·	1	47	0(

	TIME :							h	m	
3.	Birth-time as given	...	...	...	...	...	*a.m., p.m.	3	35	0
4.	Zone Standard ...	...	...	...	...	...	*E., W +	0		
5.	*Summer (double) time ...	...	...	...	...		−	1		
6.	G.M.T. ...	...	...	...	...	...	*a.m., p.m.	2	35	0
7.	G.M.T. date 21 : 6 : 1924									

							H	M	S
8.	Sidereal Time noon G.M.T.	...	...	...	...	5	57	3
9.	Interval *TO or FROM noon	...	...	*p.m. + a.m. −		2	35	
	Result ...	...	...	...	...	8	32	3:
10.	Acceleration on interval ...	...	...	*p.m. + a.m. −				2(
11.	Sidereal Time at Greenwich at birth	...	...	...	...	8	33	0:
12.	Longitude equivalent							
	Long. × 4 = result in minutes ...	...	...	*E + W −			7	0(
13.	LOCAL SIDEREAL TIME AT BIRTH	...	...	...	...	8	25	5:
	Subtract 24 hours if necessary	...	...	...				

14. From Tables of Houses for Lat. 51° 32′ N.
    Asc   25° 34′ ♎
    M.C.   4° 0′ ♌

FOR Lat. .... S. add 12 hours   + _____
     Reverse signs
     Asc. ....   M.C. ....   _____

*Strike out whichever is not required.

Calculation form B.

Designed by M. E. Ho

Closer Approximation by Proportion

If the calculated Sidereal Time had not been so near to the Sidereal Time shown in the Table of Houses, an adjustment to the Asc. could have been made proportionate to the difference, again using the nearest degree for the result.

For instance if the Sidereal Time had been $20^h 59^m 52^s$, it would have been almost exactly half-way between the Sidereal Time already used and the next ($20^h 57^m 52^s$ and $21^h 1^m 53^s$). The relative Asc. would also have been half-way between the two which correspond (20° 25′ ♊ and 21° 28′ ♊).

As the difference between these is 63 minutes, half of it (roughly 31 minutes) added to the earlier Asc., gives 20° 56′ ♊. The nearest degree to use would then be 21° ♊.

METHOD FOR FINDING THE DEGREE OF ECLIPTIC CULMINATING AT THE MERIDIAN

This is usually termed " THE MIDHEAVEN " and is shortened to M.C. since these letters are the initials of the Latin *Medium Coeli* (see p. 112).

In Raphael's Table of Houses, the first column after that for the Sidereal Time is headed " 10." This is because in the system for the arrangement of the degrees on the house cusps by these Tables (Placidean) the culminating degree is *invariably* used as the cusp of the 10th house (p. 138).

For the Sidereal Time of $20^h 57^m 52^s$ which was found to be the nearest to the calculated Sidereal Time of $20^h 58^m 04^s$, the figure under " 10 " is 12, and the sign above it is ♒.

Hence, for the example given :—

Asc. is 20° ♊

M.C. is 12° ♒

Reference Tables for Rising and Culminating Degrees (Asc. and M.C.)

The most recent are contained in "The Time-Saver Tables of Asc. and M.C."* in which these degrees *only* are given.

Raphael's† Tables give these two required degrees which *are astronomically correct* and which are the basis of many systems of house division (see Chapter 7). *The other degrees given for the intermediate house-cusps are optional and in this case are solely for the system used, which is that of Placidus.*

The use of any one system is a matter of choice and *the student should not think this is better than any other because it has been the only one for which Tables have been widely printed.*

The arguments about the different systems of house-division are not easy for a beginner to follow. They are discussed in Chapters 7 and 16 and in a good and simple statement in the foreword to the " Time-Saver Tables." The student will understand these better when he re-reads after some practice.

* *The Time-Saver Tables of Asc. and M.C.*, by Colin Evans.
† (a) *Raphael's Tables of Houses for Great Britain* (Placidean).
  (b) *Raphael's Tables of Houses for Northern Latitudes.*

Formula for Interpolation for Time and Latitude*

If the given time is known to be precise, the M.C. and Asc. can be calculated for the exact time and latitude, though between the two nearest times and the two nearest latitudes given in the Tables. This is interpolation.

For Exact Time (at nearest lat.)		*For Exact Lat. (at nearest time)*	
Nearest later time		Nearest greater lat.	
Nearest earlier time		Nearest lesser lat.	
Difference		Difference	
min. × 60 = seconds	A.	° × 60 = ′	E.
Nearest later time		*Notice whether Asc. has more longitude at nearest*	
Given time		*HIGHER lat. (Case 1) or at nearest LOWER*	
		lat. (Case 2) then :—	
Difference		*CASE* 1	
min. × 60 = seconds	B.	Nearest higher lat.	
		Given lat.	
M.C. at later time			
M.C. at earlier time		Difference	
		° × 60 = ′	F.
Difference			
° × 60 = ′	C.	Asc. at higher lat.	
		Asc. at lower lat.	
Asc. at later time			
Asc. at earlier time		Difference	
		° × 60 = ′	G.
Difference			
° × 60 = ′	D.	*CASE* 2	
		Given lat.	
B × C ÷ A =		Nearest lower lat.	
′ ÷ 60 = °	H.		
		Difference	
B × D ÷ A =		° × 60 = ′	F.
′ ÷ 60 = °	J.		
		Asc. at lower lat.	
M.C. at earlier time		Asc. at higher lat.	
′ + H		Difference	
= M.C. required		° × 60 = ′	G.

The " Least Ascendant " is Ascendant for nearest earlier time and nearest LOWER latitude in *CASE* 1 but Ascendant at nearest earlier time and nearest HIGHER latitude in *CASE* 2.

F × G ÷ E =			Least Ascendant	
′ ÷ 60 = °	K.		+ J	
			+ K	
			= Ascendant required	

Adjustments for Southern Hemisphere

In the following examples, it will be seen that exactly the same method is followed in the example of calculation for a birth in Australia as for a birth in England (p. 123). The only change is by a final adjustment since the Tables of Houses customarily used are for the northern hemisphere. Tables are now obtainable for the southern hemisphere.

1. Twelve hours must be added to the Local Sidereal Time obtained.

2. On reference to the " Tables of Houses " for the appropriate northern latitude the sign *opposite* in the zodiac to the one given must be used.

Example.—For Cancer, read Capricorn.

The sign and degree on the M.C. will now be the same as they would have been for the northern latitude, but the degree of the sign ascending and possibly the sign itself will be different because of the different inclination of the ecliptic.

*The beginner may ignore this formula until later.

Examples (using calculatory part of Form B).

Example 1.—For birth at Liverpool.

		D.	M.	Y.
1.	Birth-date	6	7	1916
	Birth-place .. .. '	LIVERPOOL		
		°		″
2.	Latitude	53	25	0.N
	Longitude	2	58	0.W

	TIME	h.	m.	s.
3.	Birth-time as given .. .. a.m., ~~p.m.~~*	3	15	00
4.	Zone Standard .. .. *~~E W~~+	0	—	—
5.	*Summer- (~~double~~) time .. .. .. —	1	—	—
6.	G.M.T. .. .. *a.m., ~~p.m.~~	2	15	00
7.	G.M.T. date 6 : 7 : 1916			

		H.	M.	S.
8.	Sidereal Time noon G.M.T.	6	56	32
9.	Interval *TO ~~or FROM~~ noon .. *~~p.m.~~ +, a.m. —	9	45	00
	Result	21	11	32
10.	Acceleration on interval .. .. *~~p.m.~~ +, a.m. —		1	38
11.	Sidereal Time at Greenwich at birth	21	9	54
12.	Longitude equivalent			
	Long × 4 = result in minutes .. *~~E +~~ W —		11	52
13.	LOCAL SIDEREAL TIME AT BIRTH	20	58	02
	Subtract 24 hours if necessary .. .. —			

14. From Tables of Houses for Lat. 53°.25′ N.
Asc. 20 Ⅱ
M.C. 12 ♒

FOR Lat. .... S. add 12 hours   +

Reverse signs
Asc. ....   M.C. ....

*Strike out whichever is not required.

Example 2.—For Kingston, Jamaica

		D.	M.	Y.
1.	Birth-date	19	6	1917
	Birth-place	Kingston,		Jamaica
2.	Latitude	18	0	0 N
	Longitude	76	52	0 W

	TIME :	h.	m.	s.
3.	Birth-time as given .. .. .. *a.m., p.m.	5	50	00
4.	Zone Standard .. .. .. *E——, W +	5	—	—
5.	*Summer (double) time	—		
6.	G.M.T. .. .. *a.m., p.m.	10	50	00
7.	G.M.T. date 19 : 6 : 1917			

		H.	M.	S.
8.	Sidereal Time noon G.M.T.	5	48	34
9.	Interval *TO or FROM noon .. *p.m. +, a.m.——	10	50	0
	Result	16	38	34
10.	Acceleration on interval .. .. *p.m. +, a.m.——		1	48
11.	Sidereal Time at Greenwich at birth	16	40	22
12.	Longitude equivalent			
	Long. × 4 = result in minutes .. *E——+, W —	5	7	28
13.	LOCAL SIDEREAL TIME AT BIRTH	11	32	54
	Subtract 24 hours if necessary ..	—		

14. From Tables of Houses for Lat. 18° 0′ N.
Asc. 16 ♐
M.C. 22 ♍

FOR Lat. .... S. add 12 hours   +

Reverse signs

Asc. ....   M.C. ....

*Strike out whichever is not required.

Example 3.—For Melbourne, Australia

						D.	M.	Y.
1.	Birth-date	..	..	..	..	I	3	1944
	Birth-place	..	..	..	..	Melbourne		
						°	′	″
2.	Latitude	..	..	..	..	37	45	0 S
	Longitude	..	..	..	..	145	0	0 E

						h.	m.	s.
	TIME:							
3.	Birth-time as given	..	..	..	a.m., ~~p.m.~~	10	0	00
4.	Zone Standard	..	..	..	*E —, ~~W + ~~	10	—	—
5.	†Summer ~~(double)~~ time	..	..		—	I	—	—
6.	G.M.T. ..	..	..	..	~~*a.m.,~~ p.m.	11	0	00
7.	G.M.T. date 29 : 2 : 1944							

					H.	M.	S.
8.	Sidereal Time noon G.M.T. ..	..			22	32	43
9.	Interval *~~TO or~~ FROM noon	..	*p.m. +, ~~a.m.~~		11	00	00
	Result	..	..	..	33	32	43
10.	Acceleration on interval	..	..	*p.m. +, ~~a.m.~~		I	50
11.	Sidereal Time at Greenwich at birth				33	34	33
12.	Longitude equivalent Long. × 4 = result in minutes		..	*E. +, ~~W.~~	9	40	00
13.	LOCAL SIDEREAL TIME AT BIRTH				43	14	33
	Subtract 24 hours if necessary				— 24	—	—
					19	14	33
14.	From Tables of Houses for Lat..........:.N.						
	Asc.						
	M.C.						

FOR Lat. 37° 58′ S. add 12 hours	+ 12	—	—
Reverse signs (Asc. 15°♎, M.C. 17°♋)			
Asc. 15° ♈	31	14	33
	— 24		
M.C. 17°♑	7	14	33

*Strike out whichever is not required.
†Daylight Saving Time used only in periods of years of war.
See Chapter 11 for full Example Charts.

CHAPTER 7

METHODS OF CHARTING AND SYSTEMS OF HOUSE DIVISION

THE results obtained must now be charted. To do this, a SYSTEM OF HOUSE DIVISION must be used. Up to the present time, there is no unanimity, even amongst the most thoughtful and careful astrologers, as to which of the many systems is the best.

It is difficult for the student to get any guidance on the subject as there is no book on it* (see Chapter 16). There are many articles in old astrological magazines, but each writer endeavours to prove his own chosen system is best.

The variation of the systems may be more easily understood if it is realised that, as the centuries have gone by, men have learnt more about the ways of measuring the earth and the positions of the bodies seen in the sky.

In each age, the mathematicians were the astronomer-astrologers and their astrological systems of measurement kept pace with their knowledge of astronomy.

It has been the habit of writers of text-books to explain the use of one system only, with the expectation that students might consider others later. The effect of this has been to condition the minds of students to the acceptance of that system, and to the rejection of others. At the present time of writing, astrologers are more alive to the differences between house divisions than they have been for many years, and various systems are being taught by different teachers.

For this reason, the main systems will be explained briefly and the student must choose which he is to use ; at first according to the preference of his teacher, but later on, when he is more adept at the interpretation of *the meaning of each planet in each house* he can make his own judgment by comparing the different placings which result from the various systems, as seen in maps of people well-known to him.

The Equal House system is explained first as it is the simplest to use, and as it is the choice of the writer, arrived at after much work in comparing each system and in the testing of many maps erected by each. However, a properly informed student of astrology MUST understand all systems in general use and these are explained in turn.

MAIN SYSTEMS OF HOUSE DIVISION

1. Equal House System.
2. The Quadrant Systems.
3. Variations on both.

* See Article "Let's *Face* The Problem," by M. E. Hone, *Astrologers' Quarterly*, June, 1949, and relevant Chapters in *Casting the Horoscope*, by Alan Leo.

1. EQUAL HOUSE SYSTEM

This is one of the oldest systems and, after a period of disfavour, is becoming more generally used to-day, especially by those who merit attention by reason of their long and careful work. The most recent pronouncement in its favour is by Charles E. O. Carter who says :—

" This ancient and simple method of house division, fallen into disuse during the would-be ' scientific ' age, when mathematical considerations outweighed the much more profound symbolism of astrology, has of late years had a strong revival in Britain and is now being accorded some attention on the continent of Europe.

" Without totally rejecting the significance of the Placidean cusps, I must state that *only by using equal houses for natal work* will the student be able to do justice to himself and his art.*

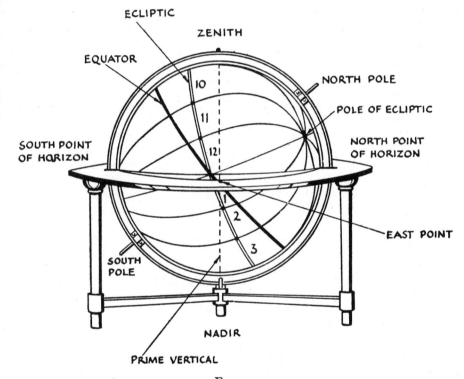

FIG. 12

THE LUNES OF THE HOUSES BY THE EQUAL HOUSE SYSTEM

* From " Tomorrow's News " by Charles E. O. Carter, B.A. An article in the magazine *American Astrology* (October, 1950).

This seems particularly true of *psychological* astrology.

In England, the present older generation of astrologers was much influenced by the excellent work of Alan Leo*, who dismissed the system as " rough and ready " and " now practically abandoned." In his day, argument raged as to the advantages of one trigonometrical calculation as against another, and the simplicity of the E.H. system made no appeal.

As the houses carry the meaning of the signs into practical everyday affairs, it would seem that the sequential meaning of these (beginning from Aries, but working in human life as 1st house, i.e., *personal* affairs), is presumed to begin its cycle again with the Ascendant as its first point.

The great circle taken is the ecliptic which is divided into twelve parts. The twelve equal houses are bounded by great circles passing through the degree of ecliptic ascending over the horizon and through every subsequent 30th degree from this, all meeting at the North and South Poles of the ecliptic.

Many users of the Equal House System prefer not to think of " the houses " as precisely drawn mathematical space-divisions, but rather as a symbolic repetition of the meaning of the twelve signs.

To Chart by the Equal House System (Example in Fig. 12)

On a chart form for use with this system (such as No. 1, " The Ecliptic Chart," facing p. 201) will be seen this circle, divided into 360°, with spaces for the symbols of the twelve signs of 30° each in an outer ring. It is usual to consider the upper and lower parts of the charted circle as those parts of the ecliptic lying to the south and north of the horizon, and the left and right sides as the easterly and westerly parts.

Culmination (degree of M.C.) is always *due south* (in northern latitudes) and ascension is always *on the eastern horizon*.

Confusion has been caused in the minds of beginners by certain chart forms on which the words " East Point " are printed beside the cusp of the first house, where the ascending degree is to be written. The Ascendant is *due* east only when the equinoctial points, 0° Aries and 0° Libra, are rising. It is more towards the north point of the horizon when signs of *long ascension* are rising and towards the south point when signs of *short ascension* are rising.

Fig. 13 shows the amount of ecliptic (123°, over one-third of the whole, between ascension and culmination when a sign of long ascension is rising in the north-east, while Fig. 14 shows the much smaller amount (56° 30', almost one-sixth of the whole) when a sign of short ascension is rising in the south east.

It would be both convenient and correct to write the degree of culmination always at the top of the circle, and the ascending degree at its given distance away. This is done by many Continental astrologers who are willing to turn their maps around when looking at the houses, but English and American astrologers are so used to the visual aid of the Ascendant being *always* on the extreme left of the chart that, as with words, so with charting, *an incorrect usage is habitual*, because it is easier, and no harm is done, *so long as the facts are realised*.

* *Casting the Horoscope*, Alan Leo.

Figs. 15 and 16 show *the more customary method of charting*. In this way, the
1st house is always immediately below the ascendant which is on the extreme left.
Note the difference in its placing in the two pairs of figures.

The calculated degree of ascendant is marked and equal houses of 30° each are
marked all round the ecliptic. The lines dividing the houses are drawn. (The use of a
stencil makes this easy, see p. 315).

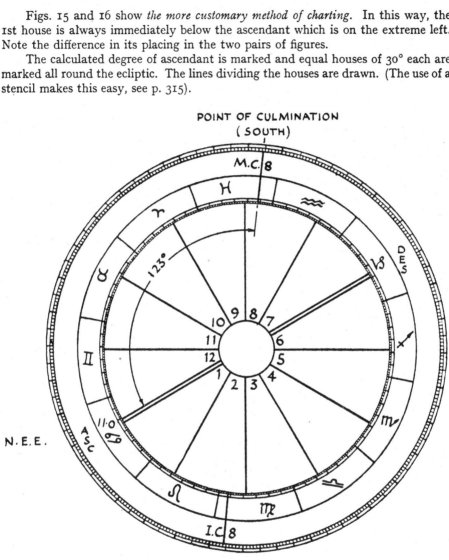

FIG. 13

CHART OF THE ECLIPTIC SHOWING SIGN OF LONG ASCENSION RISING.

(Actual position in sky.)

Sidereal Time 22 h. 38 m. 50 s.   London.

* "No. 1. The Ecliptic Chart" is the chart-form used. See page 315.

It is unnecessary to repeat the number of the degree at every house cusp (beginning point), as it is understood to be the same throughout. House numbers are put in until the student is accustomed to the work and can do without them.

It should be noticed that, since an early degree of a sign is rising in Fig. 15, it is more convenient to use the space *below* the extreme left as that for the sign

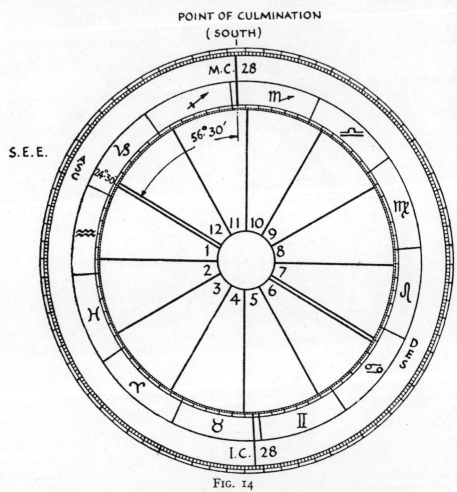

FIG. 14

*CHART OF THE ECLIPTIC SHOWING SIGN OF SHORT ASCENSION RISING.
(Actual position in sky.)
Sidereal Time 15 h. 42 m. 57 s. London.

* " No. 1. The Ecliptic Chart " is the chart-form used. See page 315.

ascending, since the early degree will then come nearer to the required position on the left.

In Fig. 16, *the reverse* is the case, so the space above is used.

The M.C. is put in at the correct ecliptical degree, even though the south is thus not placed at the top of the figure.

To Insert the Planets (example in Fig. 15)

Mark the degree occupied by each planet at birth, as calculated. Write its symbol and degree from left to right, followed by ℞ if retrograde.

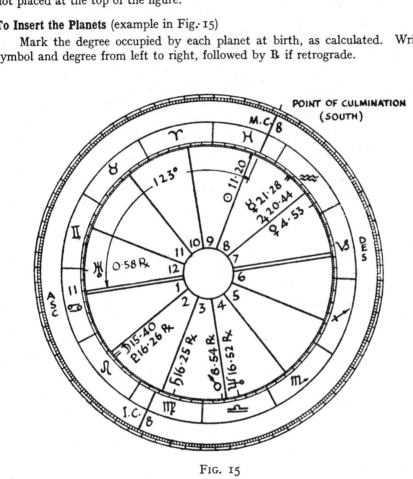

FIG. 15

*USUAL METHOD OF CHARTING BY THE EQUAL HOUSE SYSTEM.

(As for Fig. 10 but adjusted to place Asc. in customary position.)
(Note position of M.C.)

Sidereal time 22 h. 38 m. 50 s.   London.   Planets for Noon, March 2nd, 1950.

* " No. 1. The Ecliptic Chart " is the chart-form used.   See page 315.

If No. 2, " The Houses Chart," is preferred, the planets must be inserted by eye, approximately in their relative positions.

For full example, see Chapter II.

Signs of Long and Short Ascension

In every 24 hours, all signs ascend over the eastern horizon (in latitudes below the Arctic Circle). Each degree of each sign culminates in the south at the upper meridian; each descends, then transits the lower meridian below the northern horizon and completes its circle, ascending again in the east.

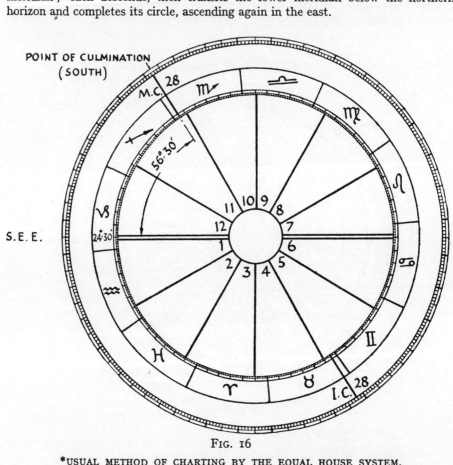

FIG. 16

*USUAL METHOD OF CHARTING BY THE EQUAL HOUSE SYSTEM.

(As for Fig. II but adjusted to place Asc. in customary position.)

(Note position of M.C.)

Sidereal Time 15 h. 42 m. 57 s.   London.

* " No. I. The Ecliptic Chart " is the chart-form used. See page 315.

In northern latitudes, the signs Cancer to Sagittarius are referred to as signs of *long ascension,* while those from Capricorn to Gemini are called those of *short ascension.* The opposite is the case in southern latitudes.

It will be seen from Fig. 11 that these terms do not apply in equatorial regions. In polar regions some signs do not rise at all. Hence the terms are applicable only in those middle latitudes of the countries in which astrology has been mainly studied.

The signs in the centres of these divisions of six ascend more uniformly, but no special term is used for them.

The reason for the difference is that all rising occurs parallel to the celestial equator, and, as the ecliptic lies obliquely across the equator (Fig. 9) some parts of it rise over the horizon at a much quicker rate than others.

The use of a celestial globe will make this clear.

2. THE QUADRANT SYSTEMS

It must never be forgotten that the early cartographers worked under great difficulties and had to *find out* how to chart their findings, both terrestrial and celestial. In making spherical observations, it was necessary to lay down fixed bearings for the purpose.

" The determination of the East and West line, i.e., the parallel of latitude, was one of the earliest triumphs of the human mind.

" Simple trial and observation showed that a stationary point was to be found in the North Pole of the firmament and the star lying nearest to it." Thus the north–south line was found and the observer projected his meridian upon the celestial vault.

" The East and West points of the horizon and the meridian of the observer having been ascertained, the earliest facts of observation regarding the paths of the planets could be brought into relation therewith. Because of the rotation of the Earth, there is an apparent daily revolution of all stars around the position of the observer, each of them crossing his meridian once in 24 hours, while, if they be on the equatorial circle, the intersection takes place exactly 6 hours after they rise in the east and 6 hours before they set in the west."*

Hence, the observer's celestial equator, too, was laid out in 12 segments corresponding to the 12 signs of the Zodiac.

At every two hours interval, for an observer at the equator, this would have corresponded with a change of 30° of the zodiac. These were the divisions known as houses. These were sometimes divided into two, which led to the division of the day into 24 hours. This " quadrature " of the heavens *was the basis of all the " quadrant " house systems.* All measurement was relative to it. In medieval times there were no specialists in mathematics, astronomy, astrology, and so on. Those who could compute, did so for all these branches of knowledge, as they would now be called.

* Introduction to " Sun, Moon and Stars," Baron Felix von Oefele. *Encyclopedia of Religion and Ethics,* edited by James Hastings, 1921.

In relation to astrology, the difference between the various systems of house division is in the different methods of marking the ecliptic *to denote the three houses in each quadrant.* So long as this was done in equatorial countries, the variety of the systems made little difference to the result, since the apparent revolution of the heavens took 6 hours to each quadrant with regularity. The resultant houses were then equal, or very nearly so, *as in the equal house system.*

Just as the word Midheaven does not mean in medium or northern latitudes, what it actually *is* near the equator, so these quadrants, in the higher latitudes, do not contain anything like a similar number of degrees, the one with the others, as they do on, or near, the equator. But the habit came north with other astrological usage and has persisted.

The points on the boundaries of these quadrants are those already described as the M.C. and Asc. and their opposites. These are also known as the *Angles.* Reference to Figs. 13–16 shows that very varying proportions of the ecliptic can be in the quadrants. Only at the daily risings of the equinoctial signs, Aries and Libra, is the proportion equal. They are called equinoctial because about 21st March and 23rd September, 0° Aries and 0° Libra respectively are on the horizon at sunrise. At these times, day and night are equal the world over. (Latin *aequus*, equal; *nox*, night.) When other signs rise, there are differences which become greater as the latitudes become further north. When the northern countries, such as Norway, Sweden and parts of Russia are reached, the difference is very great indeed at those times of day when the signs of longest and shortest ascension are rising. The charts produced become abnormal, but the abnormality has existed to a certain extent ever since the equator was left. It has not been noticed because not extreme, just as it is not remarked that a middle-aged person is growing old, though that process begins from birth!

These northern countries were relatively unknown to the early astrologers and their inhabitants were thought to be very different from those in more civilised places. In the present day, many of these countries are as modernised as any others, and are becoming of greater importance because of their geographical position in the line of flight between the two great countries of the U.S.A. and the U.S.S.R. Their people mix more with those in more southern latitudes because of greater ease of travel, so they cannot be separated in astrological usage. *In the Arctic regions, these charts reach the limits of impossibility,* but it is hardly necessary to go into this fully at the moment as it is discussed in Chapter 16.

Basis of the Quadrant Systems

The basis of each system is to take one of the great circles, to divide it equally into the four quadrants and then to subdivide each again into three sections. Through the points of such divisions and subdivisions, great circles are placed which go through other important points, each in its way effecting a twelvefold celestial dividing. These circles crossed the ecliptic wherever it might be at the time, and the degrees at which they crossed were thus decided on as the *house boundaries or cusps.*

As the ascending degree was *always* taken as the cusp of the 1st house, and the culminating degree (M.C.) was *always* the cusp of the 10th house, reference to Fig. 15 will show that, in this case, 123° would have to be charted as if cramped into one quadrant, while reference to Fig. 16 will show that, in this case, 56½° would have to be charted as if stretched to cover the same quadrant. In the former case, the resultant houses in that quadrant would be larger than 30° each, while in the latter, they would be smaller. The opposite quadrant would be a repeat of the first, while the fourth would be a repeat of the second. To sum up, the effect *on the ecliptic* was that it was unequally divided in regard to these pairs of quadrants.

Main Quadrant Systems

The student must read extensively to understand *all* these—only those in general use will be described here. These are known by the names of their introducers, as follows :—

(A) Campanus—died about 1297   ⎫
(B) Regiomontanus—died 1476   ⎬ Space System
(C) Placidus—died 1688   Time System

The systems will be described in chronological order, *though the third will be chosen for use, since it is the most widely known.* This is mainly because, until 1953, it was the only system for which reference Tables were currently published.

Space Systems

A. Campanus   ⎫   These two may be called " space " systems
B. Regiomontanus ⎬   since distance (on great circles) is divided.

(A) Campanus (1297)

The great circle taken is the Prime Vertical which is divided into twelve parts.

Degrees of house cusps are obtained by finding out (trigonometrically) what degrees of the ecliptic are cut by six great circles (circles of position) passing through the points of division of the Prime Vertical and the north and south points of horizon (Fig. 17).

Prime Vertical

All great circles which rise vertically from the horizon and pass through the Zenith and its antipodal point are *Vertical circles.* That one which passes through the *EAST Point of the Horizon* is the first, or *Prime* Vertical.

Current Use of System

This system is used by certain modern astrologers who have seriously studied this controversial question, and have decided that the traditional idea of the Quadrant systems must be adhered to, and that, in their opinion, this is the one most *mathematically* acceptable, and conforms to their requirements.

(B) Regiomontanus (1476)

The great circle taken is the celestial equator which is divided into twelve parts.

Degrees of house cusps are obtained by finding out (trigonometrically) what degrees of the ecliptic would be cut by the six great circles passing through these points of division of the equator, and the north and south points of horizon (Fig. 18).

Note that at the equator the celestial equator would coincide with the Prime Vertical, so the two would be the same (cf. Fig. 11).

Lunes

The moon-shaped divisions between the house circles.

Current Use of System

This system had a great vogue until about 1800, due largely to the fact that printing had been discovered and its description could be circulated in astrologically interested countries. It is still used on the Continent.

The following figures show the six houses located on one side of the celestial sphere, as seen from the east.

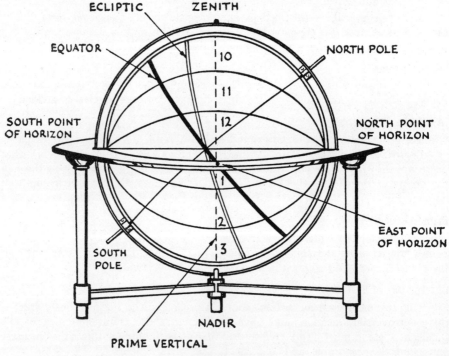

FIG. 17

THE LUNES OF THE HOUSES BY CAMPANUS

(diagrammatically shown)

They are almost identical, it being impossible to show in so small a diagram, the slight difference in the size of each house, as measured along the ecliptic, but the average amount of difference can be seen by reference to comparative Tables on p. 136.* Very few copies of these Tables were printed, so making it difficult for astrologers to compare the differences made by the use of the three systems.

In Fig. 17 (by Campanus), *the Prime Vertical* is seen to be divided into six. The circles of position running through the points of division cut the ecliptic at six places.

In Fig. 18 (by Regiomontanus), *the Equator* is seen to be divided into six, the circles of position again cutting the ecliptic.

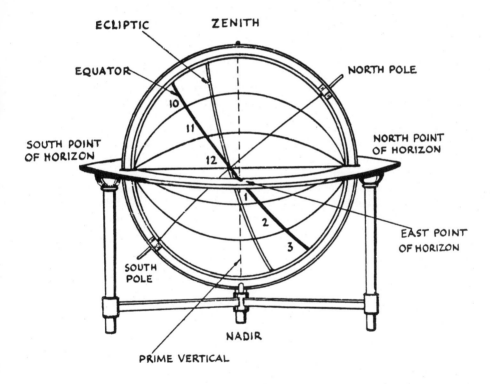

FIG. 18

THE LUNES OF THE HOUSES BY REGIOMONTANUS

(diagrammatically shown)

* From Dr. E. Williamson's *Astronomical Ephemeris* for 1936.

Latitude 50° N.   Ecliptic 23° 27' 0".

S.T.	Æ	X	I Ascend.	Placidus				Regiomontanus				Campanus			
				XI	XII	II	III	XI	XII	II	III	XI	XII	II	III
h m	°	° '	° '	° '	° '	° '	° '	° '	° '	° '	° '	° '	° '	° '	° '
8 0	120	27♊54,5	21♎30,5	2♍20	0♎0	18♏1	20♐38	4♍9	0♎0	14♏53	16♐40	23♌48	20♍37	26♏10	29♐
8 4	121	28 51,9	22 13,4	3 15	0 49	18 49	21 31	5 0	0 45	15 38	17 32	24 41	21 24	26 57	0♑
8 8	122	29 49,4	22 56,2	4 9	1 37	19 36	22 25	5 51	1 30	16 23	18 24	25 35	22 11	27 44	1

FIG. 19

COMBINED TABLES OF HOUSES ACCORDING TO THE SYSTEMS OF PLACIDUS,
REGIOMONTANUS AND CAMPANUS.*

(Note that with 21° 30' Libra ascending, the cusps of the 12th house by Placidus and Regiomontanus are the same and that, 4 minutes later, there is a different sign on cusp 3 by Campanus.)

(C) Placidus (1688)

This is called a time system because what is divided is *time, taken to cover space*. In this system, no lunes are formed. In fact, the boundaries of the houses are not formed by great circles converging to the north and south points of the horizon *or to any other pair of points*. In this respect, Placidus made a complete departure from the principles followed by all previous systems, and no other subsequent system has followed him.

It is often referred to as the *semi-arc* system because the times (in right ascension), taken for *each degree of the ecliptic* to rise, on its own parallel of declination, from lower meridian to horizon (nocturnal semi-arc) and from horizon to upper meridian (diurnal semi-arc) are trisected.

At any moment of time, one degree of the 360 will have completed one-third of *its own* n-s-a and will be in the position to be that on the cusp of the 3rd house; at the same moment, another will have completed two-thirds of *its own* n-s-a and will be in the position to be that on the cusp of the 2nd house. At the same moment, another degree will have completed its n-s-a and will on the horizon (cusp 1) ; another will have completed one-third of its d-s-a (cusp 12) ; another will have completed two-thirds of its d-s-a (cusp 11) while another will have culminated at the upper meridian (cusp 10). Their opposites will be cusps 9, 8, 7, 6, 5, 4.

The essential factor of this system is that there should be semi-arcs to trisect. It is obvious that, in latitudes greater than 66° 33', where many degrees are circumpolar (never touching the horizon), these will not have diurnal *and* nocturnal arcs, their whole arcs being *either* diurnal *or* nocturnal. Since there are no semi-arcs to trisect, the basic requirement of the system is missing.

Certain degrees can therefore never form house-cusps nor be included in houses. Sun, Moon and planets in those degrees at that time cannot appear in any charting attempted by this system, so must also be omitted. No complete chart can be made.†

* From Dr. E. Williamson's *Astronomical Ephemeris* for 1936.
† For fuller discussion, see Chapter vi, the new *Waite's Compendium of Natal Astrology* by Colin Evans. Routledge and Kegan Paul.

The diagram below is an attempt by a mathematician* to show the houses at a given time and place.

This shows that the idea held by many astrologers of a twelvefold division of such houses, surrounding the person at his birth-place, in anything like even sizes, as might be gathered from the customary chart form, is completely erroneous.

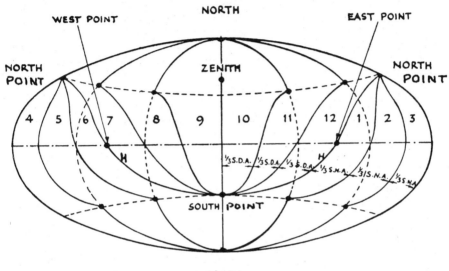

S.D.A. = SEMI-DIURNAL ARC.
S.N.A. = SEMI-NOCTURNAL ARC.
    H = HORIZON

FIG. 20

THE HOUSES BY PLACIDUS AT A SPECIFIC MOMENT OF TIME.

The above description and diagram are given so that the reader may gain some idea of the complexity of the discussion, but it is not expected that he should understand these in detail.

Current use of the System

This system was violently opposed by astrologers of the day when brought to England (1711). It gained ground because it was preferred by the editor of one of the

* Chief Engineer A. Ludwig, *Les Cahiers Astrologiques*, Nov.–Dec., 1949, page 324.

earliest of astrological magazines, and by the compiler of a general almanac of the time which included planetary data amongst much else.

He was one of the first in England to calculate and print Placidean tables for various latitudes. Since these were thus made generally available, their use became habitual and their publishing, together with the astrological section of the Ephemerides, has continued.

At the time of the great recrudescence of astrology, due to Alan Leo and writers of his day (the turn of the century), this system was strongly approved. From then on, with one notable exception,* writers of all text-books in English have taught this system, with no more comment than that the controversy is too difficult to put before students, and with no admission of the fact that *some mathematically minded astrologers condemn this system as the least worthy of attention*. Some French and German astrologers have taught otherwise.

During this time, astrology spread greatly through the U.S.A. This vast country lies in the main further south than the European countries where astrology is chiefly practised, so the distortions of this and all quadrant systems in the higher latitudes (where they are in practice unusuable) are not immediately apparent to Americans. (See Chapter 16.)

To Chart by any Quadrant System

The method is the same for all three, but as Tables of Houses for Regiomontanus and for Campanus are less readily obtainable, those for the *system of Placidus* will here be used.

The degrees of Ascendant and Midheaven are found as before from the Tables of Houses at the end of Raphael's (or other) Ephemerides and are entered on to the chart form *using the degrees of the other four houses as given*. (See Fig. 21)

This is the type of chart form *customarily used* in England and America for charting by any *quadrant system*, but continental astrologers are more precise (see Fig. 22).

Note that, on the printed form, *house spaces are now given*, not the ecliptic, and, because in these systems the culminating degree *must* be the cusp of the 10th house, it is placed thereon. Degrees for cusps 11, 12, 2 and 3 are entered as given in the Tables of Houses. Their naturally opposite signs with same degrees are entered across the chart.

Beginners will find it more difficult to see the aspects between planets when working with this method (Chapter 10).

Fig. 22 shows the charting much used on the Continent but rarely in England or America. This is surprising because, though it is slightly more trouble to put in the varied houses correctly, the advantages are that the sizes of the houses can be seen in their actual inequality, and the calculation of aspects is simpler.

Intercepted Signs

It will be seen that the signs Cancer and Capricorn cover two cusps each, while there is no cusp for Taurus or Scorpio.

* P. J. Harwood. Set of text-books using Equal House System.

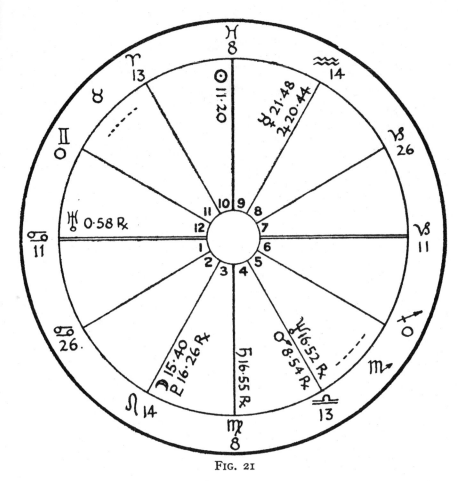

FIG. 21

*USUAL METHOD OF CHARTING BY THE PLACIDEAN SYSTEM.

(As for Figs. 13 and 15 but with the type of chart used generally for this system.
Note position of M.C.)

Sidereal Time 22 h. 38 m. 50 s.   London.   Planets for Noon, March 2nd, 1950. ·

    Reference to Fig. 13 will show that there were 123° between Asc. and M.C., so that, by this type of house division, more than the 30° of one sign will have to lie within one house while, in the lower quadrant of 57°, these must be as if stretched out to cover three houses.

  * " No. 2. The Houses Chart," is the chart-form used. See page 315.

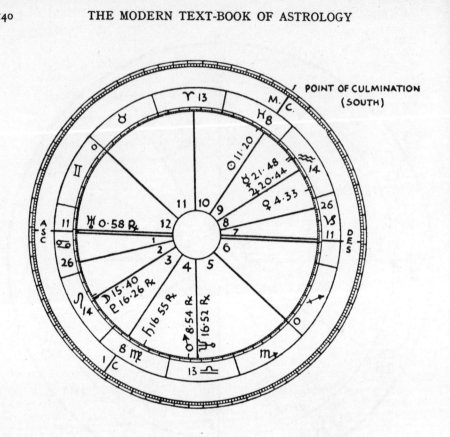

FIG. 22

*CONTINENTAL METHOD OF CHARTING BY THE PLACIDEAN SYSTEM.

(As for Figs. 15 and 21 but showing the unequal houses in their exact sizes in regard to the ecliptic.   Note position of M.C.)

A sign which comes entirely into one house but on to neither cusp is called *intercepted*.

There is no agreement amongst astrologers as to the meaning of this in the interpretation of charts.

In a recent discussion on this point, varying opinions were expressed, some considering that the house was thereby strengthened because it was thus connected with three signs, others that the sign was weakened because it was not on the cusp

* "No. 1. The Ecliptic Chart," is the chart-form used. See page 315.

of a house. Others suggested that the sign carried a more " inward " meaning in relation to the character of the person concerned.

The beginner is reminded that interception is not an *astronomical* fact but is due solely to the mathematics of the particular system of house division used.

In view of the absence of agreement on interpretation, he is recommended not to pay too much attention to this point.

To Insert Planets

Planets are written near to the line of the cusp bearing the sign in which they are to be charted, and on the side of it to which they naturally go numerically, in relation to the number of the degree on this cusp.

Any planet in an intercepted sign is written *across* the house, as indicated by the dotted lines. (See p. 139 and example Chart facing p. 222).

House Position of Planets

The student will now see that with the exception of Uranus, no planet is in the same house as it occupied in the same chart by the Equal House system. This is an extreme case. Charts with the equinoctial signs rising will not show this difference. It will never occur in charts for equatorial regions *whatever sign* is rising. It will occur with even greater frequency as charts are done for localities further north.

Conclusions to be Drawn From Planetary Placing

The system of Placidus has not yet been used for a half of the time that the Regiomontanian has existed, nor for a third of the time that the Campanian has been known, but its period has been that of the modern spread of astrology and many astrologers have had no experience of any other. Though many opinions are expressed little statistical work has been done concerning the correctness of any of these systems as compared with the Equal House system.

At the time of writing (1950), there is a strong movement towards the latter, by reason of the proof offered by experienced workers.

The student can easily put up his first few maps by both systems, and, when he finds a change in the house position of a planet, he can refer to the meanings of " Planets in Houses " (Chapter 9), and *decide for himself* which gives the better result, in the light of his own knowledge of the person whose chart he is doing.

3. VARIATIONS OF SYSTEMS

Many modern mathematicians have made suggestions and it must be remembered that they have more data at their disposal than the earlier computators.

These suggestions all embody changes as to the three basic factors in question :—

(1) The start from the Asc.

(2) The points at which circles of division should converge.

(3) The method of sub-dividing the quadrants.

(4) Ways of combining such factors.

In a recent contribution to the subject, a mathematician has arrived at the total of fifty-four different methods !

Two ideas which are of interest are :—

(1) the house cusps should be regarded as the house-*centres*.

(2) *That the whole conception of " houses " is too rigid* and that the well known difficulty of statistically assessing correctness of house systems by actual placing of planets in houses is because there should be an " over-lapping " of their meanings, hence a planet may indeed have validity in two adjacent houses, and may be claimed as " true " in meaning by the advocates of more than one system. *

The System of Porphyry (Space system)

This must be mentioned as it is a well-known system of antiquity, and has recently been revived by a group of astrologers who wish to adhere to the division into quadrants but not to the subsequent unequal dividing usual in quadrant systems.

By this method, having made the *four unequal quadrant divisions*, the degrees *of ecliptic* in each are then *equally* divided into three.

This is frequently referred to as " the equal system," but it is an inaccurate description.

4. CHOICE OF SYSTEM FOR USE

A student cannot consider himself efficiently taught if he understands only one system which he uses customarily. He must be familiar with both *the Equal House system* and a representative of *the Quadrant systems*. Since the Tables for the Placidean system are readily available, he must use this one as an example, so that he may understand charts by this system which he will see in books and magazines.

He must also be able to convert one system to another so as to be able to make comparisons between the two.

Conversion of a Chart Erected by a Quadrant System into E.H.

Users of the Equal House system can easily re-write a chart erected by any other system, by simply placing the degree of the Asc. in its usual place, following by the same degree of the rest of the signs, in their known order, on the cusps of the subsequent houses. The house positions of the planets must then be adjusted. The important M.C. and I.C. must be inserted.

Conversion of Chart Erected by E.H. to any Quadrant System

Tables for required system must be used. The degree of the Asc. will be the same. The degree of the M.C. must be placed on cusp 10. Degrees on intermediate cusps must be inserted as given in Tables. House positions of planets must be adjusted.

See Chapter 11 for example charts by two systems, and Chapter 16 for further discussion on the house division question.

* Advanced students are referred to a pamphlet issued by The London Astrological Research Group, 1951. Obtainable from L. N. Fowler and Co. Ltd. In this it is suggested that two sets of equal houses may be used, one in which the houses follow the degree of the ascendant as cusp 1 (A houses), their rulers and the planets in them being interpreted as showing the innate predisposition of a person. The other twelve follow from the degree of the M.C. as cusp 10 (M houses), their rulers and the planets in them being interpreted as showing what a person might have to meet and adapt himself to in life, with deduction as to the way in which this would affect his character.

CHAPTER 8

FURTHER CONSIDERATION NECESSARY FOR THE COMPLETION OF THE CHART-FORM

BEFORE the interpretation of a chart can be begun, it must be dissected and examined in many ways for its strengths and weaknesses.

Taking either Chart Form No. 1 or 2 and leaving the section headed " Progressed Data " until later, the remainder of the spaces, as arranged, should be filled in as in example chart in Chapter 11.

Ruling Planet

That which rules the sign on the Ascendant. Its strength will be most important and the person will show its characteristics strongly.

Ruler's House

The house in which this planet is found. The affairs of this house are likely to be stressed.

Rising Planet

Strictly speaking, all planets are " rising " from the moment of their transit of the lower meridian (I.C.) until they reach the upper meridian (M.C.).

It seems that the phrase has been narrowed in its meaning to denote planets rising not far from the Ascendant, so that its significance is modified by them. There is no exact rule, but any within 5° *above* the Ascendant would influence it by conjunction, while those below it would influence the person if within the first house. As will be learnt later, the Ascendant " progresses " through this house, so will be further influenced by approach to such planets.

Needless to say, by house must be meant the natural 30° of the Equal House system to which a reasonably undistorted map by one of the quadrant systems would approximate. It could not be said that a planet " in the first house " would affect the Ascendant if it were 90 or more degrees from it, as would be possible for charts for certain birth times in latitudes north from about the Midlands of England, having one, or even two, " intercepted " signs in the first house by such systems of calculation.

Triplicities (Chapter 4, Group 1)

Enter Asc. and M.C. beside the Element which each occupies. Refer to Fig. 3. Count the planets in each Element and list them. Whichever Element is predominant will be strongly represented in the life.*

Positive and Negative

Add number of planets in Fire and Air for the Positive category.

Add those in Earth and Water for the Negative category.

For effect of predominance, refer p. 42 and p. 182 (Grand Trine).

* The same deduction can be made from strength by occupancy of *the natural houses of the signs* (see pp. 89 and 204), this often making up for lack in the signs themselves.

Quadruplicities

Refer to Fig. 4. Count and list planets as found. Predominance of any one quality will be shown in the life.

Angular, Succedent, Cadent

If the Placidean or other quadrant system has been used, this classification applies and the number of planets in each house so named should be listed.

If the Equal House system has been used, it is better to list those planets near an angle as " angular " *and to cross out the other two words.*

The M.C. and its opposite point are not automatically the cusps of 10th and 4th houses, and their degrees of ecliptic may be in other houses (see **Figs. 15 and 16**).

Mutual Reception

This is the term used when each of two planets is found to be in the sign ruled by the other. The position brings them into relationship as if they were in conjunction (p. 182).

Example.—Sun in Cancer and Moon in Leo.

Own Sign.   Exalted

A planet is said to be strong, or in the old term " dignified," when it is in (*a*) the sign which it rules, or (*b*) the sign in which it is exalted. The traditional exaltations are as follows :—

$\odot$ is exalted in ♈

☽ is exalted in ♉

☿ is exalted in ♍

♀ is exalted in ♓

♂ is exalted in ♑

♃ is exalted in ♋

♄ is exalted in ♎

The essential principle of the planet should manifest at its best.

Many suggestions have been made as to the signs in which the three extra-Saturnian planets may be considered to be exalted, but no generally agreed conclusions have been reached.

Detriment—Fall

A planet is said to be weak, or in the old term " debilitated," when in the opposite signs to the above in the order given. The sign of its detriment is opposite to its own sign. The sign of its fall is opposite to that of its exaltation.

The modern tendency is to give less importance to this idea.

Declinations

Under this column should be listed the declinations of the planets as given in the Ephemeris. It is sufficiently accurate to list them as for mid-day. The exception is the Moon. As stated in the chapter on Computation, it moves quickly so its declination should be calculated at the same time as its celestial longitude.

If two planets are equidistant from the celestial equator, either to its north or its south, they are said to be in " Parallel of Declination," usually shortened to *Parallel.*

An *orb* of 1° is the most that is allowed. The effect is considered to be similar to that of the conjunction. A capital P or the symbol ‖ is written in the aspect space. If the two planets concerned are already brought into connection by aspect, the P or ‖ is often omitted, though it should be thought of as an intensification of the meaning of the aspect (see Chapter 10).

Latitude

In the older forms, there is a column so headed. As only the Moon and Pluto can have enough latitude to warrant consideration, the space-wasting column is nowadays omitted, *but* there is a very strong feeling that insufficient attention has been paid to the fact that the Moon's aspects may be considerably weaker when her latitude is great. A glance at the Ephemeris for the day in question will show this and it can be stated in the NOTES column of the newer forms.

The Nodes of the Moon

☊ North Node.
☋ South Node.

As so many of the traditional terms have continued in their Latin form, these are often spoken of as Caput and Cauda, since the names were *Caput Draconis* and *Cauda Draconis*, the dragon's head and tail.

Astronomically, the nodes of a planet are the two points at which its orbit intersects the plane of the ecliptic as it goes from north to south latitude and vice versa. Those of the Moon are considered of great importance by some astrologers but not enough research has been done to form a solid opinion and very little has been written about them (except in Hindu astrology).

The mean longitude of the North Node will be found in the upper part of the right-hand page in the Ephemeris, and its opposite point in the ecliptic will be that of the South Node.

Interpretatively, it may be said that the North or Ascending Node seems to have a better reputation than the South. One theory put forward is that the line which they form across the chart may be thought of as receptive in the North and depleting in the South. It is as if the person could receive and benefit by the " head," in terms of house and sign in question, but that he is called upon to give in terms of the situation of the " tail."

Another theory is that the axis of the Nodes across the Asc.–Des. line indicates something unusual in the appearance, often exceptional shortness or tallness.

No calculation is needed and they should be inserted in the chart. (See p. 147.)

The Part of Fortune

⊕ Again the Latin term is often used. It is *Pars Fortunae* and is often shortened to " Pars," or merely " Fortuna." There are many of these " Parts " and all are formed by adding the longitude of the planet concerned to the longitude of the Ascendant, and from this sum subtracting the longitude of the Sun. Thus a point in space is indicated. In this case, the planet concerned is the Moon.

Interpretatively, it is thought that the matters concerned with the house in which it falls are those in which the person is truly interested and in which he wishes to find fulfilment, whatever he may say to the contrary. It must be said that, though this point is considered benefic, there is little agreement of opinion about it. It should be inserted into the chart.

Each sign occupies 30 degrees of zodiacal longitude:

0° Aries	=	0°	0° Leo	=	120°	0° Saggitarius	=	240°
0° Taurus	=	30°	0° Virgo	=	150°	0° Capricorn	=	270°
0° Gemini	=	60°	0° Libra	=	180°	0° Aquarius	=	300°
0° Cancer	=	90°	0° Scorpio	=	210°	0° Pisces	=	330°

Hence, in the following example, the longitudes of Ascendant, Moon and Sun are written as follows :

				Degrees	Minutes
Asc.	♎	25° 34′ (180° + 25° 34′)	=	205	34
+ Moon	♒	29° 48′ (300° + 29° 48′)	= +	329	48
				535	22
− Sun	♊	29° 54′ (60° + 29° 54′)	= −	89	54
				445	28
Since total exceeds 360°, subtract the circle				− 360	00
		Result		85	28

Therefore ⊕ = ♊ 25° 28′ (See Example chart, Chapter 11).

If the combined longitudes of the Ascendant and Moon are less than the longitude of the Sun, add 360° to the addition before making the subtraction.

A useful check is to remember that " As the Moon is to the Sun, so is the Part of Fortune to the Ascendant." Thus in the example, the Moon is *behind* the Sun *in trine aspect plus six minutes*, so the Part of Fortune should be *behind* the Ascendant *in trine aspect plus six minutes*.

It is helpful both for tidiness and for quick observation, if the Nodes and Part of Fortune are written in ordinary ink, and close to the centre of the chart-circle, while planets are written in red ink.

Dispositor

A planet is said to dispose of, or to be the dispositor of another when that other is in a sign ruled by this planet.

Example.—Mars in Taurus. Venus would be said to be the *dispositor* of Mars.

The principle of a planet is affected by its dispositor. In this case, the active energy of Mars would be, to a certain extent, stabilised and harmonised by the contact with Taurus and its ruler, Venus.

Extended Dispositorship

Sometimes a chain of dispositors may be formed, so that one planet may be said to be the final dispositor of all in the chart.

Example.—2nd May, 1942 :—

Venus is in Pisces, dispositor Neptune.
Neptune is in Virgo, dispositor *Mercury*.
Mars is in Cancer, dispositor Moon.
Moon is in Sagittarius, dispositor Jupiter.
Jupiter is in Gemini, dispositor again *Mercury*.
Pluto is in Leo, dispositor *Sun*.

These two dispositors of six planets, are with Saturn and Uranus in Taurus, so the final dispositor of all is *Venus, ruler of Taurus*. In such a case, Venus is said to be of much importance in the chart.

Note.—The above is not customarily entered on to a chart form, but it is given consideration in assessing strength of a planet.

Ruler's Sign

On chart-forms, it has been customary to note the house occupied by the ruler but not the sign. The effect has been an under-valuation of the sign position. It is *most* important that this should be taken into consideration in interpretation. Differences between people with the same ascending sign are thus indicated since its traits are intensified if it contains the ruler or modified according as this is placed in one of the other eleven signs.

Nodes of the Planets

These are not customarily inserted. Lists copied from astronomical sources are expressed heliocentrically. Such positions cannot be used in charts of geocentric positions.

CHAPTER 9

INTERPRETATIVE MEANINGS FOR PLANETARY POSITIONS IN SIGNS AND IN HOUSES AND BY THEIR SHAPING IN A CHART

THE dictum cannot be too often repeated that the student will NEVER become fluent and quick in interpretation until he so thoroughly grasps the nature of each *planet, sign, house* and *aspect*, that he can apply them, as related in any chart, without constant reference to books.

The practised astrologer reads new publications and current magazines, attends lectures and sharpens his mind by endless discussion with his astrological friends, but when at interpretative work, he needs no book but his *Ephemeris*. The beginner should also read and listen as much as possible, but he needs the help of books in his work, at first.

When interpreting, he should remember the keywords, for the basic ideas, then he should re-read the earlier paragraphs on the planet with which he is dealing and on the sign and house in which it is posited. The short descriptions which follow are only as *reminders* when these have become familiar. They are in NO way a substitute for the understanding of essential meanings. For help in the understanding of *aspects** in a fuller way a whole book is necessary and should be read. Short hints will be included here.

It must be remembered that, in general terms, the *SIGN* placing of a planet will give its *mode* of working, while the *HOUSE* placing will give its *application in the affairs of life*, but the two are complementary and partly overlapping in meaning.

These will be *modified* :—

1. By the aspects received (see Chapter 10).
    (*a*) If mainly helpful, there will be ease of working of the principles of the planet and the best of the meaning of the sign will show in the sphere of life indicated.
    (*b*) If mainly unhelpful, the planetary working will be difficult, and the traits listed under " overstress or misuse " of the planet and sign will be evinced.
2. By the strength assessed through the various placings as listed (Dignity, Debility, Angularity, Rulership, dispositor of satellitium).
3. By other indications from the rest of the map, more fully discussed in Chapters 11 and 12.

Note.—In the following condensed aids to interpretation, no detailed remarks are given about HEALTH except in regard to 6th house. Whatever bodily part, or system, is correlated with sign or house under scrutiny, will be improved by helpful planets contained and by helpful aspects to these, and vice versa (see p. 46).

---

* *The Astrological Aspects*, by C. E. O. Carter.

SUN

By Sign

The entire nature of the person will be strongly as described for the sign in Chapter 4. In a woman's map, its conditioning gives some understanding with regard to the men in her life.

By House

The affairs of the house occupied will be strongly emphasised in the life. This is often accentuated by there being a satellitium in this house, because Mercury, whose orbit is nearest to the Sun, must be within 28° of it, while Venus, whose orbit is next, must be within 48°. Therefore, if very near, these three frequently form a small satellitium or part of a larger one. The word " Stellium " is used in the U.S.A.

By Rulership

The affairs of the house which has Leo on its cusp will be brought into connection with those of the house occupied by the Sun.

KEYWORDS :—*POWER, VITALITY, SELF-EXPRESSION*

These will be expressed in accordance with aspects :—

IN SIGN

Aries (Exaltation)

Assertive, courageous, energetic, incisive, bold.

OR

selfish, crude, over-harsh.

Taurus

Possessive, steadfast, hospitable, conservative.

OR

grasping, stubborn.

Gemini

Intelligent, talkative, with a lively manner, and much versatility and duality.

OR

with lack of concentration or lack of " heart."

IN HOUSE

(The same but with difficulty if NOT well aspected.)

1st

In personal affairs, which will be thought important, resulting in much self-concentration, but which will be enlivened and strengthened.

2nd

In affairs to do with possessions, money (mainly self-earned), personal feelings. Success in the natural desire to obtain these will be according to above modifications. The ability to do so will be much strengthened by the Sun.

3rd

In affairs to do with mental pursuits, or in activity in any communicatory way either by speech or by journeying. There will be more than usual connection with neighbours, brothers and sisters. Success will be according to modifications. All such matters will be enlivened and vitalised by the Sun.

Cancer

Intuitive, emotional, guarding, domestic.

OR

with lack of reason, withholding, moody.

Leo

Proud, cheerful, gay, magnanimous, powerful, generous.

OR

conceited, despotic, wasteful.

The Principles of the Sun are at their strongest when it is in its own natural sign or house.

Virgo

Modest, practical and with keen desire to work and with attention to detail.

OR

over-cool, fussy, interfering.

Libra (Fall)

Pleasant, smiling, companionable.

OR

discontented, vacillating.

Scorpio

Intense, passionate, secretive, penetrative.

OR

resentful, vengeful.

Sagittarius

Restless, free, cheerful, with dignity and generosity.

OR

over-sporting, careless, extravagant.

4th

In affairs to do with home and family and basic necessities. Happiness and self-fulfilment in such matters will be indicated.

5th

In all affairs which are creative and enjoyable and occasionally risky. Children, love affairs, sports, games, artistic creativity.

The gay, shining Sun lights up all these happy activities. They will be successful and gratifying to the self.

6th

In affairs to do with service, with work, especially if of the detailed practical type, or to do with health and hygiene.

The Sun in this house, well aspected, indicates excellent health and ability to do good work after the manner of the sign involved. It also points to good relations with workers.

7th

In affairs of marriage or partnership. The Sun in this house indicates a successful marriage.

8th

In affairs of the strongest feelings, in sexual matters, often in connection with death and legacies and with mysticism and psychism. The Sun in this house indicates successful interest in the above matters and, eventually, a normal death.

9th

In matters to do with serious study and with distant countries. The Sun in this house indicates addiction to and success in such studies. It often indicates much time spent abroad.

Capricorn
  Practical, ambitious, but cautious.
           OR
with a stern, hard, selfish manner.

10th
  In affairs of "the world" whatever that may mean to the person. In dealings with those in authority. In the business or professional life.

Aquarius (Detriment)
  Independent, unconventional, original, free.
           OR
rebellious, perverse.

11th
  In groups and societies and amongst acquaintances brought together for a common purpose.

Pisces
  Emotional, intuitional, artistic, often psychic. Also sacrificing and kind.
           OR
confused, deceitful, and with desire to escape consequences.

12th
  In secluded or hidden ways. The Sun in this house often indicates a secluded start to life and an ability to use the unconscious side of the psyche.

MOON

By Sign
  Since the Moon is receptive and responsive, in that she reflects and gives out from what she receives, the conditioned behaviour, mannerisms, habits and ways of a person will be expressed in the mode of the sign in which the Moon is found. In a man's map, it often has reference to the women in his life, and for both sexes, it frequently represents the mother. It also refers to conditions of early childhood. In adult life, it represents the manner of dealing with the general public.

By House
  The affairs of the house occupied will be of interest to the person and will tend to colour the life.

By Rulership
  The affairs of the house which has Cancer on its cusp will be brought into connection with those of the house occupied.

  Note.—In older text-books, the Sun, Moon, and Ascendant have been said to represent *specifically* certain sides of the nature. These have been stated as Personality, Individuality, also as Spirit, Soul and Body, etc. *It is now suggested that the entire psyche of a person cannot be dissected into such divisions, but that all combine to form the whole. The art of astro-analysis is in blending the indications given by these three important pointers.*

KEYWORDS :—*RESPONSE, FLUCTUATION*

These will be expressed in accordance with aspects :—

IN SIGN

Aries
In ways and manners which will be pushful, self-assertive, quickly aroused.

OR

quick tempered, unthinking.

Taurus (Exaltation)
In possessive ways and with a liking for the good things of the earth and for Venusian things.

OR

in greedy, money-seeking ways.

Gemini
In addiction to mental and rational interests. In a lively, variable manner.

OR

in over-hard manner and over-shrewd ways.

Cancer
In domestic ways, with much sympathy and desire to care for others.

OR

over-accentuation of the feminine and the restlessly sensational.

Leo
The character seems to show the solar traits. The manners and behaviour will be sunny and gay. The tendency will be to organise and control.

OR

manner conceited and overbearing.

IN HOUSE

(The same, but with difficulty if NOT well aspected.)

1st
In a tendency to have many vicissitudes in personal affairs and to be easily changeful.

2nd
In a tendency to have changes over financial affairs and personal feelings. Money is likely to be obtained through dealings with the public, with women or through the mother.

3rd
In a tendency to changes in early education, to insufficient continuity of mental application, to changeful ideas. Many alterations in the affairs of brothers and sisters. Much activity in going " round-and-about."

4th
In interest in the home and family. Regard for ancestry. Changes in residence.

The Principles of the Moon are at their strongest when it is in its natural sign or house.

5th
In public success in games, sports and with children and women. Interest will be in all these. Aspects to the Moon will give indications about children and about creative activities such as art and literature (according to sign).

Virgo

In addiction to precise attention to detail and readiness to change the mode of work involving this. Love for clean hygienic conditions.

OR

in fussy, interfering ways.

Libra

In gentle, companionable ways and diplomatic manners.

OR

in lazy, easy going, peace-at-any-price ways.

Scorpio (Fall)

In an appearance of intensity and emotional force.

OR

in bitterness and jealousy.

Sagittarius

In a restless but mentally interesting and cheerful approach to life.

OR

in an offhand and over-casual manner.

Capricorn (Detriment)

In a reserved, cautious manner and generally thrifty, sensible ways.

OR

in cold, selfish ways.

Aquarius

In a manner which is independent and detached ; widely friendly without great affection ; liking for mental pursuits, especially of unusual and scientific nature.

OR

manner aloof.

Pisces

In a manner which is sympathetic, voluble, kindly and extremely receptive to the influence of others.

OR

weakly impressionable, over-gushing and emotional.

6th

In desire to work and to make others work. In interest in health. Possible public work in this way.

7th

In changefulness towards those in any intimate relationship. In a liking for women as intimates. In the expectation that the marriage partner will be motherly.

8th

In an interest in sexual matters, in psychic research and speculation on the after-life. In matters to do with legacies of others or contacts with their affairs (as trustee, etc.).

9th

In an interest in travel, in study of profound subjects.

10th

The life is lived much in public. The career is of interest.

11th

In a tendency to join all sorts of societies and groups and to pursue the chosen objectives with interest but with varying ends.

12th

In a tendency to retirement, and to work in secluded or isolated ways—also in a tendency to live in a world of the imagination, or to use the power of the unconscious self or to be mediumistic.

MERCURY

By Sign
The way of self-expression by any method of communication will be shown by the sign containing Mercury. The kind of nervous system and reactions will also be implied.

By House
The affairs of the house occupied will indicate those to which the mind is largely applied and there may be some indication to do with brothers and sisters.

By Rulership
The affairs of the houses which have Gemini and Virgo on their cusps will be brought into connection with those of the house occupied.

KEYWORD :—*COMMUNICATION* (Mentally and by Transport)
This will be expressed in accordance with aspects :—

IN SIGN

Aries
Speech and thought and nervous energy will be used assertively, cuttingly, strongly. The gestures will show this.

OR

hurtfully, sarcastically.

Taurus
Speech and thought and gesture and movement will be slow and smooth. Good for singing voice. The mind will not be resilient but will be turned towards practical and pleasant things.

OR

these will be expressed ponderously and dully.

Gemini
In this sign, the mind works most fluently, quickly and with the greatest versatility. Talking, writing, speaking will be easy.

OR

the above will be excessive, verbose, over-rational and under-emotional.

IN HOUSE
(The same but with difficulty if NOT well aspected.)

1st
In personal affairs which will be approached rationally and coolly but very especially according to the sign on this cusp. Mental occupations and diversions will attract. The mind will be directed towards the self.

2nd
In money-making ways in which the mind can be used, mainly clerically, educationally, commercially, rationally.

3rd
In affairs to do with reading, writing, correspondence, educational matters and the many varied interests described under " 3rd house." The affairs of brothers and sisters will matter in the life. The nervous system will be important as weakness will cause worry, often resulting in intestinal trouble (Mercury rules Gemini *and* Virgo).

The Principles of Mercury are at their strongest when it is in one of its own natural houses or signs.

Cancer
The mind is subject to the emotions. Memory is good.

OR

mind over-tenacious of its opinions and harking back to authorities of the past rather than outreaching.

Leo
Mind works fixedly and cheerfully.

OR

conceitedly, arrogantly.   The tone of voice may show this.

Virgo (Exaltation)
Mind works in a detailed, sensible, thoughtful manner.

OR

tiresomely fussy and given to worrying.

Libra
Charming in speech and manner. Speech will be slightly drawling but soft and attractive. The mind tends to enjoy friendly discussion and all beautiful objects of contemplation.

OR

wavering in manner, unable to make decisions.

Scorpio
Mentally intense.   Penetrative with depth of feeling.

OR

with the same in hurtful ways.

4th
In affairs to do with home, domesticity and any business to do with collecting. Often points to mental occupations carried on in the home.

5th
In affairs to do with creativity.   The mind will tend to occupy itself with pleasures, love-making, children, artistic creation.   The speech and letters, will be much concerned with these.

6th
In affairs connected with day-to-day work, especially if secretarial, commercial, educational.   Also in matters of health.   As with the Gemini placing, over-worry conduces to intestinal trouble through the double rulership.

As in Gemini, the principles of Mercury are strongly expressed since it also rules this sign.

7th
In affairs to do with partnership of any kind, or any matter which implies reciprocity or rapport with others.

8th
In affairs to do with possessions of others and emotions aroused by others. Occultism will attract.

Sagittarius (Detriment)

Mind works in a " far-flung " manner. It is restless because far-seeking. Can be satisfied by knowledge. Interest in travel and in acquiring languages. Speech quick and decisive.

OR

over-restless, unconcentrated. Nerves too tense.

9th

In affairs to do with the more profound studies and in foreign interests.

Capricorn

Mind practical, sensible. Forethought and patience good.

OR

with limited mentality, concentrated only on utilitarian things and forever wanting the next thing on the list.

10th

In affairs to do with the life out of the home. Business, politics and all public life will attract.

Aquarius

Here the "communicativeness" of Mercury will turn the mind to mental interests of the scientific kind and those deemed to be for the good of humanity, but also towards a linking with other minds similarly motivated.

11th

In all ways in which there may be a getting together with others for a common purpose or objective. Friends so made are mental companions rather than emotional ones.

Pisces (Fall)

Mind sympathetic and intuitional. It is confused by practical issues, but is highly receptive to artistic, psychic and benevolent ideas. The nervous system is sensitive so that elation and depression quickly alternate.

12th

In ways in which the mind can work by swift intuition rather than ordered reasoning. Excellent for occultism, for work in seclusion, for things of the sea. Likely to keep its communicativeness hidden unless otherwise brought out.

VENUS

By Sign

The power to attract others, to make good relations with them, to love and to be loved and enjoy people, beautiful things, and all the pleasant ways of life will be expressed according to the sign containing Venus.

By House

The affairs of the house occupied will show the sphere in which this ability is mainly used.

By Rulership

The affairs of the houses which have Libra and Taurus on their cusps will be brought into connection with those of the house occupied.

KEYWORDS :—*HARMONY, UNISON*

These will be expressed in accordance with aspects :—

IN SIGN

Aries (Detriment)

Affection will be strong, keen, ardent but tending to be self-seeking.

OR

selfish with others and easily quarrelling with loved ones.

Taurus

Will be steadfast in love, but possessive. Slow to make partnership but reliable when once settled. Happy when host or hostess. Inclines to music, art, good living.

OR

over-possessive of loved ones. Greedy for the good things of life.

The principles of Venus will be strongly expressed in either of its own signs and houses.

Gemini

Affection is changeable and often for more than one at a time. Expression of it is charming and fluent.

OR

inconstant. All talk rather than real feeling for another.

Cancer

Affection is sympathetic and tender and somewhat maternal or cherishing in its desire to care for the loved ones. Attractive for house-keeping ways.

OR

affection which will not let go. Over-emotional and unreasoning.

IN HOUSE

(The same but with difficulty, if NOT well aspected.)

1st

Attractive personality. Good looking. Likes to be " spoilt " and have plenty of amusement and social life. Tendency to fail in these things if Venus not well aspected.

2nd

Likes to make money by pleasant ways to do with art, beauty, lovely clothes, flowers and will be diplomatic and pleasant over money-making and will enjoy it for the sake of the lovely things it will bring. Successful and happy in the above if Venus well aspected.

3rd

Venus here gives charm to all mental activity. Going here and there for visits and social occasions is much enjoyed. Will learn if the subject is liked. Inclined to be lazy otherwise. Relations with brothers and sisters happy and they are likely to be good-looking and attractive.

If Venus not well aspected then the above are liked, but there is less benefit through them.

4th

If Venus is well aspected, the home is harmonious and delightful and family relationships smooth and loving, especially with parents. Pleasure will be taken in all matters of furnishing and decorating and the arrangement of flowers and pictures.

Leo

Warm, heartfelt affection. Faithful and generous in love. Likes to be proud of the loved ones. Likes gay, luxurious comforts.

OR

over-emotional and all for having a good time at all costs.

Virgo (Fall)

Affection is cool, undemonstrative and critical, but with a retiring modest charm.

OR

allows critical faculty and constant fuss about detail to interfere with harmony of life.

Libra

In love with love. Happiest when with a congenial " other " either for work or play. Happy, charming, lovable nature. Usually attractive and good looking. Women prettily dressed even though not well off.

OR

always seeking the " other half " and never satisfied.

5th

Happiness and success through love affairs and eventually through lovely children. Enjoys creative ability through art and the things of the theatre and any way of being prominent. Also all games and happy occupations. Success through all these if Venus well aspected.

6th

Favourable for health. Happy in work so long as it is not ugly or dirty. Ready to give the helping hand to another to make life go happily. Good at getting others to work harmoniously either as co-workers or employees. All successful if Venus well aspected.

7th

Excellent indication of happy marriage and ability to live harmoniously with others. Business partnerships run smoothly.

If not well aspected, the same desires are present but fulfilment is disappointing.

The Principles of Venus are strong in either of its own signs and houses.

Scorpio (Detriment)

Love tends to be more intense, more sexual, more secretive and passionate.

OR

love which turns to hate. Jealousy of loved one through possessiveness.

8th

Gain through partner's money or inherited money or possessions. Harmonious conditions in sexual relationships. An easy death. If the development is such that the life energies tend towards spiritual rather than physical pleasures, then these are a joy and a happiness.

Again, if Venus is not well aspected, these desires will not be harmoniously satisfied.

Sagittarius

Affection is demonstrative and gay but does not want to be enchained. Freedom often preferred to marriage.

OR

too free with affection and unstable.

Capricorn

Sincere and stable in affection but conventional.

OR

inclined to expect position through affection and to be too practical with loved ones and too strict with younger people.

Aquarius

Love is unemotional and detached. Friendship preferred rather than emotional ties. Desire for harmony for others in a widespread way results in kindly motives in humanitarian ways.

OR

too cool in affection.

Pisces (Exaltation)

Sentimental in affection. Very emotional and expressive of feelings. Easily influenced through affections. Ready to sacrifice self for love not only in an amorous way, but in a self-abnegatory way for a greater love for the weak or suffering.

OR

sloppily emotional.

9th

Fond of study and intelligent interests and of travel. Success through foreign countries and people from abroad. May marry a foreigner or live abroad after marriage—or may go into such partnership for business or profession.

Disappointment in the above if Venus not well aspected.

10th

Very happy in life in the world. Ambitions succeed. Good in public because of diplomatic manner. Happy with parents. Prefers profession or occupation as listed under Venus as planet.

Disappointment in the outcome of these things if Venus not well aspected.

11th

Good at achieving smooth working of any club or society or group to which attached. Happy amongst like-minded friends.

Disappointments in above if Venus not well aspected.

12th

Happy when alone or in quiet, secluded place. Can keep love affairs secret. Enjoys mystery and hidden matters. No neuroses through suppressions in the unconscious self. Undercurrent of life smooth. Liking for psychism.

MARS

By Sign

The energy and initiatory force of the person will be expressed according to the sign containing Mars. This will include physical strength, working ability, and, when applicable, sexual energy. Harshness experienced from others will be signified also.

By House

The affairs of the house occupied will show the sphere in which such force is used or experience suffered.

By Rulership

The affairs of the houses which have Aries and Scorpio on their cusps will be brought into connection with those of the house occupied.

KEYWORDS :—*ENERGY, HEAT, INITIATORY FORCE*

These will be expressed in accordance with aspects :—

IN SIGN

Aries

Extremely assertive and aggressive and vigorous and courageous.

OR

pugnaciously aggressive and hurtful to others.

IN HOUSE

(The same but with difficulty if NOT well aspected.)

1st

In personal affairs with great energy. Good at starting new enterprises. Quick and stirring in action, antagonistically so if in difficult aspect.

The Principles of Mars are exceedingly strong in its own sign or natural house.

Taurus (Detriment)

Possessive, stubborn and with strong affection for those possessed.

OR

obstinately forceful. Temper smouldering to outbreak.

2nd

In financial ways and also in work for the growing things of the earth. Voice powerful, but discordant if in difficult aspect.

Gemini

Energetically talkative, more than usually lively.

OR

force frittered away in constant change of direction.

3rd

In keenness to work at educational or literary pursuits. Always " on the go." Affairs of brothers and sisters call for attention.

Cancer (Fall)

Strongly emotional and intuitive. The desire will be to work for the care of others and to collect and maintain family and home.

OR

difficult touchiness quickly aroused.

4th

In home affairs with energy and quick able ways.

If in difficult aspect, there will be harsh conditions or quarrelling in the home.

Leo

With " heart " and strong purpose and creative ability.

OR

with domineering insistence on being overforceful. Hot temper.

Virgo

With keenness towards taking trouble in every minute detail.

OR

with cantankerous insistence on non-essentials.

Libra (Detriment)

With energy apt to sway one way and another. Much effort made to obtain companionship.

OR

much effort for little result. Quarrels with intimates.

Scorpio

Emotions and desires deep and very strong.

OR

emotions overstressed, causing hurtful vengefulness. Sexually strong.

As in Aries, Mars is strong in its own sign and natural house.

Sagittarius

Enthusiastic and " all-out " for far-flung ideas, for cheerful ways of enjoyment. Somewhat exaggerative and off at a tangent.

OR

tiresomely boisterous, extravagant, extreme. Caustic in argument.

Capricorn (Exaltation)

Vigorous, ambitious, works to an end and with keen desire to plan and succeed.

OR

stern in over-orderly sticking to duty without pleasure.

5th

In gay enjoyment of love-making, of children, of games and all pleasures. Harmlessly unless in difficult aspect.

6th

In hard and unstinting work. Expects same from others. Most strengthening for health. Liability to feverish complaints if in difficult aspect.

7th

Forceful in intimate relationships. Partner combative. Bad relations with partners if in difficult aspect, causing irritation and quarrels.

8th

Necessity for dealing with finance for others. Sexual life is of importance. Interest in psychic matters and readiness to work for research in such ways. Surgery and psychology attract the mind.

9th

Keen on travel and sport and enjoyment. Interest in serious study deepening as life goes on.

10th

Work and energy put into the day's work. Keenness to get to the top in material ways. Liable to suffer and cause hurt to others in the attempt, when in difficult aspect.

Aquarius

Determined in self-freedom to pursue chosen ends. Strong tendency to intelligence and scientific outlook in a wide meaning and to action through these.

OR

harsh in such determination without regard for freedom for others.

Pisces

Strong desire to exert for others and in kindly self-sacrificing ways.

OR

efforts become confused so that muddles are made. Too many irons in the fire.

11th

Keen about any idea or objective, mental, material or personal, once this is thoughtfully chosen, but if disillusioned will be equally decided about new idea or friend.

Quick to make friends but loses them through overpushfulness and quarrelsomeness.

12th

Keen to act for the good of others and often in unrecognised ways.

If in difficult aspect, many acts in secret and in harmful ways. Harsh reaction on self from unconscious severity or aggression.

JUPITER

By Sign

The power to expand the life in every benefic way, and also the indications as to the way in which the person will fortuitously benefit by what seems to be " luck " being on his side, will be expressed according to the sign containing Jupiter.

By House

The affairs of the house occupied will show the sphere in which this ability will be used and from which good fortune will accrue.

By Rulership

The affairs of the house which has Sagittarius on its cusp will be brought into connection with those of the house occupied. To a certain extent, the same will apply to the house which has Pisces on its cusp, though its correlation seems to be more with Neptune.

KEYWORDS :—*EXPANSION, PRESERVATION*

These will be expressed in accordance with aspects :—

IN SIGN

Aries

The desire to enlarge the scope of personal expression will be strong and forceful.

OR

this will be overdone, and over-accentuated in an aggressive manner.

IN HOUSE

(The same but with difficulty if NOT well aspected.)

1st

Cheerful, jovial personality, optimistic and broad-minded. If well aspected, many opportunities for the self and general good luck may be expected.

Taurus

Desires for expansion will be in material ways though with love of the beautiful.

OR

over-exaggerated desire to aggrandise the self through money and what money can buy.

Gemini (Detriment)

Self-expansion tends to be through mental alertness. Advantage through versatility. Very talkative.

OR

self-expansion through slick cleverness. Over-talkative, " too clever by half."

Cancer (Exaltation)

Self-expansion in a kind, protective sympathetic way.

OR

exaggeration of wish to keep to the self those held by emotional ties.

Leo

Self-expansion is in a noble, dignified, loyal, high-minded and good hearted way.

OR

exaggeratedly bumptious.

Virgo

Desire for more scope in life is expressed in quiet unassuming ways. Critical faculties strengthened.

OR

exaggeration of habit of constant criticism.

2nd

Excellent indication of financial success so long as well aspected ; also of contentedness with possessions.

3rd

Success through all educational matters, writings, communicative activities. Pleasant and advantageous relations with brothers and sisters. Mind capable of much development if Jupiter well aspected.

4th

Benefit through things of the home and family. Good relations with parents. Home conditions comfortable and often improved if Jupiter well aspected.

5th

Success, pleasure and happiness through all enjoyable ways of sport, love-making, children, and creativity, through art and literature if there are other indications to these. Children are likely to be successful. Speculations and risks can be undertaken if protectiveness is indicated by Jupiter well aspected.

6th

Excellent indication of good health. Work will be plentiful and lucrative. Contacts with workers cheerful and beneficial if Jupiter well aspected.

Libra

Natural desire for self-expansion is through using the ability to be companionable and well loved.

OR

cannot be happy alone.

7th

Best indication for fortunate marriage and good business or professional associates if Jupiter well aspected.

Scorpio

The self expands through ways of reserved, yet strong, intense desire for life. Feelings deep, sympathies wide.

OR

risk of overstrong feelings of all kinds, pushing the self to violence of behaviour.

8th

Prosperity through marriage, or close relationship with another in friendship or business. Legacies to be expected. Death comes as an easy release with feeling of expansion into new life. Success in psychic or occult investigation.

Sagittarius

Fineness of character through the desire to expand self being expressed in love of liberty for self and others, through generosity, and through dignity without pomposity.

OR

exaggeration of licentious behaviour, freedom at any price lacking concentration.

9th

Favourable for life abroad and dealings with foreigners. Tendency towards and success in any of the more profound lines of study.

The principles of Jupiter will be strongly expressed in either of its own houses and signs, but especially in Sagittarius and the 9th house.

Capricorn (Fall)

Scope for expression will be enlarged through ability in careful, far-seeing ways.

OR

over-stern, rigid and narrow.

10th

Excellent indication for success in affairs of the world, in business, profession, political or social life. Ease of accomplishment through frequent good opportunities.

Aquarius

Self-expansion is sought through humanitarian ways and on unconventional lines. The scientific spirit is evinced.

OR

self-freedom sought through revolutionary free-for-all ways.

11th

Success in objectives in life. Friends and acquaintances are many and much enjoyed.

Pisces

Thoroughly expansive in genial, kindly emotional ways, with strong intuitive imagination, helpful for the arts and for psychic work. Overflowing with kind desire to help others.

OR

over-imaginative to the point of self-undoing through lack of commonsense in every-day affairs. Emotions too easily stirred to exaggerative expression.

12th

Success in things of the sea, in businesses to do with oil, in art, dancing, acting, psychism, and in hidden ways, especially if connected with philanthropic work.

The principle of Jupiter will be strongly expressed in its own house and signs, but it shares the rulership of Pisces and the 12th house with Neptune.

SATURN

By Sign

The power to limit or control the life and also the indications as to the way in which the person will be limited, controlled, frustrated or delayed by what may seem to be the sternness of fate will be expressed according to the sign containing Saturn.

By House

The affairs of the house occupied will show the sphere in which the person will feel his limitations, whether from within himself or from without. This may urge him to try to overcome them, but success comes late and after long patience and work.

By Rulership

The affairs of the house which has Capricorn on its cusp will be brought into connection with those of the house occupied. To a certain extent, the same will apply to the house which has Aquarius on its cusp though its correlation seems to be closer with Uranus.

KEYWORD :—*LIMITATION*

This will be expressed according to aspects :—

IN SIGN

Aries (Fall)

Desire to achieve security keen, but initiatory impulse to do so checked and made cautious and often frustrated.

OR

caution disregarded with impatience and energy, hence trouble through unsmooth working of plans.

IN HOUSE

(The same, but with difficulty if NOT well aspected.)

1st

Feeling of personal insecurity or inadequacy, the results of which must be judged by the rest of the map. In a strong character, this may be the spur to achievement in spite of obstacles. Personal responsibilities will be heavy. In a weak one, it may lead to inability to press forward the personal concerns in the life. Likelihood of personal responsibility and also of moods of depression.

Taurus

Caution and patience and care are used in practical ways. The feelings are controlled and serious but steady.

OR

an ungenerous attitude. Feelings dull, unresponsive to love or beauty.

Gemini

Limitation and control will affect mental concepts and expression so that thoughts will be well considered and deliberate and outlook serious.

OR

slow in speech and expression. Thoughts slow and depressive.

Cancer (Detriment)

The desire for security and the realisation of need for caution will result in a strong feeling for guarding and cherishing that which is under the care of the person.

OR

over-repressed and prone to holding to the self alone, that which is cherished, whether it be family or knowledge, or valued collections of any kind.

Leo (Detriment)

Limitation is on power to express self in creative, happy ways. Enjoyment of life does not come easily.

OR

frustration of outlets causes poor organisation in affairs and resentment through being kept down.

2nd

Sensible and orderly about financial affairs or in the care of property. Responsibility likely in such matters. Rest of map as well as aspects must indicate whether such a burden causes eventual delayed success through necessary effort, or failure and depression (see comment on 1st house).

3rd

As with above house placings, other testimonies must be considered before it can be decided whether the inevitable limitation will result as wise control and caution and commonsense in all matters of correspondence and communication, all educational, or literary work. Also in willing acceptance of responsibility in any such way, or for brothers and sisters, or whether this placing is to mean depression and feeling of inadequacy and trouble to be borne because of difficulties in these ways. Often implies education scanty.

4th

Sternness or hard conditions suffered or caused in the home. Responsibility for home and often for parents. Depression caused through home matters, or through lack of proper home.

5th

Disappointment or frustration or delay in what should bring joys such as games, sport, love affairs, children. Seriousness and responsibility over these. Attraction to older people. As always with Saturn, it rests with other parts of the map to show whether willing acceptance of necessity will strengthen the character and eventually bring good results.

Virgo

The desire to limit and control, and the feeling of the need for this, will be expressed as painstaking care of detail in every way resulting in tidy, neat, punctilious ways.

OR

can result in over-dogmatic forcing onto others a rigid planning of all detail.

Libra (Exaltation)

Desire to control and need for patience are expressed in balanced reasonable ways and necessity comes to be accepted as experience.

OR

lack of reciprocity from others brings depression and loneliness and an inability to realise this as springing from within the self.

Scorpio

Caution and limitation expressed as strong reserve and secrecy. Deepest emotions very one-pointed.

OR

expression as dour jealousy. Emotional outlets desired.

Sagittarius

Desire to control and limit will, to a certain extent, be freed, scope will be widened in the mode of this free-ranging sign. Freedom of thought and action will be achieved through long study, through application and determination. Gravity and dignity will increase with age.

6th

The burden to bear or responsibility to take, will be through work (which will be taken seriously) or health, which will give trouble (usually according to sign on cusp). Difficulties come through workers or through service given to others. As above, long term results can be good, if patience can be used and the character is strong to bear what has to be borne. In this case, if weak, petulance and worry because of refusal to accept necessity will affect the health.

7th

Frustration and disappointment to be expected from others in close connection whether in marriage or business. They may bring much responsibility or cause losses. As above, these may strengthen the person by building up an ability to stand on own feet without a partner or may cause depression and loneliness because of loss of partner or inadequacy in forming happy relationships.

8th

Responsibility through affairs of others, either through financial cares or through losses caused by them. Seriousness over sexual affairs. Careful interest in psychic matters and thoughts of death and the after-life develop when older.

9th

Frustration of plans when travel arranged, difficulties abroad or with foreigners, or journeys undertaken for the carrying out of duty. Much seriousness in questions of faith and beliefs. As all above, long-term results can be good if duty realised and efforts made. Contacts with foreigners better if elderly.

OR
freedom of mind and action stultified, resulting in resentment.

If not well aspected, serious difficulties occur abroad and the person would do better to stay at home. Even so, he will then feel denied the possible benefits of travel. In the sphere of study, seriousness and concentration give good final results if well aspected, but, if not, depletion and exhaustion can result by over-concentration.

Capricorn

The expression of self in carefulness, practical ability, patience, success by long and ambitious planning, is likely to come to its best.

OR

self concentration on care for real or imagined necessities can turn to a miserly insistence on getting much out of life for selfish ends, with coldness and lack of regard for the necessities of others.

10th

Serious application to the business of getting on in life, often necessitated by pressing family responsibility. No easy path but, as in all the above, eventual success through plodding care and wise looking-ahead. If the rest of the map indicates no desire to accept such a necessity, then there will be disappointment and grudge against life because of set-backs and failures.

The Principles of Saturn will be strongly expressed in either of its own signs or houses, but more so in Capricorn and the 10th, than in Aquarius and the 11th, since the latter are deemed to be shared by Uranus (opinions not unanimous).

Aquarius

Control and seriousness are fixed in their aim which is rationally thought out, and, paradoxically, much freedom to achieve such aim is demanded.

OR

one-pointed ideas lead to non-ability to see reason in the aims of anyone but the self. Hence gloomy treading of solitary path with no one but fellow-ideologists.

11th

Elderly friends will be most satisfying. There will be lack of real friendship and a concentration on well defined objectives. If not well aspected there will be disappointment in the attaining of these, or they will become a burden.

Pisces

Philanthropy will be at the urge of duty rather than of love or pity. A sad outlook on life through lack of outlet in expression in the arts or through imaginative or psychic ways.

OR

Emotional expression chilled, with poor results on health.

12th

General lack of good spirits, often through sorrows borne in secret. These may frequently be of own making and will be resented and made a misery unless the truth is realised.

THE EXTRA-SATURNIAN PLANETS

(BY SIGN AND HOUSE)

The orbits of these three are successively further from the Sun, hence they take longer to make a complete cycle.

To make the journey through the twelve signs, the time is as follows :—

By Uranus, about 84 years.
By Neptune, about 165 years.
By Pluto, about 248 years.

From this it is obvious that the planets will remain in one sign about 7, 14 and 21 years respectively, so that all people in the world born in those years will have that placing. *They cannot be judged too individually unless prominent in the chart* (p. 148).

The same caution is not so stringently applicable in regard to the houses, though it must be realised that, except when quadrant house-systems involving " intercepted " houses are used, every similar Ascendant will have such planet in the same house for the stated number of years (e.g., Neptune is now in Libra, the seventh sign. Allowing for variation according to the early or late degree of sign rising, everyone with Taurus ascending will have it in 6th, everyone with Gemini ascending will have it in 5th, and so on).

URANUS

Note.—This MUST be read in the light of remarks on the " Extra-Saturnian Planets " in the paragraph above.

By Sign

The power to exert a free, independent and often unconventional spirit, and also the indications of the way in which a person may experience the results of independence from others as breaks in the life, will be expressed according to the sign containing Uranus.

By House

The affairs of the house occupied will show the sphere in which the person will feel change and disruption, whether started by himself, or by others, or by completely external causes.

By Rulership

The affairs of the house which has Aquarius on its cusp will be brought into connection with those of the house occupied.

This planet has recently completed its second cycle since becoming known to the world. It was retrograde and close to 25° Gemini on 13th March, 1781, when discovered.

KEYWORD :—*CHANGE (DISRUPTIVE, INDEPENDENT)*

This will be expressed according to aspects :—

IN SIGN

Aries

Self-will, independence, desire to make breaks and start anew, will find vehement and assertive expression.

OR

such eccentric self-will, etc., as above will be so strong that rebellious inability to conform to any conventions will make life disruptive and unpleasant for the self and all others in the life.

Taurus

Galvanic desire to change, working through a static medium, implies sudden outbreaks from a smouldering tensity.

OR

self-will and independent action even if upset caused to any settled conditions of others.

Gemini

Changeableness is more " at home " in this versatile mode. It works with flashing genius and quick inventiveness. Speech offhand.

OR

eccentric, quick-change mentality seeking advancement in any quick and unconventional way. Speech abrupt and without enough thought for others.

Cancer

Eccentricity shown in ways of taking care of anyone or anything.

OR

unstable emotionally.

IN HOUSE

1st

The personality will be out of the ordinary, clever, original, seeking new and interesting ways even if letting go of the old. Tendency to express this in science if chart shows application to study, or in aviation.

If not well aspected, personality will be eccentric, difficult for others to live with, ready to alter life at too short notice.

2nd

Change to be expected in financial ways. Money earned in unusual ways. Feelings galvanic.

If not well aspected, financial difficulties through unexpected changes. Feelings often upset.

3rd

Erratic, odd and interesting happenings to be expected while going about from one place to another. Brothers and sisters, or their circumstances, unusual. Separation from them likely. Thought, speech, writing and mentality vivid, unusual, scintillating, inventive and inclined towards unusual subjects for study.

If not well aspected, troubles through these.

4th

Frequent changes in the home, or separation from it and the family. If well aspected, an unusual but attractive family background.

If not well aspected, the unconventionality will not be pleasant.

Leo

Eccentricity is apt to run away with itself and desire for freedom to be too arrogant, though splendid leadership can be shown if in the right place for it.

OR

headlong freedom at any price. Revolutionary.

Virgo

Eccentricity will occur in " faddy " ways especially over health.

OR

strange ideas on " cults," with much criticism of others who are more ordinary.

Libra

Paradoxical results of disruptiveness expressed through harmonious ways. The person is charming and lovable even though somewhat odd in expressing this.

OR

unable to achieve harmony because too independent and self-willed.

Scorpio

Unusualness will be expressed in emotional ways and in independent strength of feeling.

OR

rebellion and self-will stir deepest emotions to vengeful and cruel ways.

5th

Little regard for convention in love affairs.   Unusual children but often separation from them.   Brilliance in creative ability in whatever way the map shows that to be.   Interesting hobbies.

If not well aspected, love affairs will be sudden and soon ended.   Attachments unconventional.   Odd ways of finding enjoyment in life and no interest in the hackneyed and ordinary.

6th

Changes and new ideas and " different-ness " is applied to food, and precautions about health.   Clever and inventive in ideas to aid work, especially of the designing or craftsman type or if scientific.

If not well aspected, there will be frequent changes in work and sudden upsets in health according to sign on cusp.

7th

Unusual conditions in marriage or partnership.   Changes in circumstances likely in both but agreeably if well aspected.   Partner likely to be unusual but attractively so.

If not well aspected, then changes hurtful and often unexpected.   Partner's eccentricities will exasperate.

8th

Money from others often in unusual ways.   Odd and unconventional ideas about life, sex and death, mostly kept secret.

If not well aspected, these can be unpleasant.

Sagittarius

Intense desire for free expression of self in highly-strung restive way.

OR

wild, rebellious, over-excitable and revolutionary.

Capricorn

Unusual, working through the conventional, results in a sobering of the electric ways, with consequence of excellent leadership through brilliant ideas.

OR

nervous and eccentric and restless.

Aquarius

Desire for changefulness for the betterment of humanity. Easily friendly.

OR

desire for change for everyone with comfort and stability for no one. Awkward as a friend.

Pisces

Very changeful but all with good intent. Strong intuitionally.

OR

too much at the mercy of changeful emotions.

9th

Changes when abroad and sudden events. Exciting, new, thrilling happenings while journeying.

If not well aspected, liability to sudden accident or difficulty while travelling. Study will be of the more unusual subjects but success may be uncertain through changes in objectives.

10th

A splendid leader in affairs of the world, with vision and readiness to change old ways. Awkward if not able to be in the position to lead.

If not well aspected, too unready to submit to routine if in conventional office life.

11th

Interestingly unusual in objectives in life. Ready to join societies for good 'isms. Quick to make acquaintances.

If not well aspected, the objectives are apt to change too often. Societies are broken from. Acquaintances suddenly dropped.

12th

Attracted to unusual and unobtrusive matters and quiet ways which are " different." Occultism can be positive and forceful.

If not well aspected, there will be eccentricity in odd secret ways. Life made difficult through unresolved conflicts in the unconscious.

NEPTUNE

Note.—This MUST be read in the light of remarks on the " Extra Saturnian Planets " (p. 169).

By Sign

The desire to use the imagination, to have contact with the non-material and the intangible, resulting either in vagueness or in artistic or psychic work, or to sacrifice the self for others because able to imagine their true needs, will be expressed according to the sign containing Neptune.

By House

The affairs of the house occupied will show the sphere in which the person may use these abilities and desires.

By Rulership

The affairs of the house which has Pisces on its cusp will be brought into connection with those of the house occupied.

Not until 2011 will this planet have completed its first cycle since becoming known to the world. It was retrograde and in 25° Aquarius on 23rd September, 1846, when discovered.

KEYWORD :—*NEBULOUSNESS* (or the capacity to receive impressions)

This will be expressed according to aspects :—

IN SIGN

Aries

Imaginativeness will be strongly expressed. According to the rest of the map may be found a hint as to the direction in art, psychism, etc. Ideals keen and strong. Assertiveness will be softened.

OR

too strong a tendency to imagination and the playing of a part can produce a schemer who will seek to give strength to his ideals in subversive ways.

Taurus

Imagination and psychism thought of in a practical way and yet aesthetically. Good rhythm in music.

OR

self-deceptive as to feelings. Careless about sense of ownership.

IN HOUSE

1st

The person has moods of dreaminess and inattention and can lose himself in a world of imagination. Very much depends on aspects and the rest of the map. In a strong map, well aspected, the fruits of the imagination will be used in works of art, literature, psychism or intuition in everyday and professional life.

In a weak map, or not well aspected, the planet is depleting to the self, sapping the energies in a way which is often difficult to spot. This may result in guile or, even worse, in underhandedness.

2nd

Imagination and psychism brought to concrete use and for money-making purposes. Vague about money matters. Easily loses possessions. If well aspected, idealistic about possessions.

Gemini
Mentally intuitive and receptively sensitive.

OR

too easily susceptible to influence of all kinds.

Cancer
Idealistic and imaginative in a kindly, tender way of protectiveness to others.

OR

sentimentally " woolly " in such ways. Lives in dream world and makes muddles in real life.

Leo
Vague but well intentioned ideas lead to an inflation of self-approbation and idealistic notions about own organising powers and the governments of countries. Loving-kindness in general way when organising.

OR

too easily susceptible to self-conceit and to subversive ideas politically. Affections kindly but confused.

Virgo (Detriment)
Spiritual ideas chaste and calm. Liable to be critical in psychic matters.

OR

idealism weak through over-critical coolness.

3rd
Mentality imaginative and intuitive. Mind can be used for the study of hidden or occult matters. Tendency to daydream.

If not well aspected, the mind is too vague in its working, too unstable for academic work, but, if strength of purpose shown elsewhere can be turned to artistic work or imaginative writing.

4th
Peculiar conditions to do with home. Often some " substitute " home such as an adopted one. Idealistic about home and parents.

If not well aspected, peculiar matters to do with home are kept secret. Misunderstandings with family and parents.

5th
Muddles over love affairs through idealisation of the loved one without enough common-sense evaluation. Disappointment when realisation comes. Peculiar happenings with regard to children. Investments should be in things of the sea, oil, or business to do with art. If not well aspected, all investments should be left alone. Deceit likely through love affairs. Children disappoint.

6th
Much depends on aspects. Lack of concreteness does not help in work or in the attempt to keep good health. A well aspected Saturn does much to balance the vagueness of Neptune.

If not well aspected, work will be unsatisfactory through muddles made and through two-faced-ness of work people. Health will suffer through hidden causes, often toxic. Food poisoning, drugs, gas escapes must be avoided.

Libra

Adds to gentle charm. Weakness in becoming too easily attracted.

OR

too susceptible to the attractions of others and liable to deception.

Scorpio

Highly sensitive and inspirational and receptive of impressions, either psychically, or through many forms of the arts. Much quick intuitive understanding when in love.

OR

sensitive to all slights. Subtly perceptive of the hidden feelings of others, thus able to hurt them.

Sagittarius

" Far-sightedness " can result as clairvoyance or as inspirations which can be applied to great width of ideas in writings or publications.

OR

trouble through annoying dreams and visions or mental states. Lack of clarity in ideas on philosophy of life.

Capricorn

Excellent intuition applied to concrete affairs. Castles in the air are made into reality.

OR

castles remain " in the air." Impracticability spoils progress.

7th

Peculiar conditions about marriage and partnership, or a hidden arrangement about these. Partner likely to be spiritually minded or artistic, but if not well aspected, difficulties arise through this and disillusion comes.

8th

Strongly intuitive and psychic because receptive. Dreams or visions can be pre-cognitive. Easy understanding of spiritual things with great ability to rise to heights of attainment in this way. May be mystical or mediumistic. All financial matters should be put into careful hands.

If not well aspected, deception through fantastic notions as to after-life conditions. Liable to curious disillusion in sexual matters. Whatever the aspects, death likely in sleep or under anaesthetic.

9th

Quick intuitions which can be used advantageously in serious study and for work to be published. Travel tends to be wandering and without planning.

If not well aspected, depth of study becomes confused through ideas not being sufficiently concrete. Liable to losses and confusion while abroad.

10th

Excellent if in a chart which shows life work to be inspirational or artistic or psychic. Strong idealism as to the personal prestige in life. Something hidden from outer world.

If not well aspected, difficult to find success because necessary application to the usual necessities of life of the world too careless. Success imagined but not worked for. Secret reasons for lack of this.

Aquarius

Kindly humane expression of gentle inspirational desires to help others. Interests widespread rather than personal.

OR

liable to take up vague ideas which increase rebellious independence.

11th

Friends kindly and likely to be connected with all Neptunian matters. Objectives in life inspired by " hunches " which will usually be right.

If not well aspected, liable to letting-down by friends. All " ideas " or ideologies should be carefully scrutinised and reason used with deliberate intent against the subversive and the confused.

Pisces

Most inspirational and spiritual and capable of the greatest of attunement with the infinite and the mystical.

OR

most highly susceptible to subversive influences of every kind which can drag down to depths of squalor.

12th

Indicative of intuition and psychic power at work in hidden ways and especially in any branch of mediumship, or delicate expression in art, dancing, music, rhythm.

If not well aspected, trouble through subversive effects of the above and through neuroses springing from over-repression in the unconscious life.

Note.—The present generation has no *first-hand* knowledge of Neptune in the later signs of the Zodiac, but information has been gained through study of older charts.

PLUTO

Note.—This *must* be read in the light of remarks on the Extra-Saturnian planets (p. 169).

By Sign

The desire to get rid of, to unearth, to disclose and bring to light, thus ending one phase and beginning another, and also the way in which a person may have this forced upon him, will be expressed according to the sign containing Pluto.

By House

The affairs of the house occupied will show the sphere in which the person will feel the effects as above, whether started by himself or by others.

By Rulership

As Pluto is so newly discovered, it would be dogmatic to insist that current ideas as to the sign ruled are correct. Fuller knowledge may change ideas. At present, it seems that opinion inclines to this being Scorpio, so that the affairs of the house which has that sign on its cusp may be brought into connection with those of the house occupied.

This planet was discovered on 12th March, 1930, and was in the 18th degree of the sign Cancer at the time. (This was by measurement along the Zodiac. It was in the *constellation* of Gemini.)

KEYWORDS :—*ELIMINATION, RENEWAL, REGENERATION*

These will be expressed according to aspects :—

IN SIGN

As Pluto remains for thirty years in each sign, its working through those other than Gemini and Cancer can only be surmised. Those born with it in Leo are not yet adult, so that its effects cannot be fully noted.

Gemini

At the time of writing (1950), all middle-aged to elderly people had Pluto in this sign. The generation was marked by a tendency to throw off inhibitions and conventions of earlier days and to express themselves in more open and candid ways. This was noticeable in the rejection of prudery in speech, especially about sexual matters. Though this was often crudely done and hurtful to older people, the result is a new phrase in that there is a more frank and healthy attitude. This is the forceful but finally healthy effect of Pluto.

If badly aspected, there is more violence, and less healthy reaction. There is rather a driving underground.

Cancer

Those of the generation which has Pluto in the earlier part of this sign (from 1913) were born during the 1914–18 war. They were the earliest of a generation of the nations concerned, in which family life, as it had been known, suffered a great alteration.

IN HOUSE

Referring to remarks on the " Extra Saturnian Planets " (p. 169), it will be seen that while Pluto was in Gemini for thirty years, it would be in the 12th or 1st house for *all* those with Gemini ascending, in 1st or 2nd for *all* with Taurus ascending and so on through the signs.

If very prominent through closeness to the angles, or through very strong aspects, it may be specially considered, but otherwise its effects are so general that no more detail should be noted than that its effects (as first paragraph) will *at times* be in the sphere of life of the house concerned. Such times will be when activated by cyclic action of other planets (see Chapter 10).

Note on possible rulership of Scorpio

If the current idea that Pluto is co-ruler of this sign is true, then it is also true that the planet is strong in this sign and in the 8th house.

Though the " sloughing off of the old "
which Pluto brings is always attended
with some violence to those who are hurt
by it, the result seems to be a more
healthy and open way of development.
When this generation became adult, it
bore the brunt of the 1939-45 war when
homes were rent asunder by war and
bombing in many countries. This, with
consequent supply shortage, caused less
building afterwards, and the generation
has grown up living in flats instead of the
family home, eating in restaurants instead of enjoying the meals prepared by
the almost extinct family cook. The
relative advantages and disadvantages of
this can easily be seen.

Leo

Those born with Pluto in Leo (since
1938) are not yet old enough for observation to be made about them, but current
events show that they are likely to see
changes in the notion of rulership in most
countries.

NOTE ON "SHAPING" OF CHARTS

Interpretation of the actual shaping of the planetary pattern of the chart has
been little regarded until recent times.

Marc Edmund Jones the American author* has introduced certain non-tradi-
tional classifications which are most helpful in making an overall survey of the chart
at first sight. It is regretted that only a summary can be given.

(1) *The Splash Type*.—The planets are scattered round the signs. At best, a
capacity for genuine universal width of interest ; at worst, one who scatters his
interests too much.

(2) *The Bundle Type*.—The planets are concentrated within the space of a trine
aspect. The course of life is held to certain narrow bounds of opportunism. The
man is inhibited in contrast with one whose chart is of the splash type.

(3) *The Locomotive Type*.—The reverse of the bundle in that the planets are in
the space of two trines, leaving an empty one. The temperament reveals a self-
driving individuality, the important planet being that which leads in clockwise
direction and is to be judged in relationship to the house it occupies.

* Marc Edmund Jones in *The Guide to Horoscopic Interpretation*, David McKay, Philadelphia,
U.S.A.

(4) *The Bowl Type.*—The planets lie in any one half of the Zodiac, but if the division is along the horizon or meridian line, a hemisphere emphasis is created. The bowl type " holds " something and has a self-containment because he is set off against a segment of experience from which he is excluded. Thus he seeks to scoop up and to give to his fellows, either constructively or vindictively, and in relation to the houses occupied.

(5) *The Bucket Type.*—All planets but one are in a half-section. This one gives a " handle " to the bowl, and especially if it is alone in one hemisphere when it is known as a singleton, it reveals an important direction of interest. It indicates a particular and rather uncompromising direction to the life effort.

(6) *The See-saw Type.*—The planets lie in two groups, roughly opposed to each other across the chart. The tendency is to act at all times under a consideration of opposing views or through a sensitiveness to contrasting possibilities.

(7) *The Splay Type.*—The planets are in strong and sharp aggregations at irregular points. The temperament juts out into experience according to its own special tastes, ruggedly resisting pigeon-holing.

Interpretation of Planets Apparently Retrograde

The idea has been handed down that the principle of a planet would show itself in some retarded or detrimental way in a person if retrograde at his birth.

In the knowledge that the Sun is the centre of the solar system and that retrogradation is due to the angle of vision from the moving Earth, it seems unreasonable to hold to such an idea.

No evidence can be brought in regard to this point since it is impossible to isolate what is correlative with one planet only, in order to compare its effects in various charts.

CHAPTER 10

THE ASPECTS

Part I.—*DESCRIPTIONS AND USE*

Note.—The student should unfold one of the example charts in Chapter 11 for reference while reading this section.

Astronomically, aspects are certain angular distances made at the centre of the Earth between a line from one planet and a line from another.* These are measured in degrees along the ecliptic. *Astrologically*, their interpretative significance is all-important, as it qualifies the way in which the principles of the planets manifest.

Traditionally, they were divided into good and bad or even referred to as evil. Opinion is changing. It is now seen that it is somewhat crude to judge everything on what psychologists call the " pleasure-pain " principle. What is unpleasant to us is not necessarily bad nor is what is liked always wholly good. The words easy and difficult are now preferred.

An exact aspect is very much stronger than a wide one. The extreme width allowed is called its orb. Opinions differ as to orbs allowable.

TABLE OF ASPECTS

These are given in order of orb allowed. Two more degrees of orb may be allowed if one of the aspecting planets is the Sun or the Moon.

Symbol	Name	Exactness	Orb	Implication
☌	Conjunction	0°	8°	Strength of meaning (according to nature of planets).
☍	Opposition	180°	8°	Tenseness.
△	Trine	120°	8°	Ease of working.
☐	Square	90°	8°	Difficulty of working but can be energising and constructive.
✳	Sextile	60°	4°	As trine but weaker. ⎫ Reduced by 2°
∟	Semi-square	45°	2°	Difficulty. ⎪ since writing first edition as
⟥	Sesquiquadrate (Square plus half a square)	135°	2°	Difficulty. ⎬ result of experience of several astrologers.
⚻	Quincunx	150°	2°	Strain.
⚺	Semi-sextile	30°	2°	Lack of ease.
Q	Quintile	72°	2°	See description.
BQ	Bi-quintile	144°	2°	See description.

* Such aspects are called *geocentric*. The astrologer, like the navigator, is concerned with angles to the *Earth* on which he lives. Aspects to the Sun, as the centre of the Solar System are called *heliocentric*.

Traditional Division of Main Aspects

According to nature of planets involved	*" Good "*	*" Bad "*
Conjunction	Trine	Square
	Sextile	Opposition
	Semi-sextile	Semi-square
		Quincunx
		Sesquiquadrate

It will be seen that the foregoing descriptions agree with these except for the semi-sextile.*

Theory of Formation of Aspects

Numbers have always been related to meanings. Without going into technical numerology, it may be remarked that the division of the 360° by 3 *and* 6 (△ and ✻), would seem to be harmonious as partaking of the nature of Jupiter and Venus, while the division by 4 *and* 8 (☐ and ⌞) would seem to be inharmonious as partaking of the nature of Saturn and Mars.

Relation by Triplicity and Quadruplicity. Example of use of orb.

Reference to Fig. 3 shows that any degree of any element must be 120° from the same degree in either of the other signs of the same triplicity, i.e., 4° Leo is trine to 4° Aries. By the allowance of 8° of orb, 4° Leo would be trine to any degree up to 12° Aries. Taken backwards, it would also be trine to any degree back to 26° Pisces, but then the two signs would not be in the same triplicity. The effect would be slightly weaker. This is called a *dissociate* trine.

Similarly, reference to Fig. 3 shows that any degree of any element must be in opposition to the same degree in the sign opposite to it in the same quadruplicity, and square to the other two. Hence, 4° Leo is opposition to 4° Aquarius, but square 4° Taurus and 4° Scorpio. In the same way, as before, 4° Leo would be within orbs of square to 26° Gemini but this would be a *dissociate* aspect.

Simplicity in Counting and Recognising Aspects

Conjunctions and *oppositions* are obvious.

Trines and *Squares* are most easily seen in relation to triplicities and quadruplicities once these are familiar.

Sextile and *Semi-sextile* are small enough to be easily observable.

Semi-square and *sesquiquadrate* are best discovered by mentally adding 15° to each planet, then a further 30° (one sign) for the semi-square and a further 120° (four signs) for the sesquiquadrate. When doing this, students are apt to say " trine and 15." Confusion will be caused if any connection of *meaning* is thereby inferred. The meaning is opposite to that of the trine, it being a derivative of the square.

Interpretative Use of Aspects

Any planets brought into connection by any aspect, affect each other according to their natures and according to the type of aspect. No single factor in a chart can

* See footnote p. 239.

be judged by itself, but stands in relation to main factors. Hence, too much " ease " of aspect in a chart already shown as lazy by the Ascendant or other factors, may result in disaster rather than success. Conversely, much " difficulty " by aspect in a chart generally strong may result in success because the power is there to make the necessary effort in overcoming difficulties.

Conjunction

A strong focal point. The principles of the two planets will not be fused but will react on each other or modify each other.

Opposition

Any two planets exactly in opposition to each other in a chart, are in actuality connected with each other by *polarity*,* i.e., a great circle passing through the North and South Poles and the one planet, must pass through the other. Hence, it is possible that the principle of the one planet may supplement that of the other, though in general, a tenseness may be expected. *T-square.*—The tenseness will be aggravated if another planet (or planets) is *square* to both ends of the opposition. *Mediation.*— The tenseness will be lessened if another planet (or planets) is *trine* to one end of the opposition and *sextile* to the other. The following paragraphs will explain these terms.

Trine

Generally strongly helpful, though too much " ease " may signify an expectation of success in life through others rather than through personal effort.

Grand Trine.—The easefulness will be intensified when three, or more, planets complete a triangular formation in the chart. Some authorities think badly of this. Certainly a weak character may be ruined by too much good fortune in life. The chart should be examined for compensatory strength of purpose in other ways. Also it is true that a person of bad character with such a configuration may find it all too easy to achieve his ends successfully.

If more than three planets compose the trine, the life is liable to be marked by an over-expression of the element so accentuated. The extra easy flow in life frequently comes because such a person is at ease with himself, hence a pleasant person whom others like to help and favour. A weak character may come to rely on this and bank on it, hence the idea expressed sometimes that those with a grand trine are " parasitical."

Square

Generally obstructive or disruptive. But obstructions can be used as stepping-stones by determined people, who will thus be energised to further action. This effect is accentuated when the formation is a T-square. Charts of those who are successful in life and strong in character usually show both trines and squares.

Grand Cross.—The obstructiveness will be increased when four or more planets complete a four-cornered square, which will also form two oppositions. Even a strong character could find life very hard in face of so much difficulty. The chart should be examined for compensatory help. The crosses formed by planets in the different quadruplicities are different in effect.

* In the same way, two signs or two houses which are opposite to each other are said to be connected by polarity.

Cardinal Cross.—The out-going nature of the signs included implies an intention to surmount the difficulties.

Fixed Cross.—The steady but settled nature of the signs included implies an inclination to let matters remain as they are and put up with them. A person in whose chart this configuration exists, often becomes patiently conditioned to trying circumstances.

Mutable Cross.—The greater adaptability in the nature of the signs included implies an adjustment to conditions and an attempt to by-pass them, though this is rarely done without nervous stress.

Sextile

Helpful, but less so than the trine. There will be an accentuation of Positivity or Negativity.

Quincunx

Stressful. As the orb of this is small, unless the two planets concerned are respectively at the very end and very beginning of the two signs occupied, they will form this aspect from two signs which have no relationship between each other by either triplicity, quadruplicity, positivity or negativity. Such a forced relationship implies *strain*. The aspect is most often to be seen in charts of lives in which strain has to be borne.

Semi-sextile

Slightly stressful. As with the quincunx, there is no natural relationship between the signs from which the planets aspect each other. This seems to be mitigated by the fact that the semi-sextile may, to some extent, partake of the nature of the sextile. For this reason, older books describe it as weakly good. Nowadays, there is doubt about this.

Semi-square

Difficult, since it partakes of the nature of the square.

Sesquiquadrate

Difficult, and for the same reason.

Quintile

This is little used and can be ignored in general work. Seventy-two is the resultant of the division of the circle by 5 which, numerologically, is connected with Mercury. Hence it is said to be strengthening to the mind if Mercury is one of the planets involved.

Bi-quintile

Little used. Said to be helpful.

Division of 360 by 7

As there is an aspect for the division of the circle by all other numbers, it has been suggested that, if two planets are between 51° and 52° apart, there should be an effect of an intangible or spiritual nature, since 7 is said to be the number of Neptune. No such aspect is generally used.*

* For note on tredecile (108°), decile (36°), vigintile (18°), see *The Principles of Astrology*, Chapter, I Section 5. C. E. O. Carter. Fourth Edition, 1952.

Manner of Listing Aspects

The student will find that the simplest method is to put his finger on the place of the Sun in the chart under consideration and to count (as indicated in foregoing paragraphs) from it to every other planet, in the order as given in the space provided on the form. Enter the symbol for any aspect found.

The Moon should be taken next. It has already been considered in relation to the Sun, so its first possible relation is to Mercury. It will be seen that one less has to be considered each time. Symbols need be written once only, on the upper side of the diagonal line. (If using older charts, draw a line, as in example chart, Chapter 11.)

Visual Indication of Aspects

On the Continent, it is the habit to show planetary linking by aspect, by drawing lines in ordinary ink between those in difficult aspect to each other and in red ink between those in easy aspect. The idea has only recently been used in England *and is of the greatest help*, not only to students in early days, but to anyone teaching from a chart, or talking from it to a client or friend. When there is no time for scrutiny, the planetary pattern can be seen at a glance. It is useful to indicate a quincunx or a sesquiquadrate by a dotted line to differentiate it from the opposition since they are so nearly similar.

Exactness of Aspect

An exact aspect, and even one which is within 1° of exactitude, is very considerably stronger in effect than a wider one. For these, it is helpful to put a small " E " in the space with the symbol (see example chart) and a small "W" if an aspect is so wide that it is only just within the orb allowed. These little extras are no trouble while listing and are valuable aids to quick recognition if a chart is to be studied after being put away for a long time.

Part 2.—*INTERPRETATIVE MEANINGS*

Preliminary Note

(A)   The working of every aspect is " two-way."

(B)   The principle of each planet is modified by the principle of the other.

(C)   An aspect is of more importance if one of the planets is the ruler of Ascendant or Sun, or is particularly strong for any other reason.

(D)   No aspect must be judged as itself alone, but as against the general showing of the map.

(E)   It is important to note whether two aspecting planets are themselves further modified by other aspects, for example, both planets in a conjunction may receive helpful or unhelpful aspects from others, which completely alter their interpretation.

(F)   An aspect does not *only* unite planets, but it emphasises the sign (if conjunction) or the triplicity (if trine) or the quadruplicity (if square or opposition) in which it functions.

Absence of Aspect Between Two Planets

This is *important* and very often passes unnoticed.

The bringing together of the principles of two planets by aspect creates an interchange between those two principles. Often, it is the *lack* of such an interchange which is the key to a character. An energetic, busy person may use his energy in futile ways unless one or more of his most important planets (Sun, Moon, Ascendant-ruler or Sun-ruler) receive aspects from Saturn which will give him the necessary braking-power, and the ability to order and plan his enthusiasms.

An able, practical person may remain of little account in life if his important planets have no aspect from Jupiter which would bring him ways of expansion, and opportunities through which to use his abilities.

It must be remembered that the so-called good or easy aspects are helpful but the so-called bad or difficult ones can be used constructively by a strong personality.

Unaspected Planets*

Occasionally a planet is found to receive *no* aspects whatsoever. (The student should be wary of failing to notice the semi-square and the sesquiquadrate.) This does not seem to have been the object of much research. The idea is expressed here that such a planet will not be weak or ineffective (unless otherwise so adjudged), but, failing the interchanges with other planets, its principles, and especially its drive or urge when considered as an instinct or a force in the unconscious self, will not be properly integrated into the wholeness of the person. If a forceful planet, it will lack ways of using its drive. If a more receptive planet, it will at times be as if left out of the scheme altogether. For instance, a person with an unaspected Mercury will have moments of acting from sheer emotion, without the inclusion of any reasoning whatsoever.

Aspects Between Two or More Planets, not aspected by Any Others*

Very rarely, it is found that the planetary pattern falls into two groupings. Two or more planets are connected. The rest are all connected, but there is no link between the two sets. This usually implies a definite rift in the nature. It can indicate the type of person who has a distinct second side which he keeps separate from his main personality or activity in life.

SHORT INTERPRETATIONS

Note.—As with the condensed interpretation given for planets by sign and by house, no detailed remarks with regard to health will be made in the following.

Bodily parts and systems signified by certain planets will be considered to be indicated as in good working order if these are helpfully aspected, but the opposite if unhelpfully aspected. (See p. 46.)

ASPECTS OF THE SUN

Any planet aspected by the Sun will be strengthened and vitalised.

Matters ruled by that planet will be affected.

The principles expressed by the two planets will be united for good or ill.

* For fuller discussion, see Chapter 14, *Applied Astrology* by same author. L. N. Fowler & Co. Ltd., 1954.

The nature of the person as a whole will be much affected by any planet aspected by the Sun.

CONJUNCTION	*EASY*	*DIFFICULT*

TO THE MOON

General harmony, particularly at home. Emphasis on traits of sign since containing both Lights.

The nature is at one with itself. No rift. Home matters happy.

Often a cleavage in the life relating to parents or early childhood. Disharmony of the nature can urge to accomplishment.

TO MERCURY

Traditionally, a close conjunction (within 5°) is called "combust" and implies poor mental faculties, but experience does not confirm this. Sign emphasised since mentality and self-expression will both be of its nature.

Cannot occur, as the two are never more than 28° apart.

Cannot occur, as the two are never more than 28° apart.

TO VENUS

Self-expression is through the affections, through beauty and art and gentle ways. In men, can give effeminacy.

Only the semi-sextile can occur as the two are never more than 48° apart. Happiness, love of peace and beauty mildly indicated.

Only the semi-square can occur. Inclination will be towards beauty and ease, but too irresponsibly and lazily.

TO MARS

Self-expression energetically shown. Bold, strong, forceful, brave, initiatory. Physical robustness. Hard working. Quick.

The same expressed with good result and without annoyance to others.

Though much may be achieved, the tendency is to overstrain through overdoing, thus impairing the vitality. Pugnacious and bad tempered. Liable to minor accidents.

TO JUPITER

Cheerful, contented with own surroundings and ways. Has plenty of opportunities in life and a feeling that "good luck" is to be expected.

As before, but with even greater success.

Too much reliance on luck. Showy. Exaggerated. Conceited. Imprudent. Extravagant.

TO SATURN

Limitation to the self and its expression. Sometimes through father. Life rigorous or hard but lessons of duty and self-control learnt. Feeling of inadequacy in matters of house tenanted.

Limitations as before but with better acceptance. Becomes conditioned to what is lacking. Wisdom, patience, constructiveness grows and brings success in later life.

Self-expression hurtfully limited. Life hard, causes self-pity. Tendency to falls, chills, orthopaedic troubles.

CONJUNCTION	EASY	DIFFICULT

TO URANUS

Independent, interesting, dramatic, magnetic, tendency to scientific thought. Rebellious. Original.	The same with tendency to genius and leadership and success in inventive, flashing thought.	Self-willed, revolutionary, self-insistent. Disruptive, awkward, brusque, sudden.

TO NEPTUNE

Tendency to the intangible. Hence lack of concreteness. Attraction to music, art, dancing, psychism and to the spiritual and mystical. Tendency to all matters to do with the sea.	Tendencies to the intangible resulting in strong imaginative faculties, visions, ideals, boundless aims. Can be of the most ethereal and inspirational kind but need strength in the map in order to actualise them. Person is a good sleeper.	Intangibility results in vagueness and muddles. Many ideas but poor fulfilment. May be deceitful or the object of treachery. Escapist. Tendency to avoid the concrete by daydreaming or by effect of drugs or alcohol.

TO PLUTO

Ready to get rid of the old and begin the new.	Tendency to free the self from bounds or ties. Easy elimination of the unwanted.	Tendency to advance self through ruthless behaviour to others.

Note.—It must be remembered that Pluto is but 20 years " old " in astrological knowledge. Also that his influence seems to be general rather than individual. As he is in one sign for about 20 or more years, the conjunctions can only be in *that one sign, the trines in that triplicity and the squares and oppositions in that quadruplicity,* during that period (with the exception of dissociate aspects, page 181).

ASPECTS OF THE MOON

Any planet aspected by the Moon will give rather than take, since the Moon is receptive in its action.

Matters ruled by that planet will be subject to fluctuation and changes.

A person's own power of changeable receptivity and response, eventuating as manner and as the self in a deep instinctive way, will be modified by any planet aspected by the Moon.

CONJUNCTION	EASY	DIFFICULT

TO MERCURY

Mentality active and sensitive. Nervous system responsive.	Good common-sense mentality and nervous force.	Mind acute but restless and excitable and acrimonious. Nervous system poor.

TO VENUS

Good balanced outlook. Love of beauty.	The same but more marked. Tendency to interests in the arts. Happiness in domestic conditions.	Uneasy expression of the affections and lack of harmony in the home.

CONJUNCTION	EASY	DIFFICULT
	TO MARS	
Robust, courageous manner, though over-active at times and over-quick in response.	Excellent strength physically and emotionally. Ability to work and push on in life.	Moody, or quarrelsome nature. Unpeaceful in the home.
	TO JUPITER	
Extremely helpful, since it implies optimism in the nature, good health and a tendency to a lucky journey through life.	The same but with even more tendency to success, to the meeting of good opportunities and helpful people.	The same but with tendency to squander gains and to be extravagant and to trust to luck too easily.
	TO SATURN	
The manner appears cool and cautious and the person more limited than he really is. Duty, conscience and orderliness are of importance. Tendency to be timid through feeling of personal inadequacy.	The benefit lies in the willing acceptance of duty and success through orderly and practical ways, even though these may cause personal limitations otherwise and lack of gaiety.	The sense of lack intensifies the shyness and prevents easy response to what could bring happiness. Relations with women and mother not easy. The practical is over-valued. Tendency to meet hardships.
	TO URANUS	
Emotional response is galvanic and tense. Desire is for the unusual and unconventional, especially in the home. Independent behaviour.	Intuitions are strong. Desires are towards achieving good through unusual objectives. Moods are suddenly changeable resulting in ability to throw off the static and start new receptive ways. New friends often made.	Ideas and intuitions strong through heightened receptivity, but may be carried out in a perverse or cantankerous manner and with nervous tension. Frequent breaks with friends.
	TO NEPTUNE	
Great sensitivity. Hence to be judged by the rest of the map as to what this will receive and give out. Tendency to retirement and philanthropy and to day-dreaming.	The sensitivity of this contact opens the psyche through the unconscious and much may be given out through the reception of ideas and influences. This may be in the sphere of art, music, dancing, acting, psychism, or, more practically, as love of the sea. Highly imaginative.	The tendencies may be the same and may be brought to better fulfilment by the compulsion of difficult aspects. If in a lazy map, the tendency to escapism may prevail, and to deceit or self-gullibility.
	TO PLUTO	
The moods and ways can be changeful in an acceptable way since new phases in life are liked.	Changeful happenings, even though violent, are turned to good account.	Subject to upsets and forced new phases.

Note.—See note after Sun-Pluto.

ASPECTS OF MERCURY

Mercury is often spoken of as a neutral planet ; in other words, it takes colour from the planet united to it by aspect, rather than giving to it.

The mentality and nervous system, the general communicatory ability, and the mental and personal agility of the person will be affected.

CONJUNCTION	*EASY*	*DIFFICULT*
	TO VENUS	
The mind and the mental outlook are improved by this contact in so far as charm of speech, pleasantness of manner and the generally benefic results of harmoniously working nervous system are concerned. Balance rather than worry is in evidence. A writer or a speaker benefits in this way, but ease rather than strength is gained.	These planets cannot be more than 76° apart so the quintile, the semisquare, the sextile and the semisextile are the only aspects which can be formed. As conjunction.	There is so little harm in either planet that the semisquare cannot be very difficult. It is more constructive in the use of the mind for the expression of beauty and harmony and any way of " communication." This includes the hand and arm work of Mercury in painting, designing and all forms of craftsmanship.
	TO MARS	
Mercury receives the strength of Mars, hence the mind is forceful, incisive, downright, good at debate. Bodily communication, i.e., walking, motoring, etc., will be keenly undertaken and with speed.	The same but more beneficially. The mind is powerful, courageous, enterprising. Nervous system strengthened, hence good eyesight, hearing and sense of touch.	The mind and nervous system can now be energised to the point of being overstrained. Breakdown can occur and irritability and temper. Incisiveness becomes satirical and carping.
	TO JUPITER	
The mind is jovial and optimistic, hence contented and with good nervous system. There may be a certain amount of mental inflation leading to conceit. There will be width of mind rather than grasp of detail.	A cheerful, humorous, witty mentality and success through its exercise.	The mind is over-widened so that it loses grasp and the results are carelessness and woolly thinking and indiscretion. The usual comment on this aspect is that the judgment will be poor. In all aspects to Jupiter, the liver must be considered and it is probable that lack of correct working between it and the nervous system may be at the bottom of these results.

CONJUNCTION	EASY	DIFFICULT

TO SATURN

The combination of communication and limitation can have disastrous results if the conjunction is itself badly aspected. Mental and nervous powers will be limited and dullness results. If well aspected the limitation will result as a mind without width but with great power of concentration and drive. Through apprehension, prudence will be increased. Depression will be frequent.

Even if well aspected, Saturn will limit. The mind will not wander but will order and control in practical, cautious, methodical ways.

Though constructive in a narrow one-track way, order now becomes rigid discipline and dreary planning. Mental loneliness results, often because of the fear and apprehension of Saturn. Lack of poise forces brusque speech and writing.

TO URANUS

Communicativeness and changeful disruptiveness produce a mentality which is sudden in action, but full of power and revolutionary intent. Hence refusal to tread the beaten path resulting in inventive genius, scientific "new" thought, brilliance of ideas in an independent and unconventional way. The unusual is preferred as a study, so, since Uranus and Aquarius are thought of in connection with astrology, this may be one way in which the inclination may result.

Usually brilliant and inventive and scientific. The hands will be used with cleverness. The speech will be quick and dramatic. The outlook will be independent and self-reliant.

Though conducive to strong mental action through revolutionary thought, the communicativeness in every way becomes too brusque and independent so that it loses good contact with others. The addiction to the unusual and unconventional is so strong and so awkwardly expressed that the person becomes eccentric and odd and tiresome.

TO NEPTUNE

The sensitivity and impressionability of Neptune conjoined with Mercury make a mind which can take varied patterns as wax takes an imprint, and a nervous system exposed to all that touches it.

The rest of the map and the aspects to the conjunction must decide the final effect of this. Imagination will be fertile and there will be a gentle kindliness. Though talkative, times of quiet and withdrawal are needed.

The sensitivity can now be used to bring impressions to the mind so that it is the channel for all inspirations, ideas, dreams. Hence it becomes the mind of the writer, the visionary, the artist, the poet, the dancer, the mimic, the mystic, the medium, the spiritualist.

The more difficult aspects can be more forceful of result of this sensitivity, but the outcome is likely to be vivid imagination which is gullible and confused so that the mind is not well directed.

Touchiness induces escapism. The mind schemes in an involved way. Action is from intuition rather than from reason.

CONJUNCTION	EASY	DIFFICULT

TO PLUTO

CONJUNCTION	EASY	DIFFICULT
Mind throws off worries easily and begins thought anew.	As before but with good results in relief to nervous tension.	As before, but over-violently and explosively with resultant nervous stress.

Note.—See note after Sun-Pluto.

ASPECTS OF VENUS

Any planet aspected by Venus will be softened and harmonised.

A person's affections and general ability to make happy relations with others will be modified by any planet aspected by Venus.

CONJUNCTION	EASY	DIFFICULT

TO MARS

CONJUNCTION	EASY	DIFFICULT
Ability to love and to enjoy sexual life and all things of beauty is strengthened and made more robust but less delicate.	Warmth and enthusiasm enter into relationships of affection, both in sexual life and as expressed to young people in a family.	A cutting harshness enters into affectional relationships. Feelings are strong but cause and receive hurt. Sexual relations are likely to be intense but not without quarrels. Partnerships not easy.

TO JUPITER

CONJUNCTION	EASY	DIFFICULT
Popularity and much social life are likely to result from the widening of the scope of the desire to form harmonious relations with others. This would especially apply to women and young people. Artistic inclinations strong. Love affairs numerous. Better in partnership than alone.	Again, popularity. Ease of attracting others or the public in general, by sheer innate charm. Love affairs numerous and very happy. Partnerships beneficial and very successful.	Easy charm will be intensified but overdone. Troubles caused by too many love affairs, too much love of the easy, the beautiful and the pleasant at any price, unless a tougher note given by other parts of the chart. Desire for partnership overdone, with restless lack of ability to be happy alone.

TO SATURN

CONJUNCTION	EASY	DIFFICULT
Duty or some form of limitation stops the full expression of love and harmony, but the duty appears to be accepted or less heavy because of some happiness which it brings. Partner often older. Marriage delayed.	Limitation of affection or of happy social life has its reward in a serious, one-pointed direction. Love may mean sacrifice or a life lonely except for the chosen one. Partnerships will be a serious matter but successful in a practical way.	Affection most difficult to express. Life tends to be solitary. Any partnership brings responsibility. Sorrow or loss through affections.

CONJUNCTION	EASY	DIFFICULT

TO URANUS

Ideas on love, art, beauty are out of the ordinary, hence more exciting and attractive, but there is a tendency to be "off with the old and on with the new."

Unusualness in expression of love or in artistic accomplishment or in any kind of partnership is delightful and intriguing and fascinating. There is an easy slipping away from one attraction and the quick forming of another. Partings are likely but for good reasons and with pleasant replacements or reunions.

Unusualness is apt to be just as fascinating and compulsive but less pleasantly. Partnerships are unconventional and apt to be broken because of insistence on freedom. Partings are likely through unhappy causes. There is a tenseness which is hard to relax and which causes nerve storms.

TO NEPTUNE

Receptive sensitivity, harmony, rhythm and beauty are combined. The results are sweetness of character and behaviour, tendency to all forms of artistic expression, including dancing and things of to the sea, and to a psychic sensitivity which needs rapport for expression. The self may be deluded as to the realities of life through too much living in the clouds, lovely though they may be. Partnerships may not be what they seemed. Conditions often kept hidden. Ideas and "hunches" come easily. Imagination strong.

As before but with likelihood of much success through the use of the tendencies listed. Music, dancing, poetry, painting are necessities of life and bring happiness and benefit. Psychic sensitivity is rarely absent and can be developed like any of the other gifts. Glamour and "Clouds of glory" are more to be expected than any delusion. Ideas and "hunches" should be acted upon. Happiness sometimes secret.

Tendencies are the same and more constructive effort is made to develop them, but success is less sure and delusion more probable, unless commonsense strongly shown elsewhere in the map. Partnerships disappointing and independable and if in business, these should be made as fool-proof as possible. Ideas which seem inspirational are better well scrutinised. Confusion occurs in love affairs and even deception. Secret partnerships may be formed.

TO PLUTO

Affections and partnerships subject to disclosures and upheavals and new starts.

The same but with good results in the end.

The same but with trouble and unpleasantness.

Note.—See note after Sun-Pluto.

ASPECTS OF MARS

Any planet aspected by Mars will be strongly enforced.

The forcefulness of the person will be modified according to the principle of any other planet aspected by Mars.

CONJUNCTION   *EASY*   *DIFFICULT*

TO JUPITER

Energy is vastly increased. Desire for enjoyment and widespread activity of mind and body is keen. Daring, courage and argumentativeness are increased.

Much the same but with even more gaiety and fun and humour, though this can be - teasingly caustic. Fortunate in material results because opportunities offer for the use of the enthusiasm and energy.

The overdoing of the unison of these two planets can be disastrous unless control is shown elsewhere in the chart, or there is a legitimate outlet in sport or career which uses this excess. Otherwise the indication is towards wild extravagance of thought and deed, extremism both in work and play, leading to overstrain.

TO SATURN

Energy and limitation do not combine well, unless it can be seen from the rest of the chart that it is a good thing that excess energy be controlled or that inertia should be energised. Force and initiative are canalised and ordered, while caution and patience are enlivened, but these results can be depressing to the energetic and hurtful to the slow-and-solid.

Similar relationship between the two planetary principles but with better hope of harmonious interplay. Hence helpful for all arduous, rough or pioneering conditions or for the bearing of personal hardship.

The constructiveness of the aspect can force to a patient working out of what is begun, but not with ease. Results must be battled for. The narrowness engendered produces selfishness and egocentricity. Hardship is endured and sternness given. Danger of accidents by burns and scalds (Mars) and falling (Saturn). Physical overstrain is risked.

TO URANUS

The combination of initiative and will-power in unusual ways can produce unusual results. But there is likely to be great nerve tension resulting in nervous irritability and disruptive behaviour.

There is a strong galvanic force engendered which points to results of outstanding nature, particularly if the rest of the chart indicates interest in such work as engineering and science and aviation. The personality will be compulsive and magnetic, so that leadership is either obeyed or violently broken. Physique muscular.

There may still be the magnetic leadership and the unusual ability, but results can be drastically ruined unless the chart has redeeming features (such as helpful Saturn). Explosive temper and wilful impatience and nervous strain do not make for easy partnership in marriage or business. Tactlessness antagonises friends. Breaks of personal relationships occur. Accidents to limbs likely.*

* For general discussion on accidents :—" The Astrology of Accidents " by Charles E. O. Carter.

CONJUNCTION   *EASY*   *DIFFICULT*

TO NEPTUNE

Interest in the sea, in mysticism, in hidden things is pursued with energy and with desire to experiment in new ways. The connection with the sea can result as work such as ship's engineer, ship building, etc. The more intangible side can be expressed as enthusiasm for the arts, dancing, psychic sensitivity, or any form of idealism.

Much the same but with good result and with high ideals. Work is done to achieve these, even though they may be visionary and unattainable. Life on or by the sea is liked.

As with all difficult aspects, the chart must be examined for something which balances them, or an outlet which uses them. Very hard work may be done for idealistic ends. Results may be disappointing and elusive because all was too imaginary. The tragedies of the worst of this aspect are those of a weak chart, so that vivid over-imagination without commonsense produces chaos. Irregular, over-glamorous, escapist ways bring downfall. Strange fears prey on the nerves, health can be undermined by these and by susceptibility to fish poisoning or harm from impure water.

TO PLUTO

Explosive and likely to end conditions and force new beginnings.

The same but with good results after a crisis which was painful.

The same, but more forceful action and less happy results.

Note.—See note after Sun-Pluto.

ASPECTS BETWEEN JUPITER, SATURN, URANUS, NEPTUNE AND PLUTO

Important Note.—The aspects between these planets will be within orbs for a considerable period, and unless either of the planets is emphasised by position or rulership of Ascendant or Sun, they will not be unique to the person, but may be understood to have a general effect on all those born in these periods of varying length.

ASPECTS OF JUPITER

The principles of any planet aspected by Jupiter will be given more scope and opportunity will be made more benefic.

The expansiveness of a person and his propensity towards cheerful, happy " good luck " in life will be affected by any planet aspected by Jupiter.

CONJUNCTION   *EASY*   *DIFFICULT*

TO SATURN

The conjunction and opposition recur every 21 years (refer to p. 194).

The joining of the principles of limitation and expansion is contradictory. There are usually alternations of gay optimism and of depression. Great things can be done by those in whose charts it appears if they will understand themselves and work hard in the expansive periods and use every opportunity that arises. Similarly they must take a long view and be cheerful in the depressive times.

Betokens success in material ways since commonsense control is well combined with optimism and desire to expand both the viewpoint and the circumstances. Extremism is kept in bounds and fortunate results accrue.

As usual, the compulsive effect of the more difficult aspects must be realised and, in this case, assessment must be made as to the relative strength of the two planets concerned. Success may be achieved but at much cost of hard work or personal hardship and may be long delayed. Overmuch limitation of what the person conceives to be his or her way of self-expression and self-gratification bring exaggerated depression, often with tragic results. Overmuch careless optimism when caution is calling produces unhappiness and guilty conscience.

TO URANUS

The conjunction and opposition recur every 14 years (refer to p. 194).

Excessively wilful, independent, and in unconventional and expansive ways. Not likely to pass unnoticed. Helpful for a person whose conditions are big enough and free enough for this to find vent, but indicative of resentful rebellion otherwise.

Forceful, magnetic, determined, conducing to results through sheer dramatic, scintillating bigness of personality and belief in self. Often indicates genius.

The same strength and freedom-loving expansiveness is present, but with less ease of expression. Wilfulness and insistence on being " different " produce tactlessness and bluntness which offend others. The view is highly egocentric, so the ideas and ways of all others are scorned. " Every one is out of step but our John."

CONJUNCTION   *EASY*   *DIFFICULT*

TO NEPTUNE

The conjunction and opposition recur *about* every 13 years (refer to p. 194).

The sea and all its ways, attraction and pursuits, is emphasised. Emphasis is also on everything summed up as " the values," " the intangibles," everything rhythmic such as the sea, music, dancing, colour harmonies. Kindness, philanthropy, good-Samaritan work is extended to others and also received. Over-idealism is indulged in but the rest of the map must show whether this is shaped into results in art or work or religion, or whether it ends in fantasy and day-dreaming and deceit of self and others (subversive side of Neptune). All intuitions and subtle impressionability is increased, hence telepathy, psychometry, and all forms of mediumistic and psychic ability are developable.

The easy flow of benefit from all matters under " Conjunction " is increased. Benefit is often from hidden sources. Sleep will be good. Dreams will be frequent. Anaesthetics well taken.

As ever, there is more compulsion to achievement with the more difficult aspects, but more trouble can arise. If the exaggerative effects (Jupiter) on the over-receptive sensitivity (Neptune) are predominant in a not otherwise controlled and not moral character, escapism, treachery, foolishness, craziness about " -isms " will ensue. Sleep will be over-heavy. Danger may come from gas, drugs, poisons, anaesthetics.

TO PLUTO

The conjunction and opposition recur *about* every 12 years (refer to p. 194).

Reaction to explosive, expulsive ways will be increased. Many new beginnings in the life. Prominence in life at certain times.

Benefit through easy casting off of old contacts and ways and by readiness to start anew. Successful prominence.

Compulsive desire to achieve through violence in bursting away from existent conditions. Results often cause further bondage.

Note.—See note after Sun-Pluto.

ASPECTS OF SATURN

Any planet aspected by Saturn must be thereby limited in its expression, but also controlled.

The orderly, cautious ambitions of a person and also his sense of inadequacy will be affected by any planet aspecting Saturn.

CONJUNCTION   *EASY*   *DIFFICULT*

TO URANUS

The conjunction and the opposition are exact about every 91 years (refer to p. 194).

Practical planning and determined self-will in an unusual way unite to produce brilliant results if opportunity is shown elsewhere in the chart. Nervous tension is likely since freedom and limitation do not go easily together. Self-will and self-control do not blend and are apt to alternate. Danger is likely through accidents of the falling, crashing, limb-breaking kind.

The same but with greater ease of accomplishment. Brilliance will be shown in management, in science, in unusual ways. Accident-prone.

The same, but the awkward contradictoriness of the two principles is more emphasised. Much may be achieved in the ways indicated but with nerve strain, and many breaks and new starts. Nerves suffer badly both through suppression and outbreak. Such a person is often not happy because he gets from others the repercussion of his own awkwardness as a companion.

TO NEPTUNE

The conjunction and opposition recur *about* every 35 years (refer to p. 194).

Can be excellent in a strong character because ideals and imaginative intuitions are kept in bounds and given shape and form so that they are useful in this material world. Limitation is felt through difficulties which are hard to grasp and come to terms with, or which have to be kept hidden.

The same but with greater ease. Intuitions help in accomplishment. Orderliness and caution stop ideas from being too vague. Limitations are through maze-like worries but tend to clear up in the long run, through patient endurance and quiet keeping out of the limelight.

The same but with less ease. Schemes come to frustration because they are too impractical. There is an undermining of the power of control and of completion of purpose. Sometimes scandal.

TO PLUTO

These aspects occur so rarely and last so long when they happen, that it is unwise to think of them with too personal an effect, unless Saturn is highly important in the chart. In this case, the limiting and controlling effect of Saturn would be forced to combine with the explosive, clearing effect of Pluto. Even if well aspected, the results could hardly be pleasant, though in the long term, the end might be wholesome if drastic.

Note.—See note after Sun-Pluto.

ASPECTS OF URANUS

Any planet aspected by Uranus will be made more galvanic, more unusual in its working.

A person's urge to freedom and his independence of behaviour will be modified by any planet aspecting Uranus.

CONJUNCTION	*EASY*	*DIFFICULT*

TO NEPTUNE

The conjunction and opposition recur *about* every 171 years (refer to p. 194).

It will not be found in current maps as its last appearance was 1820 and this modern book will be old-fashioned by 1991.

Imaginative idealism and intuition are made unusual and directable. It is the unison of positive and negative mediumship and was in charts of those who were adult when the spiritualist movement began after the entry of Neptune into human consciousness in 1846. Genius of science gains from unison with inspirational ideas.

The last trine was in orbs during the years 1937–41. In the last two of these years, there was also a Jupiter–Saturn conjunction, so it is to be expected that among those who are children at the time of writing (1950), there will be some outstanding characters. Their charts would be likely to have the planets forming these aspects prominent by position or rulership.

Ideals carried into actuality by unusual power of leadership in practical, scientific and advanced ways. (Trine in the Earthy Triplicity.)

The last opposition occurred several times and was within orbs for many months between the years 1905 and 1913. This was because both planets went Retrograde and again Direct. The next square will be within orbs in the latter half of 1951, again in parts of 1952, exact in autumn 1953, when Saturn, Jupiter and Mars will also aspect it. It will continue in varying degrees of closeness till early 1958. It will thus be in *all* charts of the time and must not be considered unique unless by position of rulership of the planets. Another way of prominence is by the squaring of both ends of the opposition by another planet as Saturn did in 1909–10, or by the square forming part of a T-square, or Grand Cross, or itself being joined by other planets.

A state of nervous tenseness. Effort is made to attain the ideals in unusual ways, but tension can snap, causing much tragedy, especially when Saturn is concerned in this. In all tensions, relief may be found in the attempt to let the energies free themselves in the ways indicated by the happier parts of the chart.

TO PLUTO

The rare aspects formed between two planets moving so slowly would be in all charts for so long that their effects would be on that generation, rather than to be considered personally, unless the aspect is unique because prominent.

Note.—See note after Sun-Pluto.

Aspects of All Planets to Ascendant and Midheaven

If the birth-time is accurately known, *these are of great importance*, but if not they are misleading, and are better omitted. An orb of 5° may be allowed.

Detailed interpretation of all is not necessary in this chapter. The student will now have realised by the preceding paragraphs that effect of each planet will be *according to its nature*, modified by the *kind of aspect* formed.

Those to the Ascendant will have a closely personal implication, very often in relation to health.

Those to the M.C. will affect the self-expression in the outer life, hence influencing prestige, standing, and the career ; also the relationship to those in authority and sometimes to a parent, more probably the father.

Those to the Descendant will affect others in close connection, or the relationship made with them.

Those to the I.C. will affect the self-expression in the home, or through family connections ; also the relationship to a parent, more probably the mother.

Any planet aspecting one angle must also aspect the opposite angle, and by an aspect of a similar kind ; the exception to this being that a planet in conjunction with one angle will be in opposition to another. Interpretation *must* be in accordance with *the nature of the planet*. Though the opposition may indicate a tenseness, no serious harm can be expected from the opposition of a benefic, but difficulties will result from both the conjunction and opposition of planets which are mainly malefic.

Even so, their helpful and strengthening sides *must not be forgotten*, also other aspects to the planet in question *must* be taken into consideration.

Interpretation of the Aspect Pattern

When lines are drawn to indicate interplanetary relationships (p. 184), the resulting pattern, as a whole, focuses the attention on to the intricate interweaving of the urges or drives in a person, correlating with this design. The outstanding difference between the emphasis on planets with many aspects and those with few should be interpreted accordingly in terms of the principles of these planets, as modified by sign and house position.

CHAPTER II

SCHEME OF CHART INTERPRETATION, WITH EXAMPLE

(1) Example charts with detail of work.
(2) Working plan for preparation of interpretation.
(3) Case history.
(4) Notes for interpretation (using No. 1 Chart and Equal House System).
(5) Finished example analysis with astrological marginal references on astrologer's copy only.
(6) Alterations if using No. 2 Chart and the Placidean House System.
(7) Comment on accuracy of analysis.
(8) Possible additions to information given.

Part 1.—*EXAMPLE CHARTS (facing pp. 201 and 222) WITH DETAIL OF WORK*

Birth is given as *3.35 p.m   21st June, 1924.   Swindon, England.*

As instructed in Chapter 6 :—
(1) Birth time examined to find if given in G.M.T., and adjusted since Summer Time was found to be in use at the time.
(2) Reference is made to atlas for latitude and longitude of Swindon.
(3) Calculations are made on forms A and B :—
   (*a*) To find planetary positions (see p. 108).
   (*b*) To find Local Sidereal Time at birth (see p. 118).
   (*c*) To find position of Part of Fortune (see p. 146).
(4) Reference is made to Table of Houses for given latitude :—
   (*a*) To find degree of ecliptic ascending (under Ascen.).*
   (*b*) To find degree of ecliptic culminating (under " 10 ").*
(5) Above results are charted according to House System used. (Two are illustrated.)
(6) All details about chart entered as indicated in spaces provided (see Chapter 12).

Charting by No. 1.   The Ecliptic Chart

Ascending degree is marked.
House lines are made (see Chapter 7, Fig. 15).
Symbols of signs are inserted.
M.C. and I.C. are inserted at the degree they occupy.

* Or as given in the Time-saver Tables of Asc. and M.C. by Colin Evans.

EXAMPLE CHART
by
EQUAL HOUSE SYSTEM
using
No. 1. The Ecliptic Chart

(For same example
by
PLACIDEAN SYSTEM
see Chart facing p. 222)

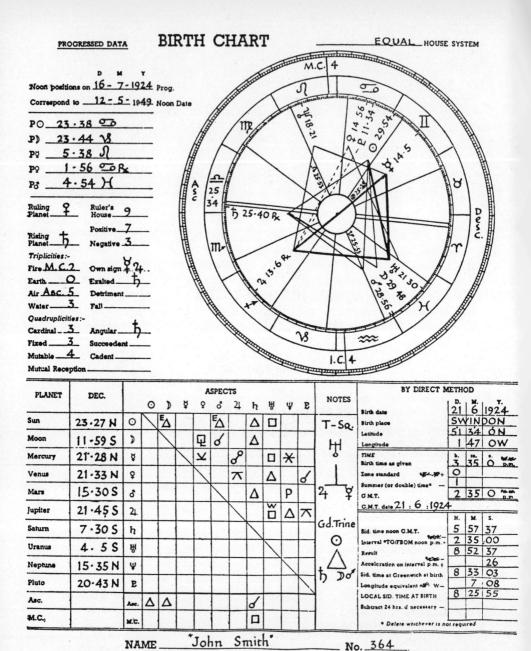

BIRTH CHART

EQUAL HOUSE SYSTEM

PROGRESSED DATA

Noon positions on 16 - 7 - 1924 Prog.

Correspond to 12 - 5 - 1949 Noon Date

P⊙ 23.38 ♋
P☽ 23.44 ♑
P☿ 5.38 ♌
P♀ 1.56 ♋ R
P♂ 4.54 ♓

Ruling Planet ♀   Ruler's House 9

Rising Planet ♄   Positive 7
  Negative 3

Triplicities:-
Fire M.C.2   Own sign ♀ ♃
Earth 0   Exalted ♄
Air Asc.5   Detriment ___
Water 3   Fall ___

Quadruplicities:-
Cardinal 3   Angular ♄
Fixed 3   Succeedent ___
Mutable 4   Cadent ___

Mutual Reception ___

PLANET	DEC.	ASPECTS										NOTES	BY DIRECT METHOD			
		⊙	☽	☿	♀	♂	♃	♄	♅	♆	♇			D.	M.	Y.
													Birth date	21	6	1924
Sun	23.27 N	⊙	E△			E△		△	□			T-Sq.	Birth place	SWINDON		
Moon	11.59 S		☽		⊡	☌		△				♅	Latitude	51	34	0N
Mercury	21.28 N			☿	⋎		☍		□	✳			Longitude	1	47	0W
Venus	21.33 N				♀		⊼		△		♂		TIME	h.	m.	s.
Mars	15.30 S					♂		△		P		♃ ♀	Birth time as given	3	35	0 p.m.
Jupiter	21.45 S						♃		W□	△	⊼	Gd.Trine	Zone standard	0		
Saturn	7.30 S							♄					Summer (or double) time*	1		
Uranus	4.5 S								♅			⊙	G.M.T.	2	35	0 p.m.
Neptune	15.35 N									♆		△	G.M.T. date 21 : 6 : 1924			
Pluto	20.43 N										♇	♄ D☌		H.	M.	S.
Asc.		Asc.	△	△						♂			Sid. time noon G.M.T.	5	57	37
M.C.		M.C.							□				Interval *TO/FROM noon p.m. –	2	35	00
													Result	8	52	37
													Acceleration on interval p.m. †			26
													Sid. time at Greenwich at birth	8	33	03
													Longitude equivalent ☞ W–		7	08
													LOCAL SID. TIME AT BIRTH	8	25	55
													Subtract 24 hrs. if necessary —			

* Delete whichever is not required

NAME "John Smith"   No. 364

No. 1 - The "ECLIPTIC" Chart. DIRECT METHOD   Designed by M.E.HONE.

Moon's nodes are inserted in line with their degrees, but nearer centre of chart to lessen possibility of confusion with planets.

Part of Fortune is inserted in the same way.

Planets are inserted, as tabulated, each at the degree calculated. (Planets should be written in red ink, which should also be used for a small mark at the degree itself.)

Charting by No. 2.   The Houses Chart (using Placidean system)

The signs containing the Asc. and M.C. and the degrees in which these are found, are written at cusps 1 and 10, and their opposites at cusps 7 and 4 (see Chapter 7, Fig. 21).

Signs and degrees of intermediate houses are copied from Placidean Tables of houses at end of Ephemeris. Their opposites are inserted and also any omitted signs which are " intercepted."

Moon's nodes are inserted near centre but are written along cuspal line of sign in which they are. They are written before or after it according as their degree is before or after that of the cusp.

Part of Fortune is inserted in the same way.

Planets are inserted as tabulated but near house lines, in numerical order with cusp. Any planets in an intercepted sign are written crossways.

Note on Charts

It will be seen that the Moon and Mars are the only planets which vary in house position. Reference to meaning of these by house (pp. 152, 160 and 161), will show which is the more applicable to the person.

Remainder of Both Charts

Name of House System used is entered.

All details from Form A entered.

Number of planets in triplicities and quadruplicities are entered with all other information necessary for assessment of chart as indicated by spaces provided.

Aspects are calculated and entered.

Planets are connected by light lines for easy aspects and heavy lines for difficult ones, since red cannot be used for printing. (This is optional but strongly advised.)

While doing this, it is realised that the chart contains both a Grand Trine and a T-square and notes are made to that effect in the column provided.

Declinations are inserted. It is seen that, with the exception of Mars and Neptune, all pairs of planets found to be in parallel of declination are already noted as brought into connection by aspect, so the parallel between these two is the only one to be inserted.

Date of day taken for year of progression is entered, with date in all years, to which the noon positions of the planets correspond (refer noon-date, p. 226).

Progressed positions of more quickly moving planets are entered.

Note on Last Two Entries

These should never be omitted as they are the facts from which any other astrologer seeing the chart, but without access to Ephemeris, can draw many deductions as to present condition of the person's life. The student himself may return to a chart many years after he made it, and be glad of this information at a glance.

Instruction will be given in Chapter 12.

Part 2.—*WORKING PLAN FOR PREPARATION OF INTERPRETATION*

There are no " rules " for this, and each worker will develop his own technique in time, but the student's great difficulty is that, at first, he has no experience from which to evolve such a technique. Many books only help him by *astrological comment* on example charts, which is not the same as giving an example of *interpretation* and explaining how this was deduced. He will hear practised astrologers talking fluently straight from a chart, but he cannot do this without notes at first.

What follows is a workable method which each can adapt to suit himself later. Detailed preparation may not appeal to all students, but it saves time in the end. When proficient, only skeleton notes are required.

Step 1.—Notes are made in the following order, with marginal abbreviation of the category under which each note is to be assembled.

(*a*) General notes about the chart. These should record any outstanding factor which influences the whole chart, such as :—

> Strong formations by aspects (Grand trine, Cross, exactness of aspects).
> " Shaping " by M. E. Jones methods (p. 178).
> House or sign emphasised by containing many planets (p. 47).
> Planets outstandingly strong by position or aspects.
> Classification by triplicity and quadruplicity.
> Comments drawn from Nodes and Part of Fortune.

(*b*) Notes on Ascending sign, the placing of its ruler by sign and house. Notes on aspects made by ruler.

(*c*) Notes on Sun by sign, house and aspect.

(*d*) Notes on Sun-ruler in same way.

(*e*) Notes on Moon in same way.

(*f*) Notes on other planets, not yet covered, in their order from Sun.

To begin with, such notes must be made by looking up instructions in Chapters 9 and 10. This is tedious. The only way to avoid it is by *work*. The more the student practices, the sooner he learns the actual nature of each planet, sign, house and aspect and becomes fluent in interpretation in his own words. He should first write *the keyword interpretation*, making a reasonable sentence out of the words which cannot help but be stilted. By schooling himself to this at first, he will find that he forms the habit of looking for basic meaning which can then be *translated* rather than trying to arrive at " end-results " at random.

Step 2.—Categories or headings are decided on for classifying these notes. Abbreviations for these are placed in the margins for easy collecting. List of suggested cate-

gories follows, but choice must be according to the requirements of the case.
Several can be combined if desired. Others can be stressed singly when necessary.

For final writing, the student must take the first category as decided and go
through the notes on it only, selecting as the abbreviations indicate.

The house or houses connected, as indicated in list must then be observed.
Their signs and rulers must be considered. Judgment must be made also by planets
in the house, their aspects and strength. Notes can be made on this if desired
though most points will have been covered already.

It is not to be expected that every detail of a chart can be included in an interpretation. The notes of the category must be read and *a good, interesting synthesis*
of them under that heading must be made. Each must be taken in turn in the same
way, until all is welded into one whole.

SUGGESTED CATEGORIES

Abbreviation	*Category*	*Refer also to :—*
Char.	1. General Characteristics	1st house. Sun and Moon in full detail. Any-thing outstanding in general formation.
Ment.	2. Mentality, creativity. Intuitional ability	3rd and 9th mental trends, 5th creativity, 8th and 12th intuitional ability. Mercury and other planets for special abilities (as Chapter 3).
Car.	3. Career, money, work-ing ability	10th career, with all general tendencies. 6th work and ability for it. Contrasted strengths of Jupiter and Saturn for success and obstacles to overcome. 7th for partners and associates. 2nd and 8th for money.
Sp. time	4. Spare time occupations	1st general. 5th pleasures. Sun and Moon and ruler general indications.
Friends Love Marr.	5. Personal contacts. Friends, attachments, Marriage	11th friends, 5th love, 7th marriage, 8th sexual love. Venus for ability for " rap-port." Sun in woman's map. Moon in man's. Mars for outreaching force.
Fam.	6. Family contacts	4th and 10th mother and father, also Moon and Saturn. 3rd brothers and sisters, also Mercury. 5th children.
Health	7. Health	1st type of person. 6th health. 12th sometimes hospitalisation. Sun vitality and heart. Moon functional disorders. Saturn chills, falls. Mars burns, scalds, cuts, fevers. Jupiter liver trouble. Uranus circulation, also breaks, sprains. (See Chapter 3.)
Trav.	8. Travel	3rd and 9th. Mercury–Jupiter.

Displacement of Natural Sign on House Cusp

It must be remembered that *the affairs of a house are correlative with the mode of expression of its natural sign,* and that, if any sign other than Aries is on the Ascendant, *the natural signs all round the chart are displaced by others in their turn.* These are noted, with the strength, or weakness, and placing of their rulers. To make notes on all this would be lengthy but the import of it can be easily observed while writing.

Importance of Ascendant

The ascending sign must always be kept in mind. *Whatever else the chart shows can only act through the medium of that type of Ascendant.* For instance, a strong Mars may be shown. The effect of it must be judged very differently if in the chart of a strong dominant ascending sign such as Leo, or in a gentle, weaker one such as Pisces.

Repetition

It will be found that the same remarks recur from more than one source. This is to be expected, as *an outstanding characteristic is usually shown by more than one factor in a chart.*

Style of Writing

The person for whom the reading is being prepared must be considered and the style suitably adapted.

For instance, different phraseology would be applicable for a young girl, an elderly woman or a business man. The chart of a small child is usually written as to the parents about the child and with special attention to giving help in bringing up, according to the tendencies shown.

Interpretation should not be interlarded with astrological terms which the reader does not understand. The style which reads " Your Sun is square Saturn, so you will be such and such," may be delineation but it is not an interesting analysis.

Another style which makes painful reading is that which changes frequently. Beginning with " the native of this chart will be so and so," it changes to " this lady will so and so," then, mentioning the ascending sign, " Librans are always so and so," then, switching to the Sun sign, "but Capricornians are this and that" and finally " you " will be such and such.

If the person for whom the chart is done is knowledgeable about astrology and wishes to learn from the work done, then the aim is completely different, and astrological comments on the chart should be included.

Step 3.—All that has been written should be re-read for corrections in English, in grammar and in punctuation. Variety in wording can be attained by the use of *a Dictionary of Synonyms and Antonyms.*

An outer page should be arranged for descriptive name for work, such as " Horoscope," " Character Analysis," etc., and for name of the person for whom the work has been done and signature of astrologer.

An introductory page should be written on which some statement should be made to the effect that what has been written is not intended to " foretell the future," but to indicate possibilities. It is also advisable to state that notes of all astrological factors have been kept and can be supplied if required.

On the first page a preliminary paragraph should be written in which Ascending and Sun signs are stated. People like to be able to quote their astrological " make-up."

Step 4.—Good typescript with carbon copy should be made, or sent to trained typist to be done.

Step 5.—In case there may be errors to alter in the top copy, the carbon should be checked from the rough, as the astrological significators in its margin can be copied on to it at the same time. This should be kept in alphabetical box-file for future reference when more work on it may be needed.

Step 6.—A copy of the working chart should be made and pasted to the left of the inside of a double folder. The typing should be attached to the other side by the top only, as each page can then be folded over as read, leaving the chart clear for reference.

Step 7.—Both charts should be numbered. The working chart should be kept in a snap-back file. Alphabetical file cards must be kept when many charts are collected.

Step 8.—Before putting away the Ephemeris which has been used, the name of the person whose chart was done should be written outside. This is a most valuable help for comparison when others of the same year are done later.

Part 3.—*CASE HISTORY*

(This chart is published by the permission of the young man for whom it was made. The name and birthplace are fictitious. It is chosen because it is a chart of a typical young life of modern times, deterred by the war and striving towards fulfilment.   It is hoped that this will be more helpful to the student than the many published example charts of royal or long dead personages.)

" John Smith " is a young man of 25, about to take examination to qualify as teacher. Settlement of career delayed owing to sudden death of father in 1944 and sale of business owing to inability to carry on during war conditions. No brothers or sisters. Unmarried.

Chief Interests.—Judo, collecting of semi-precious stones and a scientific study of their composition, all usual sports, study of psychology.

Reason for Request for Work Done

Mother, knowing some astrology, required general character-analysis to confirm own assessment. (See present chapter.) She also wished to know whether tendencies for coming year were favourable for passing of exam (see Chapter 12).

Lastly, being sure of the birth-time within half an hour, she wanted to know whether it was possible to decide whether the ascending sign was Libra or Scorpio.

Part 4.—*NOTES ON WHICH TO BUILD INTERPRETATION*

(**Note.**—The words " Benasp " and " Malasp " are used to shorten " well aspected " and " not well aspected.")

CATEGORY	SIGNIFICATOR	DEDUCTION
	General Indications	
Char.	" Splash "	Spreads his interests.
Char.	Grand Trine in Air	Emphasises Air element. Easeful conditions frequently helpful and often through kindly help from others.
Char.	♄ strong by exaltation and by aspects	Strength to offset possible tendency to depend on above.
Char.	T-square in Mutables	Tenseness will set up urge to overcome implied difficulties, which will be circumvented when possible.
Char. Ment.	Early change of sign by Asc. Sun and Moon (all Air to Water)	Mental and physical agility soon to receive an " overlay " of emotional and intuitive development.
Char.	Mutable-Air	Adaptable, lively, intelligent.
Char.	Asc. Air Sun Air Moon Air	Very strong tendency to self-expression through intelligent, varied, lively ways, constant contact with others mentally and personally.
Char.	♄ ☌ Asc. benasp	All other tendencies subject to deliberate control and planning. Also to limitation in action and development. Responsibility inevitable, but well aspected.
Home Spare time	Nodes 11th–5th benasp	Likelihood of success in objectives and in friendships but need to give in matters relating to sport, love-making, children, and other creative activities.
Home	(By Placidean System. Nodes 10th–4th)	(Gain as above in career, need to give in home affairs.)
Char.	⊕ cusp 9	Real desire is to widen scope through serious study and through travel.
	Ascendant	
Char.	♎	Active, expressive, communicative, beauty loving, peacefully inclined, balancing, companionable, graceful, vacillating.

Health		Possible headaches and kidney trouble later in life.
Career Spare time		Professional and using contact with others. Pleasant social activities.
Love	Early Prog. to ♏	Addition of more strongly emotional force, more initiatory drive, more deeply penetrative ability.
Ment.	♂, ruler of ♏, benasp	More intensity and reserve.

Ascendant-Ruler, Venus

Char.	♀ in ♋ in 9th (aspects mixed)	Keywords :—Urge to *harmony* working *cherishingly* in regard to *profound mental interests* or to do with *matters abroad*.
Char.	♀ in ♋	i.e., Strong innate desire for harmony, beauty and for entering into relations with others. Affections tender and cherishing, will express such desires in enjoyment of study, love of travel possible life abroad and the study of young people.
	♀ in 9th	
Love	♀ △ ♅ 9th–5th	Unusualness in expression of love and in any kind of partnership is delightful and fascinating. Easy making and breaking of attractions. Partings likely but with pleasant replacements or reunions.
Career		
Char. Mon.	♀ ⚼ ♃ ♃ 2nd	At times, love and personal contacts cause strain and restlessness and become expensive.
Love. Career	♀ ☌ ♇	Affections and partnerships subject to sudden disclosures and upheavals and new starts.

Sun

	☉ in ♊ in 9th (mainly benasp)	Keywords :—*Power* and *vitality* expressed in *lively*, *versatile* ways when dealing with matters to do with serious studies and beliefs.
Love Char. Career	☉ in ♊	i.e., Agile, talkative, quick in thought and movement, cool in affection. enjoys mental pursuits, diffusive, literary. Good at use of hands, likes getting about, tends to writing, lecturing, educative work.

Career Travel	In 9th	Above will tend to deepen in seriousness as regards studies and widen in scope as regards travel.
Char. Home	☉ △ ☽ (exact)	Happy nature at one with itself. Home matters and family background good.
Char.	☉ △ ♂ (exact)	Self-expression strong. Mentally and physically robust, courageous, hard working, quick, incisive.
Health		Strong heart.
Char. Family Char.	☉ △ ♄	Self expression limited, possibly by reason of father and his affairs. Life hard at times, but lessons of duty and control learnt. Feeling of personal inadequacy spurs to achievement.
Char.	☉ □ ♅	Tendency to allow independence and dramatic tensity to become self-willed and self-insistent. Sudden disruptive action possible with brusque manner.
	(Note ♎ Asc. counters this)	
Ment.		Tendency to originality and scientific thought.

Sun-Ruler, Mercury

	☿ in ♊ in 8th	Keywords :—Principle of *communication* working in *lively, alert* way especially when to do with feelings aroused by, or matters to do with *others* and their *possessions*.
Ment. Health Career	☿ in ♊ (Strong in own sign)	i.e., Mind and nervous reaction quick. Speech fluent. Learning and teaching congenial and successful.
	in 8th	Above will show in the more intense emotional relations to others. At some time in life, thoughts will turn to psychic interests and consideration of meaning of life and what follows it.
Ment.	☿ ☍ ♃ (Neither planet harmful) (♄ controls this)	Mental scope tends to expand. Care must be taken to keep it within bounds lest too much is attempted.
Love	8th–2nd	Judgments, especially as regards feelings and financial matters, must be taken slowly and well thought over. Memory is not good.

Ment.	☿ □ ♅ 8th–5th	Mental action, inventive, revolutionary, independent ; will be excited in unusual ways and in unusual pleasurable occupations to the point of being considered " different " and odd by some people.
Spare-time Char.		
Ment.	☿ ✶ ♆	Mind is good channel for inspirational ideas of the kind to use in art, poetry, imaginative writing and in thoughts of mysticism.
	(♆ in 10th)	This will affect the career, giving vision and imagination in planning.
Char.	☿ ⊻ ♀	Pleasant mind reflects in speech and manner.

Moon

	☽ in ♒ in 5th	Keywords :—*Response* to life, *detached, independent, scientific*, especially as regards *pleasures* and *children*.
Char.	☽ in ♒ (benasp)	i.e., Responses to conditioning in life, ways and manner independent, friendly, detached, unemotional and with tendency to mental interests of unusual or scientific nature.
Love Children	in 5th	Interests will be in sports, games, in love-making, in children's affairs and many kinds of creative activity.
Spare-time	(in ♒)	These will be unusual and inventive.
Home Family	(By Placidean System⎫ in 4th)⎭	(Interests will be in home and family matters. Many changes in residence.)
Char.	☽ ☌ ♂	Robust, courageous, very active. Quick in retort and response. This is likely to be taken for quick temper.
Char.	☽ △ ♄	Excellent sense of control and order in practical and personal ways. Tends to seriousness and to willing acceptance of duty and responsibility.

Mars

	♂ in ♒ in 5th	Keywords :—*Energy* used *detachedly* and *scientifically* especially in regard to *pleasures* and *children*.
Char.	♂ in ♒ (benasp)	i.e., Energy will go into determined self-freedom to pursue chosen ends.
Ment.		Strong tendency to intelligence and wide scientific outlook.

Love Children Enjoyment	In 5th	Energy used in gay enjoyment of love-making, of children, of games and all pleasures and with much personal satisfaction through these.
Home	(By Placidean System, in 4th)	(Energy used in home affairs and in quick able ways.)

Jupiter

	♃ in ♐ in 2nd	Keywords:—Urge to *expansion* working in a *free ranging* way especially in regard to *feelings and possessions*.
Char.	♃ in ♐ (Mixed asp. strong in own sign) (♄ helps)	i.e., Fine character through desire to expand self in love of liberty for self and others, generous, dignified but without pomposity. Must guard against putting freedom before everything and against lack of concentration.
Finance	In 2nd	Good financial success to be expected if care is taken.
Char.	(See aspects)	Appreciation of own possessions.
Char. Char.	♃ □ ♅ (wide) (Asc. in ♎ will moderate this)	Care must be taken to avoid consequences of too wilful and extreme egocentricity.
Love Children	(♅ in 5th)	The strong desire to be "different" and free must be expressed with tact and acted on with thought for others, especially for loved ones and children and when relaxed and enjoying life.
Char.	□ can be constructive (T-square)	If this is done, then the unusual creativity and inventive ability, affecting mind and desire to self-expansion will be constructively used.
Career Finance	♃ △ ♆ (2nd–10th)	Self advancement in the life of the world and in the career in general will be enormously improved by helpful opportunities which will arise and be promptly taken.
Spare-time		Good ideas, swift inspirations, will grow and find expression in the arts and in music and in all touch with the intangibles. Source of benefit may sometimes be kept hidden.
Health		Sleep will be good. Anaesthetics well taken and harmless.

♃ ⊼ ♇
(♇ in ♋)

An upsetting tendency must be guarded against. This is the desire to upset existing conditions and make new starts. The desire is for freedom, but the result may be a greater tie.

Saturn

♄ in ♎ in 1st

Keywords :—*Limitation, harmoniously* expressed and felt as a *personal* matter.

Char.

♄ in ♎
(exaltation)
(benasp)

i.e., Desire for control and need for patience are splendidly expressed in balanced reasonable ways. Necessity is wisely and cheerfully accepted as experience.

♄ in 1st

This will do a great deal to calm rebellious tendencies.

Career
Char.

(♂ Asc)

Feeling of personal insecurity and inadequacy which will be the spur to achievement in spite of obstacles. Personal responsibilities will be robustly shouldered.

♂ strong

Home

(♄ rules 4th)

These are likely to be connected with home and family.

(By Placidus rules 3rd)
(Aspects already dealt with)

(These are likely to be connected with educational matters.)

Uranus

♅ in ♓ in 5th

Keywords :—*Changefulness* working *nebulously* and *impressionably* in dealing with *pleasures* and *children*.

Char.

♅ in ♓
(General for 7 years)
(Mainly malasp)

i.e., Emotionally changeful in a self-freeing, unconventional way but with strong intuitions.

Love
Children
Spare-time

In 5th

Above has much effect on relations with girl friends, children, pleasures. There will be little regard for conventions in dealing with these, but originality of idea.

Char.

(Important as point of T-square)
(Aspects already dealt with)

The strong originality and will-power which works creatively is an extremely powerful force acting on the mind, the ego, the affections and the desire to expand the life. The nicety of balance between this urge to unconventionality and freedom of thought and action, and the equally strong urge to control and planning will be decisive in the life.

(♄

	Rules 5th	It will have great effect on all affairs of love, children, spare-time diversions and creative activities.
	(By Placidus ♅ rules 4th)	(Changes and unusual conditions to be expected in regard to home affairs.)

Neptune

	Ψ in ♌ in 10th	Keywords :—*Nebulousness* expressed *creatively* and *joyfully* in affairs *outside the home*.
Char.	In ♌ (General for 14 years)	i.e., Vague and inspirational ideas will lead to big schemes for self-expression in an organising, managing way. This will be planned with kindly, generous, magnanimous feelings towards those under control.
Career	(Mainly benasp) (⚹ ☿, ⊾ ♂, △ ♃)	
Career	In 10th	The above will influence to aims towards which the intentions are directed in the outer world. The objective is not to remain an assistant, but to be in control of staff and an administrator and organiser.

Pluto

	♇ in ♋ in 9th	Keywords :—Urge to *eliminate* and *begin anew* works *protectively* and *in relation to life abroad* or *serious studies*.
	In ♋ (General for 30 years)	i.e., Any upsetting phase that arrives connected with those under the care, whether family or pupils, will be easily and tactfully dealt with, but with consequent strain on the feelings and endurance. When the desire is strong to end one period in life and to begin afresh, care must be taken that the financial considerations are well thought out lest there is an over-stepping of income.
Career	(Aspects mixed) (☌ ♀, ⊼ ♃)	
Career Travel	In 9th	This will specially apply when there is any consideration of change by way of taking on extended studies, or involving life abroad.

Part 5.—*FINISHED EXAMPLE ANALYSIS (IN ACTUAL WORK, ASTRO-LOGICAL MARGINAL REFERENCES WOULD APPEAR ON ASTRO-LOGER'S CARBON COPY ONLY)*

ASTRO-ANALYSIS

for " JOHN SMITH "

(Published by his kind permission)

BY

MARGARET E. HONE

PROLOGUE*

Owing to the prevalence of certain misunderstandings, it has been thought well to place the following statement before all work.

ASTROLOGY does not constitute an art by which the future can be foretold in detail. This would be fortune-telling and is not possible.

The modern attitude to this age-old knowledge is more or less as follows.

The universe is *one* and all parts of it work in unison, but our unaided senses are too inadequate to perceive this. It is possible that, by measuring parts which are observable, i.e., the planetary movements, we can deduce this working in the lives of human beings.

The deductions from the birth map are according to the experience of astrologers through the ages and especially those working on modern psychological lines.

Any remark on the possibilities for the future should be preceded by the phrase " the likelihood is that " and should be understood to be the probable outcome of the development of the potentialities of the birth-moment ; and as conditions of life, not as actual events. As it is impossible to re-iterate the phrase, it should be understood.

ASTROLOGY attempts to indicate a life-pattern, but there are more ways than one of this being worked out.

NOTE ON CHART*

The signs of the Zodiac are of varying importance in different natal charts. " Popular " astrology has emphasised the one in which the Sun is placed, since everyone can know it by knowing the date of birth.

Serious astrologers know that the sign ascending over the horizon at birth is of equal, or even greater importance. The actual degree rising in this sign can only be computed when the *moment* of birth is known, and is therefore individual to the person for whom the chart is made.

Your chart shows that :—

The sign ascending is *Libra*.

The sign containing the Sun is *Gemini*.

You would therefore describe yourself astrologically as :—

" *Libran, with Sun in Gemini.*"

Hence, subject to the many subtle modifications imposed by the angular relationships of the planets at your birth-moment, and the emphasis on the other signs, you are very largely a compound of the characteristics known to be observable in those for whom the above signs are important.

Technical astrological terminology will not be used in the following analysis. The main astrological correlatives of every deduction made from the chart will be entered in the margin of the copy filed for future reference, and can be obtained by arrangement, if required.

* These two sections should be second and third pages of typescript.

GENERAL CHARACTERISTICS

Asc. ♎, ☉ ♊, ☽ ♒,
♄ strong
Mutable—Air

YOUR NATURE, as seen from your chart, is rational, balanced, reasoning, active, academic, versatile and adaptable, but yet controlled.

Early change of Asc. and Sun from Air to Water
♎ ☉ ♋

♃ 2nd

Now to expand that statement, you may be said to be as above but with great capacity to soften and improve what might be a too coolly " mental " outlook by the addition of much that tends to a fuller life, including an interest in the more intuitional and emotional things of life, such as music, dancing, and the collecting of things of beauty with fine appreciation of the lovely and valuable.

☉ ♊, mainly benasp

You are so versatile that no curt description will fit you, but alternatives must be given. In fact, you will generally be found to be interested in more than one thing at a time, and to run interests subsidiary to what may be your chief one at any period.

♄ exalted ☌ Asc. benasp

To this tendency to over-diffuseness you have an excellent corrective as you find it easy to exert an iron self-control when necessary, forcing yourself to a single line of thought to gain a desired end. This is a key-note in your life which could otherwise tend to be too much at the mercy of a desire to look for easy conditions through others, and an urge to be " different " in an independent and dramatic way which could easily become a rebellious self-will.

Grand Trine
☉ □ ♅

Grand Trine and T-sq.
☉, ☿ □ ♅ but ♀ ruler

Your character is complex and contains many paradoxes.

♎ Asc. ♄ rising

Asc. ♎, ♀ △ ♅

You are innately balanced, beauty loving, peacefully inclined and companionable, so you will develop the " differentness " as originality rather than eccentricity, forming a strong individuality rather than conforming to any type. Therefore you will develop in unusual ways and will have the good sense to see that you do so with delightful charm.

T-sq. in Mutables
☉ in ♊
♄ ☌ Asc.

Asc. ♎

♄ in ♎ benasp
♄ △ ♂ in ♒

9th house strong
⊕, ☉, ♇ and Asc.-ruler

♀ in ♋ in 9th

☉ △ ☽
☉ △ ♂

☽ in ♒
Asc. p. into ♏
♂ benasp
☽ ☌ ♂

Asc. ♎

☽ ☌ ♂
♃ in ♐

♊

Asc. Sun, Moon in Air
Grand Trine in Air
♐ on cusp 3

☉ in ♊

Strong ♄
Asc. ♎, ♇ ☉ ♋
☉ ☌ ♂ in 5th

♀ (ruler) in ♋
☉ p. in ♋

You will meet your difficulties in life with a tense nervous apprehension which comes from a feeling of personal insecurity. You will circumvent them when possible, preferring the easy way, but, once you have realised any circumstance as a necessity, you will accept it willingly, shouldering your responsibilities, energetically and determinedly making your plans to gain the personal freedom for which you long.

Your real desires are towards the widening of your scope in life through the acquisition of knowledge, and through travel.

To the achievement of this you will bring a pleasant diplomacy in dealing with others.

Yours is a happy nature, at one with itself, outright in its full and robust and courageous self-expression.

Your outward response to life is friendly, detached, unemotional. Your deeper feelings are intense but hidden by a controlled reserve. Reactions are quick so that the sudden retort may be mistaken for brusquerie if you are not careful to remember your true tactfulness. As a small child you were probably quick tempered. A fine, expansive generosity of nature is shown. You want liberty and growth for yourself but also for others. As you get older, this attitude will increase a dignity in your bearing which you will carry without pomposity. If a caution may be given, try not to let the expansive and the diffusive betray you into lack of concentration.

MENTALLY, your whole tendency is towards development through the use of your brain. You are conditioned to an academic life and could not have chosen a better profession than that of a schoolmaster.

You have all the qualities for success in this field. Intelligence, ability to study, to write and to teach are all shown. Then you have application, strength of will, appreciation of the arts, an interest in physical as well as mental exercise plus a desire to use your work in protective, kindly helpful ways, which really train a child, rather than merely to teach facts to it.

☿ in own sign in 8th but ⚻ ♃ □ ♅ ✶ ♆ — All reactions of your mind, your nerves and your hands are quick ; speech should be fluent and writing easy.

☿ ⚻ ♃
♂ and ♄ benasp ♂ Asc. — Memory is not good, but you make up for this by energy and application.

☿ ⚻ ♃ — Mental scope tends to expand and can press you to undertake too much.

☿ ✶ ♆ in 10th — Your mind is an excellent channel for inspirational ideas which you will use to further your career. These will also help you in regard to poetry, imaginative writing and thoughts of mysticism.

☿ □ ♅, 8th to 5th — Mental action is strong, inventive, revolutionary, independent. It will be exerted in unusual ways and occupations, to the point of being considered " interestingly out of the ordinary " by some people and " odd " by others.

☉ □ ♅
☿ □ ♅ 8th to 5th
☿ ✶ ♆
☽ and ♂ in ♒
☿ in 8th and Asc. p. into ♍
♎ △ ♃ (wide). — Your chief tendency is towards scientific thought. Research work on these lines would be a pleasure rather than a toil. Research would be on wide lines, with an interest in mankind and a wish to increase a penetrative psychological understanding of human nature.

♆ in 10th. ☿ in 8th
☉ 9th — At some time in life, thoughts will turn to the mystical and the hidden, and to a serious consideration of the meaning of life and of what follows it.

Full 5th containing ruler of ♒ on cusp, through ♎ Asc. — Creativity is strong and will be expressed in original thought and writing and occupation.

As to your *CAREER* in life, your ability to work for this and to become financially secure, the comment has already been made that your choice of profession is suitable. All that has been said of your character points to ability scholastically, educationally in the wider sense of the word, and as a disciplinarian.

Emphasis on Air
♐ on 3rd, strong ♃
Full 9th, ♊ on cusp
" Mental " planets in own signs.   Strong ♄

♓ on 6th, ♆ on 10th benasp
♃ in 2nd ⚻ ☿ — As a worker, you are idealistic and have vision and would wish to be sympathetic towards those with whom you are concerned in work. As a money-earner, you should do well so long as you can check the tendency to the diffusion of interests spoken of earlier. Alterations of policy to do with money should be carefully considered before action is taken.

♏ on 2nd ♂ benasp	Earning power should be good but subject to sudden fluctuation.
♉ on 8th, ♀ △ ♅	Inherited money and property are likely to come to you unexpectedly.
♃ △ ♆, 2nd to 10th ☊ in 11th in ♌ ♅ combines Gd. Trine and T-square	Self-advancement in the world will be enormously improved by helpful opportunities which will arise and be promptly taken. These will often be through well placed friends or connections. Your best line of activity is through anything scientific or inventive.
	You would also be interested in anything connected with radio, films, electricity or with the study of the unusual or the antique.
Cusp 10 ♋ M.C. ♌ ☽ and ☉ mainly benasp ☉p. into ♌ most of adult life ☊ in ♌ in 11th	It was remarked that education in its truest sense of guarding and helping the young was a strong point in your innate ability, but your eventual progress should be through administrative work and the use of organising ability.
Full 5th ☉ and ☽ Air ☽ ☌ ♂ △ ☉ ♅ in 5th strongly asp. working through ♎ Asc.	Much interest and energy are devoted to your *SPARE-TIME ACTIVITIES.* These would be in accord with your general make-up, in that they would be varied, intelligent, involving speed and agility and of an unusual nature. You would be keen on all forms of sport, especially those requiring quick mental reaction.
☉p. ♋, ☽ 5th	Clubs and groups for games and sport giving opportunity for constantly changing personal contact, would attract you. In these, you would like helping youngsters to enjoy their leisure also.
♒ on cusp 5 ♅ in 5th ☋ in ♒ in 5th	Unusual studies would be a pleasure to you. You have a great ability to enjoy life which is all to the good so long as it does not dissipate your energies too much.
♀ in ♉ △ ♅ ⚻ ♃ ♀ in 9th ♄ in ♎ ♀ ⚻ ♃ ☌ ♇	In your *PERSONAL CONTACTS* in life, success will be through a sympathetic charm and an unusual attraction which you will use not only in friendship but with those more serious people whom you will meet in academic life and abroad. Though companionable, you feel a peace in loneliness, and a strain and restlessness when personal ties bind you too closely or make too many calls on your pocket.

♀ ☌ ♇

Associations, whether professional or personal, are subject to sudden disclosures, upheavals and new starts.

♌ on 11th

You will make friends amongst well placed people who will advance you.

♒ on cusp 5th
♂ and ☽ on cusp, ♅ in 5th working through ♎ Asc.
Fixed sign on 5th but ☉ ♊

With your *GIRL FRIENDS* you will be charming, attractive, forceful, yet you remain coolly appraising and even critical. Paradoxical in love as in all else, you have the ability to remain fixed in your affections, yet you like change and find it hard to settle.

Asc. ♎. ♀ △ ♅
♈ on cusp 7, ♂ benasp
☉ □ ♅, ☉ △ ☽
♂ in ♒ benasp

MARRIAGE should be successful so long as the over-independent streak is kept in control. Your wife should be stimulating, active and interesting.

♑ on 4th, ruler ♂ Asc.

2♃ ruler 3rd, ☍ ☿
♀ in ♋
♂ in ♒ on cusp 5

In *FAMILY LIFE* there is likely to be much responsibility for you and a tendency to stand alone. You have a love for children and also an interest in them as a study.

♅ in 5th

When you have some of your own, they should inherit your keen activity in many ways and your tendency to be attracted by the unusual or unconventional.

♎ Asc. ♂ ♄
☉ ♊ △ ☽, ♂
♀ Ruler ♂ ♇ ⊼ ♃
☿ Sun-ruler ☍ ♃, □ ♅

♀ ♂ ♇ ⊼ ♃

☿ ☍ ♃

♄ ♂ Asc.

☉ △ ☽ and ♂

Your *HEALTH* must have been weak to start with, but soon becoming robust. As a child you were probably susceptible to every feverish, catching complaint.

All the eliminatory functions of the body should be kept in good order as weakness is shown. Chest and lung complaints will be a source of trouble at times. Nervous worry will affect your liver and an over-heavy feeling of responsibility will bring moods of depression. None of this need cause you any apprehension as you are basically sound.

☉ and Asc.-ruler in 9th
♊ on cusp

TRAVEL should be a pleasure to you since to be on the move is better for you than too static a life. Action, movement and change are all congenial to you and it is hardly likely that you will limit these to the borders of your own country. Life abroad is highly probable; the U.S.A. would be a likely country for you to visit, probably for academic rather than holiday reasons.

Planets in ♋ in 9th.
♊ on cusp

	Yours is a well rounded life with good variety of interests.
♅ key-point. Aspects already given	Success will come through strong originality and will-power working creatively and powerfully on the mind, the ego, the affections and the desire to expand the life.
♄ strong	The nicety of balance between this urge to unconventionality and freedom of thought and action and the equally strong urge to control and planning, will be decisive in the life.

Part 6.—*ALTERATIONS IF USING NO. 2 CHART AND THE PLACIDEAN SYSTEM*

Exactly the same plan is followed if the Placidean or any other house system is used, as once a planet is placed in certain sign and house, the delineation for such house will follow automatically.

The only *planets* which change their house position by this method are Mars and Moon which would both be in the 4th house. Alternative readings are given for these in the notes in Part 4. Energy and interest would now be directed less to spare-time interests, sport, girl friends and more to matters within the home. John's mother affirms that this is not so.

There are also changes in the *signs* on the house cusps, hence *the planets ruling the houses* in question will be changed.

Cancer	is intercepted in the	9th house	Ruler Moon
Leo	is on the cusp of the	10th house	Ruler Sun
Virgo	is on the cusp of the	11th house	Ruler Mercury
Libra	is on the cusp of the	12th house	Ruler Venus
Capricorn	is intercepted in the	3rd house	Ruler Saturn
Aquarius	is on the cusp of the	4th house	Ruler Uranus (and Saturn)
Pisces	is on the cusp of the	5th house	Ruler Neptune (and Jupiter)
Aries	is on the cusp of the	6th house	Ruler Mars

Again these seem less applicable.

The student is referred to introductory remarks in Chapter 7 and fuller discussion in Chapter 16.

Part 7.—*COMMENT ON ACCURACY OF ANALYSIS*

Students will be interested to know how much truth there was in this reading.

On discussion, details seemed very accurate. John's versatility and energy in 5th house matters, liking for scientific study and out of the ordinary pursuits, children and clubs, have already led him to such a varied list of spare-time activities as Judo for his main choice, collection of semi-precious stones and their scientific study as his second, pleasure in all scientific things, study of children from the psychological view-point with strong ideas as to the future bringing up of his own.

He plays football and tennis, dances and bicycles, plays several musical instruments and likes going to concerts, runs a youth club and is a scoutmaster. He likes his home and will help his mother if asked, but it is not in his character to apply himself readily to household tasks.

Part 8.—*POSSIBLE ADDITIONS TO INFORMATION GIVEN*

Description of Appearance

Older text-books are full of precise descriptions for each sign, and so on, and if astrology is non-consultative, it is understandable that the old-time astrologer might try to score a hit by describing the " native " of the nativity which he cast.

While it is easy to work backwards and to track the astrological significator for observed physical traits, it is almost impossible to know *which* significator any person may show above any other.

John has the pleasant open face and ready smile of his Libran Ascendant and the lithe, active movements of his Geminian Sun. His colouring is the fresh, good complexion of the strong Mars. Saturn at the Ascendant nearly always darkens, but not so in this case.

In a recent test of 44 people (not a sufficiently large number for real statistical work), their appearance was voted on by about 100 others well versed in astrology.

17 looked more like their ascending sign.
13 looked more like their Sun sign.
9 looked more like the sign containing their Asc.-ruler.
5 looked more like the sign containing their Moon.

This shows that, while the truth of astrological correlation can be definitely seen, truth is NOT served by hazarding a guess at which part of the map will be reflected in appearance.

Jewels, Colours, Numbers

While a case can be made for the correlation of these to the different signs, the inclusion of the possible reference to one and the other does not seem a necessary part of a modern analysis, which is more concerned with the psychology of the person and the discernable future trends in the life. Tradition is *very often* correct but not always. In the case of our example, John as a small child (Moon period, ☽ ☌ ♂) loved red, but now he likes the harmonious rose and blue of the average Libran.

Description of Father or Mother and Profession from M.C.

Parents seem different to each child and they are so frequently *not* as the M.C. or I.C. that it is better not to rely on this traditional idea.

It happens that John's father was a jeweller and this is mostly aptly signified by Leo on M.C. But, it must be remarked that everyone with the last decanate of

Libra and the first decanate of Scorpio rising (in latitudes near to the one used), will have Leo on the M.C. so it seems that " it happens " is the operative part of the last sentence !

Profession in relation to 10th house is discussed under that heading in Chapter 5. Research work is now in progress on the relative meanings of the cusp of 10th house in the Equal House system and of the M.C. which always forms the cusp of the 10th house in the Quadrant systems. It is too early to indicate any results yet, but it is likely that this may show that the sign of the M.C. (the degree of which is always inserted in Equal House charts) may indicate the more conscious and deliberate mode of self-expression in the outer world, while the 10th house cusp by Equal House may show the " born," the instinctive, or innate mode of such self-expression. In this example, John is a born educator in a Cancerian way of wishing to bring up and care for the young, while his conscious and more developed ambition is to gather experience so that he may take a position requiring more organising ability (Leo) when older.*

The Giving of Advice

While hints may be given as to the best traits to encourage and the wisdom of toning down others, it is no part of an astrologer's work to give advice to the person whose chart he is doing, *unless he has been asked* so to do. This comes back to the remark made earlier that, when a member of the public makes his request in the phrase which he thinks is correct, " Will you do my horoscope," the answer should be a kindly expressed " Why? " He may have problems on which he is longing for advice, or he may be expecting a straightforward analysis and may even resent advice. The matter should be arranged clearly before the work is begun.

Astrology was the first expression of psychology as we know it now, and by the study of human nature with its aid and the addition of commonsense, anyone with some experience of life can help and advise others, but a student proposing to do this would be better equipped to do so and would have a more up-to-date vocabulary if he made a study of modern analytical psychology also (see Chapter 18).

* Fuller discussion in Chapter 13, *Applied Astrology*, by the same author. L. N. Fowler & Co. Ltd., 1954.

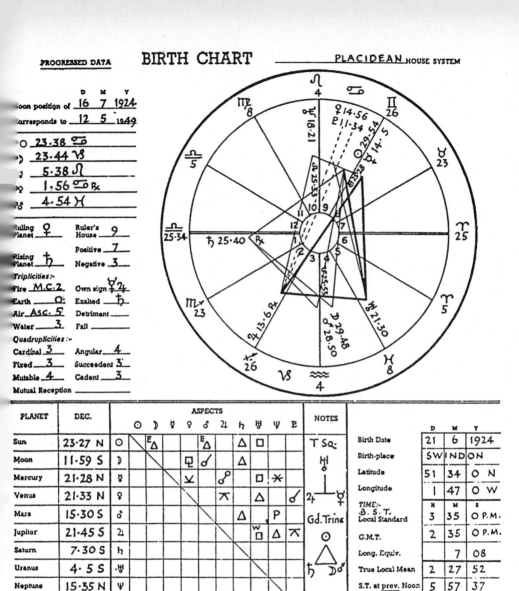

BIRTH CHART

PLACIDEAN HOUSE SYSTEM

PROGRESSED DATA	D	M	Y
Moon position of	16	7	1924
Corresponds to	12	5	1949

☉ 23.38 ♋
☽ 23.44 ♑
? 5.38 ♌
☿ 1.56 ♋ ℞
? 4.54 ♓

Ruling Planet ♀   Ruler's House 9
Rising Planet ♄   Positive 7   Negative 3

Triplicities:-
Fire M.C.2   Own sign ☿ 2↓
Earth 0   Exalted ♄
Air Asc. 5   Detriment
Water 3   Fall

Quadruplicities:-
Cardinal 3   Angular 4
Fixed 3   Succeedent 3
Mutable 4   Cadent 3

Mutual Reception

PLANET	DEC.	ASPECTS ☉ ☽ ☿ ♀ ♂ ♃ ♄ ♅ ♆ ♇	NOTES
Sun	23·27 N	☉ / E△ · · E△ · △ □ ·	T Sq.
Moon	11·59 S	☽ · · ⊡ ☌ · △ · ·	♅
Mercury	21·28 N	☿ · ⋎ · ⚹ · · □ ⚹ ·	
Venus	21·33 N	♀ · · · ⊼ · △ · · ☌	2↓ — ☿
Mars	15·30 S	♂ · · · · △ · P ·	Gd. Trine
Jupiter	21·45 S	♃ · · · · · □ △ ⊼	☉
Saturn	7·30 S	♄ · · · · · · · ·	△
Uranus	4·5 S	♅ · · · · · · · ·	♄ ☌ ♂
Neptune	15·35 N	♆ · · · · · · · ·	
Pluto	20·43 N	♇ · · · · · · · ·	
Asc.		Asc. △ △ · · ☌ ·	
M.C.		M.C. · · · · □ ·	

	D	M	Y
Birth Date	21	6	1924
Birth-place	SWINDON		
Latitude	51	34	0 N
Longitude	1	47	0 W

TIME:-	H	M	S
B. S. T. Local Standard	3	35	0 P.M.
G.M.T.	2	35	0 P.M.
Long. Equiv.		7	08
True Local Mean	2	27	52
S.T. at prev. Noon	5	57	37
S.T. Correction			25
S.T. at Birth	8	25	54

NAME. "John Smith"   No. 364

Designed by M.E.HONE.

TEN YEAR SHEET*

(Explanation on page 241)

(Interpretation on page 252)

1947

⊙ △ ♅ r and p   ☽ ♐

⊙ P ☿

1948

⊙ P ♃   ☽ ♑

☿ ♂ M.C.

1949

⊙ ☍ ☽ p

☿ ⊼ ♂ p   ☽ ♑ and 4th   See Chart No. 3

☿ ⧠ ♅ p   New moon affects life
                 Oct. Nov. Dec. Jan.

♆ ⧠ ♃ by O–D

1950

                                        T ♃ ☌ ♂ ☽   Spring
                                                           Autumn

Asc. ⌵ ♃   ☽ ♒   (Affects all Grand Trine)

                                        T ♂ ☌ ♂ ☽   April
                                                           October

---

1951

⊙ ⧠ ♄ r and p   T ♅ ☌ ♇, ♀   Summer

  ⧠ Asc.   ☽ ♒ and 5th

  ⧠ ♃   T ♂ ☌ ⊙   July

Asc. ⊼ ☿

1952

Asc. △ ♀   T ♅ ☌ ♇ ♀   Spring
                                                          Summer

                 ☽ ♓   T ♂ ☌ ♄ Asc.   January

☿ △ ♃ p   T ♄ ☌ ♄ Asc.   Winter

                                       T ♂ ☌ ♂ ☽   December

1953

                                       T ♄ ☌ ♄ Asc.   Spring
                                                          Autumn

☿ △ ♃ r and p   ☽ ♓   T ♃ ☌ ☿   Summer

☿ ⚹ ☿ r   T ♆ ☌ ♄, Asc.   Winter

                                       T ♂ ☌ ⊙   June

                                       T ♂ ☌ ♄ Asc.   December

---

* The planet (or Asc. or M.C.) written first in each entry on this sheet is understood to be that which
is progressed, so it is not necessary to follow it by "p" each time.

54
△ ♀   ☽ ♈ and 6th   T ♆ ☌ ♄ Asc.   Winter
     Autumn
       T ♃ ☌ ☉, ♀   Summer
       T ♂ ☌ ♂ ☽

955
☽ △ ☽   ☽ ♈   T ♃ ☌ M.C.   Summer
       ☌ ♆   Autumn
       T ♆ ☌ ♄ Asc.   Summer
       T ♂ ☌ ☉   May
       T ♂ ☌ ♄ Asc.   November

956
☽ enters ♌
♀ (ruler) Sta. Dir.   ☽ ♈- ☿ and 7th   T ♅ ☌ M.C.   Autumn
☿ ☌ ♆   T ♂ ☌ ♂   July

957
☉ ⋁ ♀ p   ☽ ♉   T ♅ ☌ M.C.   Summer
☿ ☌ ♆ p   T ♄ ☌ ♃   Spring
       T ♃ ☌ ♄ Asc.   Winter
       T ♂ ☌ ☉   May

1958
Asc. □ ♆   ☽ ♉ and 8th   T ♃ ☌ ♄ Asc.   Spring
       Summer
       T ♂ ☌ ♂ ☽   Spring
       ☌ ☉   Winter

NOTE.—Transits of Mars are important in this chart, since it strongly aspects ☽, ☉, ♄ in the Grand Trine. For this reason these recurrent transits are noted.

CHART FOR PROGRESSIONS AND TRANSITS

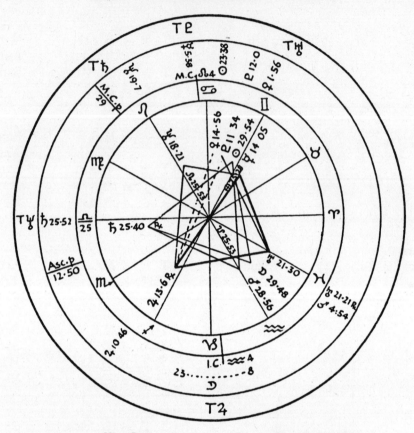

	Noon Date						
		D.	**M.**	**Y.**
Noon Positions on		16	7	1924
Correspond to		12	5	1949

House System ___EQUAL___

NAME ___John Smith___

No. ___364___

Data for Prog. Asc. and M.C.

BY DIRECT METHOD

	H.	M.	S.	
Sid. time noon G M T. (Prog.)	7	36	11	AGE
Interval *TO/FROM noon p.m. *	2	35	00	25
Result	10	11	11	
Acceleration on interval p.m. *			26	
Sid. time at Greenwich	10	11	37	D. M. Y.
Longitude equivalent *E/ W—		7	08	21·6·49
LOCAL SID. TIME	10	4	29	
Subtract 24 hrs. if necessary —				

* Delete whichever is not required

No. 3 - The "PROGRESSIONS" Chart. DIRECT METHOD

Designed by M.E. HONE.

SECONDARY, RADIX, OR "O.D.", AS REQUIRED. ASPECTS AND PARALLELS

NATAL PLANETS NUMERICAL ORDER	SOLAR		MUTUAL		Current O-D's
	⊙ P ☿ 1947	♀ Ruler	♂ Sta. ℞ 1957		Current O-D's
	△ ♄ r&p 1947	Sta. Dir. 1956			
M.C. 4.0	P ♃ 48				♆ +25°= □ ♃ 1949
♇ 11.34	☍ ☽p 49	☿ Sun Ruler	♃-♄-♅-♆-♇		
♃ 15.06℞	□ ♄ r&p 51	♂ M.C. 1948	No aspects		
☿ 14.05	□ Asc. 51	⊼ ♂ 49			
♀ 14.56	℞ ♃ 51	⊼ ♅p 49	Asc. p		
♆ 18.21	⊼ ♂ 54	△ ♃p 52	⊻ ♃ 1950		
♅ 21.30	⊼ ☽ 55	△ ♃r 53	⊼ ☿ 51		
Asc. 25.34	⊻ ⊙r 55	✶ ♃ 53	△ ♀ 52		
♄ 25.40℞	⊻ ♀p 57	☌ ♆r 56	□ ♆ 58		
♂ 28.56		☌ ♆p 57			
☽ 29.48	⊙ enters ♌ 56				
⊙ 29.54					

Date 12 Month	Moon's Long.	LUNAR ASPECTS To Natal	To Prog.	♇	♆	♅	♄	♃	♂	NOTES
1949 MAY	♑ 23.44		☍ ⊙	1 ✶ ♃	22 △ ♂	27 ✶ ⊙ / ☍ ☽ D				
JUN.	24.57	□ ♄ Asc.			8 ☌ ⊙ / △ ☽			28 ⊼ ⊙ / ⊻ ☽ ♂	30 ☌ ♅	
JUL.	26.10								22 ☌ ⊙ / △ ☽ ♂	NEW MOONS
AUG.	27.24			14 ✶ ♃					9 ☌ ♇ / 15 ☌ ♀	24 ✶ ⊙ ☍ ☌ ♂ D
SEP.	28.37	⊻ ♂			16 △ ☿		30 □ ♃	19 Near Sta. ✶ ♅		22 □ ⊙ ⊼ ☌ ♂ D
OCT.	29.51	⊼ ⊙			11 □ ♀		9 □ ☿ / 17 ✶ ♀		7 ☌ ♆	21 △ ⊙ △ ☌ ♂ D
NOV.	♒ 1.4			27 Sta ℞ / ☌ ♅				⊻ ☽ ♂		20 ⊼ ⊙ □ ☌ ♂ D
DEC.	2.17							20 ☍ M.C.		19 ☍ ⊙ ✶ ☌ ♂ D
1950 JAN.	3.30									18 ⊼ ⊙ ⊻ ☌ ♂ D
FEB.	4.44		⊻ ♂					2 △ ☿ / 5 ⊼ ♀		16 △ ⊙ ☌ ☌ ♂ D
MAR.	5.57						21 ✶ ♀	24 △ ♄		18 □ ⊙ ⊻ ☌ ♂ D
APR.	7.10						20 □ ☿	9-14 ☍ ☌ ☽ / △ ⊙		17 ✶ ⊙ ✶ ☌ ♂ D

CHAPTER 12

PROGRESSIONS

Note.—Both astrologers and clients are apt to use this word to cover all calculations from which trends in a life for any specified time may be judged.

To " do the progressions " implies that all such trends are ascertained by the use of whatever methods are customary, as described below, and by the scrutiny of transits.

It should be understood that, strictly speaking, the phrase applies only to the movement of the planets in their cycles, by which the potentialities shown in the birth-chart may be expected to develop.

The transits (see p. 238) stimulate these, often acting as minute hands to indicate the time when their effects may be noticeable in a life.

Part 1

THEORY AND METHOD

" A Day for a Year "
The Secondary System.
The Primary System.
Use of the separate " progressed horoscope."
Use of the No. 3 " Progressions " chart.
Calculations for Progression :—
    (a)   To find date in Ephemeris for use in progression.
    (b)   To find noon date.
Charting with the " Progressions " chart.
    (a)   Insertion of progressed planets.
    (b)   Insertion of Asc. and M.C.
Charting with separate " progressed horoscope."
Natal planets in numerical order.
Method of preparation for judgment.
1. Examination of double wheel for :—
    (a)   Aspects by planets, M.C. and Asc.
    (b)   Change of sign or house by planets, M.C. and Asc.
    (c)   Parallels between planets.
2. Examination of current Ephemeris for transits.
3. Various other methods of prognostication.
Recognition of classes of aspects and the duration of their effects.
Solar aspects.
Lunar aspects.
Mutual aspects.
Aspects by Asc. and M.C.
Need for caution in assessing strength of aspects.
Way of writing progressions and transits.
Scope of work.

Part 2

APPLICATION TO EXAMPLE CHART
Listing of Factors

Listing of solar aspects.
Listing of mutual aspects.
Listing of aspects by Asc. and M.C.
Reckoning of lunar aspects.
Listing of lunar aspects.
Converse aspects.
Aspects of transits.
Listing of transits.
Other methods of prognostication.
　(*a*)　The " One-degree " method.
　(*b*)　The Radix method.
　(*c*)　New Moons and eclipses.
Eclipse of the Sun.
Eclipse of the Moon.
Annular eclipse.
" How particular must I be with aspects ? "
Listing for examination of several years.

Part 3

General discussion on interpretation of progressions.

Part 4

(*a*)　Example of progressions with explanation.
(*b*)　Examination of conditions for any special day.
(*c*)　Examination of astrological indications for any year in the light of a
　　　known event.

Part I.—*THEORY AND METHOD*

" A Day for a Year "

This is the phrase generally used in reference to the way in which astrological
progressions are worked. It is the basis of the working of " directions " or " progressions " by what is known as *the Secondary System*.

No scientist has yet explained how it is that the life of every human being on
this earth is geared to its two cyclic movements, which are its daily rotation on its
own central axis and its yearly revolution round the central point of the Solar-System,
the Sun itself. Astrologers know this to be a fact but they cannot explain it.

The Secondary System

This is the system of progression in customary use. It correlates with the orbital
movements of the planets, one day's movement after birth corresponding to one

year's development of growing life. The name is given to differentiate it from the Primary System.

The Primary System

This correlates with the rotationary movement of the earth itself, the passage of 1° of right ascension over the meridian being equal to one year of life. This system involves much work and is therefore rarely used by modern astrologers. Special books* on it can be studied. For general purposes, it is only necessary that the student should know of it and be able to state its basis.

Its accuracy depends on two undependable factors. These factors are the almost invariably unknown *precise* moment of birth (an error of four minutes throwing out directions as much as a year), and the complete impossibility of deciding on the validity of the degrees on the intermediate house cusps by any of the various quadrant house systems.

Use of the Separate " Progressed Horoscope "

This has been a most popular method of using the Secondary system. It involves the re-calculation of the whole birth chart for the same time and place as before, but with the use of the planetary positions as given in the Ephemeris for whichever day is as many days ahead of the original birthday, as the number of years lived by the person up to the time of the re-calculation.

The chart is erected in the usual way and a comparison is made between the positions of the planets, in the degrees to which they have arrived and those of the planets in the birth chart. Judgment is made from the angular relationships (aspects) so formed. This separate chart is of value to the users of the Placidean or Campanian or Regiomontanian House Systems, or that of Porphyry, which some astrologers use. Each avers that the actual degrees on the intermediate house cusps, which vary with each system, are important, and assist in accuracy in prognostication. As all cannot be right, *and as it is becoming rare for the separate progressed chart to be used by modern astrologers, the method will NOT be shown* for the example chart but will be explained for any who wish to try it.

Use of No. 3 The " Progressions " Chart†

When the average astrologer wishes to take a quick look at a chart, in order to get an idea of the development of a person's planetary pattern in any one year, he decides which day in the Ephemeris of the birth year corresponds to the year he wishes to assess. He then jots down the noon positions of that day, round the edge of the natal chart, approximately near the ecliptical degrees at which they have arrived by their cyclic movement. In this way, he can judge from the aspects he observes.

In actual practice, he needs more precision and more space to record other factors. Hence the natal chart is copied on to the central part of *No. 3 The " Progressions " Chart, but without precise ecliptical places*. These are already recorded on the natal chart. *The " Progressions " Chart is designed to suit users of both " Ecliptic " and " Houses " charts, and for easy recording of factors.*

* *Key to Primary Horoscope Progressed*, by O. H. W. Owen.
† No. 3 *The Progressions Chart.* See page 315.

CALCULATIONS FOR PROGRESSIONS

The example chart will again be used and the year for required progressions will be 1949 (see reference pages from Ephemeris pp. 230–231.

(a) To Find Date in Ephemeris for Use for Progression)

	D.	M.	Y.
Birth date	21	6	1924
Age on birthday in 1949 (add as days)	25		
By addition	46	6	1924

Since the month of June contains 30 days, the required day is July 16, 1924.

(b) To Find Noon Date (also Called Adjusted Calculation Date)*

The positions in the Ephemeris are given for noon each 24 hours. Thus, if each year of growing life corresponds to each of these 24-hour periods, it is necessary to know to which *day* of each year the noon planetary positions will always apply. *Once this is done, the necessity for laborious re-calculation of the planetary places for each year of progression is completely avoided.*

Thus :—24 hours (of babyhood) = 12 months (of subsequent life)
6 hours = 3 months
2 hours = 1 month
1 hour = 0 month 15 days (about)
½ hour = 0 month 7½ days (about)
5 minutes = 0 month 1¼ days (about)

Birth hour was 2.35 p.m. (G.M.T.), i.e., 2 hours 35 minutes *past* noon. Use *time and date* as previously converted to G.M.T. By reference to table :—

2 hours = 1 month
30 minutes = 0 month 7½ days (about)
5 minutes = 0 month 1¼ days (about)

2 hours 35 minutes = 1 month 9 days (about)

The time must be *added* for an a.m. birth (and if this cannot readily be remembered at first, before its reason has been seen, it is simple to remember that both begin with " a ").

It is *subtracted* for a p.m. birth.
Hence :—

Birth date	June 21	
Subtract	1m	9d
Perpetual noon date =	May	12

* The student must understand this calculation but, in actual work, noon-date can be found by reference to Tables. See p. 315 "Reference card for finding noon-date."

To be precise, on May 12, 1924, the child was not yet born, so his age, in terms of the correspondence of the day to the year, was minus 1 month 9 days. A year later, his age on May 12 was 10 months 21 days or " nearly a year old," or " it was the year of his 1st birthday."

Since the life is now to be examined in relation to the year of the 25th birthday and since it may be examined again in future years, May 12 should be written beside the birthdate in the Ephemeris, and May 12, 1949, beside July 16. In the further margin the age, 25, should be written, and the planetary positions for the day underlined across both pages, since these are rarely level in printing and this frequently causes mistakes. If the life is to be examined in relation to many events in the intervening period, corresponding years and ages can be written at 10-year intervals from which counting is easy (see pp. 230–233).

To be entered on form :—

Noon Date

	D.	M.	Y.
Noon positions of	16	7	1924
Correspond to	12	5	1949

CHARTING WITH THE " PROGRESSIONS " CHART

(a) Insertion of Progressed Planets

Planetary positions as given for noon, on July 16, are now inserted in the second circle (preferably in contrasting ink) proportionately as they come in the ecliptic. (See example *facing* p. 223.) It will be noticed that, as always, Venus and Mercury continue their cycles not far distant from the Sun ; Mars has made some progress ; Jupiter, which is still retrograde, appears behind its natal degree, while the remaining four planets have hardly changed their positions. The most swiftly moving is the Moon. Its progressed position a year later is given for noon the next day in the Ephemeris. It is therefore better to indicate its passage by inserting both degrees as shown in example chart.

(b) Insertion of Progressed Asc. and M.C.

The calculation of the necessary LOCAL SIDEREAL TIME is made by the Direct Method* as for the natal chart.

The process is as before *except that the Local Sidereal Time for noon of the day now being used for progressions must be inserted instead of that for the natal day.*

The time interval TO or FROM noon G.M.T. and the acceleration on that interval must be added or subtracted as before.

The longitude equivalent must then be added if the place is east of Greenwich and subtracted if west, as before. Table of Houses for given latitude must be consulted for progressed Asc. and M.C. which should be inserted in the same circle as the progressed planets.

* See page 115.

12   **JUNE, 1924.**   **[RAPHAEL'S**

D M	Neptune Lat.	Neptune Dec.	Herschel Lat.	Herschel Dec.	Saturn Lat.	Saturn Dec.	Jupiter Lat.	Jupiter Dec.	Mars Lat.	Mars Declin.	Mars Declin.
1	0N16	15N44	0S46	4S10	2N40	7S38	0N41	21S59	2S49	17S20	17S14
3	0 16	15 43	0 46	4 9	2 40	7 37	0 41	21 58	2 55	17 7	17 1
5	0 16	15 42	0 46	4 8	2 39	7 35	0 41	21 57	3 1	16 55	16 49
7	0 16	15 41	0 46	4 8	2 39	7 34	0 41	21 55	3 7	16 43	16 37
9	0 16	15 41	0 46	4 7	2 39	7 33	0 40	21 54	3 13	16 31	16 25
11	0 16	15 40	0 46	4 7	2 38	7 32	0 40	21 52	3 20	16 20	16 14
13	0 16	15 39	0 46	4 6	2 38	7 32	0 40	21 51	3 26	16 9	16 4
15	0 16	15 38	0 46	4 6	2 37	7 31	0 39	21 49	3 33	15 59	15 53
17	0 16	15 37	0 46	4 5	2 37	7 31	0 39	21 48	3 40	15 49	15 44
19	0 16	15 36	0 46	4 5	2 36	7 31	0 39	21 46	3 47	15 39	15 35
21	0 16	15 35	0 47	4 5	2 36	7 30	0 38	21 45	3 54	15 30	15 26
23	0 16	15 34	0 47	4 5	2 35	7 30	0 38	21 43	4 1	15 22	15 18
25	0 16	15 33	0 47	4 5	2 35	7 31	0 38	21 42	4 8	15 15	15 11
27	0 16	15 32	0 47	4 5	2 34	7 31	0 37	21 41	4 15	15 8	15 5
29	0 16	15 31	0 47	4 5	2 33	7 31	0 37	21 39	4 23	15 2	
30	0 16	15 30	0 47	4 5	2 33	7 32	0 37	21 39	4 26	15 0	

D M	D W	Sidereal Time H.M.S.	☉ Long.	☉ Dec.	☽ Long.	☽ Lat.	☽ Dec.	MIDNIGHT ☽ Long.	☽ Dec.
1	S	4 38 46	10♊41 22	22N 3	28♉37 9	5S 0	14N58	4♊33 6	16N11
2	M	4 42 42	11 38 51	22 11	10♊28 55	4 51	17 13	16 24 47	18 5
3	Tu	4 46 39	12 36 19	22 19	22 20 52	4 29	18 45	28 17 22	19 12
4	W	4 50 36	13 33 46	22 26	4♋14 29	3 56	19 27	10♋12 28	19 29
5	Th	4 54 32	14 31 13	22 33	16 11 33	3 12	19 18	22 12 4	18 53
6	F	4 58 29	15 28 38	22 39	28 14 21	2 18	18 16	4♌18 46	17 25
7	S	5 2 25	16 26 2	22 45	10♌25 45	1 18	16 23	16 35 45	15 8
8	S	5 6 22	17 23 25	22 51	22 49 16	0 13	13 42	29 6 47	12 6
9	M	5 10 18	18 20 47	22 56	5♍28 52	0N54	10 21	11♍56 0	8 26
10	Tu	5 14 15	19 18 8	23 1	18 28 43	2 0	6 24	25 7 28	4 16
11	W	5 18 11	20 15 28	23 5	1♎52 39	3 2	2 2	8♎44 34	0S15
12	Th	5 22 8	21 12 47	23 9	15 43 25	3 55	2S34	22 49 12	4 54
13	F	5 26 5	22 10 5	23 13	0♏ 1 46	4 36	7 11	7♏20 45	9 24
14	S	5 30 1	23 7 23	23 16	14 45 35	4 59	11 30	22 15 27	13 27
15	S	5 33 58	24 4 39	23 19	29 49 22	5 3	15 11	7♐26 7	16 40
16	M	5 37 54	25 1 54	23 21	15♐ 4 24	4 45	17 53	22 42 48	18 46
17	Tu	5 41 51	25 59 9	23 23	0♑19 56	4 8	19 19	7♑54 28	19 31
18	W	5 45 47	26 56 24	23 25	15 25 7	3 13	19 22	22 50 52	18 52
19	Th	5 49 44	27 53 38	23 26	0♒10 48	2 6	18 4	7♒24 17	16 59
20	F	5 53 40	28 50 52	23 27	14 30 52	0 53	15 38	21 30 20	14 6
21	S	5 57 37	29 48 5	23 27	28 22 38	0S21	12 22	5✶ 7 53	10 31
22	S	6 1 34	0♋45 19	23 27	11♓46 21	1 32	8 34	18 18 25	6 32
23	M	6 5 30	1 42 32	23 26	24 44 32	2 35	4 28	1♈ 5 13	2 23
24	Tu	6 9 27	2 39 45	23 25	7♈21 0	3 30	0 18	13 32 30	1N46
25	W	6 13 23	3 36 58	23 24	19 40 12	4 13	3N48	25 44 44	5 46
26	Th	6 17 20	4 34 12	23 22	1♉46 37	4 44	7 39	7♉46 22	9 27
27	F	6 21 16	5 31 25	23 20	13 44 29	5 2	11 10	19 41 23	12 45
28	S	6 25 13	6 28 38	23 17	25 37 30	5 7	14 12	1♊33 10	15 30
29	S	6 29 10	7 25 51	23 14	7♊28 46	4 59	16 39	13 24 33	17 37
30	M	6 33 6	8 23 4	23 11	19 20 49	4 38	18 24	25 17 47	18 59

Marginal figures added by student (left / right):

• May 12 '24	(row 21)	— 1 M 9 D
,, ,, '25		+ 10 ,, 21 ,,
,, ,, '26		2 yrs.
,, ,, '27		3 ,,
,, ,, '28		4 ,,
,, ,, '29		5 ,,
,, ,, '30		6 ,,
,, ,, '31		7 ,,
,, ,, '32		8 ,,
,, ,, '33		9 ,,

From Raphael's Ephemeris for 1924.

* Underlining and marginal figures as added by student (see p. 227).

EPHEMERIS.]							JUNE, 1924.		13
D	Venus.			Mercury.			☽		
M	Lat.	Declin.		Lat.	Declin.		Node.		
	° ′	° ′	° ′	° ′	° ′	° ′	° ′		
1	2N30	24N56	24N47	3 S42	13N20	13N37	26♌56		
3	2 15	24 38	24 29	3 36	13 55	14 14	26 50		
5	2 0	24 19	24 9	3 27	14 35	14 56	26 44		
7	1 42	24 0	23 50	3 15	15 19	15 43	26 37		
9	1 23	23 40	23 30	3 1	16 8	16 33	26 31		
11	1 2	23 19	23 9	2 45	17 0	17 26	26 25		
13	0 40	22 59	22 48	2 27	17 53	18 21	26 18		
15	0 16	22 38	22 27	2 7	18 48	19 16	26 12		
17	0S 9	22 17	22 6	1 46	19 43	20 10	26 6		
19	0 36	21 55	21 44	1 24	20 37	21 3	25 59		
21	1 3	21 33	21 22	1 1	21 28	21 52	25 53		
23	1 32	21 11	21 0	0 38	22 15	22 36	25 47		
25	2 0	20 49	20 38	0 14	22 56	23 14	25 40		
27	2 28	20 27	20 17	0N 8	23 31	23 44	25 34		
29	2 56	20 6		0 29	23 56		25 27		
30	3 9	19 55		0 39	24 5		25 24		

Mutual Aspects.

1. ⊙ P ♃.
2. ⊙ ⚼ ♄. ☿ □ ♆.
3. ♂ ⊻ ♅.
6. ⊙ ☍ ♃. ☿ ✱ ♅.
8. ⊙ ⊻ ♀. ☿ □ ♂, P ♆. ♀ ± ♂.
9. ⊙ ✱ ♆.
10. ☿ P ♂, ∇ ♄.
12. ⊙ P ♀, □ ♅.
13. ♂ Q ♃, △ ♄.
14. ☿ ∠ ♀, ± ♄.
15. ☿ Q ♅.
17. ⊙ △ ♄. ☿ Q ♆.
19. ⊙ △ ♂. ☿ ⊥ ♀, ⚼ ♄.
20. ♀ P ♃. ♂ P ♆.
21. ☿ ⊻ & P ♀, ☍ ♃.
22. ☿ P ♃. ♀ ⚼ ♂.
23. ☿ ✱ ♆.
25. ⊙ ∠ ♆. ☿ □ ♅.
26. ⊙ P ☿. ♀ ∇ ♃, ⊥ ♆.
27. ☿ △ ♄.
30. ☿ △ ♂.

	D M	♆ Long.	♅ Long.	♄ Long.	♃ Long.	♂ Long.	♀ Long.	☿ Long.	Lunar Aspects. ⊙	♆	♅	♄	♃	♂	♀	☿
		° ′	° ′	° ′	° ′	° ′	° ′	° ′								
	1	17♌54	21♓16	26♎13	15♐36	20♒28	16♋15	16♉53							∠	
	2	17 55	21 17	26℞11	15℞29	20 57	16 32	17 43	☌				☍			
	3	17 56	21 18	26 8	15 21	21 25	16 47	18 37		✱	□	△		△	⊻	⊻
	4	17 58	21 19	26 6	15 13	21 53	17 0	19 35		∠				⚼		∠
	5	17 59	21 20	26 4	15 6	22 20	17 12	20 35	⊻	⊻	△				☌	✱
	6	18 0	21 21	26 2	14 58	22 48	17 21	21 40	∠			□	⚼			
	7	18 1	21 22	25 59	14 51	23 15	17 28	22 47			⚼		△			
	8	18 3	21 23	25 57	14 43	23 41	17 32	23 58	✱	☌		✱		☍	⊻	□
	9	18 4	21 24	25 56	14 35	24 7	17 35	25 12				∠			∠	
	10	18 5	21 25	25 54	14 28	24 33	17℞35	26 29	□	⊻	☍		□		✱	
	11	18 6	21 25	25 52	14 20	24 59	17 32	27 49		∠		⊻				△
	12	18 8	21 26	25 50	14 12	25 24	17 28	29 12	△	✱			✱	⚼	□	⚼
	13	18 9	21 27	25 49	14 5	25 49	17 21	0♊38			⚼	☌	∠	△		
	14	18 11	21 27	25 47	13 57	26 14	17 11	2 7	⚼	□	△		⊻		△	
	15	18 12	21 28	25 46	13 50	26 38	16 59	3 39				⊻		□	⚼	☍
	16	18 14	21 28	25 45	13 43	27 2	16 45	5 14		△	□	∠	☌			
	17	18 15	21 29	25 44	13 35	27 25	16 28	6 52	☍	⚼		✱		✱		
	18	18 17	21 29	25 42	13 28	27 48	16 9	8 33			✱		⊻	∠	☍	
	19	18 18	21 30	25 41	13 21	28 11	15 48	10 17			∠	□	∠	⊻		⚼
	20	18 20	21 30	25 41	13 14	28 33	15 24	12 3	⚼	☍	⊻		✱			△
1924	21	18 21	21 30	25 40	13 7	28 54	14 59	13 53	△			△		☌	⚼	
'25	22	18 23	21 30	25 39	13 0	29 15	14 31	15 45				⚼	□		△	□
'26	23	18 25	21 31	25 39	12 53	29 36	14 2	17 39			☌			⊻		
'27	24	18 26	21 31	25 38	12 46	29 56	13 31	19 37	□	⚼			△		□	
'28	25	18 28	21 31	25 38	12 39	0♓16	12 58	21 36		△	⊻	☍		∠		✱
'29	26	18 30	21℞31	25 37	12 32	0 35	12 24	23 38	✱		∠		⚼	✱		
'30	27	18 31	21 31	25 37	12 26	0 54	11 49	25 41		□					✱	∠
'31	28	18 33	21 31	25 37	12 19	1 12	11 13	27 47	∠		✱			□	∠	⊻
'32	29	18 35	21 31	25D37	12 13	1 30	10 36	29 54	⊻			⚼	☍		⊻	
'33	30	18 37	21 30	25 37	12 7	1 47	9 59	2♋ 2		✱	□					

From Raphael's Ephemeris for 1924.

14   **JULY, 1924.**   [*RAPHAEL'S*

D M	Neptune Lat.	Dec.	Herschel Lat.	Dec.	Saturn Lat.	Dec.	Jupiter Lat.	Dec.	Mars Lat.	Declin.	
1	0N16	15N30	0S47	4S 5	2N33	7 S32	0N37	21 S38	4 S30	14 S57	14S55
3	0 16	15 29	0 47	4 6	2 32	7 33	0 36	21 37	4 38	14 53	14 51
5	0 16	15 28	0 47	4 6	2 32	7 34	0 36	21 36	4 46	14 49	14 48
7	0 16	15 27	0 47	4 6	2 31	7 35	0 35	21 35	4 53	14 47	14 46
9	0 16	15 25	0 47	4 7	2 31	7 36	0 35	21 34	5 1	14 45	14 45
11	0 16	15 24	0 47	4 8	2 30	7 37	0 35	21 33	5 9	14 45	14 45
13	0 16	15 23	0 47	4 8	2 30	7 39	0 34	21 32	5 16	14 45	14 46
15	0 16	15 22	0 47	4 9	2 29	7 40	0 34	21 31	5 24	14 47	14 48
17	0 16	15 20	0 47	4 10	2 29	7 42	0 34	21 30	5 31	14 49	14 51
19	0 16	15 19	0 48	4 11	2 28	7 44	0 33	21 30	5 39	14 52	14 55
21	0 16	15 18	0 48	4 12	2 28	7 46	0 33	21 29	5 46	14 57	14 59
23	0 16	15 17	0 48	4 13	2 27	7 48	0 32	21 29	5 53	15 2	15 5
25	0 16	15 15	0 48	4 14	2 27	7 50	0 32	21 28	6 0	15 9	15 12
27	0 16	15 14	0 48	4 15	2 26	7 53	0 32	21 28	6 7	15 16	15 22
29	0 16	15 13	0 48	4 16	2 26	7 55	0 31	21 28	6 13	15 24	15 29
31	0 16	15 11	0 48	4 17	2 25	7 58	0 31	21 28	6 19	15 33	

D M	D W	Sidereal Time H. M. S.	☉ Long.	☉ Dec.	☽ Long.	☽ Lat.	☽ Dec.	MIDNIGHT ☽ Long.	☽ Dec.	
1	Tu	6 37 3	9♋20 18	23N 7	1♏15 41	4S 4	19N22	7♋14 42	19N32	10 yrs.
2	W	6 40 59	10 17 31	23 3	13 15 2	3 20	19 28	19 16 53	19 11	
3	Th	6 44 56	11 14 44	22 58	25 20 26	2 26	18 41	1♌25 53	17 57	
4	F	6 48 52	12 11 57	22 53	7♐33 27	1 25	17 1	13 43 23	15 52	
5	S	6 52 49	13 9 10	22 48	19 55 56	0 19	14 32	26 11 23	13 1	
6	☉	6 56 45	14 6 22	22 42	2♑30 2	0N49	11 21	8♍52 13	9 32	
7	M	7 0 42	15 3 35	22 36	15 18 16	1 56	7 35	21 48 33	5 3½	
8	Tu	7 4 39	16 0 47	22 29	28 23 21	2 59	3 22	5♎ 3 2	1 10	
9	W	7 8 35	16 58 0	22 22	11♒47 51	3 53	1S 5	18 38 1	3S21	
10	Th	7 12 32	17 55 12	22 15	25 33 41	4 36	5 36	2♏34 52	7 48	
11	F	7 16 28	18 52 24	22 7	9♓41 31	5 3	9 56	16 53 22	11 56	20 yrs.
12	S	7 20 25	19 49 36	21 59	24 10 55	5 12	13 47	1♈ 31	15 26	
13	☉	7 24 21	20 46 48	21 50	8♈55 41	5 1	16 51	16 23	17 59	
14	M	7 28 18	21 44 1	21 42	23 52 10	4 29	18 50	1♉22	19 20	
15	Tu	7 32 14	22 41 13	21 32	8♉51 28	3 39	19 31	16 19 24	19 20	
16	W	7 36 11	23 38 26	21 23	23 44 45	2 44	18 50	1♊18	0	25 yrs.
17	Th	7 40 8	24 35 39	21 13	8♒23 48	1 20	16 53	15 35 53	15 31	
18	F	7 44 4	25 32 52	21 -2	22 42 12	0 2	13 55	29 42 19	12 8	
19	S	7 48 1	26 30 7	20 52	6♋36 1	1S13	10 14	13 ✕ 22	8 12	
20	☉	7 51 57	27 27 21	20 41	20 3 57	2 23	6 7	26 38 26	4 0	
21	M	7 55 54	28 24 37	20 29	3♈ 6 56	3 22	1 51	9♈29 51	0N16	
22	Tu	7 59 50	29 21 54	20 17	15 47 37	4 10	2N22	22 0 45	4 24	
23	W	8 3 47	0♌19 11	20 5	28 9 46	4 45	6 23	4♉15 14	8 16	
24	Th	8 7 43	1 16 29	19 53	10♉17 43	5 7	10 3	16 17 46	11 43	
25	F	8 11 40	2 13 48	19 40	22 15 59	5 15	13 16	28 12 52	14 40	
26	S	8 15 37	3 11 8	19 27	4♉ 8 58	5 9	15 50	10♊11 44	17 0	
27	☉	8 19 33	4 8 29	19 14	16 0 43	4 50	17 54	21 57 15	18 37	
28	M	8 23 30	5 5 51	19 0	27 54 46	4 19	19 7	3♋53 38	19 25	
29	Tu	8 27 26	6 3 14	18 46	9♋54 8	3 36	19 29	15 56 35	19 21	
30	W	8 31 23	7 0 38	18 32	22 1 14	2 43	18 58	28 8 16	18 22	
31	Th	8 35 19	7 58 3	18 17	4♌17 54	1 41	17 33	10♌30 17	16 31	

Left-margin figures (added by student):
May 12, '34 (row 1); May 12, '44 (row 11); ,, ,, '45; ,, ,, '46; ,, ,, '47; ,, ,, '48; May 12, '49 (row 16); ,, ,, '50; ,, ,, '51; ,, ,, '52; ,, ,, '53; ,, ,, '54; ,, ,, '55; ,, ,, '56; ,, ,, '57; ,, ,, '58; ,, ,, '59; ,, 1960 (row 27).

From Raphael's Ephemeris for 1924.

* Underlining and marginal figures as added by student (see p. 227).

EPHEMERIS.]	JULY, 1924.							15
D	Venus.			Mercury.			☽	
M	Lat.	Declin.		Lat.	Declin.		Node.	
	° ′	° ′	° ′	° ′	° ′	° ′	° ′	
1	3 S23	19N45	19N34	0N49	24N12	24N15	25♌21	
3	3 48	19 24	19 15	1 6	24 16	24 14	25 15	
5	4 11	19 5	18 56	1 21	24 10	24 2	25 8	
7	4 32	18 47	18 39	1 32	23 52	23 39	25 2	
9	4 51	18· 31	18 24	1 41	23 24	23 6	24 56	
11	5 7	18 17	18 10	1 47	22 46	22 24	24 49	
13	5 21	18 4	17 59	1 49	22 0	21 34	24 43	
15	5 32	17 54	17 49	1 49	21 7	20 38	24 37	
17	5 41	17 45	17 42	1 47	20 7	19 35	24 30	
19	5 47	17 39	17 37	1 42	19 2	18 28	24 24	
21	5 51	17 35	17 34	1 34	17 53	17 17	24 18	
23	5 54	17 33	17 82	1 25	16 40	16 3	24 11	
25	5 54	17 32	17 33	1 14	15 25	14 47	24 5	
27	5 53	17 33	17 34	1 1	14 9	13 30	23 59	
29	5 51	17 36	17 37	0 47	12 51	12 12	23 52	
31	5 47	17 39		0 31	11 32		23 46	

Mutual Aspects.

1. ☉☌♀.
3. ☿☌♀.
4. ☉▽♃. ☿▽♃.
5. ☉☌☿, ⊥♆.
7. ☿±♃.
8. ☿⚼♂.
9. ☉±♃. ☿△♅.
10. ♀△♂.
11. ☉⚼♂, ⊻♆. ☿⚼♃, □♄.
12. ☿±♂. [♀∠♆.
14. ☉P☿, △♅. ☿⊻♀, P♃.
15. ☉P♃. ♃∠♄.
16. ☿▽♂, ⚼♅.
17. ☿⊥♀.
18. ☉⚼♃, □♄.
19. ☿△♃.
21. ☿Q♄, ±♅.
22. ☉±♂. ☿∠ & P♀.
24. ☉⊻♀. ☿☌♆.
25. ☿P♂, ▽♅, P♆.
27. ♂P♆.
28. ☉▽♂. ☿✱♄.
29. ☉⚼♅.

	D	♆	♅	♄	♃	♂	♀	☿	Lunar Aspects.								
	M	Long.	Long.	Long.	Long.	Long.	Long.	Long.	☉	♆	♅	♄	♃	♂	♀	☿	
		° ′	° ′	° ′	° ′	° ′	° ′	° ′									
1934	1	18♌38	21♓30	25♎37	12♐ 1	2♓ 3	9♋22	4♋11		∠		△		△		☌	10 yrs.
	2	18 40	21℞30	25 38	11℞55	2 19	8℞44	6 21	☌	⊻				⚼	☌		
	3	18 42	21 30	25 38	11 49	2 35	8 7	8 31			△	□	⚼				
	4	18 44	21 29	25 39	11 43	2 49	7 30	10 42	⊻		⚼		△		⊻	⊻	
	5	18 46	21 29	25 39	11 38	3 3	6 54	12 52		☌		✱			∠		
	6	18 48	21 28	25 40	11 32	3 17	6 19	15 2	∠					☍	✱	∠	
	7	18 50	21 28	25 41	11 27	3 29	5 45	17 11	✱	⊻	☍	∠	□			✱	
	8	18 51	21 27	25 42	11 22	3 42	·5 12	19 20		∠		⊻			□		
	9	18 53	21 27	25 43	11 17	3 53	4 41	21 27	□				✱				
	10	18 55	21 26	25 44	11 12	4 4	4 11	23 33		✱		☌	∠	⚼		□	
1944	11	18 57	21 25	25 45	11 7	4 14	3 44	25 38			⚼		⊻	△	△		20 yrs.
	12	18 59	21 25	25 46	11 2	4 23	3 18	27 41	△	□	△	⊻			⚼	△	
	13	19 1	21 24	25 48	10 58	4 32	2 54	29 43	⚼			∠	☌	□		⚼	
	14	19 3	21 23	25 49	10 54	4 40	2 32	1♌43		△	□	✱					
	15	19 5	21 22	25 51	10 50	4 47	2 13	3 41		⚼			⊻	✱	☍		
1949	16	19 7	21 21	25 52	10 46	4 54	1 56	5 38	☍		✱	□	∠	∠			25 yrs.
'50	17	19 9	21 20	25 54	10 42	5 0	1 41	7 32			∠		✱	⊻		☍	
'51	18	19 11	21 19	25 56	10 38	5 5	1 29	9 25		☍	⊻	△			⚼		
'52	19	19 14	21 18	25 58	10 35	5 9	1 19	11 17	⚼			⚼	□	☌	△		
'53	20	19 16	21 17	26 0	10 32	5, 12	1 12	13 6			☌						
'54	21	19 18	21 16	26 2	10 29	5 15	1 7	14 54	△	⚼				⊻	□	⚼	
'55	22	19 20	21 15	26 4	10 26	5 17	1 4	16 40		△	⊻		△	∠		△	
'56	23	19 22	21 14	26 7	10 23	5 18	1D 4	18 24	□			☍	⚼		✱		
'57	24	19 24	21 12	26 9	10 20	5℞19	1 6	20 6			∠			✱	∠		
'58	25	19 26	21 11	26 12	10 18	5 18	1 10	21 46		□	✱					□	
'59	26	19 28	21 10	26 14	10 16	5 17	1 16	23 25	✱					□	⊻		
'60	27	19 31	21 8	26 17	10 14	5 15	1 25	25 2	∠	✱	□	⚼	☍				
	28	19 33	21 7	26 20	10 12	5 12	1 36	26 37				△			☌	✱	
	29	19 35	21 5	26 23	10 10	5 9	1 49	28 11	⊻	∠				△		∠	
	30	19 37	21 4	26 25	10 9	5 4	2 3	29 42		⊻	△	□	⚼	⚼			
	31	19 39	21 2	26 29	10 7	4 59	2 20	1♍12	☌		⚼		△		⊻	⊻	

From Raphael's Ephemeris for 1924.

		H.	M.	S.
Sidereal Time noon G.M.T. (Prog.)		7	36	11
Interval *~~TO~~/FROM noon†	*~~a.m.~~ p.m. +	2	35	00
Result		10	11	11
Acceleration on interval†	*~~a.m.~~ p.m. +			26
Sidereal Time at Greenwich		10	11	37
Longitude equivalent *~~E~~ + W —			7	8
LOCAL SIDEREAL TIME		10	4	29

AGE

25

D.   M.   Y.

21   6   1949

By reference to Table of Houses for Lat. 50° 32′ N :—
    Prog. Asc   12° 50′ ♍
    Prog M.C   29° 00′ ♌

It is important that the addition or subtraction of the longitude in time should be the last part of the calculation so that it can be changed if required.

There are astrologers who think that if the person whose chart is under consideration is living at a different place from the birth-place, the equivalent of this new longitude should be used for the progression.

It is also suggested that when doing a Solar Return (see Chapter 15) the same change should be made if the person is living at a different place at the time of the Return.

Charting for Separate " Progressed Chart " if Required

Forms can be bought for this purpose, but not uniform with those listed on p. 315, as their use is not advised. The degrees of the progressed Asc. and M.C. are placed on the cusps of houses 1 and 10, as in No. 2 the " Houses " Chart. The signs and degrees of the intermediate houses are placed on cusps of the 11th, 12th, 2nd and 3rd houses. Their opposites and any intercepted signs are inserted. These are now called the progressed houses. Progressed planets are written in them, as in No. 2 the " Houses " Chart.

METHOD OF PREPARATION FOR JUDGMENT

(1) The double wheel (or separate chart) must be examined now to find out :—
    (a) Whether any of the progressed planets have arrived at degrees from which they form aspects to planets in the natal chart or their progressed position, or to Asc. or M.C.
    (b) Whether the progressed Asc. and M.C. or any of the more important planets have recently changed their sign or house.
    (c) The Ephemeris for the year of birth must be consulted to see whether any Parallels have been formed.

* As Explained on Form B (page 108) the Student should delete that which is not required.
† These two calculations can be combined in one, as soon as the student has understood the method.

(2) The *current* Ephemeris must be used to find out whether in the year under consideration any planets have arrived at degrees from which they form aspects to natal or progressed planets. These are called *transits*. Explanation is easier by example. (see " Listing of Transits," pp. 234 and 239.)

(3) Various other methods used in prognostication may be followed. Of these, some astrologers prefer one and some another. The chief ones will be described later and are as follows :—

> (*a*) " Symbolic " methods of which that mainly used is known as the " One-Degree " method.
> (*b*) The Radix method.
> (*c*) The effect of positions of New Moons (Lunations) and eclipses. These will be found in the current ephemeris and are, in fact, transits, though not customarily referred to as such.

Natal Planets in Numerical Order

The above processes are much simplified by listing the natal planets in order in the space provided. If the Asc. and M.C. are accurately known, their degrees should be included in this list, so that main aspects to them will not be overlooked.

RECOGNITION OF CLASSES OF ASPECTS AND DURATION OF THEIR EFFECTS

Solar Aspects

Progressed aspects from the Sun are stronger than from any other planet. When the Sun arrives at a degree from which it aspects any other planet, the trend of the life deduced from this will be effective for the whole of the twelve months of which its exactitude is the central time, but its effectiveness will have gradually begun a year before this and will remain in lessening power for a year to follow. It is most likely to be effective over the period of exactitude, or when emphasised by similar aspects or transits.

Lunar Aspects

These are of minor importance. When the Moon arrives at a degree from which it aspects any other planet, the deducible effects will not be noticeable for much more than the four weeks of which the exactness is the central time. To this there is an *important exception*. When the Moon is ruler or Sun-ruler of the chart, its aspects and also its position by sign and house as it moves through the chart, are of great importance.

Mutual Aspects

These are made when any planet, other than the Sun or Moon, arrives at a degree from which it aspects any other planet. The time over which they are effective *varies according to the speed of their movement*, and their strength on the natal map. The deducible effect may begin to show from the time when the progressed planet is within an orb 1° *of exactness* of the aspect which it is about to form with the other planet. *It will be at its strongest in the year of its exactness.* It will be effective until it has again separated by 1° from exactness. The student should now look at any

Ephemeris and see for himself that from one noon to the next (i.e., from one year to the next by progression), Mercury and Venus in any year will be approximately within an orb of 1° of the position to be occupied the next year, while they will have passed that orb a year after the next year. Mars will be slower. Jupiter may hold varying minutes of the same degree for four or five years, hence if it forms an aspect to another planet from that degree, its effect can be observable in the life for some eight years. Saturn may take ten years to pass through a degree, hence its effect will colour a life for twenty years when it is forming and separating from an aspect. Uranus, Neptune and Pluto move so slowly that they cannot do more than complete an inexact natal aspect or slightly separate from an exact one.

If any planet is about to become stationary, either from direct or retrograde motion, its movement will be slower, hence its effect will last longer. As with solars, these are likely to be most effective when exact, or when emphasised by other similar aspects or transits.

Aspects to and from Asc. and M.C.

If the birth moment is exact, these are of great importance. If not, they are most misleading. They affect the whole year in which they are exact.

Aspects by Transiting Planets

As with progressed aspects, the period of effect of a transit is taken to be from the time when such an aspect is within an orb of 1° of exactness, to the time when it separates from it by a similar orb. It is most effective while within the period of exactness. As before, this period lasts according to the speed of the planet. Actual movement in the *current* Ephemeris is now being considered. Mercury and Venus will remain within orb no more than a day, so their transits are of little importance *unless* the matter under consideration is of a Mercurian or Venusian nature. The duration of the effect of the others increases with the slowness of their motion, so that the outermost may effect a life for *weeks* if aspecting an important degree in a natal chart.

Need for Caution in Assessing Strength of Aspects

The discerning student will now see that he may much under-estimate the effect of an aspect by progression or transit, if he charts these respectively in reference to a certain year, or a certain day, without proper understanding of these varying durations of effect.

Way of Writing Progressions and Transits and Parallels

Different methods are used but the most customary is to write " p " and " r " after the planetary symbol to indicate progressed or radical (Latin, *radix*, root).

When using No. 3, the Progressions Chart, it becomes unnecessary to use " p " after a progressed planet when it is already indicated as such by its placing in the outer circle of the double wheel or under an appropriate heading such as Solar or Mutual. Neither is it necessary to insert " r " for the planet to which the progression is made, as this also is understood. If the planet to which the progression is made is a progressed planet, then " p " must be used to show this.

The parallel of declination is denoted by the capital " P ". The symbol ‖ is sometimes used. " T " is used before a symbol to denote a transiting planet.

Examples :—

☉ p △ ♃ p   = Progressed Sun trine progressed Jupiter.
☽ p □ ♆ r   = Progressed Moon square natal or radical Neptune.
☉ p P ♃ p   = Progressed Sun parallel progressed Jupiter.
T ♃ ☌ ☉ p   = Transit of Jupiter conjunct progressed Sun.
Asc. p □ ♀ r   = Progressed Ascendant square natal Venus.

Scope of Work

This must depend on the final shape which the work is to take. A fully comprehensive astrological " reading " should include :—

(1) A personal analysis.
(2) An assessment of the life at the time of writing.
(3) A detailed comment on the trends at work in the coming twelve months, with the listing of outstanding dates.
(4) A brief survey of the coming ten years pointing out any years which are outstanding for any reason.

Each astrologer must make his own arrangement with friend or client as to how much of this shall be done and in what detail.

He will find that the average person is far more interested in knowing the future trend of his life than in his personal analysis. In fact, the request " will you do my horoscope ? " usually means " will you try to tell me what is likely to happen to my life in the future." -It is the business of an astrologer *to assess these future trends, as states of being through which the life must pass,* but if he attempts to declare incontrovertibly that definite events *will* result from these trends, he is putting heavy strain on his powers of deduction and may find himself mistaken.

Unless the chart is one to which he is never likely to refer again, it saves time in the end to list the progressions for ten years at a sitting*. Once these are completed and filed away, if progressions should be required for any of these years, no more work is necessary than to add the details for the current year.† For speed in this part of the work, it is helpful to continue to write the year of progression beside its corresponding day in the Ephemeris on both pages for easy reference (p. 230).

Part 2.—*APPLICATION TO EXAMPLE CHART*

Listing of Solar Aspects

These must be considered first as they are the most powerful.

Taking the example chart, progressed Sun is seen to be in 23° 38′ Cancer. From the list of planets in their numerical order, it can be seen that Uranus is in the 21st degree of its sign. Since this is Pisces, the aspect is a trine. Since the Sun moves about 1° a year, this must have been exact about two years ago. Reference to the Ephemeris shows that the Sun was in 21° 44′ Cancer on July 14, corresponding to 1947. As

* The beginner should start with less.

† These should be entered on to a half-sheet of a No. 3 chart and clipped to the first work in place of the details for the earlier year.

the double wheel shows that Uranus has only moved a few minutes by progression, the aspect is to its progressed place also. This is written as ☉ p △ ♅ r *and* p, 1947 and entered into the column headed SOLAR. As this is solely for progressed positions the p after ☉ can now be omitted.

The Ephemeris itself gives all aspects between progressed planets, but they are a little confusing to find at first.

Under " Mutual Aspects " at the top right of the page, for the 14th day, will be found ☉ P ☿, △ ♅, followed by other aspects of less duration. The parallel between ☉ p and ☿ p can be observed by comparing the declinations of the two on the 14th, both being in the 21st degree N. In the next year, the Ephemeris lists ☉ P ♃ which is the next entry.

The Sun's aspects to the Moon are in the Ephemeris under "Lunar Aspects" where the opposition symbol will be seen on the 16th. The chart shows that this is so. It is written in the solar column ☉ ☍ ☽ p and entered for 1949.

The next planet on the numerical list is Saturn in the same degree as the Asc. Sun p arrives at that degree on the 18th, Saturn is still in the same degree by progression, and we see, under Mutual Aspects, that ☉ p is also ⚼ ♃ on that day.

After these, the aspects to Mars, Moon and Sun itself are the only ones to natal planets to be made in the ten year period, and the semi-sextile to ♀ p is the only one of sufficient importance to be taken from the list of Mutual Aspects. The first two are quincunx and are written ☉ p ⚻ ♂ p 1954, and ☉ ⚻ ☽ p 1955, the solar one is semi-sextile, thus ☉ p ⚺ ☉ r 1955.

As the Sun moves 1° every year, it should be noted that this last aspect is general for everyone at the age of 30.

On July 23, the Sun enters Leo. This correlates with 1956 and is entered.

Listing of Mutual Aspects

The order in which the planets were examined when making notes for chart interpretation is again used.

The ruler of the chart is taken next after the Sun. In this case it is *Venus*. It will be seen to be in 1° 56′ Cancer, making no aspect to any planet, either radical or progressed. The Ephemeris shows it to be moving very slowly preparatory to its change of apparent motion on July 23. Change of motion, particularly when from retrograde to direct, is said to mark a change in a life. Opinions differ on this point. It is entered Sta. Dir. 1956 (stationary and changing to direct).

The Sun-ruler is the next in importance. In this chart it is *Mercury*. The same procedure is followed. The conjunction with the M.C. in 1948 is sufficiently important to be noted. Those in the ten-year period are as listed and should be checked by the student.

Mars is the next in order from the Sun. It makes no aspect but note must be made of its change of apparent movement on July 24 which corresponds to 1957.

Jupiter is next and is moving slowly, preparatory to its change to direct motion 22 days later. It makes no aspect.

Saturn, Uranus and Neptune neither close nor leave any natal aspect and *Pluto* rarely does so in a life. These are merely entered in this way, so that it does not appear that they have been forgotten.

If these slow-moving planets close a birth-aspect, it is advisable to follow the entry by a note such as " Within orb of 1° ten years." This will prevent a wrong interpretation through over-emphasis on the year of exactitude.

Listing of Aspects by Asc. and M.C.

If the birth time is correctly known, these should be included. Reference to any Table of Houses will show that the degree of the M.C. is one later each year. Reference to several Tables of Houses will show that the corresponding degree ascending *varies according to latitude.* Reference to the appropriate Table of Houses for the example shows that M.C.p makes no aspect during the ten years under review, while Asc.p makes the minor aspects of ⋁ ♃ in 1950, ⊼ ☿ in 1952, and the happy major aspect of △ ♀ in 1953. These can be listed in a spare part of a column.

Reckoning of Lunar Aspects

As the Moon moves so swiftly, its position must be calculated for each month, but it is sufficiently precise to make a rough division of the year's movement, thus avoiding exactitude to seconds, as follows :—

Movement of progressed Moon from May 1949
$$\begin{aligned} \text{to May 1950} = \quad & ≈ 8°\ 23' \\ - \ & ♑\ 23°\ 44' \\ \hline & 14°\ 39' \end{aligned}$$

14° 39' ÷ 12 = 1° 13' and 3' over.

The monthly difference added to the longitude given for the first day in question gives the longitude for the same day of the next month and so on through the year. At three times of such addition, an extra minute must be included to cover the " three over " of the division. As follows :—

Moon's Long. 1949,	12th May	23° 44' ♑
	12th June	24° 57'
	12th July	26° 10'
	12th Aug.	27° 24'
	12th Sept.	28° 37'
	12th Oct.	29° 51'
	12th Nov.	1° 4' ≈
	12th Dec.	2° 17'
1950,	12th Jan.	3° 30'
	12th Feb.	4° 44'
	12th Mar.	5° 57'
	12th Apr.	7° 10'
	12th May	8° 23'

These positions are from noon date of one year to noon date of the next. It may be required to begin the study of the progressions from the beginning of a year, or from the month when the work was begun. In such a case, subtractions could be taken further back or additions further on, as required. The twelve months in question are then entered.

The noon date should be entered in the space at the top of the column so that the *date* of the month corresponding to the entry is obvious.

Listing of Lunar Aspects

The degrees covered by the Moon's passage for the year can now be compared with the list of those occupied by the *natal planets*. It will be seen that the first aspects on the list are those to Asc. and Saturn.. The aspects for September and October are semi-sextile and quincunx, which are not of great importance for so swiftly moving a body. The aspects to the *progressed planets* can be taken as listed in the Ephemeris under " Lunar Aspects," though they must be checked as to month of exactitude.

These are the opposition to the progressed Sun in May and the semi-sextile to progressed Mars in February, 1950.

Converse Aspects

Many astrologers believe that regressions are as effective as progressions. Experts on time theories such as Hinton and Ouspensky imply that our ideas on time are incomplete. It may be that the effects of any one moment extend around us in every direction like the ripples round a stone thrown into a pond. There is no way of measuring these laterally, but if it is desired to work out the converse directions the same routine must be followed, in the backwards order of the years.

In the case of the example, the noon positions of May 27 would correspond to May 12, 1949. They will not be included now as the work would be too much for a first example.

Aspects by Transit

No astronomical explanation can be given of the working of transits any more than for the working of progressions.

The ecliptical positions taken are those in the current Ephemeris. For a student to study his own transits for the day on which he is now studying the subject, he would refer to the actual day in the Ephemeris of the year* he is in now, at the time of reading. If a planet actually in the heavens, at the moment, was found to be in a degree which aspected a planet in his natal chart, it would be said to be transiting over or in square or trine, etc., to his natal planet. But, in actuality, it would be in such angular relationship to the place of that planet years ago at his birth.

Similarly, without understanding the still hidden laws of nature, it is observable without doubt that the transits of a planet are of the nature of that planet and affect the person according to the angular relationships made to degrees in his chart, made sensitive to such impacts by reason of planetary tenancy. Inasmuch as a person tunes in with the planetary pattern of his birth moment, so the passage of a planet in its transit of the day appears to stimulate that which is already an

* If the period of twelve months under consideration runs into a calendar year past that of the current Ephemeris, future transits can be seen by reference to *Fowler's Ephemeris 1955–1959*, inclusive, or, in less detail in that by Raphael, footnote, p. 241.

essential part of his being. It is customary only to consider transits by conjunction, opposition, trine and square.

Listing of Transits

In the present example, aspects to natal planets only will be considered. It is doubtful whether transits to progressed planets are as effective as those tᵣ natal planets but if it is wished to consider them the method of assessing them is the same. The more slowly moving planets remain within 1° of an exact aspect to another planet for *weeks* at a time. This is also true of the more quickly moving ones when they are slowing down before change of apparent direction. It is therefore nothing but misleading to take the central date of this effect and to enter this only as the date of the transit (see p. 106).

In the 1949 Ephemeris, it will be seen that Pluto is transiting within 1° of the conjunction of Neptune from mid-September onwards, being Sta. ℞ on November 27. The effect of this transit will colour the life for the whole of this time and should be indicated so when entering (see example form).

With Neptune, a glance through the Ephemeris shows that the earliest degree touched by it in the year is 12° 24′ in June, while the latest is 17° 16′ in December. It is then obvious that no aspect need be looked for except to planets listed as between these degrees. These are Jupiter, Mercury and Venus. It remained within the square to Venus and the trine to Mercury for the whole of March.* When it again contacts these planets in the autumn, the central dates are in two different months, but the effect will again be combined. In the same way, though the exact dates of the two formations of the sextile to Jupiter are entered, Neptune does not separate as much as a whole degree from it during the interval. This must be taken into consideration.

With Uranus, the Ephemeris shows that it can only form aspects to any planets between 26° Gemini and 5° Cancer during the May to December period. The list shows these to be Mars, Moon and Sun and their dates are noted. The aspect to the M.C. is only a semi-sextile which is too minor to include as a transit. Saturn and Jupiter are dealt with in the same way.

Mars transits so swiftly that only its major aspects are noticed. Its effects are slight *unless* the year in question is heavily stressed by many other Martian contacts by Sun, Moon and other planets.

In the example, only conjunctions are noted as these are the strongest transits.

Other Methods of Prognostication

(a) *The "One-Degree" Method,* This is one of the "Symbolic" measures. To understand these fully it is necessary to read a special book.† It is commonly shortened to "O-D," and is the most generally used. It is extremely reliable and has the advantage of being easy to apply. Degrees corresponding to the age at the time of progression are added to each planet and any resulting aspects are considered. For

* It can now be seen that one reason for the interpretation of "strain" when two planets are in close quincunx or semi-sextile to each other is that when one receives an easy aspect from a progressing or transiting planet, the other receives a difficult one at the same time (see p. 183).

† *Symbolic Directions.* Charles E. O. Carter.

further exactitude, a proportion of the year can be taken in order to decide on the month when results are to be expected.

If several measures fall due within a few weeks, it is often found that an average of these will decide the time of exactitude. In the example, the age is 25, and the only addition from which a result is obtained is that to Neptune, as follows :—

Neptune 18° 21′ Leo + 25° = 13° 21′ Virgo, which within minutes is square to Jupiter. This is entered in the spare column. See further example, p. 256.

(b) *The Radix Method.* To understand this fully, it is again necessary to read a book on it.* It is less simple in application as the amount added for each year of life is 59′ 8″. If in constant use, there are Tables to which reference can be made for easy reckoning. In the example by this method, Neptune will not come to the square of Jupiter till the age of 25½.

(c) New Moons (Lunations) and Eclipses

The date of the *New Moon* of each month is printed at the top of the page in the Ephemeris. A New Moon is the monthly conjunction between Sun and Moon. In other words, the swifter Moon arrives at the same degree of Ecliptic as the Sun. As the lunar cycle is 29½ days and the calendar months are 30 or 31 days with the exception of February, the date of the N.M. becomes a little earlier each month and the degree of the lunation is a little earlier also. If the N.M. aspects a degree occupied by a planet in a natal chart, it will continue to make a series of aspects to it for several months and its effect will continue. A simple way of noting these is to underline the Sun and Moon positions on the dates indicated in the current Ephemeris, so that they are outstanding when doing any progression. In the example (*facing* p. 223) these recur for several months and are entered in the " Notes " column.

An *eclipse of the Sun* takes place when, at the monthly *conjunction* with the Moon (New Moon) the latter has no latitude, so the two are not only in the same degree of Ecliptic but also precisely in line with each other as seen from the Earth.

An *eclipse of the Moon* takes place when at the monthly opposition to the Sun (Full Moon), the former again has no latitude. The two will be in opposing degrees of Ecliptic and precisely in line with each other, but with the Earth exactly between them.

These eclipses may be partial or total. The dates of their occurrences are marked in the Lunar Aspects in the Ephemeris by the symbol ☾ for eclipse of Sun and ☽ for eclipse of Moon. They are listed under " Phenomena " on p. 29 of the Ephemeris for each year.

If the N.M. making an aspect to any planet is also a *Solar eclipse*, then the effect is much increased.

The effect of the Full Moon is not usually noted, but when it is also a *Lunar eclipse*, it is of more importance.

Annular eclipse of the sun (ring-shaped) is like a total eclipse, but the Moon is so

* *The Radix System.* Vivian Robson.

far from the Earth that it does not completely cover the Sun, so a ring of light is seen round the Moon.

" How Particular Must I Be With Aspects ? "

This is a constant question from the student. The answer is that he must suit his work to the purpose for which he is doing it. He would go without much of the enjoyment of astrology if he insisted on calculating every minor progressed aspect whenever he wanted to form a quick idea as to the main shaping of the tendencies of a life. For this the major aspects to natal planets, seen at a glance, are enough with the addition of the major transits. Even for ordinary work, minor aspects can be disregarded except for detailed work on an important year. For examination work, the student should expect to find an indication given as to aspects to be listed.

Listing for Examination of Several Years

Having ruled off two pages of paper for the number of years required to survey, the year should be noted in each space.*

The solar and mutual (and O-D or Radix if used) aspects should be entered, as noted on the chart form. By inspection of the Ephemeris, the sign in which the Moon will be, for each year, should be added and changes of house noted. By reference to the positions of the transiting planets† for future years, the *main* transits made should be noted. Any change of sign by Asc, M.C. or Sun should also be noted and any change from retrograde to direct or vice versa made by any planet and any other details according to importance (see example sheets, *between* pp. 222–223).

The student should practise with 2 or 3 years of a life before doing too much at a time, interpreting each year from the indications collected on this sheet.

Part 3.—*GENERAL DISCUSSION ON INTERPRETATION OF PROGRESSIONS, WITH EXAMPLE CHART AS ILLUSTRATION*

Case History

If the work is done in order to be of use to the person to whom it applies, some knowledge of conditions in the year of progression must be given. Astrology is the *applied use of symbols and it is impossible to apply them unless it is known to what they are to be applied.*

If this is not given, then the work is merely a test of the astrologer's skill in deduction and his success will depend a great deal on his intuitive use of what has been called "the selective factor." Any given tendency may result in any one of several end-results. If existing conditions are known, it is possible to suggest which end-result is the most likely.

Progression by the Ascendant and M.C.

If the natal Ascendant is in a sign of short ascension, it will be possible for the progressed Ascendant to travel through several signs in a lifetime, whereas there

* Printed sheets can be bought. See page 315.
† " The Geocentric Longitudes and Declinations of Neptune, Herschel, Saturn, Jupiter and Mars," by Raphael.

may be no more than two changes if the natal Ascendant was in an early degree of a sign of long ascension.

The years of these changes in the past or any about to take place in the future will mark a deep psychological change when the person gradually and unconsciously adopts some of the traits of that sign into which his Ascendant has entered or is entering. He never loses his essential basic make-up but it is added to *according to the nature of* the new sign. Often, a person is heard to remark, " I wonder why I was so this, that, and the other, up to a few years ago. I think and feel differently about many things now." Such a change can be traced to the change of Ascendant. The psychological change is often accompanied by changes in the outer life in accordance with this. (This cannot be noted unless the birth time is certain.)

For example, a person with a Taurean Ascendant natally comes to a time when his progressed Ascendant is in Gemini. He will not lose his solid, practical, stable and stubborn personality but it will be expressed in a lighter, more versatile manner. Events may happen in life which cause him to move about more from place to place and be more communicative and chatty with people. On the other hand the person whose natal Ascendant is Aries will not lose his fiery enthusiasm and dash while his progressed Ascendant is in Taurus but it will be moderated by a more practical outlook. Events will probably force this on him.

By reference to the Table of Houses used for the example chart, it will be seen that the M.C. is given as 1° further on for about every four minutes of sidereal time. This corresponds to a year of life. The corresponding movement of the Ascendant is according to its speed of ascension. It will be seen that, when the M.C. p. is about 10¼ Leo, the Asc. p. enters Scorpio. At this age the child would have become more emotional, more intense. In a childish way he would have begun to develop that keen desire to penetrate into life, which he has in later years.

The progression of the M.C. into a new sign will show a change in the manner of self-expression in the outer world. This may indeed be no more than an altered way of meeting life in terms of the new sign, but this is apt to cause changes, or it may be caused by changes in the life and is likely to affect the career.

To assess any one of such changes the student must re-read a description of the sign in question and think out the impact of the new on to the old in terms of the adopted or over-laid traits which will gradually show forth.

Progression of the Sun

In exactly the same way, the progression of the Sun from one sign to another correlates with a new upspringing of desires, feelings, urges and traits which were but latent before. Events may seem to " cause " these or they may seem to " cause " events. The ideas of *correlation* and *synchronisation* with the planetary pattern give a better picture than those of " cause and effect." As the Sun's progress is virtually constant in its 30 years through a sign, it is obvious that only centenarians would have such a change more than three times in adult life. The dates are easily seen in the Ephemeris.

In the example chart, John's Sun progressed into Cancer in his first August

(☉ 29° 48′ Gemini in May — ¼ of the Sun's daily passage = ¼ year by progression ; Sun would be in 0° 3′ Cancer on August 12). This change was referred to in the personal analysis. The next change will be into Leo at the end of 1955. No " mathematics " are necessary to see this. The noon date is already noted in the Ephemeris and the year 1956 is written beside July 23. The noon position of the Sun is 0° 19′ Leo on May 12, so it would enter Leo almost four months earlier. Closer precision is not necessary as these changes are periods of development not sudden alterations.

At this time, John's Cancerian " looking after " tendencies will be overlaid by a more dictatorial spirit. He will want to order and organise the looking-after rather than do it himself. He will probably apply for an administrative appointment and will think he has " chosen " to do so, but he will be synchronising with his pattern of development. It would be necessary to examine the aspects of the natal Sun (ruler of Leo) to know how this change will suit him, and the rest of the progressed aspects and transits for the year to know whether he will be successful and happy in the new way of more Leonine self-expression which he will adopt.

The aspects made by the Sun in its progress are more important than any. Effects will be noticed according to the nature of the aspected planet and correlative events will occur. The aspects of progressed Sun to the natal Moon invariably produce changes and those between progressed Sun and progressed Moon generally mark the change-over of varying phases in life. (See paragraph on progression of Moon.)

Progression of Ruler and Sun-Ruler

These may also be examined for developments in the life due to change of sign. In the example, the ruler, ♀, has not changed its sign but ☿, the Sun-ruler, has entered Leo and has recently passed over the M.C. (♌ 4). As Mercury is not only John's Sun-ruler but also significator of the mentality, this is added testimony that he is developing a more autocratic and " managing " way of thought especially as regards his self-expression in the life of what is to him, " the world " (☿ p. ♂ M.C. 1948). It should be remembered that Mercury is never far from the Sun so it frequently happens that change of direction in mental outlook will precede, accompany, or soon follow, the more personal changes which correlate with the Sun's progression.

Progression of the Moon

The Moon changes sign about every 2½ years. With the use of the Equal House system the changes in house position will be at much the same intervals, though not necessarily at the same time. With the use of any of the Quadrant systems, the time of stay in a house *must vary with the varying house sizes.*

The changes are again as an overlay to the basic person and less deep and more passing than those of the Sun. The keywords given for the Moon were response and fluctuation. While progressing through any sign, the response to life and its conditioning, and the necessary day-by-day fluctuations will become rather more *of the nature of* that sign than they were before. No wholesale change is to be expected but the inclinations will change. In a very free map, they will have observable results whereas in a very bound map they may have to be suppressed. Such a suppressed person limited in nature by overmuch Saturn, overmuch Earth or over-much Fixity, will assure the astrologer that ·" no change whatever happened " in this period. If the astrologer expects every progressing trend to crystallise *as an event*, he will indeed be disappointed and may even begin to doubt the truth of astrology. Without a psychological approach and quiet consultative work, he may never find out the longings and urgings which pressed for satisfaction but were denied.

Outwardly, the affairs of the house through which the Moon is passing are likely to be of more concern than at other times.

In the example, for the year 1949, the Moon is passing through the latter degrees of Capricorn. This is the third decanate, ruled by Mercury. It was thoroughly in keeping with the nature of this sign and planet that the year was one of hard work and of application to practical things in order to rise in life by passing an examination to begin on a career. This also applied to the year before, when the Moon was also in Capricorn, as John was doing a two-year course at a training college for teachers.

The time of the passing through the Mercury decanate was one of intense concentration on detail in the necessary mental work.

When the Moon reached 25° Capricorn and entered the 4th house, John returned from his resident training college and began life at home (4th house).

In another way his thoughts soon centred on home, as he was about to become engaged and a beginning was made on the discussion of plans for the house itself, for structural alteration into two houses, for his mother and for himself and wife.

By the Placidean system, the Moon would not enter the 4th house until it reached the I.C. in 4° Aquarius in February, 1950. This would be late.

(When the work has become more habitual and the student can quickly put up his maps by both the Equal House and the Placidean or other systems, he will be able to compare their respective effectiveness at such times as the above.)

Progressions of Sun and Moon

As the Moon encircles the chart every 29 years (about), it makes the aspects of conjunction, square, opposition and again square to the progressed Sun with regularity every 7 or 8 years. These times mark minor phases in the life. The conjunction generally means a change, either in outlook or circumstance, while the opposition usually correlates with a time of fruition of what has gone before.[*]

In the example, John's ☉ p. was ☍ ☽ p. in May, 1949, just as he was about to pass his examination and begin to take up a teaching career, the fruition of his efforts in the past.

The Use of Triplicities and Quadruplicities in Assessing Changes of Sign by Asc., M.C., Sun and Moon

The broad classifications of the triplicities and quadruplicities are of great help here. Progression into any Water sign will bring a more emotional, intuitional response to life, because more emotion and intuition will be *given* to life. In Cancer

[*] For extension of this. *The Moon*, by Dane Rudyar.

which is Cardinal Water, a more energetic expression will ensue for this ; in Scorpio which is Fixed Water, the response will be emotionally slower, but deeper and more intense, while in Pisces which is Mutable Water, the response will be shifting, variable, but highly sensitive and receptive. This line of argument should now be followed by the student and applied to the other signs.

Progressed Aspects

No progressed aspect stands alone, nor should one be interpreted as a solitary factor. *It is only effective in relation to the aspect (or lack of same) made by the two planets in the natal chart.*

If no natal aspect, the effect of a progressed aspect will be weak.

If the natal aspect is favourable, and the progressed aspect unfavourable, it will accentuate the potentialities of the natal aspect though difficulties may rise before results come.

Conversely, if the natal aspect is unfavourable and the progressed one is favourable it will activate the natal situation, possibly alleviating it for a while, but it will not turn basic difficulty into ease.

If an inexact natal aspect closes by progression, its effect is very strong in the year or years of its exactitude when transits set it into action, either because being of a similar nature they intensify it or because they themselves are intrinsically energising.

If a planet forms two progressions of a contrary nature at the same time they will not cancel each other out but will paradoxically both affect the life.

When a progression covers some months or even years, there will be a general psychological effect *in accordance with its nature* for the whole time, but its effect will be more apparent, both in the personal reaction to it and in events of its nature when transits are of the same nature. For instance, if Saturn is 5° behind the Sun natally, it is conjunct but not exact. If by slow progression the aspect becomes exact in later life, a time of frustration or limitation will occur. (See "duration of effects" p. 233.)

The power of a planet in progression depends very much on its strength in the natal chart.

To sum up :—

The *nature* of each planet forming the aspect and their *relation* in the natal chart are of more importance than the *kind* of aspect.

Parallels of Declination

If a planet, by progression, is parallel to a radical or progressed planet, it is said to be as strong as if the two were in conjunction. Opinions differ on this.

Transits

These must be understood to affect the transited planet *according to the nature of* that one which transits, as with progressions, in accordance with the natal relation of the two planets. It is rarely possible to tell *exactly* what the effect of a transit will be, though it will certainly affect the affairs of the house through which it is passing. Some idea may be had from reading the descriptions of planets natally in houses.

Examples.—Saturn transiting through 1st house will be depressing and personally frustrating ; more so if the natal Saturn has any difficult aspects, less so if it has easy aspects. Jupiter, as the opposite, brings optimism and success and opportunity in whichever house it may be transiting. Uranus will bring changes and Neptune confusions at its worst, idealisms at its best ; Pluto will emphasise and bring to prominence the things of a house. Mars will energise them. When it returns to its natal place each two years, this is a time of extra energy, to use or to be wary of (according to natal aspects). If natally in aspect to Sun or Moon, its recurring transits to them are also times when action should be taken, or carefully watched. Venus may have minor fleeting happy results. Mercury may stress similarly minor busy details.

In trying to assess the possible effect of a transit by that one which *receives* the transit, the effect may be through those things of which the planet is the general significator.

Examples.—T. Saturn over Venus; a limitation or denial of love or happiness. T. Jupiter over Mercury; an increase of activity in mental output and in getting about.

The effect can then be applied to the house.

Example.—T. Saturn over Venus in 2nd ; harmony or happiness spoilt through financial stress.

The effect may also extend to the house of which that planet is ruler.

Example.—T. Saturn over Venus in 2nd; it being ruler of 5th, happiness, upset through loss of money, it having been needed for children.

To a certain extent, some effect can be noticed of the transit of planets through signs, but mainly if such sign contains several planets.

Example.—In John's chart whenever Mars in its two yearly transit round the map contacts the three corners of the Grand Trine, this will be favourably activated.

When Uranus transited the Sun to which it is square natally, he received a sudden serious injury.

Time of Transits

Saturn often delays its effects. Jupiter and Mars hasten with theirs. Events do NOT always coincide with the *exact* days of transits but are seen to correlate with several transits *near* such a date, usually leading up to and culminating in an event.

Minor Transits

In interpretation, it is not necessary to delineate every minor transit but it is necessary to *list* them so that they may be taken into account with others.

Part 4.—(a) EXAMPLE OF " PROGRESSIONS " WITH EXPLANATION

Except for a little editing, the following is exactly as it was written in March, 1949. When spectacular events and changes happen in a life, many aspects and transits usually combine to show this and the work is easy ; but the customary work of an astrologer is to deal with the ordinary men and women, intent on the normal development of their lives at home and at work. This chart is chosen as representative of such.

POSSIBLE DEVELOPMENT OF POTENTIALITIES OF THE BIRTH-CHART KNOWN ASTROLOGICALLY AS " PROGRESSIONS "*

for

" JOHN SMITH "

(Published by his kind permission)

by

MARGARET E. HONE

---

* Dates given in this section are calculated as nearly as possible for the chart under consideration, but they mark the time of *trends* at work in the life rather than definite " events."

PRESENT TIME

1949

Significators to be marginally entered on astrologer's carbon copy only, unless otherwise requested. (Bracketed notes give confirmations as given a year later.)

☉ △ ♅ r and p

The complete change which took place in your life in 1947, when you suddenly heard that you were accepted by the college for which you had been making application for 3 years, is well indicated in your chart. It seems to have been a time which brought you an excellent opportunity of using your brain and intelligence to the full, for the furtherance of your career. This must have been most welcome to anyone of your type after the indecision as to your future.

☉ P ♃
☿ ♂ M.C.

The year is most definitely marked as a time of climax caused by the fruition of plans. The results should be most advantageous to you in every way. Your coming examination fits in with this well and the inference is that you will pass it, thus bringing to an end the time of preparation and beginning a new phase.

☉ ☍ ☽ p
(natal △)

New Moon aspecting ♂, ☉ and
☽ r 4 months. ☽ enters 4th

As the year goes on, there are many minor changes and unsettlements, especially with regard to home affairs. As you will need to make definite living arrangements when you take up an appointment, it looks as if you are working out your life pattern with great exactness.

(Began settled life at home after living away.)

☿ ⊼ ♂ p, ⊡ ♅ p

(☿ □ ♅ natally)

There is a minor indication that you should be deliberate and critical over any new plans or agreements. For you, second thoughts are usually best, having had time to mature.

In the main, the year is a time when you will be serious-minded and when application and aspiration mean much to you. Watch your expenditure.

☽ in ♑
♆ □ ♃, O-D

DETAILS OF 1949

Note.—Following dates must *NOT* be taken as exact but as the centre of a period of action.

MAY

☉ ☍ ☽ p exact

This is the centre period of the time of " climax " to which I referred.

1st

T ♆ ✳ ♃ (natal △)

(♃ in 2nd)

A day of heightened idealism and ability to gain through metaphysical or occult or abstract interests rather than practical ones. Financially good.

T ♅ △ ♂
(♂ rules 7th)

T ♄ ✶ ☉ ☍ ☽ ♂ (natal △)
(T ♄ will work *in the nature of* itself, even if well aspected.
Astrologer should try to counter-
act this, not depress further.)

☽ □ ♄ and Asc. (natal △)
(He felt extremely worried and
responsible about the examination.)

. T ♅ ☌ ☉ △ ☽

(☉ rules 10th)
(☽ women in man's map.)

(On this afternoon in the middle
of the exam week, he was suddenly hit on the eye with a cricket
ball and had to have six stitches
near it. But the exam work was
excellently successful.)

(T ♂ ☌ ☿)

☿ natally ☍ ♃

No lunar aspect
T ♂ ☌ ☉, △ ☽ ♂

(☽ in 5th)
(Exam had been passed. Excellent holiday, sailing, bathing, etc.,
with girl friend, making plans for
future.)

22nd
Events are likely to happen suddenly and sur-
prisingly. Your mind may turn more directly to
marriage. Your own mood will be tense and a little
strained.

27th
Take no notice of any frustration or depression just
now. It is only temporary and you need all your
vitality for your work. Take no risks about colds.
Take care of yourself and try not to get overtired.
A tiresome few days but easier to get through if you
recognise it as part of your pattern, to be dealt with
rather than to be annoyed with. The great thing is to
realise that you should *pay attention* to any physical
upset or mental depression. It is no time to neglect
yourself in view of the coming exam.

JUNE

The month in general appears to be a time of effort
and work and with a feeling of stress. This is quite
concomitant with the natural worry and apprehension of exam time.

8th
This has various repercussions in that it is suddenly upsetting, but actually pleasing. It seems
to be good for your career and congenial to your
mother.

It would seem only natural to translate this into
your success in the exam, but I prefer to indicate
tendencies rather than to attempt to forecast
" facts." Also there is a great element of surprise in
this, so something else quite different may happen !

30th
You are very energetic mentally and should watch
yourself critically, lest you overstep the mark in some
way. Guard your speech and refrain from exaggeration. It is a time when you can put on an extra spurt
in anything to do with writing or study.

JULY

22nd
Such days as this are worth knowing about in
advance. It is a time of vital forcibleness when your
mind and brain and physique are working perfectly
in tune. At such times, you should use this force
for making new beginnings, for setting new plans
on foot, for going " all out " for thorough enjoyment.

AUGUST

No lunar aspect
T ♂ ☌ ♇ and ♀. T ♆ ✱ ♃
(Holiday still delightful. Became engaged. Announced on 20th.)

10th–15th
A period to be a little cautious. You will be sexually and emotionally stirred and very full of ideals for life. Finance good.

SEPTEMBER

New Moon affects ♂ and ☉ and ☽ r for 4 months. Now ✱ ☉ ☍ ☽ ☍ ♂ (24th August.)
♇ within 1° ♆ in 10th 5 months

This begins a period of four months in which each month has indications of movement, change and unsettlement.

T ♆ △ ☿ (natal ✱)
(Pleasure at first teaching post but unsettled because children lowest grade of intelligence and unresponsive.)

16th
This should be a time of mental upliftment.

♃ within 1° of ✱ ♅ in 5th
Sta. Direct on 19th
(Engagement month before. Note that ♂'s transits hasten matters.)

19th
You are likely to make a change in your "girl-friend" relationship and to open up a new phase. From one point of view this will be agitating to your feelings, while from another it will bring you much more harmonious conditions.

T ♄ □ ♃ (no natal aspect).
(Valuable stone lost from engagement ring necessitating replacement.)

30th
Either you will be called on to spend extra money or you will find some difficulty about it.

OCTOBER

(Displeased with post.)
☽ ⊼ ☉ and New Moon (22nd September.) □ ☉ ⊼ ☽ ♂

Time of worry about changes.

T ♂ ☌ ♆ in 10th
♇ within 1° of Sta. ℞ ☌ ♆
(5 months)

7th
Agitation over difficulties in career.

T ♄ □ ☿

9th
Avoid today for agreements or contracts.

T ♆ □ ♀

11th
Happiness spoilt through carelessness. Try to be alert and on guard.

T ♅ ✱ ♀

17th
Improvement of happiness through will power and control.

NOVEMBER

☽ into ♒
New Moon (21st October) near Asc. (△ ☉, ☽, ♂.)

Tendency towards more detached scientific independent thought. The changes are more personal and more congenial.

♇ Sta. Dir. ☌ ♆ in 10th
(Still unable to feel post was good.)

27th–30th
Likely to throw off or get rid of something to start different phase in work.

DECEMBER

New Moon (20th November)
□ ☽ ♂ 木 ☉
(Very upset month. Mother ill. Had to manage at home.)

Still upset and changeful and not a good time for any women folk connected with you.

(Heard of better job; maths and science master in technical school.)
Note.—☽ into ≈ (science) November.

Possible financial opportunity.

Asc. p ⊻ ♃
☽ into ≈ in 4th and 5th

T ♃ through 5th, ♂♂☽, △ ♄ and Asc., △ ☉ affecting Grand Trine spring and summer.
T ♂ ♂ ♂ ☽ April and October, also △ ☉, ♄ and Asc.
(Work to do with *excellent new post begins 17th April*. Teacher of science in technical school. Marriage arranged for August.)

1950

The year shows personal success and happiness both in career and in love. Attention is more on home affairs than before. April seems especially marked for success. Your interest in scientific matters is intensified. A splendid year to start new ventures.

DETAILS OF EARLY MONTHS OF 1950

New Moon (19th December)
☍ ☉ ✶ ♄, ♂ and ☽
T ♇ still aspecting ♆ in 10th.

JANUARY

Still very changeful but with better outlook.

☽ ✶ ♂ p ♂ r
T ♇ still within 1° of ♆ in 10th.
T ♃ △ ☿
(Had successful interview for new position.)

FEBRUARY

2nd
This should be a time of excellent opportunity in mental or scholastic matters.

No lunar aspect.
T ♄ ✶ ♀

MARCH

21st
A seriousness enters into your happiness.

T ♃ △ ♄. (♄ at Asc., rules 3rd.)
New Moon (16th February) ♂ ♂ and ☽, △ ☉.

24th
Improvement in personal conditions and mental outlook.

No lunar aspect.
T ♄ □ ☿ (no natal aspect)

APRIL

2nd
Slight depression soon thrown off.

T ♃ ♂ ♂, to ♂ ☽ △ ☉
New moon (26 ♓ 16th March partly affects month. Next on 17th April, important as ☍ ♄)
✶ ☉ ✶ ♂ ☽.

9th–14th
It is pleasant to end on such a splendid day as this when opportunities should be opening to you, which you will undoubtedly take with success.

FUTURE YEARS

Note.—The most important remark to make is that 1953 stands out as the most successful year of the near future.

1951

☉ p □ ♄ and Asc. from cusp 10 E.H. (natal △) ⚼ ♃
Asc. p ⚻ ☿
☽ in ♒ in 5th
T. ♅ ruler 5th ☌ ♇ and ♀ in the summer.
T ♂ ☌ ☉ July

The year is marked by an access of greater responsibility in the career. Some limitation may accompany it, giving it a feeling of weight, but with gratification for success. Love and happiness are emphasised. There is also an indication which might mean the birth of a child.

1952

Asc. p △ ♀
☿ p △ ♃ p
☽ ♓
T ♅ ☌ ♇ and ♀ spring
T ♂ ☌ ♄ and Asc. January
T ♂ ☌ ♂ and ☽ December
T ♄ ☌ ♄ r and Asc. winter

The year brings much indication of personal happiness and of expansion of mental scope. Your outlook becomes somewhat softened and more intuitive and emotional.

An important time is reached when aspirations reach fulfilment. Health may suffer slightly and it may be necessary to moderate the activities a little.

1953

☿ p (Sun-ruler) ⚹ ☿ r and △ ♃ in 2nd
☽ ♓
T ♄ ☌ ♄
T ♃ ☌ ☿
T ♆ ☌ ♄ and Asc.
T ♂ ☌ ☉ June
T ♂ ☌ ♄ and Asc. December

After possible health difficulties early, *this should be a peak year*, when you should be able to take advantage of an extremely favourable opportunity. It should improve your position academically and financially. A journey abroad is likely.

1954

☉ p ⚻ ♂ (natal △)
☽ in ♈
T ♆ ☌ ♄ and Asc.
T ♃ ☌ ☉, ♇ and ♀ summer
T ♂ ☌ ♂ ☽

Life is considerably active and at times tiring and with strain in dealing with others. There is personal worry and health must not be neglected. Intuitional powers increase and also an interest in abstract thought and ideals. Even so, keep all accounts in good shape and see to general routine practical matters, not permitting any muddle or slackness.

The summer should be a splendid time for home affairs and married happiness.

1955

☉ p ⚻ ☽, ⚺ ☉ r, enters ♌
☽ ♈
T ♃ ☌ M.C. summer
☌ ♆ autumn
T ♂ ☌ ☉ May
T ♂ ☌ ♄ and Asc. November
T ♆ ☌ ♄ and Asc.

Towards the end of this year and onwards, you should become conscious of a change in yourself, in that you become much more managing and organising, *being better fitted for administrative work* and a position of more authority. This is important. You should keep it in view and work towards it. Don't lose your head about this as the little tendency to confusion or escapism still exists.

T ♃ ☌ M.C.
☉ p ☌ M.C. 1959

Opportunity will undoubtedly come to you both now, and again in 4 years' time.

1956

♀ p (ruler) Sta. Dir.
☿ p ☌ ♆
(♆ △ ♃ natally)
☽ ♈ — ♉
T ♅ ☌ M.C. autumn
T ♂ ☌ ♂ ☽ July

This is a year to be careful. It *can* be very successful, and indeed it probably will be, especially financially. Your mind is becoming much more interested in the study of the abstract and the intangible. The only caution is to keep your feet on the ground. While reaching greater heights than before in ways of imaginative thought and inspiration and possibly greater interest in music and art, you may tend to carelessness in things nearer to hand. Unfortunately, it is necessary to advise you to be on your guard against petty thieving, or deceit or laying yourself open to being let down by others, with financial loss. See that insurance is in good shape, and so forth.

1957

☉ p ⚹ ♀ p
☿ p ☌ ♆ p
☽ ♉
T ♅ ☌ M.C. summer
T ♄ ☌ ♃ spring
T ♃ ☌ ♄ and Asc. winter
T ♂ ☌ ☉ May

The caution of last year must be repeated. Changes in the career are likely. Financial affairs must be safeguarded in the spring. Health and spirits good.

1958

Asc. p □ ♆
☽ ♉ and 8th
T ♃ ☌ ♄ Asc. spring
T ♂ ☌ ♂, ☽ spring
☌ ☉ winter

Health must not be neglected. Outlook generally is stable and sensible. New ventures can be successfully started.

(b) *EXAMINATION OF CONDITIONS OF ANY SPECIAL DAY*

It is often necessary to assess an important day to decide as to the probable outcome of what is to be begun that day. Nearly a year after the progressions of the example map were written, John was advised that his duties in his new post as science master were to begin on 17th April, 1950. This day will be used as example.

17th April, 1950

Main Aspects in Operation

☉ p ☍ ☽ p 1949 (see p. 248)
(natal △)

A completely new phase in the life was begun at this time.

☉ p going to □ ♄ 1951
(natal △)

Main future indication is of seriousness and the necessary acceptance of personal responsibility.

☽ p in ♒

Excellent indication of scientific trend.

Main Transits Leading up to Exact Day

♆ 15° 41′ ♎ □ ♀ △ ☿

As this has no natal aspect to Venus, it is of little account, probably indicating some lack of clarity about happiness. As it is natally sextile to Mercury, the present trine will intensify the natal aspect, indicating idealism in scholastic matters.

♅ 1° 36′ ♋

This is leaving proximity to the actual conjunction with the Sun, thus indicating that the changefulness of that aspect has passed and settlement may begin.

♄ 13° 14′ ♍ ✳ ♀ □ ☿
No natal aspect

These aspects have been formed recently, indicating the mental depression of the earlier post. Of little importance because of lack of natal aspect.

♃ 0° 24′ ♓. ♂♂ and ☽ △ ☉

Though not in aspect at birth, this powerful planet, in such strong aspect to important planets a few days before the 17th and still in orbs of aspect, indicates an expansion in the life of the most favourable nature.

♂ 23° 41′ ♍ ℞
Just past ⚺ ♄ and Asc., ⚼ ♂ and ☽
and returning to them in May and
June (natal ⚼ and △)
Exactly ✳ ☉ p

These technically " difficult " aspects activate the excellent trines and indicate success by energetic achievement.

♀ 10° 41′ ♓ △ ♇ (natal ⚼)

Usually a minor transit, but, since it forms the trine which pleasantly emphasises the natal conjunction, it indicates pleasurable new beginnings.

☉p 26° 54′ ♈ ☍ ♄ ✳ ☉ ♂ △ ☽
☽ p 26° 54′ ♈ (at midday)
(natal △)

This *New Moon* is exact at 9.25 a.m. B.S.T. It unites the luminaries which are trine at birth. It is in the 6th house of work, aspecting the whole of the Grand Trine. If possible, any new matter should be started soon after the new of the Moon. At this time, necessary arrangement of classes for the first day of term will be taking place, so it is to be expected that teaching would begin soon after.

So many indications of good, new beginnings are splendid testimonies for successful results in the future.

(c) EXAMINATION OF ASTROLOGICAL INDICATIONS FOR ANY YEAR IN THE LIGHT OF A KNOWN EVENT

It is not difficult to " do astrology backwards " and it is a very helpful way to learn to do it " forwards." In earlier chapters, astrology was usefully compared to medicine. In neither branch of study can the practitioner be *sure* of the future, he can only deal in *probabilities* based on experience of past results.

The student should now take a definite event of which he knows all the details and study the astrological conditions at the time of its happening. The event must be in the life of a person whose birth time is reasonably accurate, or the work will merely be misleading.

Again using our example chart :—

Sudden Death of Father, 17th October, 1944

Firstly, in the light of knowledge of the *nature of the planets*, what would be expected at such a time ?

A death of a loved parent is a loss and a blow, and with this a Saturnian condition correlates. This may be found by progression or transit *OF* or *TO* Saturn in the map.

This death was sudden. Hence Uranus should be in evidence.

The son's natural financial expectation was disappointed through loss of the family business. The 2nd house should show this, either in relation to planet in it or ruling it.

The 8th house should be in evidence through planets in it, through its rulers or natural rulers.

(It may be objected that this gives much too wide a choice. For instance :— given two planets in the house, and a sign with double rulership on the cusp and t'e natural sign (Scorpio) having double rulership, it is more than probable that *some* aspect will be made *TO* or *BY* these six out of the ten planets. This may be thought to be a weakness of astrology. On the other hand, there *are* only ten planets, four of which hardly move by progression. If all the multifarious objective and subjective conditions of life are to be correlative with their movement in sign and house, they need some lee-way in which to express them.)

Method of Working

Underline noon-time planets in the Ephemeris for *the day corresponding to the year in the life* (July 11, 1924). Enter the year in the margin, with noon date. (This should have already been calculated for any chart which has been thoroughly worked on, and should have been entered on chart in readiness for any such inspection as this. Refer pp. 230, 231.)

Check by calculating age in the year under consideration and enter in other margin.

Following the routine given in Chapter 12, Part 1, note positions of prog.: Asc., M.C., planets, parallels (though these last can be omitted for a quick look) and transits. For a beginner, it will be easier to use No. 3 Progressions Chart. Copy natal chart into centre, place progressions in their cyclic order round it, enter Solar, Mutual and Lunar progressions and all *main* transits (omit minors).

When more accustomed to the work, it can be done straight from the Ephemeris and listed as follows :—

Refer to natal chart, and 1924 Ephemeris, and calculate Moon's place for October.

Noon positions are as follows :—

Progressed Aspects in Operation 17th October, 1944

(exactness not calculated to minutes)

☉ p	⊻	♆ in ♌ in	10th	Close spring
☽ p	△	♀ in ♋ in	9th	Close previous month
	⊼	☿ in ♊ in	8th	Close previous month
☿ p	□	♄ in ♎	Asc.	Close at time
	□	Ascendant		Close at time
♀ p	⊻	M.C.		Close spring
	∟	♆		
♂ p	⊼	M.C.		Close previous year
♃ p	⊼	♇		Closer than at birth
♄,	♅, ♆, ♇			No movement

Inspection of column of *mutual aspects in Ephemeris* for July 11 1924 adds :—

⊙ p ⊡ ♂ p
⊙ p ⋎ ♆ p
☿ p ⊡ ♃ p
☿ p ☐ ♄ p
♀ p ∟ ♆ p

" O-D's " for Age 20 Years 4 Months (= 20⅓°) Give

(ruler 4th) ♄ △ ♀ (ruler Asc.)		Exact earlier
⋀ ☿ (sun ruler) in 8th		Exact earlier
♂ ⋀ ♆		Exact earlier
♅ ☐ ♇		*Exact at time*
☿ ⋎ M.C.		*Exact at time*

Transits Near Date (from Ephemeris, 1944)

T. ⊙ ☌ ♄ and Asc., △ ⊙, ☽ and ♂ during next few days.
T. ☽ ☌ ♄ and Asc., △ ⊙, ☽ and ♂ during day.
(i.e., it was a New Moon in the early morning.)
T. ☿ ☌ ♄ and Asc., △ ⊙ ☽, ♂ during next few days.
T. ♀ ☐ ♂ and ☽, ⋀ ⊙ during next few days.
T. ♂ ☌ ♄ and Asc., △ ⊙ ☽ ♂ during previous week.
T. ♃ ⋎ ♆ exact within a degree.
T. ♃ ☍ ♅ four weeks later.
T. ♄ ☌ ♇ within a degree for over a month.
T. ♅ through 8th house and within 1½° of ☌ ☿ ☍ ♃ for weeks.
T. ♆ ✱ M.C. long lasting.
No transits by ♇.

Asc. p makes no aspect.
M.C. p nears sextile Asc. r and Saturn.

Would it have been possible to foretell the death of the father from the above ? It is much to be doubted, though the indications can easily be seen in retrospect.

One of the greatest difficulties in astrology, if used for prediction, is to know whether traditionally good aspects are to bring good results, and bad ones bad results. The modern tendency is to rely far more on *the nature of the planet* than the nature of the aspect, it being considered only as marking a time when the principles of the planets in question are brought to inter-relation.

Also, when considering transits to a birth-chart, it must be remembered that though the transiting planet is actually in the heavens in the Zodiac, as listed at the time of transit, *it is not then actually making an angular relationship to any planet similarly in the heavens, but to the degree in which that planet was years before at the birth time* as listed in the natal chart.

It must therefore be understood that *the human being correlates with the planetary pattern at his birth,* and because of this correlation, he responds *in the manner of* his pattern, to stimuli *of a like nature,* as they occur.

It is in this fashion that the person born with weak lungs will have pneumonia if exposed to certain conditions, or the person with an active sense of rhythm will begin to move his hands or feet in time if he hears dance music or a military march, whereas others will remain oblivious to such stimuli.

A re-examination of John's chart shows that the pattern of his birth moment *predisposes* him to :—

(*a*) Suffer by sudden deaths   *Uranus, planet of sudden changes, is square to Mercury, his Sun-ruler, in the 8th house,* connected with the stages of life, death being one of these. At birth he lost his sister. Looking to the above list to see whether there was any stimulus to this in October, it is seen that :—

Prog. Mercury in Cancer (the sign of mother and home) has come to the square of Saturn (r and p) and the Ascendant.   *Mercury,* as Sun-ruler, represents himself ; and being in the 8th and ruling the sign mainly occupying the 8th, it brings an 8th house significance with it ; also, as ruler of Virgo, which mainly occupies the 11th, it brings a significance of objectives with it. From this must be deduced that, by death, he and his objectives in life came to a time of loss and deprivation (Saturn) which affected him very personally (Ascendant). Moreover, Saturn whose metallic significator is lead, not only signifies a blow to be met but a weight to be carried, hence responsibility. As an only son this now came to John.

Mercury, as significator of the mind, by its square to Saturn, signifies mental depression and sadness.

Further stimulus is given to this by :—

Progressed Moon to quincunx *Mercury* (aspect of strain).

Saturn by O-D also quincunx *Mercury.*

P. *Mercury* itself sesquiquadrate Jupiter p in 2nd (affecting expansion financially).

Transit of *Mercury* to conjunction of Saturn in the next few days. Note that it is then *trine* Sun, Moon, Mars and conjunction Ascendant.

Ordinarily, the transit of *Mercury* is of little importance. But, in this case, it is John's *Sun-ruler,* and also it was bad *news* that he received. This was of the nature of Saturn and meant loss or limitation in any case. Saturn is the wise control and guiding principle in life and frequently thus signifies the father, the person in authority (♑). From the accompanying trines may be inferred that John's self (Sun and Moon) and his energy (Mars) worked well and smoothly at the time to do all he could for his mother and the business and that conversely, the necessity to take up early responsibility for self and later on for his mother, would in actuality be to the good since it would bring out the best in him and " make a man of him."

Uranus, at the other angle of this natal square, is the planet of sudden change. It is too slow to move far by progression ; by O-D however, it has this year come to the *exact* square of Pluto, thought to be part ruler of the natural 8th house, and significator of new phases in life, of which death is one. Too much significance must not be placed on the fact that it is in Cancer, the sign representative of home, since it was in that sign for everyone for 30 years, but it is clear that a new phase in life was to begin and that this would be through sudden happening.

Further stimulus was given to this by :—

Transit of Uranus through *8th house*, close though not exact, to conjunction *Mercury* and opposition Jupiter for some weeks.

His natal pattern also *predisposes him* to :—

(*b*) Sudden financial crises (*T-square between Mercury his Sun-ruler and Jupiter in the " money " houses, and Uranus*), though it must be pointed out that the excellent trines will help him through at any time. The progression of *Mercury* to sesquiquadrate *Jupiter* (natal opposition) has already been mentioned. At this time *Jupiter* p is closer to the exactness of its natal quincunx to Pluto; Mars p, *ruler 2nd* is quincunx to M.C. and by O-D is quincunx Neptune in 10th. The current transit of *Jupiter* semi-sextile to Neptune, though minor, is strong because exact.

Neptune is often in evidence at the time of a death. It can be thought of as an escape from life, and as a translation to the intangible or the spiritual from the material, but for those who suffer from the death there is often confusion of affairs.

Sun p comes to semi-sextile Neptune in 10th (house of worldly affairs).

Venus p, ruler of chart comes to semi-square Neptune r and p. Mars, by O-D, has come to quincunx Neptune.

Transits which further stimulate these are :—

T. Jupiter semi-sextile Neptune (exact).

T. Neptune sextile M.C. (long lasting).

Venus is significator of love and happiness and must be thought of in connection with such matters when interpreting ☽ p △ ♀ in the previous month, but Venus is important in this map as ruler, and as well as being semi-square to Neptune r and p, it is trine Saturn by O-D (ruler of 4th E.H.), hence a sobering of happiness, a second testimony of personal responsibility.

M.C.p coming to sextile Asc. and Saturn hints again at responsibility taken up for the affairs of life.

Transits of Sun and Moon though swiftly moving are often correlative with special happenings on a certain day. In this particular chart, Sun, Moon and Mars are extremely strongly placed, being all trine to Saturn and Ascendant. The time of this event is marked by the fact that *all three of them* conjoin Saturn (deprivation and loss) within a few days, the Moon doing so on the exact day.

Finally, the transit of Saturn, though too slow to mark out any degree for one day only, is *within a degree of Pluto* (connected with death) for over a month, and stationary during the coming week.

Note the frequency of the quincunx at " crisis " times, the unhelpful nature of the semi-sextile, and the support for the idea that the 28° and 29° emphasised in a chart denote predisposition to crises.

CHAPTER 13

THE PROBLEM OF THE UNCERTAIN BIRTH-MOMENT

1. THE USE OF RECTIFICATION
2. SOLAR CHARTS

1. The Use of Rectification

(a) *If a birth-time is known no more nearly than within the 24 hours* it is not wise to attempt to rectify it. A certain amount can be gathered from the positions of the planets in their signs and from the aspects made between them. The *noon-time positions of the day* can be taken for this. Any attempt to place the map in relation to any ascendant is known as a *SPECULATIVE chart*, and should always be clearly marked as such. It is preferable to *omit* asc. and house-lines.*

If a person is known, and has outstanding characteristics, an attempt may be made to use the sign which best signifies these, as the ascending sign. Choosing any degree as cusp of 1st, and using the same for the other cusps, the planets can then be entered and interpreted according to house positions.

The chart can be adjusted one way and another to try what house positions seem to fit. If any success is obtained, further work may be done, as with a closely known birth-time, but the chart must still be considered as speculative.

(b) *If a birth-time is known within two or three hours*, charts may be put up for the beginning, the middle and the end of this time to see whether the Ascendant of any seems applicable to what is known of the person.

(c) *If the birth is closely, but not exactly known*, then the best method of rectification is by the use of the "One-Degree" system. The number of degrees from a planet to an angle will almost always correspond with the age at which an event *of the nature of that planet* and in the sphere of life denoted by that angle, will occur. Such measurements to Ascendant and M.C. are the strongest and most obvious, since they affect the self and the outer self-expression.

The chart used as example for analysis and progressions was rectified in this way which has the advantage of being extremely simple. There are elaborate methods in use (such as by the Pre-Natal Epoch—see Chapter 15) and other ways greatly approved of by some astrologers, but these cannot always be relied on. There have been many examples of maps so made to the complete satisfaction of their makers, who are very discomforted when the actual time is discovered later and they are found to be wrong.

Rectification of Example Chart (Chapter 11)

John's mother stated that she thought the birth was 3.45 p.m. B.S.T. and that she was sure she was right within a quarter of an hour. Note that parents nearly always give an exact hour, or the half or quarter. This gave a Sidereal Time of 8 h. 43 m. 7 s., with Asc. 29° Libra and M.C. 9° Leo. She wondered whether the birth was earlier or later than this time.

* See *Applied Astrology* by the same author, p. 72.

Had it been later, the Ascendant, the Sun and the Moon would all have been in Water signs. They very soon enter them by progression in any case but if actually in them at birth, John would have been markedly emotional, intuitive, artistic, rather than active, intelligent, academic.

From the point of view of the Equal House map, this would have shown in his attitude to his girl friends and to his ways of enjoying himself, since the Moon is on the cusp of the 5th.

From the point of view of the Placidean chart, the 4th house would have been affected.

Since 1st, 5th and 9th are the houses mostly to be affected, questions were put to John about himself (1st), his girl friends and enjoyments (5th), his feelings about children (5th), his ideas on more profound subjects (9th). In every case, his answers were cool, thoughtful and reasoned. In no case were they emotional or given with feeling. The decision was therefore that the Asc., Sun and Moon were in the Air triplicity and not in Water.

The next question was, if not later, then how much earlier?

With the Asc. in 29° Libra and Saturn in 25° 40' of the same sign, Saturn came to the Ascendant by the "One-Degree" measure, at the age of 3 years and 4 months (29° 00' − 25° 40' = 3° 20'). If this had been so, it would have been expected that its principle would have been in evidence in his life at that time. He would have suffered some limitation (Saturn) personally (1st). This might have been through serious illness or through a fall, or through a loss in the family which affected him. On questioning, he was quite certain that no such event happened and this was later confirmed by his mother. The trial was then made to bring the Ascendant even nearer to Saturn, but no such drastic event had happened at the age of 2 or 1 and the attempt was given up.

It chanced that just as his interview was ending, a remark was made as to the similarity between his map and another one with Grand Trine containing the same planets, the Moon being robustly conjunct Mars, both they and the Sun strengthening each other by a close trine. The owner of this one was described as rather like John in that she was strong and healthy-looking, but had nearly died at birth. John's laughing reply was " and to look at me now, you'd never think *I* was an incubator baby ! "

The problem was solved. John had very nearly died *at birth*, moreover he and his parents had suffered the loss of the one who should have been his greatest companion in life, his twin sister. Since this was *at birth*, the supposition was that the Ascendant was closely conjunct Saturn. It was then placed at 25° Libra, for which the M.C. was 4° Leo, in that latitude, and a further test was made.

If the M.C. was correct at 4° Leo, then by " O-D," Venus came to it *at the age of* 19°. On being asked when he first fell in love, *he replied that it was at* 19.

Three and a half years later Pluto came to the M.C. by " O-D." This planet is often in evidence at the beginning of a new chapter in life. When nearly 23, John suddenly heard that he was accepted for his teachers' training college after three years of trying for this. His old life was completely closed and a new chapter begun. This added confirmation seemed to prove the rectification.

When a map is rectified in this way, it should be watched for further confirmation. As the Sun, by secondary progression, moves at about 1° per year, its natural movement is about the same as if by " O-D." It reaches 4° Leo in 1960, at which time, if he takes some more prominent administrative position, it will give added proof to the rectification.

Two points should be noted. First that the M.C. is used rather than the nonagesimal because it is a mundane point of great significance and seems to be connected with the world of *events* more than the 10th cusp E.H. John's Sun reaches the latter late in 1951. He will probably come to some satisfaction of *personal* ambition which he will value greatly.

Secondly, Saturn rules most of the 3rd house by E.H. and is part-ruler by Placidus, since Capricorn is intercepted, so in either case, matters of the 3rd house affect him personally. (Saturn conjunct Asc.) This can be seen fully in his academic life, but at birth the effect was from the other meaning of the 3rd house, since the loss was of *his sister* and the difficulty of the birth was accentuated through it being of twins.

The time given by the new Ascendant is 3.35 p.m. B.S.T., which differs by ten minutes from 3.45 p.m., the time given by the mother who said she was " right within a quarter of an hour."

2. Solar Charts

There are astrologers who consider that the twelve houses may have significance if started from any planet or from the M.C., but it will be in relation to that point.

The strongest planet is the Sun which shows the vitality and self expression of a person, hence the Solar Chart is most popular, especially in the U.S.A.

The Sun in its degree for the noon of the day, is placed as cusp of the 1st house. The mistake of calling this the Ascendant must not be made. Equal houses follow from this in the usual way as from the Ascendant ; they are referred to as *the Solar houses*. The other planets are entered in their noon positions and judgment is attempted. (This should not be confused with the *Sunrise* chart, in which the Sun is placed on the cusp of the first house in the degree and moment which it occupied at sunrise at the latitude of the birth-place ; the zodiacal longitudes of the Moon and all other planets being calculated for this moment also. When this chart was used by astrologers favouring the quadrant systems, the M.C. and intermediate cusps correlative for the Ascendant were used also. Such precision seems of little use when the time is not known. Deductions from inter-planetary relationships can be made just as well from the noon positions.)

CHAPTER 14

THE COMPARISON OF CHARTS

" Synastry "

THIS is the old word of which the dictionary meaning is " Coincidence as regards stellar influences." (Greek *syn*, together with, *astron*, a star.) The practising astrologer is frequently asked to compare two charts to see whether any such coincidence exists. Certainly, it would be no use telling two people who were violently in love that there was little coincidence in their planets, but many young people especially men, are anxious to have confirmation for their feeling that " this is the right one " before making an irrevocable step.

As with much of astrology, there is no one rule, but the only way to assess charts for this purpose is the way in which all real astrological work must be done, that is, by thoroughly understanding *the nature of each planet* and then deducing from the inter-relationship found between the maps in question.

The method is to make a list of the points of likeness and unlikeness between the charts, as to shaping and house and sign-emphasis and then between the aspects made by the planets in the one to the planets in the other, and to judge by what has thus been noted.

In no pair of maps will everything be found to be harmonious, but, if the inquirer is asking for astrological aid with real intent to be helped to make the very best of a marriage, then if tactfully done, the likely causes of occasional disharmony can be shown and thus allowed for and minimised.

The great lesson of modern " depth psychology " is that neuroses and psychoses arise from those things in ourselves which we refuse to face and accept. If suppressed, they remain in the unconscious but break out in some other form to hurt us. It is therefore better if two people realise they do *not* combine well in certain ways. After being able to admit this openly, they may even begin to laugh at themselves for it and then all is well.

The principles of the planets are the same, whatever may be their application. The Ascendant refers to the person and often his health, Sun to his self-expression in general, the M.C. to the expression of self in the outer world. The Moon in its response and fluctuation refers to the way of living, the habits and ways, Mercury to the mental outlook, Venus to love as true uniting affection, Mars to the energy, which from this point of view, is being expressed as sexual love. Jupiter tells of the expansiveness and the power to make life gay and delightful for another, Saturn of the limitations and the power to crush or be too much for another. These must not be taken as all good or all bad.* Jupiter in bad aspect may mean too much extremism and licence; Saturn in good aspect may mean wise control. Uranus galvanically excites the other. Neptune raises to heights of ecstasy or deceives, according to aspect. Pluto is not sufficiently personal to take into account. Moreover, he is in the same sign for all those near in age. This applies also to Uranus and Neptune. As with interpretative work, the closer the aspect the stronger it is, an orb of 3° being the widest allowed.

* Traditionally, the planets were called benefic and malefic. Modern astrologers do not divide them so sharply.

Good aspects between like planets produce a harmony of relationship which brings friendship, whether between two of the same sex or the opposite, and this in itself goes towards the making of a happy marriage. Such aspects between Suns show an alikeness in the basic selves of the two. They will see eye to eye. If between the two Moons, they will react to moods and changes similarly and have the same ways, hence share common interests. If between the two Mercuries, the tie will be mental, between the two Venuses it will be more in the line of pleasures and social entertainments, between the two Mars, they may share a fighting spirit but quarrel if the combining degrees are otherwise badly aspected. A shared Jupiter is excellent as each will vie with the other to open up life and make it free and prosperous. A shared Saturn may even unite in calm and sober ways, but both will be depressed at the same time when the shared degree is afflicted by difficult transits.

With the other three planets, if in conjunction between maps of people of about the same age, it must be remembered that this is the same for all and only means that they share a certain outlook and tendency common to all their generation. If the two are far apart in age, the result of the aspects will be according to the nature of the planets.

For a lasting marriage relationship, perhaps the strongest tie is that formed by good aspects from the Ascendant of the one to the Sun of the other.

Equally strong are those between Sun of one and Moon of the other. Next may be taken those between rulers, also Sun-rulers and Asc., Sun and Moon of the other.

Those between Venus of one and Mars of another show normal male-female attraction, but when Uranus enters into this the attraction is more unusual, magnetic, compulsive, inescapable.

Difficult aspects from Mars imply sharp ways which may cause quarrels. Difficult aspects from Saturn cause a feeling of weight to the other and depression and responsibility.

The work of examining the natal planetary relationships by aspect is not enough for a full inspection. The charts should be compared to see whether planets in the one are coming or have come to planets in the other by progression.

Most frequently, when love begins, the Sun of the one will come to aspect with the Venus of the other, of if the attraction is mainly physical it will be the Mars which makes the aspect or is aspected. In charts which show basic linkage together, it is excellent to find these progressions, but, if they occur when there is NO basic link, then they show a passing attraction. The two have been brought together, but once the progressions are past, will wonder what they ever saw in each other. If this is found to be the case, it will be no use to say so while the progressions are in effect but if advice can be given that it would be wiser to delay a formal engagement for a while, this may avoid trouble when the attraction is over.

The example comparison which follows is of a pair who were determined that nothing should keep them apart. It is an extreme case of happy links, the aspects being within close orbs. It is not very likely that the student will often find such a one, but a marriage can be a success with less than half this number of links, so long as some of the main ones are in evidence.

"JACK AND JILL"

(Published by their kind permission)

Orb of aspect	HIS	HER	
	Shaping of Both		Both charts are "bowl" shaped showing similar personal "make-up" and attitude to life.
2°	♀	♂ ♀ in 7th	Unison of basic affection.
2°	☉, ruler	♂ ☉ on 5th	Similarity of basic self-expression.
Exact	☉	△ ♆, Sun-ruler	She idealises him.
2°	Asc.	♂ ♂, ruler	Strong physical attraction.
Exact	♃ in 5th	△ ♂	She can be happy without inhibitions with him, as he is good fun and encourages her to " be herself."
			He finds her responsive.
1°	♃ in 5th	✱ ♀ in 7th	He increases her innate ability to form a partnership and does it gaily.
			She gives him affection abundantly.
3°	♅ in 5th	✱ ♀ in 7th	Inescapable attraction.
Exact	☿	♂ ♃	She delights his mind, his mental ability brings her out.
Exact	M.C.	✱ ♅	In an unusual way, she tries to help him to professional success.
1°	♄ in 5th	△ ☽	He is older than she, so while there is the most perfect accord, and on her part, acceptance of certain limitations, he is liable to cause difficulties and to necessitate a giving-way on her part.
5°	♄ in 5th	△ ♀ ruler 7th and in 7th	
Exact	♄ in 5th	✱ ☿ and Asc.	
3°	♄ in 5th	☍ ♇	This affects her in her ways (Moon), her affection (Venus), her mental and nervous reactions (Mercury), her physical self and reactions (Asc. and Pluto). A tendency to depression or lack of self-confidence in him is enormously helped by her love, her mental outlook and her personality.
1°	Asc.	□ ♀ in 7th ruler 7th	At times, he can spoil her desire for complete " rapport."
3°	♆, Sun-ruler	□ ☉	Also at times, she feels he escapes from her understanding and does not come up to her ideals.

Note.—Only major aspects are taken. With the exception of Saturn trine Venus (taken because Venus is in 7th and ruler 7th), none has an orb of more than 3°.

Allowing for differences of circumstance, all that has been said applies to other ties as well as to that of marriage.

In charts of parents and children, the same emphasis as to planet, sign, house, type of aspect, triplicity or quadruplicity will repeat again and again, indicating the hereditary traits observable in them. Such charts can be compared with due regard for 5th house planets and ruler in the parents' maps in their relation to the children ; in the children's map 4th and 10th house planets and rulers will relate to parents, and also Saturn as authority. Sun and Moon also refer to fatherhood and motherhood. Progressions in the chart of a parent to a position in the chart of a child, or vice versa, often indicate a time of special nearness and added sympathy between them, especially when the Sun of the one comes to the Asc. or Venus of the other. A longer period of such happiness would be indicated when Venus p is slow in movement, when about to change its apparent motion, and remains near an important point in the chart of the other for some years.

In business or professional relationships, the comparison of charts is most important. Again the *nature of the planet* and the nature of the relationship must be thought out. If the Saturn of an employer or senior partner is on the Sun or ruler of employé or junior partner, then so long as other factors make for smooth running, it is only reasonable and will not matter that the less important person should feel the other as in authority over him and something of a weight and a causer of responsibility ; *but* if this should be the other way round, then another employé or junior had better be found, since no one can get on with his work if his so-called helper is a heavy-weight and a responsibility.

For a junior or underling of any kind, progress and advantages should be possible under anyone whose helpful planets (such as Sun and Jupiter) are conjunct or trine to his M.C. or nonagesimal, or to prominent planets in his chart.

Those whose charts have strong linking-points should watch the transits over them with care, trying not to irritate each other when Mars affects such points or depress each other when Saturn is in aspect, but should go all out for enjoyment when Jupiter and Venus are operative.

At times of stress in two lives, charts should be compared for effects of slower transits and progressions. As an example, a professional man found it unbearable to continue to work with his junior partner who seemed to be approaching a mental crisis. Inspection showed that indeed the progressed Sun was within orbs of conjunction of Uranus in the junior's 7th house, showing complete breakdown of the *ability* to sustain a partnership, while in the senior's map, the transit of Uranus was approaching Mercury in the 10th house, showing a break in professional agreements, unpleasant and upsetting, but to be put right in course of time. In this case the astrologer could show the senior that the break was inevitable and had better be made and forgotten as soon as possible. This was actually done by him without further worry as it was then felt to be part of his pattern that it should happen.   The unfortunate pattern of the junior was also fulfilled.

Another way of comparison is by noticing that two people have progressions of similar nature in their charts. In a case of a husband and wife, the one had the Sun progressing to his Saturn, while the other had Venus, ruler, also progressing to her Saturn at the same time, while several long transits added to the stress. On hearing the explanation of the astrologer that this, in the nature of things, must take another two years to blow over, each became intensely interested in watching for the crisis-times as indicated by transits and almost turned their troubles into a game of watching to see " the way the wheels went round." They learnt to accept the current difficulties with less resentment, as being part of their joint pattern and to look forward with confidence to the better time ahead.

Failing the whole map for comparison, the Sun-degree of any person is known by his birth date. The other can then compare this one strong factor with important points in his or her own known chart.

CHAPTER 15

INTRODUCTION TO OTHER ASTROLOGICAL TECHNIQUES

THERE are many ways of using astrological symbolism. The student should have general information on these so that he knows what is implied by each, but to be fully informed, it is necessary to read special books on each or to take lessons from the few who have specialised in them, so that he may try for himself these techniques, on most of which much more research is needed before authoritative statements can be made.

The following subjects will be briefly discussed :—

1. Electional Astrology.
2. Mundane Astrology.
3. Horary Astrology.
4. Degree Meanings.
5. Solar and Lunar Returns.
6. The Pre-natal Epoch.
7. Astrology in Relation to Eras of Time.

1. ELECTIONAL ASTROLOGY

BOOK SUGGESTED :—*Electional Astrology*, by Vivian Robson. 1937

An astrologer is often asked to choose a favourable time for some action to be taken. Procedure depends upon whether a period of time within certain limits has to be chosen, or whether the project is to be begun at an exact moment.

If the matter is a personal one, then the natal chart of the person, with its progressions and transits, must be studied in relation to current planetary positions. No carefully chosen moment will make a matter successful if these are unfavourable, though the careful choice may help.

Even with an impersonal matter such as the formation of a business company, or the starting of a club, it is better to have the map for the beginning moment as harmonious as possible with that of the managing director, chairman, president or whoever is to be in control.

The traditional phrase used for the wider process is the making of an *election* which simply means making a choice, but, if the matter is to be planned *to begin at a definite moment*, then alternative maps may be made of various possible moments in order to decide not only when the interplanetary positions are favourable but when the ascending degree and resulting houses and planetary house-positions are also favourable. The one decided upon will then be called an *election map*.

If the beginning of such a matter is arranged to be at a definite moment, and *hence the question of choice does not arise*, a map for that moment is called an *inceptional map*, meaning the map of a beginning. Full rules cannot be given but examples will help the student to see how to work.

Example 1.   Inceptional Map

A ship was launched at a certain time according to arrangement. At the appointed moment, Saturn and Mars were each side of a Leo Ascendant (conjunction) and all three squared by the Sun. (Weakness and liability to suffer in the back.)

There was an opposition to Jupiter (success) from Uranus (breaks). At the time of an eclipse a year later, Uranus by transit became *exactly* opposition Jupiter, and the ship broke her back on rocks.

Example 2.   Election Map

The formation of a society was proposed. The final decision was to be taken at a committee meeting. The chairman asked for astrological advice for the best moment within the available time for this to happen. Alternative maps showed that if a decision was forced early in the proceedings, Jupiter would be in 1st house but near to cusp of the second, whereas later on it would become conjunction the Ascendant. He was able to bring forward other business so as to delay the decision until the time advised.

Another example is that given in Chapter 17 of Flamsteed's map for the Founding of Greenwich Observatory, the continued success of which is apparent.

Any such map is to be judged in the same way as a natal map. The Ascendant, Sun, etc., will show the character ; the 2nd house planets and ruler will show the financial outlook, etc., while current progressions and transits will show its vicissitudes as the years go on.

Example 3.   Election Within a Period

In May, 1947, when flats were almost unobtainable in London, an astrologer wished to get one. His own progressions were reasonably good. A little earlier, his progressed Moon had returned to its natal place, always an excellent time for *change* and *new beginning*, especially if the natal degree is well aspected as it was in this case. There were good aspects to planets in the 2nd house, indicating financial ability to cover expenses of buying a lease and removing.

The current Ephemeris showed that, *six months ahead*, the transit of Saturn would enter his 1st house indicating personal frustrations, while the transiting Jupiter would leave his 4th house where it was then indicating excellent opportunity as regards *home affairs*.

It was therefore advisable not to delay the start of the new home to any quarter-day later than that of September.

Inspection of that month showed that the New Moon before the quarter day would be *September* 14, and that the Moon, always important in personal matters and changes, would be conjunct important and well-aspected planets in the natal chart on the next day, *September* 15.

As the move would entail both a legal agreement and a short journey, Mercury, ruler of Gemini, was considered to be the significator of the matter. It would arrive at the conjunction of the Moon on this same day, *the* 15*th*, so this was decided upon as the best day to move after the September Lunation.

The inescapable difficulty was that the slow transit of Neptune was near his Sun, indicating on its less favourable side the possibility of being let down.

The search began, only to be thwarted in this very way since both in *June* and *July* landlords broke agreements after making apparently secure arrangements. It was then decided that a day for the next attempt to search must also be astrologically chosen.

No combination of planets seemed favourable in what was left of *July* so, though it meant leaving the matter over-late, it was decided that no step must be taken until *after the New Moon of August* 16, at which time Sun and Moon were conjunct natal Venus, which was his Sun-ruler and well aspected, hence a favourable indication for happiness.

A day had to be found when other suitable planets backed this up. On *August* 22 T. Jupiter was still well within the 4th house E.H., and *on the same day* T. Venus (happiness, also pleasant things, furniture, etc.), and T. Mercury (agreements) were within 4° of conjunction with each other, the degree of the Sun-Moon conjunction and the natal Venus being exactly between them.

The astrologer decided to do nothing until this day. In spite of drastic scarcity, the first house-agent visited when the day came *had exactly the flat required.* It was taken and a removal firm in the country was asked which would be their best day for the journey to London. Their reply was that they could go on Mondays *only,* and that the day *must be September* 15, *the date already pre-decided for this purpose in May.*

2. MUNDANE ASTROLOGY

Books Suggested :—*An Introduction to Political Astrology.* 1951. (Charles E. O. Carter.)

Periodicals :—   Many articles in bound volumes of *Astrology.* War years.

As its name implies, this is the astrology of " the world " (Latin, *mundus*) in contradistinction to that of " the people " the old name for which is *genethliacal astrology* (Greek, *genethle,* birth).

In its narrower and more customary usage it means political astrology. For good work to be done, a much wider knowledge is required than of astrology only. As has been remarked before, astrology is an applied symbolism and is therefore useless unless there is an understanding of that to which it is to be applied.

A good knowledge of world affairs is necessary also of the history of the various countries and of the personalities of their leaders.

A large collection of charts is required so that those relative to any country that comes into the news may be studied at once.

Time is necessary for reading in order to keep well-informed as to changing conditions. This is a special branch of astrology and better left alone by those who have no aptitude for it.

The maps customarily studied are as usual, those of beginnings. Instead of beginnings of *lives,* they are beginnings of *periods.*

If there is a definite date on which it can be said that a country " began " in its present form, and if a certain *time* can be given such as the signing of a constitution, then continuous work can be done in regard to it since there will be a basic chart on which to work, watching progressions, symbolic measures and transits.

The inadequacy and failure of much Mundane Astrology is due to the fact that few reliable maps can be produced either for the countries or their leading statesmen.

Royal births are the most usually correct of all, being officially recorded. The birth-chart of a king, a president, or even anyone in control of a business organisation frequently reflects the vicissitudes of that country or business.

Charles Carter has coined the excellent expression, " The doctrine of subsumption." Again the dictionary helps. " Subsume " is defined as " to place any one cognition under another, as belonging to it."

In Mundane Astrology, though maps of definite beginnings can stand alone, the general usage is to refer current, or even natal maps of important people, to basic maps (subsume) and to compare them by aspect, much as was done for personal maps in Chapter 14.

In Great Britain, the basic maps generally used are three :—
*1. The crowning of William the Conqueror. Midday. December 25th, 1066.
2. The Union of England and Scotland. Midnight. May 1st, 1707.
3. The Union of Great Britain and Ireland. Midnight. January 1st, 1801.

Of the three, the last seems to be the most valid and the one mainly used.

Each year, charts are made for minor beginnings. The most important of these are the times of the entry of the Sun into the Cardinal signs. These are called the *Solar Ingresses*. Their exact times are tabulated at the end of each Raphael's Ephemeris.

Of the four, the Spring (or Vernal) Ingress is regarded as the most important, as the entry into Aries begins the round of the Zodiacal signs once more† (p. 276).

These are " subsumed " under the 1801 map, and under them are the *Lunation* charts which are cast for the times of the *New Moon* of each month. The exact times of these are at the head of each page for each month in the Ephemeris.

Other phenomena for which maps are cast are the *conjunctions of the major planets*, since these constitute the beginnings of new cycles of such planets, also the moments of the exactitudes of *eclipses*, since these are but special conjunctions or oppositions of Sun and Moon, indicating further sub-cycles of their perpetual Soli-Lunar relationship.

The times of these are given under " Phenomena " at the end of the Ephemerides. When conjunctions of the major planets occur, they are dated under " Mutual Aspects " on the page for the month.

The most important of the conjunctions are said to be those of *Jupiter and Saturn* which occur about every 20 years. They occur in a sign of the same triplicity always for 240 years.

* See *Astrology*, Vol. 14, No. 2.
† The point of the autumnal equinox coincides with the entry of the Sun into 0° Libra. The entries into Cancer and Capricorn are referred to as the summer and winter *solstices*. The Sun is at its farthest from the equator, at the turning point of its apparent course and its declination is almost the same for three days, hence the name. (Latin: solstitium. Sol, the Sun; sistere, to make to stand.)

The whole cycle through the four triplicities takes 960 years. At present, the conjunction takes place in the signs of the Earthy triplicity ; the most recent in Taurus, having occurred three times because of retrogradation. The dates and times were :—

    1. 0.58 a.m. G.M.T., August 8th, 1940.
    2. 5.22 a.m. G.M.T., October 20th, 1940.
    3. 6.10 a.m. G.M.T., February 15th, 1941.

It is thought that the markedly materialistic dull practicality of the present age correlates with this fact, the industrial revolution having come into being at about the time of the beginning of the succession of conjunctions in Earth. The first of these was in 9° Capricorn on January 26th, 1842.

On December 28th, 1980, there will be a conjunction in Libra, the first to take place in the Air triplicity. This will be followed by others in Earth again.

The chart for the moment of the first conjunction of an unbroken sequence in a new triplicity is referred to as the *Mutation Chart*. This will be in 1° Aquarius on December 22nd, 2020.

It is to be hoped that a more intelligent management of national and international affairs will accompany this change from Earth to Air.

In judging maps of Ingresses, Lunations, and so on, the principles of the planets are given the usual traditional meanings but are used with regard to mundane events rather than psychological trends.

The houses have the same meaning but with national application. Whereas the 2nd house of a natal chart refers to a person's money, in mundane charts it refers to the financial conditions of the nation, the Exchequer and Banks.

In any book on the subject, traditional connections are given between the various countries and certain signs. There is much diversity of opinion over these and as little research has been done, they should not be too readily accepted.

Many prognostications are made from the monthly Lunation maps, but the student should not be content with reading these. Correct research into their validity necessitates careful entering into a book, leaving the opposite page blank for a factual record a month later as to their correctness or otherwise.

3. HORARY ASTROLOGY

Books Suggested :—*Lilly's Astrology*. First written 1647, edited by Zadkiel, 1834 and reprinted several times since
Raphael's Horary Astrology. 1931

This also is a special branch of astrology but needs no special knowledge such as the grasp of politics which is required for Mundane astrology. Its practice consists in the erecting of charts for the moment when a question of pressing importance comes into the mind. The chart is judged as to the answer.

It is obvious that the heavens do not arrange themselves to fit the query of any inconspicuous one of the millions of human beings on the earth, so the supposition is that as remarked in an earlier chapter, all people are indissolubly part of the universe, and exist in unison with it, but so conditioned are they to this that they are unaware of it.

In moments of stress and anxiety, a person seems to feel that he has correlation with something outside himself. It may be that this instinctive feeling springs from his unconscious knowledge of his oneness with the universe, and as the saying goes, " the question asks him " rather than that " he asks the question."

If the question comes to an astrologer's mind, he casts the chart for the moment of his thought, using the latitude and longitude of the place where he is. If a person comes to an astrologer and puts his request, the time of the request is taken.

Diversity of opinion exists as to the procedure to follow when there is delay through the post. Some astrologers say that the time of opening the letter should be taken, others stating that the querent should give the time when the idea came to birth in his own mind. This seems the more reasonable way.

The chart having been cast, the ruler of the sign on the first cusp is reckoned to represent the querent, and the ruler of the sign on the cusp of the house connected with the affairs of the question is taken as its significator. Judgment depends mainly on the aspect formed between these two, but many minor rules to be followed have bearing on this.

As it is by no means always easy to decide which house is to provide the correct significator, and as it is all too easy to change the mind once the map is seen, it is vital that the question should be clearly stated and *written* in its final form, and the house to be taken decided upon before the map is cast.

The question must be *exact* in meaning. The map cannot be expected to answer the question " will the business prosper? " (10th house significance) if the real question is " Will it make enough profit that my salary may be raised? " (2nd house significance).

Undoubtedly, the most clear and convincing maps may be seen, cast for questions thus asked. The veracity would seem to depend on the sensitivity or intuitive ability of the querent to be so in tune with the unseen universe that the question is asked at the right time.

The practice of Horary Astrology was very popular in the Middle Ages, and its best known exponent was William Lilly (1602–81). His *Life and Works* may be read, also a book of his aphorisms and maps, edited by the astrologer Zadkiel (Commander R. J. Morrison). He states that every rule must be meticulously followed, but unfortunately he himself begins the book with Tables of Houses calculated for the Placidean system of house division and follows by Lilly's maps, all calculated according to the system of Regiomontanus.

As many astrological students have accepted the Placidean system because its Tables are the only ones easily accessible, and as few realise that Lilly died before this system was introduced into England, it may be wondered why Zadkiel did not mention this.

In Horary work, aspects to house cusps are held to be as important as those to planets. This presented no problem to most astrologers of the last few generations, since they accepted the Placidean system and said their maps " worked."

In the full knowledge that Regiomontanian, Campanian, and Equal House degrees may differ widely on the cusps of the intermediate houses, even altering the sign on the cusp, hence its ruler, the matter is not so simple to the modern astrologer.*

Method of Procedure

To each practitioner of Horary astrology, the method seems straightforward since each has, in the words of one of them, "a way of his own with Horaries," and they by no means all agree in their "ways." Nor is it easy to find a book in which the rules of procedure are shortly and simply set out.

Lilly's *Astrology*, written in the middle of the seventeenth century, still seems better than those which have followed and it has the added charm of the old-fashioned terminology in which the student is instructed "to know whether a thing demanded will be brought to perfection, Yea or Nay?"

Having mastered the rules, if judgment is to be made by reason and not by intuition, then there is only one course to follow :—the testimonies for "Yea" and "Nay" must be separately listed and decision must be made as to which are the stronger.

The question asked should be definitely written at the head of the map. The testimonies and the judgment should then be written, and if the question involves waiting for a certain time of fulfilment, that time should also be written as judged. The result should also be entered when the time comes.

It is only natural that when Horary Astrology is the subject of a lecture or an article, maps which "worked" should be chosen as examples.

In actual practice, since these charts are so easily set up, the casual worker tends to lose them unless worth keeping because successful, and therefore an incorrect idea of the proportion of successful ones arises.

No satisfactory statistical work on this branch can be done unless the decision is firmly made to file *all* work and truthfully record results.

4. DEGREE MEANINGS

BOOKS SUGGESTED :—*Encyclopedia of Psychological Astrology*, by C. E. O. Carter. 4th Edition, 1954.

The student will be confused to find that some astrologers believe firmly that there is a certain meaning inherent in each of the 360°, while others do not agree.

In most of the books of "symbolic" meanings the claim is made that they have been received by clairvoyance, thus even if correct, they are not to be thought of in the same category as astrological deduction from basic principles of interpretation.

There are no less than eight such books in which a degree may be looked up and a different meaning found in each. This does not encourage trust in any of them but yet it is true that they are sometimes startlingly appropriate. As in lectures

* See Tables, p. 136.

on Horary astrology, a very good case can be made if all the examples given are chosen for their applicability. It can hardly be supposed that if examination were made over a wider field of inquiry, the same "symbolic meaning" for the Sun degree would be fitting for a large number of people born all over the world on that day in successive years.

In *The Code of Ethics* written by the Principal, C. E. O. Carter, for the students of the Faculty of Astrological Studies, is the following paragraph: " 3(d). In work stated to be astrological I will not insert anything that is not founded upon true astrological science. Should I desire to impart advice or information from other sources, I will write this on a separate sheet with an express statement that it is not based upon astrology."

" Encyclopedia of Psychological Astrology "

This work stands in a different class from the others as it is the result of careful study of actual maps. The Foreword should be carefully read. At the end will be found a list of degree-areas which have been found to be significant for various reasons. (See also p. 280.)

5. SOLAR AND LUNAR RETURNS

BOOK SUGGESTED :—*Solar Returns and Revolutionary Periods*, by Walter Leon, M.A.

Each year, the Sun returns to the exact degree, minute and second which it occupied at birth. Each month, the Moon does the same. The times of such returns can be calculated from the Ephemeris of the year to be considered.

The charts for these times are additional aids in detecting the tendencies in a life and often of the type of events to be expected.

These charts are more used on the Continent than in England. It has recently been suggested that a more accurate chart can be made if the difference of time caused by precession (see Section 7) in the life is allowed for. This difference is trifling in youth but amounts to $1°$ for the Sun at the age of 72.

The charts may be judged in their own right, but should also be considered as important *transit* charts, and as such, compared with the natal chart.

The most indicative *Solar Returns* seem to be those in which important planets appear near the angles or receive exact or very close aspects from others.

If the thirteen *Lunar Returns* for the ensuing year are then cast, the outstanding months will be those in which the same planets are again prominent or again in aspect.

Naturally, the slower-moving planets will remain in the same mutual aspect for some time while the quicker-moving ones will catch up the slower, again forming aspects but of a different nature.

Both of these charts are of added importance if they aspect the natal chart.

The use of Ternary Proportional Logarithms simplifies calculation. (See Chamber's 7-figure *Mathematical Tables*, page 398.)

According to some astrologers, the contacts of the Sun and Moon with other planets, during the year and the month, are indicative of times when events may be expected.

More research is required to confirm this.

6. THE PRE-NATAL EPOCH

BOOK SUGGESTED :—*The Pre-Natal Epoch*, 1929, by E. H. Bailey

Clarity of meaning is again helpful. The dictionary defines an epoch as " A point of time fixed or made remarkable by some great event from which dates are reckoned."

The particular point of time known as the Pre-Natal Epoch (P.N.E.) occurs at about 273 days (the average period of gestation) before birth, when the degree ascending on the eastern horizon and the longitude of the Moon at that time, interchange with those same two points in the birth map, or their respective opposite points.

It must be clearly understood that this is not an attempt to ascertain the moment of physical *conception* since this is never definable. According to medical sources, it can take place at any time up to about three days after coition.

After following various rules for choice in special cases, a chart is erected for the chosen moment.

The system is said to have two uses, the first being as a method of rectification of uncertain birth-times, and the second as an additional indicator of characteristics appertaining to the person in question.

Though a few astrologers still hold to belief in the theory, it is more generally thought that, as stated in its present form, it is impossible to use it.

The reasons are as follows :—

1. When writing the first edition of this text-book the opinion of the author was influenced by the conclusions of a doctor who had thought that the epoch-map frequently gave the key to physical abnormalities in a person, these being perhaps not fully indicated in the natal chart. Since that time, this doctor has found that more research has invalidated his ideas.

1. Since the time of writing, the author arranged a test in which ten birth-times accurately taken by a doctor-astrologer, were very slightly altered, as would be the case if rectification were needed. These were " rectified " by six astrologers who believed in the theory. Their answers were checked against the known times. *In not one instance was* the " rectification " correct.

3. Also since the time of writing, it became obvious to the author that, since birth is the same in all parts of the world, the theory, if correct, must be usable in all parts of the world.

In the early days from which it has been handed down, little was known about the northern parts of Canada, Norway and other countries in the Arctic and Antarctic zones where there are now good-sized towns.

No attention was paid to the fact that for nearly one-third of a year it is *im-*

possible that the required interchange could take place. The reason is that for two periods of about five days each in every month, the Moon is in degrees which are circumpolar in those latitudes, the period being longer as the latitude is more northerly. (That is, the Moon neither rises nor sets, thus it is not on the horizon as required by the theory.)

Inquiry from two sources, the Maternity Hospital in a town in Latitude 64° 42' N. and the Statistical Bureau of Oslo, gave figures showing the numbers of children born on these " epoch-less " days on which, according to the theory, *no child could possibly be born.* (64 in 91 days in a given year.)

7. ASTROLOGY IN RELATION TO ERAS OF TIME

BOOK SUGGESTED*:—*Towards Aquarius*, by Vera W. Reid. 1944

The Great Year

This is the name given to the period of time (about 25,800 years) which is taken by the Poles of the Earth's axis to complete an entire circle round the Pole of the ecliptic. This is done by an oscillatory movement described as being like that of a spinning top with a swinging motion called nutation. (Latin, *nutare*, to nod.)

Its *cause* is the unequal gravitational pull of the Sun and Moon on the Earth's equatorial protuberance.

Its *effects* are :—

Firstly, *the gradual changing of the position towards which the Pole points*. The nearest star to which it points is known as the Pole Star. This changes through the ages. About 4–5,000 years ago, it pointed to Alpha Draconis, now almost to Polaris in Ursa Minor, but in another 5,000 years or so it will point to Alpha Cephei and in A.D. 13,000 to Wega.

Secondly, the phenomenon known as *the Precession of the Equinoxes*.

The Precession of the Equinoxes

The point referred to by astronomers as ♈ or the vernal equinox and by astrologers as 0° Aries, is seen each year from the earth as slightly *before* its position in the previous year, as against the background of the constellations. This is the point in space where the Sun in its apparent path crosses the equator. Thereafter it begins to have northerly declination instead of southerly. In other words, it is seen as north of the equator so the days begin to lengthen for the countries in the northern hemisphere. At the time of the equinoxes (vernal and autumnal) the days and nights are equal the world over (Latin, *Equi*, equal, *nox*, night).

Constellations

Much confusion of thought exists because the constellations have the same names as the signs of the Zodiac. Those who look into astrology in a casual way have often been known to remark that astrologers are ridiculous since they do not reckon with the fact that, because of the precession of the equinoxes, the signs do not now correspond with the constellations of the same name and that therefore astrology must be wrong. Such remarks can only come from those who do not understand that,

* Also see Chapter 5 in *An Introduction to Political Astrology*, 1951. C. E. O. Carter.

in the main, astrologers are dealing with the *Zodiac* and its signs and NOT with the constellations. In India and by a few astrologers in the West,* the ecliptic is divided, not in a manner dependent on the moving equinoctial points but on the positions of certain fixed stars, thus being related to the unequal constellations.

It must be understood that the constellations which are marked on a star chart or on a celestial globe, as definite groups of stars, are in actuality not groups at all. What is seen from Earth is the grouping of several points of light, taking many million light-years to arrive and coming from some stars relatively near to the earth and from others many million miles farther away. The groupings have no definite boundary lines but interlock very much as the counties on a map of England.

At the time when these were named and their names gradually became generally known, the 30° of ecliptic, starting from the point of the vernal equinox, was called Aries and the constellation which appeared as its background was also called Aries. This cannot have taken place suddenly, so no exact dating can be given, but the fact of Precession was not known until 134 B.C. when it was discovered by Hipparchus (see Chapter 17).

Hence it is clear that the thirty degrees of ecliptic known as Aries are always the thirty degrees as counted from the vernal equinox (and the other signs follow on) and that the equinox is slightly further back, in relation to the background of the constellations, each year.

The Twelve Months of the Great Year

Just as one civil year is divided into twelve months, so is the Great Year similarly divided into twelve. These are the periods of time when the equinox is to be judged as being against the background of each in turn of the twelve constellations which appear to lie roughly around the ecliptic. These periods cannot be reckoned with exactitude because of the interlocking already mentioned, but must be about 2,000 years each. Nor can the beginning of each period be fixed because the boundaries of the constellations are not accurately defined. As the movement is backwards from the end of a constellation to its beginning, so the periods of time are in the backward order of the signs. (See note, p. 280.)

Historical Allusions

Written history does not go back very far, but what exists confirms that the last 2,000 years have had definite Piscean characteristics, while the previous 2,000 were as clearly Arien, the next before were Taurean and the next before that Geminian. Only surmise, built on this evidence, can allow the thought that the period before that was Cancerian, preceded by an age of Leo. This would take us back some 12,000 years.

This goes back to the time of the fabled Atlantis.†

It cannot be thought that Plato was romancing when he talked of the sudden destruction of that great centre of culture which he said did exist. No proof of this can be given, but its existence would supply the answer to the problem of the many varied sources of the beginnings of astrology, so similar and yet to be found in

* Fagan's *Ephemeris*. Introduction by Gleadow.
† See all publications of the Atlantis Research Society, 9 Markham Sq., London, S.W.3.

such widely separated lands. Plato places this cataclysm at about 9,500 B.C. In each age, the characteristics of the sign are to be observed and a cult to do with the sign sprang up and continued on into the later ones. Historians puzzle over these and try to trace the resemblances between the different gods and goddesses of the times. By an understanding of the natures of the zodiacal signs, they would find the prototype of each.

The Leonian Age (about 10,000 B.C.)

Regality, rulership, pleasures, creativeness, both of children and of art-forms, are connected with this sign. The Sun is its planet. It is a Fire sign. Its metal is gold. Its animal representative is the lion. It is to be surmised that the myths and legends of a happy golden age and of Sun-worship may indeed be true.

Temples have been found in South America, with carved lions' faces, said to be dedicated to the Sun.* Each sign connects with its opposite by polarity and it may be surmised that this age of rulership included an Aquarian circulation of what was the scientific thought of that day.

The Cancerian Age (about 8,000 B.C.)

This is a Water sign ruled by the Moon. Traditions of every land tell of a catastrophe which struck the earth, of a deluge of water. According to some theories, the cause was the "capture" of the Moon by the Earth.† Moon-cults and female goddesses of the "fertile mother" order probably began at this time.

The Geminian Age (about 6,000 B.C.)

At the time of this mental, Mutable-Air sign, writing probably began in some form. The prevailing cult was that of the Twins. Sacred pillars dedicated to pairs of gods were found in Babylon and Assyrian temples. The island of Samothrace was dedicated to this cult. Later, the Romans had their Castor and Pollux, the Dioscuri, sons of Zeus. Romulus and Remus were supposed to be the original founders of Rome.

The Taurean Age (about 4,000 B.C.)

Records now tell of the age of this Fixed-Earth sign, of cultivation in Egypt and of the worship of the Bull in that country. The tombs of the Sacred Bulls are still to be seen. Taurus is connected with solid building. The pyramids and temples of Egypt still stand as witness to this. The likeness between these and others in Mexico and Central America makes the idea of a common source very tenable.

The Arien Age (about 2,000 B.C.)

It is only to be expected that in the age of this sign of Cardinal-Fire, a pioneering spirit should begin with much initiatory work, energy, courage, but also pugnacity, as expected from a sign of Mars. Exploration and conquest went on. Empires rose and fell.

The Ram, animal of Aries, gave its name to the original wooden battering-ram, carved at the end in its image. The lamb, as a burnt offering, was part of Jewish ritual, while the worship of the Golden Calf (Taurus) was forbidden. The gods

---

* *Moon Myths and Man.* H. S. Bellamy.
† Hoerbiger's *Cosmogonic Theory.* See above.

changed their names in accordance with cosmic pressure. Mithra, the Sun-god who had been the " Sacred Bull "* in Taurean times, now became the Slayer of the Bull. Ashur, Sun-god of the Assyrians, formerly known as " Great Bull," became a Martian god of war. The Greeks dressed Pallas Athene in the armour of a soldier with ram's horns on her helmet, while the Roman soldiers wore the same emblems on their uniforms.

The Piscean Age (about A.D. I, but by astronomical computation 60 B.C.)†

This transition was greater than any of the preceding because it was a new beginning of the circle of the Zodiac. A real " New Year " began for mankind. Great teachers had been born who inspired the nations with new ideals consonant with the Mutable-Water sign of Pisces, with the expansion of Jupiter and with the boundless idealism but also the capacity for muddling of its co-ruler Neptune.

Buddha, Zoroaster, Confucius and Lao-tse were born within a hundred years of each other between 660 and 560 B.C.

Much of the zodiacal symbolism appears in the records of the Christian Church. Early Christians used the sign of the Fish. Jesus was called Ichthus, the fish. He was welcomed by the shepherds (Aries) as the Lamb of God, but chose the fishermen (Pisces) as His disciples. The Bible story repeats the symbolism again and again. The Church keeps it up in the fish-head shape of the bishop's mitre and the eating of fish on Friday, the day of Venus, the planet exalted in Pisces. Rome aimed at world peace and a smooth working of the Pax Romana but fell into decay so typically Piscean. Jesus, the spiritual leader of the age, has been called the Prince of Peace, but also the Man of Sorrows, again both Piscean phrases. Something of the opposite sign is always to be noticed and in this case it is very evident as the Virgin Mother is the representative of the sign Virgo. The symbolism of the two opposite signs repeats in stories of wine and corn goddesses and again in the parable of the loaves and fishes.

The Aquarian Age (about A.D. 2,000, but by astronomical computation 2740 A.D.)†

The austerity of Saturn and the disruptive changefulness of Uranus, coupled with the worship of science and the development of flight and of all wave and ray theories, are too obviously already part of the present time for us to doubt that these Aquarian things are fore-runners of the developing age.

Perhaps the discovery of Uranus (1781) has hastened the coming of the age of the sign which he is said to rule. It is to be hoped that the opposite sign will soon make itself evident and that some true Leo organisation will clear up the remaining muddles of the world-wide tragedies which have marked the Neptunian decanate of the Piscean age. The cool, detached, impersonal Aquarianism is already replacing the sentimental but kindly, if sometimes muddled, Pisceanism. Each age plays its part in the evolution of the world, which can no more escape its correlation with the cosmic pattern than can the tiny human beings living on its surface. *Only*

---

* *Towards Aquarius.* Vera Reid.

† Pisces is one of the longer constellations, covering 39° of the ecliptic. The figures are taken from *Elementary Mathematical Astronomy*, p. 97. Barlow and Bryan. Revised by Sir H. Spencer Jones, Astronomer Royal, 1944.

a belief in a dual relationship, to the world, and to something other than the world, can help humanity to make the very best of that pattern inherent in the planets and their signs.

When these eras of time are spoken of, the second-mentioned result of the Soli-lunar cause, i.e., the precession of the equinoxes, or the changing relationship of the signs to the constellations, is referred to far more often than the first mentioned, which is the changing pointing of the earth's axis. Cosmic magnetic energy is said to enter the earth through the Magnetic Poles, while occultists have frequently thought of the North Poles of the equator as symbolic of the place of entrance of " that which is other than the world." It may well be that the first phenomenon is the more important and that behind it may lie the cause of the differences between the twelve signs.

Note on the Use of the Fixed Stars in Interpretation
Book Suggested
THE FIXED STARS AND CONSTELLATIONS IN ASTROLOGY
By VIVIAN E. ROBSON, B.Sc., 1923.

In relation to section 4 of this chapter, it may be that certain degrees or the areas around them have a special meaning because they are occupied by stars. These are alluded to as the fixed stars since, unlike the planets, they always maintain the same configurations relative to one another. Astronomically, their positions are given in Right Ascension but for astrological purposes, they are stated in zodiacal longitude like those of the planets.

In a natal chart, if any planet is on the degree of an important fixed star, it seems to be strengthened and to act more strongly in combination with the nature of that star.

Allusions to these will be found throughout Mr. Carter's *Encyclopedia of Psychological Astrology*. Mr. Robson's preface should be carefully read since he takes trouble to explain that his object in compiling the known information was neither critical nor originative but in order that further research could be built up on the work done.

Example :—*Regulus* is a star of first magnitude in 28° 43' Leo. It is said to have the nature of Mars and Jupiter. It is often called Cor Leonis, the Heart of the Lion. It was one of the four Royal Stars of the Persians in 3,000 B.C., when, as Watcher of the North, it marked the Summer Solstice.

The area in which it is, is known as one of *power*. In particular, 27° Leo and its opposite degree in Aquarius, are known as *The Astrologers' Degrees*. Many well-known astrologers have their Ascendant, Sun, or other important planet in one of these degrees.

As another instance, the areas 8 Gemini-Sagittarius and 6° Leo are said to be connected with sight. The first two are the degrees of Aldebaran and Antares, while the third is that of the Aselli.

Note on the Constellations

In 1954, the attention of the writer was called to two publications.

The first is called *Delimitation Scientifiques des Constellations* by E. Delporte. Cambridge University Press, 1930. In this are maps which show how the constellations, though still as nearly as possible in their unequal shapes so as to include the stars, were subjected to a delimitation by The International Astronomical Union, this now being used by all astronomers. The boundaries now consist of portions of meridians and parallels of declination.

The second is *The Names of the Stars* by E. J. Webb, Nisbet and Co. Ltd., 1952. In this modern and scholarly inquiry into the origins of the zodiac and star-names, we are assured that, contrary to the assertions of those who use the sidereal zodiac, the constellations were always of unequal lengths, that the zodiac was devised by the Greeks, probably in the sixth century B.C., that we have the assurance of Hipparchus that, though Eudoxus in one of his works had placed the equinoctial points in the middle of the signs, the great majority of the old astronomers had placed them, as Hipparchus himself, at the beginning.

In the Introduction is mentioned *The Exact Sciences in Antiquity* by Dr. O. Neugebauer, in which it is stated that a zodiac of 30°-long sections was needed for computing purposes and that it first appeared in a text in 419 B.C.

Thus from modern scholarship, we have support for the use of this circle and this beginning, at the intersection of ecliptic and equator, emphasising the Earth-Sun relationship, so important as the link between us as earth-dwellers and the power which we postulate as being that upon which the working of astrology depends.

CHAPTER 16

THE HOUSE DIVISION QUESTION

THIS chapter should not be read until Chapters 5, 6 and 7 have been properly grasped and the student has examined a celestial globe. It is then highly necessary that he should understand something of this important question. It would be dogmatic to insist on the rightness of any one system of house division to the exclusion of all others when there is no topic on which astrologers disagree more heartily.

However, it cannot be too strongly pointed out that the system for which Tables are customarily included at the back of Raphael's Ephemerides is one that is not only often condemned on mathematical grounds by users of other quadrant systems, but also by those who prefer the Equal House system, in which method the houses do not coincide with the quadrants at all.

Students will be puzzled to find this system of house division, the Placidean, is the most customarily used and that charts erected by it are to be seen in the pages of most astrological publications.

It must be clearly stated that most astrologers of this century have taken little interest in the house division controversy, leaving the discussion of it to keener specialists. They have accepted the Tables so conveniently to hand, not properly understanding how they are compiled but believing that, since given to them with the Ephemerides, year by year, they must bear the stamp of unimpeachable authority. This, however, is not the case.

The main variations of quadrant house systems have been described in Chapter 7. That of the monk, Placidus, was vehemently rejected when first brought to England. In 1711, a writer denounces it in scathing* terms referring to " the doctrine of Ptolemy nicely Placidianised " and saying, " Here is nothing but Egyptian Absoluteness and the power of monkish infallibility, zealously urged in Billingsgate rhetorick, all of which I could not read without just abhorrence and detestation."

Before 1825, there was no easy distribution of ideas by the circulation of magazines. In that year was started one called *The Spirit of Partridge or the Astrologer's Pocket Companion*. It happened that the promoter of this periodical fancied the Placidean system and so passed it on to his readers.

What really brought the Placidean system into habitual use, however, was that it was chosen by the first " Raphael," R. C. Smith, to calculate the Tables which he included in his early almanac of mixed information in 1821. As he was only 26 years of age at the time, his experience cannot have been great. From this, the astrological part eventually became separated and so began the present Ephemerides with Tables of Houses following. By the time the present publishers bought the firm which prints these, several such Tables by the Placidean system were included, and are still so printed by habit.†

Quadrant Systems or Equal House System ?
The crux of the matter lies in the answer given to the question, " Which is the more important thing in astrology ":—

* *Flagellum Placideanum*, by Gibson, 1711. British Museum.
† See Introductory chapter to "The Time-Saver Tables of Asc. and M.C." by Colin Evans. See also full discussion in *Waite's Compendium*, re-edited by the same author.

1. The ecliptic, which is the circle of the apparent path of the Sun, as seen from the Earth, in the plane of which lie the planets which, with the Sun, convey to the inhabitants of the Earth that which is understood to be the source of astrological working

OR

2. The twelve mundane houses, each containing varying numbers of degrees of ecliptic according to the many systems of division thought out by mathematicians through the ages?

Those who think the houses are the first consideration must agree with an American writer* who speaks of " zodiacal density within the houses," referring to the houses containing more degrees as those with " zodiacal degrees gathered thickly together " while in the others they are said to be " spread out."

Those who think that the ecliptic is the first consideration must think of the houses as a secondary division analogous to the signs, *superimposed on the unalterable ecliptic*, starting from the ascending degree.

If THE QUADRANT SYSTEMS are preferred, then the arguments for and against each one must be gone into, but it must be remembered that all these systems fail in the far northern countries, since in charts set up by them, persons born during the time of day when signs of long ascension are rising have nearly the whole of the diurnal arc (180°) in the last three houses and their opposites, while the first three houses and their opposites can consist of no more than one or two degrees each.

Twelve hours later, with signs of short ascension rising, the difference is as astounding, but no evidence has been brought forward to show that inhabitants of these countries, class for class, are so very different from those of others, or that there are two very different types of people born during each day.

With the use of the Placidean system in such latitudes, its curves do not even form sections which can be used.

At the arctic circle (lat. 66½) there is a moment in each day when the ecliptic lies exactly on the horizon, all degrees then rising simultaneously.† Above this latitude, at times, some signs are *always* above the horizon, those opposite being below, so no degree of these can form an ascendant. At other times, the signs which rise do so in reverse order, presenting a further problem to the astrologer.

The suggestion has been made that the discrepancy in the sizes of the houses is because they are seen in perspective and are not really so different. However this may be, for the purpose of a horoscopic chart *they can be measured in no other way but in degrees of ecliptic*. The planets within them natally and the duration of time of a transit through them depend on this only.

If THE EQUAL HOUSE SYSTEM is preferred, some of the above difficulties do not occur, since, so long as there is an ascendant, 12 equal houses can be measured from it along the ecliptic.

In the charting of this system, there is no difficulty about charting the position

---

* Dane Rudhyar, " Intercepted signs and cusps," *Horoscope Magazine*, May, 1950.

† It has been suggested that no chart could be made for this place and time, but as both would be fractional, this does not seem impossible.

of the Sun at midnight above the arctic circle. The charts represent *the ecliptic* and the Sun is placed in the degree which it occupies, whether above or below the horizon. In the charts used for the quadrant systems, the horizontal line from Asc. to Des. represents *the horizon*, the six houses below it are below the horizon. The situation then arises that the Sun at midnight, when above the horizon in the ecliptic, must be charted as if below it.

It must be understood that the Equal House system is not " a rough and ready system," in which words it was dismissed by Alan Leo in the early part of this century, but is a reflection of the signs in their everyday working in life. This would be better understood if they were called by the same names. The personal meaning of the first house would not have to be learnt as a separate thing if it were referred to as " the Aries house," nor the possessive character of the second if it were called " the Taurus house " and so on all round. This ordered sequence is no more rough and ready than the sequence of the signs.*

The Quadrature of the Equal Houses

A sphere can be divided into four in different ways. The basis of the division of the quadrant systems has been that a natural quadrature results from the intersection of the two circles of the horizon and the north-south meridian.

The importance of the meridian (as indicating a house cusp in the quadrant systems) has been insisted on since it is the great circle which passes through the *North and South Poles of the equator*, and the observer's *Zenith*, thus making it personal to his individual situation in longitude especially in the astrological significance of this as his birth-place.

The degrees at which it cuts the ecliptic have invariably marked the cusps of houses 10 and 4 in such systems.

What has *not* been realised is that the degrees of ecliptic which mark the cusps of houses 10 and 4 in the *Equal House System* are *also* cut by a great circle which passes through the observer's *Zenith*, and that this passes through *the North and South Poles of the ecliptic*, hence it is just as individual to a person at any birth-place but includes the Poles of the circle which is being used, and not any other.

The degree of the ecliptic cut by the upper meridian (M.C.) has also been stressed in importance because it is at that point of culmination that any degree reaches its *highest point in the day*.

Again there is an equally important fact which has *not* been realised, which is that the nonagesimal, i.e., the degree forming the cusp of the 10th house E.H., is at any time in the day the *highest degree of the ecliptic* in the heavens.†

Having contrasted the arguments for and against these systems, they must next be compared as to results in interpretation. This is not easy as bias usually comes in. Only by a rigid system of marking, used in the scrutiny of map after map, can a fair test be made. Strict adherence must be kept to the exact interpretation of the

* Another difficulty of the quadrant systems is that a planet with great latitude can be in one house by zodiacal longitude and another by latitude. Equal houses are vertical to the ecliptic and cover such a planet both by longitude and latitude.
† For further discussion, see *The Fundamentals of House Division*, page 7, by Cyril Fagan.

nature of each planet in each house. Even so, this is not always simple, as a planet may sometimes appear valid in more than one house.

Example 1.—Jupiter may be in the 8th house by one system and in the 9th in another. A person who inherits a great deal of money is more than likely to travel extensively.

One of the best ways of testing without personal bias is to watch unknown Placidean charts displayed for interpretation and to note the frequency with which the change of house position by Equal House smoothes out the acknowledged difficulties found in the map.

Example 2.—By the Placidean system, the chart of a well-known public character had Virgo on the 5th cusp, its ruler Mercury not being strongly aspected. This sign, so cool in its affections, did not fit the affectionate father of several children by two marriages. The change to Libra, by E.H., with its ruler Venus sextile the expansive Jupiter, portrayed the situation exactly.

Example 3.—In the Placidean chart of a girl who rose from humble circumstances to world-wide fame, Jupiter was in the 9th house. She did travel but not extensively. The change to Equal House put Jupiter in the 10th house, a position consonant with her overwhelming public success.

Simplification of Work by the Use of the Equal House System

An expert astrologer looks at the planets in the signs and sees the chart as a whole. When starting to learn, the awkwardness of the varied degrees on cusps and the doubling of signs on cusps with the consequent " intercepted " signs, slow down the task. Though no system should be adopted *merely because it simplified the work*, it is a fact that with E.H. these difficulties are eliminated. The aspects are seen with ease, since the planets are written (in No. 1 The Ecliptic Chart) in the angular relationship to each other in which they actually are in the heavens, so that a trine is immediately recognisable as such and the same with all other aspects. Even to an able astrologer this is a great convenience in looking quickly at charts.

Interpretative Significance in Modern Thought

It is highly probable that the present change of opinion about house division amongst those astrologers who are most qualified to form one, is in tune with a change that is obvious in much modern astrological thought.

The quadrant systems were evolved and became popular in the centuries when events and physical happenings were the main concern of astrology and it may be that such systems are still preferable for purely factual work as in Mundane astrology.

The planetary principles which are the basis of astrological understanding are also the basis of the psychological interpretation of a natal chart, towards which is the modern trend in astrology.

It is therefore significant that the modern tendency is towards the use of that system which emphasises that circle, in the plane of which lie the planets, namely *the ecliptic*, forming its quadrature by the use of the two circles which come from the *Poles of the ecliptic*, using the culminating degree (M.C.) as a highly important point of mundane significance in the interpretation of worldly ambitions and experience.*

* See footnote, p. 142.

CHAPTER 17

THE HISTORICAL BACKGROUND OF ASTROLOGY

ASTROLOGY through the ages was once pictorially represented as a river, curving along in its broad sweeps. At each curve was a date of a bygone century and beside each date stood an irate little man, saying, " Stop this, it is nonsense ! " but the river increasingly rolled on, ever getting fuller and wider. It now seems to have reached vast proportions and is in danger unless in the future, it is fed by tributaries from healthy sources and controlled by banks as in the past.

Its modern necessity is the " banking " given by sensible, well informed, well practised students, who will exert the control necessary to stop " woolliness " and vague repetition of unproved statements and will press for the clarity which the present age demands and will work to add to proof and reasoning and not be content merely to listen comfortably to others.

SOURCES

The original source of this river is unknown. There are statements that the world-known Sun-symbol has been discovered carved on the oldest stones in all lands. Later are found the glyphs of the signs and the symbols of the other planets. In the earliest stage of development of every nation, the priests formed the educated class. Its members studied and taught from the information then to hand.

An astrologer in early days was one who tried to find out the facts of what we now call astronomy and who also had the belief that men's movements could be correlated with those of the heavenly bodies. In those days, it was thought that what was not caused by men must be caused by gods. These were the deities of the planets. The same gods, names and stories in one form and another are the bases of the myths of all countries. The " history " of astrology in its early centuries must therefore be also the early history of astronomy as we know it now.

The earliest records of such knowledge come from those races which inhabited the valleys of the Euphrates and Tigris 5,000 years ago; from the Sumerians, then the Babylonians, the Assyrians and later the Egyptians. The finest account of these origins, these tributaries which fed the great river, is given in a modern encyclopedia* in which the contributions of the various countries are discussed. The alphabetical list is as follows :—

American (American Indian and Mexican).
Babylonian.
Buddhist.
Celtic.
Chinese.
Egyptian.
Greek and Roman.

* *Encyclopedia of Religion and Ethics.* Edited by James Hastings, 1921. Vol. 12, page 48.

Hebrew.

Hindu.

Iranian.

Japanese.

Jewish.

Mohammedan.

Semitic.

Teutonic and Balto-Slavic.

The story is told of the beginnings of celestial measurement and of the early stages when all work was observational, since there were no records or Tables for calculation. On such observation, early attempts at necessary calendar-making were made. Astrology, religion and medicine went hand-in-hand. Correspondences were realised between them. The richest vein of astrological records was found in the library of Sardanapalus. From these it appears that there was a system of observatories covering the whole kingdom, with an established scheme of relays for the professional astrologers and of serial reports regarding their work. A State Library was established for the purpose of supplying all needful information. But it must be understood that this was for the purpose of prognostication concerning " times and seasons " for agriculture, and portents for the king and the state, *not for individual astrological work such as is done now.*

It was through Egyptian culture that Babylonian astronomy and astrology were brought to the west. The High Priest of Heliopolis was the supreme State Astrologer until the Imperial Age of Rome.

The Mohammedans, using the Arabic language for this, as for all scientific literature, did much for astrology, in that they prepared Tables and taught exact calculations. With them, astrology became an art which required a solid scientific preparation and which tended to give an even greater mathematical complication and exactness to its methods of research among celestial phenomena. This was the greatest influence on European thought in the later Middle Ages from the beginning of the twelfth to the end of the fifteenth century. Such names as ALBOHAZEN (A.D. 1040), ALBUMASAR (A.D. 805), ALCABITUS (A.D. 950), MESSAHALA (A.D. 860), are those of the great thinkers and teachers of the period. To men of their nation we owe the translation of Ptolemy's works, the famous Tetrabiblos or Quadripartitum in A.D. 827.

A school for astronomy and astrology was founded in Bagdad in A.D. 777. It was the Arabic astronomers such as the above who first realised that the obliquity of the ecliptic had not a constant value as the Greeks had taught (ERATOS-THENES 320 B.C.). They also confirmed the idea of the continuous precession of the equinoxes discovered by HIPPARCHUS (about 150 B.C.) accepted by Ptolemy, but doubted by Greek astrologers who thought that the advance of the points would be followed by a similar retreat. They founded trigonometry in a modern sense, thus furnishing astronomical science with an excellent instrument for its work. Not until the time of TYCHO BRAHE (1546–1601) do we find observers and observations comparable to those of the Mohammedan Middle Ages.

Much of the modern difficulty in writing any history of the earliest times is due to the fact that few records remain and we are thus dependent on histories written long after events. (See later note, p. 280.)

Greek historians have written of the work of Egyptians, Babylonians and Assyrians, while travellers and missionaries in comparatively recent times have given us information about the early work of the Chinese.

The re-entry of astrology into Europe was through the Moors when they occupied Spain. Astrological books then available in Europe were written in Latin only. The dissolution of the monasteries caused the spread of those who could translate them.

The period was one in which better instruments for precise work in astronomy were being invented, so that this branch of the work became an exact science, while with certain notable exceptions astrology fell into the hands of less educated and more credulous people, who stressed the fortune-telling application of its truths and cared little for research and clear thinking. Writers repeated what others had said and there was no modern presentation until the days of such men as A. J. PEARCE (died about 1923), SEPHARIAL (died 1929) and ALAN LEO (died 1917). To these and their band of helpers must be given the credit for the great spread of astrology in the English-speaking world of today.

CHANGE IN THE USAGE OF ASTROLOGY

In the very early " observational " days, it was seen that changes followed on such happenings as eclipses and great conjunctions of planets, hence astrology dealt with affairs of countries and of rulers whose lives affected those of countless others in an obvious way.

In the Middle Ages, with the ability to calculate personal maps, *first introduced by the Greeks*, attention was more on the individual, but mainly in a very material way and on the actual outer events of his life.

In late Victorian times, with better text-books and even more personal application, " character " was studied as something apart from " events."

In modern times, with the growth of psychology, it is found that the astrological natal chart is the key to those deeper urges and drives which are the very core of a man and which give the clue to the understanding of the psyche as a whole. It is realised that the quality of certain *trends and periods* in a life may be assessed by the chart, but that to attempt to make a shot at foretelling actual events is only likely to bring disbelief on what is an interpretative and deductive art, *not a system of fortune-telling*. It is true that precise prediction is sometimes successful, but who can say how much of this is due to the astrologer's innate intuition or even to flashes of precognition ?

The work of Einstein has shown the closeness of every part of the Universe and all that is in it. It is for astrologers to control and clarify their work so that they may have a workable tool to offer if ever its value is to be properly appreciated by those studying on other lines.

CHRONOLOGICAL SEQUENCE OF GREAT NAMES

From some of these comes the present astrological knowledge. Others have built up astronomical knowledge on the work of their predecessors and on this depends the ease of the calculation of modern astrological data.

BABYLONIAN

669–625 B.C. Assurbanipal

King of Assyria. Records were found in tablets which once formed part of his library. It is stated by Diodorus Siculus (time of Caesar and Augustus) that " the Babylonian priests observed the position of certain stars in order to cast horoscopes, and that they interpreted dreams and derived omens from the movements of birds and from eclipses and earthquakes." The Chaldeans, the most ancient Babylonians, held the same dignity in the State as did the Egyptian priests.

280 B.C. Berossos

A priest of Baal. He founded a school of astrology on the Island of Cos.

EGYPTIAN

The priests of the Pharaohs are said to have been instructed in astrology by the Chaldeans, its knowledge being part of their religion. The earliest instance of the erection of a horoscope is connected with NECTANEBUS, King of Egypt in 358 B.C. Many monuments exist which show a knowledge of astronomical principles. Carvings of the Zodiac are to be seen in the temples of Thebes and Denderah.

GREEK

639–546 B.C. Thales

He studied in Egypt and left nothing in writing, but is said to have predicted an eclipse which caused much alarm and ended the battle between the Medes and Lydians. AIRY (7th Astronomer Royal, in 1835) fixed this date as 28th May, 585 B.C.

569–470 B.C. Pythagoras

Also studied in Egypt. He also left nothing in writing but is supposed to have said that the Earth, Moon and planets and fixed stars revolved round the Sun. Copernicus in the sixteenth century claimed him as the originator of the system which he revived.

500–428 B.C. Anaxagoras

Also studied in Egypt and thought the Sun went under a flat Earth each night.

429–348 B.C. Plato

Also studied in Egypt and elsewhere, was a pupil of Socrates, fellow student of Euclid, follower of Pythagoras. The problem which he set to astronomers was the keynote of all investigation until the time of Kepler in the seventeenth century. It was the problem of representing the courses of the planets by circular and uniform motions.

408–355 B.C. Eudoxos

He is said to have travelled with Plato to Egypt.

460–359 B.C. Hippocrates

Used astrological deduction for medical prognostication.

384–322 B.C.   Aristotle

He held that the Earth was fixed in the centre of the world.

190–120 B.C.   Hipparchus

May be regarded as the founder of observational astronomy. He measured the obliquity of the ecliptic. Making use of Chaldean eclipses, he was able to evaluate the Moon's mean motion. In 134 B.C. he discovered a new star. He then set to work to catalogue all stars to know if any other new ones appeared. In so doing and comparing with earlier lists, he found that all stars had changed their places with reference to that point in the Heavens where the ecliptic is 90° from the poles of the Earth, i.e., the equinox. He found this could only be explained by a motion of the equinox in the direction of the apparent diurnal motion of the stars. This was the discovery of the *precession of the equinoxes* and was necessary for the progress of accurate astronomical observations.

135 B.C. (born).   Posidonius

A Syrian, founded a school in Rhodes. He was learned in astrology ; was visited by Pompey and Cicero and is said to have inspired the " Astronomica " of Manilius.

A.D. 100–178.   Claudius Ptolemy

Wrote the " Almagest " and the " Tetrabiblos." There is no evidence beyond his own statement that he was a practical observer. It is impossible to go into the system of the epicycles of Apollonius and the excentric of Hipparchus* which he used as the responses to the demand of Plato for uniform circular motions. In the seventeenth century the accurate observations of Tycho Brahe enabled Kepler to abolish these purely geometrical makeshifts and to substitute a system in which the Sun became physically its controller.

ROME

The early Roman Emperors placed unbounded faith in their appointed astrologers. Their coins sometimes bore the astrological sign under which they were born. In those days, it was the sign of the Moon which was considered thus important and which will be found on the coins. They are too many to quote separately. In their days the Alexandrian Neo-Platonists included some of the wisest men of their time.

48 B.C.–20 A.D.   Manilius

Probably Chaldean by birth. Wrote his famous poem which fell into the hands of Julius Firmicus Maternus who gave it to the world. In five books, it deals with the motion of the heavenly bodies and the properties of the zodiacal signs.

A.D. 205–270.   Plotinus

He said, " It is abundantly evident that the motion of the Heavens affects things on Earth."

A.D. 232–304.   Porphyry

Wrote a commentary on " The Tetrabiblos of Ptolemy." To him is ascribed the house method which equally divides the unequal segments of ecliptic necessitated by the quadrant systems.

* For details, see *History of Astronomy*, 1921. George Forbes.

A.D. 300.   Julius Firmicus Maternus
Wrote eight books on astrology in which he summarised all the knowledge available in his day.

A.D. 411–485.   Proclus
Wrote a paraphrase of Ptolemy's " Tetrabiblos."

From this time onwards, interest in astronomy in Europe sank to a low ebb, but the Arabs became the leaders of science and philosophy, the Moors gradually bringing back knowledge to Europe.

EARLY MIDDLE AGES (from about 1200)

By this time, the practice of astrology had branched into three divisions.

(1) *Judicial Astrology*, for the ascertaining of the fortunes and destiny of an individual by his natal chart.

(2) *Horary Astrology*, for the answering of a question by a chart of the moment of its asking.

(3) *Natural or Mundane Astrology*, for the forecasting of events of national importance, the weather, famines, etc.

1256.   Johannes de Sacrobosco
Came from Halifax, England ; was professor of mathematics and wrote the first astronomical text-book of the west.

1297.   Johannes Campanus (Died about this date)
Chaplain and physician to Pope Urban IV and his successors. He was a mathematician. To him is attributed one of the earliest systems of dividing up the celestial sphere into " houses " after the manner of the early measurers, who based everything on first dividing it into four quadrants.

1265–1321
This was the time when the poet Dante lived. Astrology was universally believed in, and was referred to by writers of the time, including Dante in both the *Purgatorio* and *Paradiso*. At later dates, Chaucer and Milton and Spenser and Shakespeare frequently introduced astrological allusions into their work.

1436–1476.   Regiomontanus (Johann Muller)
Professor of Astronomy at Vienna. Translated the " Almagest of Ptolemy." Printed some of the earliest Ephemerides and books on trigonometry. To him is attributed one of the well-known systems of house division of the quadrant type.

1473–1543.   Nicolai Copernicus
A Slav born in Polish Prussia. His great object was to increase the accuracy of calculations by providing better tables. He accepted the views of Pythagoras and others, that the Sun is fixed and the Earth revolves, but he could give no proofs of his theory. By popular writers he is generally spoken of as the initiator of the idea that the Sun is the centre of the solar system as it is now accepted to be, but astronomers give the praise for this to KEPLER who used the observations of TYCHO BRAHE, the successor of COPERNICUS.

1493. Paracelsus

Famous physician and alchemist. He believed that " all influences that come from the Sun, the planets and the stars, act invisibly on man, and if these are evil, they will produce evil effects." For instance, he directed that if a person is deficient in the element whose essence radiates from Mars and consequently suffers from poverty of blood, he should be given iron. He said, " If a man gets angry, it is not because he has too much bile, but because the Mars correlative element in his body is in a state of exaltation."

1501–1576. Jerome Cardan

Learnt the astrology of the Arabians from his father. Teacher of mathematics. In his commentary on Ptolemy, he explained the rational manner of Regiomontanus, but he preferred a system which approximated to it and which later on was used by Placidus as the basis of his " fundamental proportion."

1503–1566. Michael Nostrodamus

Born St. Remy, Provence. Studied medicine. Astrologer and prophet. From stories told of him it would seem that he had psychic precognitive power as well as astrological deductive ability. His " Centuries," which were collections of prophecies, contained some which have proved to be amazingly accurate. Like many others of his time he believed that knowledge of medicine must include astrological knowledge.

1510–1593. Valentine Naibod

Professor of mathematics in the University of Cologne and then in Padua. Writer of many books on astrology, commenting on Alcabitius and Arabian astrology.

1523–1580. Franciscus Junctinus

Another translator of the " Tetrabiblos " with extensive commentary and a collection of the aphorisms of all known astrologers with some 600 nativities.

LATER MIDDLE AGES (from about 1500)

The invention of printing, the downfall of the Byzantine Empire and the results of the Reformation, the voyages of the Spaniards and the Portuguese were among the causes of the spread of knowledge through the world at this time.

1546–1601. Tycho Brahe

A Dane. The most distinguished and accurate observer of the heavens since the days of Hipparchus, 1,700 years before. He grasped the hopelessness of the old deductive methods of reasoning and decided that no theories ought to be indulged in until preparations had been made by the accumulation of accurate observations. *(Only by the adoption of such principles as his will astrology be brought to a high status.)* For him may be claimed the title of the founder of the inductive method. He carried out his life's work in Denmark, under the patronage of King Frederic.

In his mechanical workmanship, he was satisfied with nothing but the best. Instruments were designed by him in metal instead of wood, including armillae, mural quadrants and large celestial globes. He prepared and used more accurate tables than before, correcting those of COPERNICUS. His most fruitful work was on the motions of the planets, and especially of Mars, for it was by the examination of these results that KEPLER was led to the discovery of his immortal laws. After the death of King Frederic, the observatories were not financially supported and TYCHO BRAHE was received by the Emperor Rudolph II under whose patronage he worked in Prague with KEPLER as one of his assistants. He did not accept the Copernican theory that the Earth moved, saying, "the heavy and sluggish Earth is unfit to move, and the system is ever opposed to the authority of Scripture."

1550–1617. Lord Napier

Born near Edinburgh. The practical application of the mathematical process of reasoning was enormously facilitated by his invention of logarithms. All astrologers must be deeply grateful for this.

1561–1626. Francis Bacon, Lord Verulam

Born in London. Student of law at Cambridge. In 1619 he was Lord Chancellor of England and in 1620 he became Viscount St. Albans. He wrote " Astrologia Sana." He expressed the opinion that astrology had rule over the fate of Princes and peoples.

1527–1608. John Dee

An outstanding figure, a scholar of St. John's College, Cambridge. A mathematician and astronomer who gave such work up for the then more lucrative art of astrology.   Royal patronage gave him prestige.   He calculated the maps of Mary Tudor and of Queen Elizabeth.   He ruined his career by association with persons less worthy than himself and died in poverty.

1571–1630. Johann Kepler

Of all those who contributed to the advance of astronomical knowledge, this man's place would have been the most difficult to fill by any other. He was born in Wiel, in Würtemberg, and joined TYCHO BRAHE in Prague.

Plato's demand for uniform circular motion was responsible for the loss to astronomy of good work during 1,500 years, until the insight, boldness and independence of KEPLER opened up a new world of thought and intellectual delight. He compared the Ptolemaic, the Copernican and the Tychonic theories. His three great laws contain implicitly the law of universal gravitation. Some astrologers may wish to know these. They are as follows :—

(1) That the planets describe ellipses with the Sun at a focus of each ellipse.
(2) That a line drawn from a planet to the Sun, sweeps over equal areas in equal times.
(3) That the squares of the periodic times are proportional to the cubes of the mean distances from the Sun.

Even so, the meaning of these laws was not fully understood, until expounded by the logic of NEWTON'S dynamics. He was the first to suggest that a telescope made with both lenses convex could have crosswires in the focus, for use as a pointer to fix the positions of stars.

He was convinced that mundane events could be predicted by astrology, and, in an address, given at the request of King Frederic at the University of Copenhagen, he urged its value and importance to mankind and said, " We cannot deny the influence of the stars, without disbelieving in the wisdom of God." " Man," he said, " is made from the elements, and absorbs them as much as food or drink, from which it follows that man must also, like the elements, be subject to the influence of the planets." He also believed that man was not altogether bound by the influence of the stars, but the Creator had so made him that he might conquer that influence as there was something in man superior to it.

In 1577 he prepared a horoscope for the heir to the throne of King Frederic. The famous Wallenstein had horoscopes cast for him by Kepler. Though he was appointed Imperial Astronomer, he could hardly keep his family from starvation and died from a fever worsened by disappointment and exhaustion.

An anti-astrological book remarks regretfully that it was evident that even scientific astronomers of the period found astrology a more profitable branch of the art. Kepler wrote that " for a hundred years past, this wise mother (astronomy) could not have lived without the help of her foolish daughter " (astrology) !

1564-1642. Galileo Galilei

Born Pisa. Contemporary of Kepler. His work dealt with terrestrial dynamics. Experiments with the pendulum gave the principle necessary for HUYGHENS to use in the middle of the seventeenth century, for the making of the pendulum clock, perhaps the most valuable astronomical instrument ever produced.

But it was chance that led Galileo to the originating of a new branch of astronomy. In 1609, he heard of a Dutch spectacle-maker who combined a pair of lenses to magnify distant objects. This led to the making of one of the first telescopes ever used and to the discoveries which made him famous. These were spots on the Sun, hills and valleys on the Moon, moons around Jupiter, Saturn's rings. He died on the day of Newton's birth. KEPLER'S grand discovery of the true relation of the Sun to the planets and GALILEO'S telescopic discoveries spread a spirit of inquiry throughout Europe and astronomy rose in estimation. He was also an astrologer and prepared horoscopes as is shown in two of his books.

1583-1656. Jean Baptiste Morin

Born Villefranche. Doctor of medicine, and student of philosophy, professor of mathematics at the Paris University. In 1660, he learnt astrology from a Scot named Davison. He was the author of many works, the principal one being " Astrologia Gallica." In the opinion of his contempories, he was the most outstanding astrologer of his time. He was the astrologer of Cardinal Richelieu, whose death he predicted within ten hours. He also predicted exactly the deaths of Gustavius Adolphus, of Louis XIII and of Wallenstein.

1603-1668. Placidus de Tito

Born in Italy. A monk and a professor of mathematics in the University of Padua. To him is attributed the system of house division, the tables for which are in the end of all Raphael's Ephemerides.

When his ideas were brought to England, they were rejected by the astrologers of the day. In 1711 was written :*

" What a *desperate* distraction it would be ! to renounce the worthies of all ages, the famous LILLY, the renowned GADBURY, the admired COLEY, the great and learned SIR GEORGE WHARTON and trust to none but PLACIDUS and to PTOLEMY Placidianised ! "

1602-1681. William Lilly

In the purely astrological field, men of a different class from the scientific astronomer had now been able to read the books translated from Latin and to experiment for themselves. In England, one of the best known was William Lilly. Being denied the continuance of his education as he desired, he went into domestic employment.

He learnt astrology and began to write and issue one of the earliest prophetic almanacs with considerable success.

* *Flagellum Placideanum*, by Bishop, 1711. (British Museum.)

In 1666, he was summoned to appear before a Committee of the House of Commons, appointed to inquire into the cause of the Great Fire of London which he had accurately predicted. He was cleared of any complicity with regard to this event. He then studied medicine and received a licence to practice. He is most famous as a practitioner of Horary Astrology. His maps which are all cast by the system of Regiomontanus, are in the book *Lilly's Astrology* edited by Zadkiel.

Contemporaries of Lilly

During Lilly's life, several astrologers formed a group with him in the City of London. They wrote many books, but do not seem to have added much to current knowledge, but rather to have recorded what was then known. Some of their names are :—

Born 1601.   John Booker, Secretary to two Aldermen.
Born 1633.   Henry Coley, Mathematician.
Born 1610.   Joseph Blagrave
Born 1617.   Sir George Wharton
Born 1644.   John Partridge

ELIAS ASHMOLE, the founder of the Ashmolean Library, took a great interest in these men and attended their gatherings in London.

1627–1692.   John Gadbury

Born in Oxfordshire. He was a pupil of Lilly and wrote *Genethliacal Astrology* and other books.

1631–1700.   John Dryden

Born Northampton. Poet and astrologer. Buried in Westminster Abbey. Calculated precisely various accidents in the life of his son Charles and also his death by drowning in the Thames. Also the time and manner of his own death through a burn on his leg.

1616–1654.   Nicholas Culpeper

Doctor, botanist and herbalist. He used astrological correspondences in this connection. He said, " Only astrologers are fit to study medicine and a medical man without astrology is like a lamp without oil."

1646–1719.   John Flamsteed

First Astronomer Royal. He prepared an election map,* which exists to this day, for the time of the laying of the foundation stone of Greenwich Observatory, the lasting reputation of which is a fine testimony to the value of such maps.

1662–1675

Within these thirteen years were founded the Royal Society of London, the Royal Observatory at Greenwich, with Flamsteed as first Astronomer Royal, the French Academy and the Paris Observatory. Gravitation was much discussed, but a master mind was needed to make things clear.

1643–1727.   Isaac Newton

His work was to study the laws of motion, the meaning of Kepler's three laws, the shape of the Earth and the cause of the tides and finally to enunciate *the law of universal gravitation.* " Every particle of matter in the universe attracts every other particle

* See Chapter 15, section 1.

with a force varying inversely as the square of the distance between them and directly as the product of the masses of the two particles." This led to his explanation of the flattening of the Earth's poles and to the tilting of the Earth and hence to the cause of the precession of the equinoxes discovered by Hipparchus about 150 B.C. To him is ascribed the famous remark made to Halley, the discoverer of the comet, who expressed doubts about astrology and received the answer, " Sir, I have studied it, you have not."

1700-1800

After the deaths of the great astrologers MORIN and PLACIDUS, astrology on the Continent deteriorated even more than before into superstition. In England, however, astrology flourished under WILSON, MORRISON (" ZADKIEL," born 1795), ASHMAND, COOPER, SIBLY (born 1757)—bank director and translator of books by Placidus. R. C. Smith (" RAPHAEL," born 1795). The liking of the last named for the Placidean tables of house division is largely responsible for their spread, since he issued Almanacs and Ephemerides of the time, so that for lack of others, they are commonly used in the British Isles and in the U.S.A. today.

At the end of the century, English astrology reached France where CHOISNARD, SELVA and others were seeking to build it on a rational scientific basis.

1835. Richard Garnett (A. G. Trent)

Keeper of the department of printed books of the British Museum. He was an able astrologer, and wrote a small but valuable book on astrology and mental disease, pointing out the frequency of afflictions between Mars and Mercury in these cases.

THE TURN OF THE CENTURY

1860-1917. William Frederick Allan (Alan Leo)

This man must be acclaimed as the father of modern astrology.

Working with his wife and a devoted group of friends, he travelled all over England, lecturing on astrology. He edited the magazine *Modern Astrology* and was an indefatigable worker as a professional astrologer. His major achievement was the writing of thirty books, in which he made a complete restatement of astrology. From now on, the emphasis lay on the study of the human being, events in his life being shown to be largely, though not entirely, consequent on his own character.

In 1915, he founded the Astrological Lodge of London, which still carries on the spirit of his teaching. The high principles of Alan Leo and his understanding of the ancient wisdom through theosophical teachings, gave pure astrology an ethical status and lifted it away from fortune-telling and commercialism. Through the world-wide ramifications of the Theosophical Society, his books and teachings spread to all countries.

1864-1929. Walter Gorn-Old (" Sepharial ")

Born Birmingham. A most profound, prolific writer on occultism, on the Kabbala, and on astrology not only as understood in the west, but as taught by the Hindus and the Hebrews also.

1865-1921. Gerald Encausse (" Papus ")

Born Spain. Writer on astrology and the Tarot.

1867–1930. Paul Choisnard

Born at Tours. An artillery officer. Author of thirty astrological works, the best known being *Langage Astral*. He conducted much astrological research.

Fomalhaut (Pseudonym of French astrologer)

In 1897, in his book *A Manual of Spherical and Judicial Astrology* on page 316 he prophesied the name and nature of the planet Pluto which was first discovered in 1930.

1890–1942. Vivian Robson

Born England. Practised and taught astrology. Wrote excellent and concise text-books.

1865–1919. Max Heindel

Born Copenhagen. Lived and worked in San Francisco. Wrote many books on astrology and founded the Rosicrucian Fellowship.

Brandler-Pracht

In 1905, he spread English astrology to Germany, where it was then studied historically, critically, theoretically, experimentally and statistically.

PRESENT DAY ASTROLOGY

1950

The war years were disastrous for Continental astrology, as Hitler, infuriated by the uncongenial predictions of his astrologers, ordered their books to be burnt and themselves to be thrown into concentration camps. Over the length and breadth of Europe, devastation of homes scattered astrologers and ruined their libraries and records.

In England, though there was less devastation, most astrologers were too occupied to continue their work.

In the United States of America, further removed from the actual scene of war, great strides took place, because of the comparative ease with which astrological knowledge could be spread to the vast magazine reading public. Unfortunately, communication with Europe has been difficult and it is therefore not possible to prepare a list of best known names. Because of the prohibition against sending English money to the U.S.A. the books of writers of that country are little read in England. Among those who have become well known are the following two : —

1895. Dane Rudhyar

Born Paris. Bachelor of Philosophy. Composer of music, painter and writer no many subjects. Of his books on astrology, the best known is his *Astrology of Personality*, in which he shows astrology in its most modern form, as a companion study to that of psychology.

1888. Marc Edmund Jones

Born St. Louis, U.S.A. A most versatile personality. Starting life as a free-lance writer and pioneer motion picture author, he began astrological researchin 1913.

His great work has been the founding of the Sabian Assembly, 1922. This is a co-operative enterprise for the critical examination of philosophy, religion and science in every possible aspect.

Sixty sets of mimeographed lessons are issued, twelve of these being on astrology, and also four books on astrology. He has gained degrees from three universities. He is a Presbyterian minister and is also engaged in writing lyrics for stage productions.

1887. Charles E. O. Carter, B.A. (London), D.F.Astrol.S.

Born Dorset, England. He graduated at London University and was called to the English Bar in 1913. After his return from four years of service in the first war (1914–18) he helped to carry on the work begun by Alan Leo in the Astrological Lodge of London (Lodge of the Theosophical Society). He became President in 1922 and still holds that office. He has made this Lodge the main centre for astrological lectures in England and a training ground for many other astrologers. He has edited its quarterly magazine *Astrology* since its first appearance in 1926, and has corresponded with astrologers all over the world. In 1948, the Lodge sponsored the founding of the Faculty of Astrological Studies, a teaching and examining body in London, electing him as its first Principal. On his retirement in 1954, he was given the title of Principal Emeritus.

His many scholarly books continue to reflect deep thought and careful research on astrology and their use by students in all countries has raised the status of astrology.

It is fitting that this history should close with the name of one who is worthy to be ranked amongst those of the finest exponents of the art.

BOOKS FROM WHICH THE INFORMATION IN THIS CHAPTER IS GATHERED, AND OTHERS TO WHICH REFERENCE HAS BEEN MADE

Encyclopedia of Religion and Ethics
Edited by James Hastings. T & T. Clark, 38 George Street, Edinburgh ; Charles Scribners Sons, 153–157 5th Avenue, New York, 1921.

The History of Astronomy
George Forbes. Walls & Co., 1921.

The Mystery and Romance of Astrology
C. J. S. Thompson. Brentano's Ltd., 1929.
(Of much interest but regarding astrology as something antiquated and to be banished to the realms of romance.)

The Story of Astrology
Manly Palmer Hall. David McKay Co., Philadelphia, 1943.

Life or Times of Wm. Lilly
Wm. Lilly, 1715.

Lilly's Astrology
Zadkiel. George Bell & Sons, London, 1882.

The Astrology of Personality and other books
Dane Rudhyar. Lucis Publishing Co., New York, 1936.

The Guide to Horoscopic Interpretation and other books
Marc Edmund Jones. David McKay, New York, 1941.

Principles of Astrology and many other well-known books
Charles E. O. Carter. The Theosophical Publishing House, London, 1931.

Zenith
To a special number of this periodical entitled " Outline of the History of Astrology," by Hubert Korsch (killed by Nazis), published in Dusseldorf, 1935, grateful thanks are due for the exactness of all dates mentioned.

CHAPTER 18

THE USE OF MODERN PSYCHOLOGY IN MODERN ASTROLOGY

OLD-TIME astrology was mainly connected with the *events* in the world and in the lives of people and with a classification of people into types, according to the nature of the signs, modified according to aspects. This was the first systematised scheme of psychological assessment of the person.

As with astronomy and medicine, so also psychology has in modern times undergone a special development. This science, in its modern meaning, comprises a study of human behaviour, and, in its medical aspects, of mental derangement and its far-reaching effects, together with the classification of individuals from the psychiatrical point of view.

Depth Psychology

This is a further development which is more in line with astrological work. Those who have written about it have given the world a new vocabulary which is most helpful to the astrologer.

In the early years of this century, astrological development in England was mainly through workers connected with the Theosophical Society. No praise can be too high for this, since it kept pure astrology to a high ethical level sharply differentiating it from the merely commercial. The study of it on these lines was spread through the world by the wide ramifications of the Society.

Unfortunately, the deeper understanding of the human being in the light of the eastern religions, meant constant use of the phraseology of those religions, excellent to those familiar with it, but meaningless to others. The man-in-the-street of the latter half of the century has been familiarised with psychological terms through the press and the cinema, and the modern astrologer might with advantage re-phrase his age-old truths accordingly.

Of the great names which stand out in the history of the growth of psychology, that of Freud comes first to mind. After him came Adler, and lastly came C. G. Jung, whose " analytical " psychology correlates more closely with the work of astrology than do the ideas of his predecessors. Believing in astrology himself, and having those on his staff who are experts in it, he is accustomed to the realisation that he can get help in difficult cases under his care from astrological aid. The average psychologist in England is more conservative. Not being of the calibre of a free investigator like Jung, but being dependent on his connection with the medical profession, he has never given time to the study of astrology and has been taught by others similarly unversed. He has seen something labelled " Astrology " in the popular press and has looked no further. Fortunately all are not " average " and many have realised that even a knowledge of the Sun-sign of each patient helps them in their work. Others use astrology by getting an astro-analysis of their patients from an astrologer and others by sending the patients to an astrologer for discussion, knowing the therapeutic value of this clearing of the mind.

Jung tells us that it is nearly 200 years since Leibnitz postulated " an unconscious psychic* activity," over a century since Kant spoke of the " unmeasurable . . . field of obscure ideas " and more than half a century since Carus formulated the concept of the unconscious. If it is once accepted that the unconscious is a vaster part of the whole psyche than the conscious and that in it lie the mainsprings of much conscious activity, then a new meaning is given to the customary astrological remark that a certain planetary configuration in a natal chart, or a certain progression may work inwardly or outwardly. It is then realised that outward behaviour is the result of inner urges and that it is therefore natural that the same astrological significator applies to both.

Very often the conscious mind denies or refuses what the unconscious mind holds ; often it seeks to compensate for what is inwardly lacking. Unhappiness and neuroses result if perpetual denial and perpetual lack of compensation continue. In such a case the astrologer, by examining the progressions of the chart, will find long-lasting ones which have coloured the life for years, or slow transits similarly long in their effects. He can give immediate help to the psychologist by stating the nature of these and by filling that gap in the psychologist's equipment caused by his inability to estimate the probable time that the patient's trouble will last.

It will be no use for the astrologer to state in astrological terminology, " This will go on for two years because he has Progressed Sun conjunction Saturn in Leo in his 2nd house." Doctors have learnt long ago that it is no use talking about coryza when they mean the common cold. But let him say, " For two years, this person will be driven to try to compensate for a lack which he feels. It is intolerable to him to feel inferior and mean-spirited because, through financial stress, he cannot show himself as the big-hearted, generous person he wishes to be."

Jung places the sum total of " findings " of analytical psychology under four headings of confession, explanation, education and transformation.†

He says that the beginnings of all analytical treatment are to be found in its prototype, *the confessional*. Astrology by post has completely ignored this truth. Astrology by interview, followed by the usual valuable written report, recognises it.

A well-known psychologist once said to an equally well-known astrologer, " My patients tell me what is in their unconscious in the first few moments of a consultation " ; the astrologer's reply was, " And my clients come in and literally speak their maps." Hence it will be seen that " map " equals " unconscious " and that the opportunity for relieving what Jung has called " the cramp in the unconscious " is of the greatest benefit to the worried or nerve-ridden client and the greatest help to the astrologer in interpreting the symbolism of what he has calculated. A secret or an anxiety *confessed* becomes a conscious concealment instead of an unconscious one. It is then less likely to become a complex and will not become " an autonomous portion of the psyche which develops a peculiar fantasy-life of its own." If repressed, such fantasies take form and drive unintegrated natures to endless trouble. The

* " Psychic " is here used as meaning " of the psyche," which is the totality of the conscious and the unconscious, the Ego having a share in both.
† Quotations are from *Modern Man in Search of a Soul* by C. G. Jung and *The Secret of the Golden Flower* by Richard Wilhelm and C. G. Jung.

catharsis of full confession may prevent this. One way by which the psychologist seeks to " educate " and thus help to integrate a person is by getting him to set down his " inward pictures " of his dreams or fantasies, either in writing or in paintings. By doing this, the person externalises what is within his unconscious and is able to feel it as liberated and, by the help of the psychologist, it can be interpreted and understood. A completely new use of astrology is beginning through the discovery that, in such symbolic pictures, people portray unmistakably the difficulties shown in the natal chart, and in some cases even indicate the nature of their progressions and transits as the years go by. Further research in this fascinating field of inquiry should link the two studies together in mutual aid.

Under Jung's second heading of *explanation*, comes the astrologer's next aim, which should be giving to the client an *insight into himself*. Helpfully done, this can supply the driving force to carry him forward to self-reliance.

Under the heading of *education*, an astrologer can then try to lead his client first to recognise his weaknesses and strengthen or allow for them, and then to see where his opportunities for expansion (Jupiter) lie and where he should try to fulfil himself. If this is done in the light of progressions and transits forming for the next few years, much help can be given.

Lastly, the *transformation*. Here Jung states clearly that the consultant " must consistently try to meet his own therapeutic demands if he wishes to assure himself of a proper influence on his patient." His rule is " *Be* the man through whom you wish to influence others." He says, " Who can educate others while himself uneducated? " Further, " The medical diploma is no longer the crucial thing, but human quality instead." Substituting the word " astrological " for " medical," every astrologer who wishes to *use* astrology for the benefit of mankind, rather than merely *doing* astrology for the benefit of himself, must realise that it is his own " quality " which matters, and through which the " transformation " of the client must be effected.

Jung says, " Each of us carries his own life-form—an indeterminable form which cannot be superseded by any other." The astrologer knows that he can determine this fairly accurately if he is given the correct birth hour. Hence when the client complains of dissatisfaction with life and a feeling of frustration, the astrologer should know that it is his business to assess this " life-form," to try to restore the person to whatever is, *for him*, a rightness of being, and so give true meaning to his individual life.

Complexes and Conflicts

Having disclosed the difficulties in a map in the light of the awkward placings, the hindering aspects and the general disharmonies, the astrologer sees where these are leading a person. Already it has been noted that " complexes are psychic contents which are outside the control of the conscious mind." This is understood as the principle of any planet which, being in a certain sign, must work through the mode of that sign whether the person wills it to or not. The force and energy of Mars will mean an aggressive person who fights to get things done if that Mars is natally in

Aries, but, if in Pisces, his energy often fizzles out in a series of dissolutions and muddles. The *actions* correlative with this Mars spring from the depths of the unconscious. " Complexes always contain something like a conflict," " they are vulnerable points, skeletons in the cupboard." Here is the " difficult " astrological aspect which the astrologer seeks to define. " Something incompatible, unassimilated and conflicting exists, perhaps as an obstacle, but also as a stimulus to greater effort, and so perhaps as an opening to new possibilities of achievement. Complexes are therefore local or nodal points of psychic life which we would not wish to do without." Can the astrologer not see in this the meaning of the squares and oppositions in a chart ? and can he not thus see how to use the " explanation " part of his work so as to help the client to the stimulus rather than depress him by mere statement of unpleasant fact ?

Types of Humanity

Jung pays tribute to the astrological type-theory, saying that " to the astonishment of the enlightened, it remains intact today, and is even enjoying a new vogue." He says that the habitual reactions of a person determine not only his style of behaviour but the nature of his subjective experience and the kind of compensatory activity of the unconscious which we may expect to find. He then evolves his theory of the four " functions." The predominance of a " function " in a person leads him to seek out certain situations and avoid others and *therefore to have experiences* which are different from those of others, but occasionally he reacts in a way which reveals his specific weakness. In the struggle for existence and adaptation, everyone instinctively uses his most developed function, which thus becomes the criterion of his habitual reactions. Is this not the working of the predominant planets and signs in a chart ? The four functions of Jung are those of thinking, feeling, sensation and intuition. Many attempts have been made to correlate these precisely with the four elements of astrology, but, though those of the *thinking* type, who try to adapt themselves to the world through consideration and thought, are certainly those with Air-signs predominant, while others inveterately follow a policy dictated by *feeling*, which the astrologer recognises as " Water," his classification of " *sensation* " described as " perception through conscious sensory processes " and of *intuition* as " perception by way of unconscious contents and connections," do not so well fit " Earth " and " Fire." Other attempts have been made to fit his theories to those of astrology, such as the idea of the upper part of the map representing the conscious and the lower the unconscious, but such attempts are valueless and it is better to consider each system of type-description on its own merits and to allow each to help the other.

The Unconscious and the Collective Unconscious

Though depth psychology concerns itself with the personal unconscious in which lie memories, repressed material and emotions, it also includes those deeper levels which Jung calls the Collective Unconscious. Here lies that which may irrupt from the deepest part of the unconscious and also that part which never can be made conscious.

In these depths are also what Jung calls " The Archetypes " or the primordial images. With these, it is easy to find astrological correlatives. We understand the " superior function " as the strongest part of the map, the " inferior function " as that part less developed, the unconscious as the general planetary placing by sign, and the deeper levels of the unconscious as what is signified by the Water planets, signs and houses in a chart. Of these, the 12th is the deepest, the most hidden, the most indicative of that which lies submerged in the personality. This, in the old astrological phrase, may be the root of " our own undoing " if kept *too* hidden, too suppressed.

If we search for that which Saturn by its placing tends to deny, then we may find that the person depends on one of the " Archetypes " for his compensation. He will seek for the " wise old man " by consciously or unconsciously stressing his Sagittarian or Jupiterian qualities, for the " Great Mother " through the Moon and Cancer, for the " Father " through Leo and the Sun, for his " Animus " or " Anima " through Libra and Venus.

Acceptance

This doctrine of psychology is perhaps the most helpful of all aids to the astrologer in his dealing with a client. Jung says that the most important problems of life are all *fundamentally insoluble*. They can never be solved, but only *outgrown*. He says that people do this by *accepting* the problem and developing further *by means of it*. He says that a new thing grows, sometimes from within, sometimes from without, and that this seems " to flow out of the *stream of time*." This phrase is important to the astrologer, for it shows him that the psychologist has reached the same conclusion as himself, which is that only by the acceptance of the problem as it is, can a person find relief from it, hence the astrologer must show him that problem as a part of his present pattern in life, without which he could not be himself, and then that he must wait for nature's time-lag to elapse, so that he may " grow out of it." In other words, the astrologer must study his progressions and help him to swim with the cosmic tide as it flows and not dissipate his energies by battling against it. He has to learn " the art of letting things happen." If this can be achieved, then the complexes will not turn into conflicts, there will not be the splitting-off of these contents of the unconscious, but wholeness will be achieved through what should be the aim of both psychologist and astrologer—the integration of the whole psyche.

The result of this is a shifting of the viewpoint, a beginning of a detached attitude, from which the person becomes *the observer of the doer*. The acceptance of the pattern of life, as shown by the astrologer in his attempt to interpret the progressions faithfully as the years go by, is perhaps one of the greatest lessons which can be learnt and one most likely to produce true understanding of life.

CHAPTER 19

THE DUTY OF AN ASTROLOGER

To Astrology

To add to all existing proof of actual correlation of cosmic action with human life, by all means in his power.

To avoid woolly-thinking and wishful-thinking at all costs.

To interpret the significance of what he has charted in the light of the *actual nature of planetary action*, all other considerations being secondary.

To avoid all attempt to " score hits " or to indulge in guess-work ; and to interpret with reserve rather than to go too far.

To check and re-check his work, getting all possible corroboration from another astrologer for publicised charts.

To fit himself for serious work as soon as possible, since the responsibility undertaken, and the growing ability to compare many charts, are the two finest ways of adding to his store of knowledge, from which he can give his experience in his own subsequent writing and lecturing.

To His Clients

(The word " clients " is deliberately used in order to overcome earlier notions that " one should not take money for astrological work," The old adage that " A workman is worthy of his hire " is applicable to the astrologer, as to all other workers. The public, accustomed to the facile Sun-sign interpretations of the popular press, has no idea of the hours of work which go to the preparation of a full astrological reading with progressions for some years ahead, and is only recently realising that a suitable price must be charged for this.)

His duty then is :—

To work in the spirit engendered in such professions as the medical and legal, so that he may help his own profession to attain to the status of these, thus bringing to the client that confidence in him which should be given to any professional man.

To keep the confidences of the client absolutely undisclosed, as are those given in connection with other professions. (This does not mean that interesting or informative charts should never be shown or quoted, but that permission must always be obtained first.)

To refuse completely to be drawn into foretelling anything which may be inadvisable to discuss. (One constant refusal must be to state when a death may occur. A non-astrological client is often very annoyed with such a refusal, since he thinks that a " horoscope," which " begins " at birth, must " end " at death. The expression " your " horoscope has been used so freely that he does not realise that it is not " his " at all, but is a snapshot of a fleeting moment of time, with the developments of which his life has continued to correlate. The chart shows only the trends and predispositions which are likely to produce events. Death may be the result of application of the principle of suddenness (Uranus) or of hurtful force which the body cannot stand (Mars), or it may be a gentle dissolution (Neptune) or a happy release (Jupiter). The working of such principles *may* result in death under certain physical circumstances, but at NO time is this certain.)

To avoid all sensationalism and to endeavour to help the client through all difficulties by a constructive interpretation rather than a merely factual one.

To give a time when the written report may be expected and to endeavour to stick to it, advising the client if delay is unavoidable.

To Himself

To force himself to be thorough and accurate and conservative in all work, so that he builds up a reputation for trustworthiness rather than cleverness.

To refuse to undertake work when already over-booked. *Good work cannot by done in a hurry.*

To work and practise unceasingly, since there is no other way by which experience can be gained.

THE MODERN SITUATION WITH REGARD TO BOOKS

IT is essential that the student should absorb as much astrological thought as possible in addition to text-book information. He can do this by continual reading but also in other ways.

In London he can attend the lectures of the principal Astrological Societies, where he will be able to meet others for friendly discussion. Membership of the Astrological Lodge (of the Theosophical Society) gives access to its library which contains not only books, but bound copies of lectures and of volumes of astrological periodicals. Membership also covers subscription to the Society's journal, *Astrology*. This is also available to non-members and subscription enquiries should be addressed to Mr. R. C. Davison, 70 Gravel Hill, Croydon, Surrey, CRO 5BE. The Astrological Association also issues a quarterly publication, the *Astrological Journal*, and here too subscriptions can be arranged independently of membership. Write to Mrs. V. Milne, 41 Liberton Brae, Edinburgh EH16 6AG.

Postal Tuition is available from qualified teachers and readers are referred to the advertisement at the foot of page 315.

BOOK LIST

At first, the student should not confuse himself with too many books. Once he has learnt the phraseology and the system of work, he should then widen his knowledge as much as possible.

An Astrological **Catalogue** can be obtained on request from **L. N. Fowler & Co. Ltd.,**, who supply books by mail order to all parts of the world. Address: 1201/3 High Road, Chadwell Heath, Romford, Essex RM6 4DH.

Among the many excellent books currently in print, the following may be recommended:

The works of Alan Leo.
The works of Charles Carter.
ALL the latter should be read in due course, but especially, in the order given:
The Principles of Astrology.
Astrological Aspects.
Some Principles of Horoscopic Delineation.
Works of other authors:

On Astrology in General:
From Pioneer to Poet (i.e. Aries to Pisces) by Isabelle Pagan.
Message of the Stars by Max Heindel.
The Astrologer's Handbook Series Nos. 1 to 4 (*Astrologer's Astronomical Handbook; How to Read the Ephemeris; How to Cast a Natal Chart; Planets and Human Behaviour*) by Jeff Mayo.
Teach Yourself Astrology by Jeff Mayo.
Astro-Kinetics, 3 vols. (*The Influence of the Houses; The Influence of the Planets; Aspects and their Meanings*) by Edward Whitman.
The Astrologer's Handbook by Frances Sakoian and Louis S. Acker.
Everyman's Astrology by Lyndoe.

On Methods of Prognostication:
The Technique of Prediction by R. C. Davison.
The Progressed Horoscope Simplified by Leigh Hope Milburn.
Planets in Transit by Robert Hand.

On Special Subjects of Astrology:

These are listed separately in their sections in Chapter 15 since they are essential for these studies. However, the reader's attention is also drawn to the following techniques and the books appropriate to them:

Cosmobiology. This is based on the principle of Midpoint relationships. Certain aspects, House references and the rulership factor are not taken into account. Emphasis is exclusively on the potential revealed by the various planetary pictures, an approach which may justly claim to be dynamic. For this branch of study the key book is *The Combination of Stellar Influences* by Reinhold Ebertin.

Synastry: being the comparison of horoscopes with a view to assessing their interaction. The Astrological Association booklet of the same name is a useful introduction. Readings for its detailed application are provided in *Planets in Composite* by Robert Hand and in *The Astrology of Human Relationships* by Sakoian and Acker.

Harmonics: very briefly, the study of cosmic rhythms and sub-rhythms in the context of Astrology. Although it has come to the fore relatively recently, John Addey's pioneering work, *Harmonics in Astrology* was the fruit of twenty years' research.

No implication of less worth is inferred for the omission of any book from the above list, which is necessarily short.

———————

Addendum to Chapter 16: **The House Division Question**. Readers are also referred to R. W. Holden's *The Elements of House Division* in which the problems connected with the subject are very thoroughly examined.

STANDARD TIMES

THE information given below is adapted from the *Nautical Almanac* of 1955 by permission of H.M. Stationery Office.

The dates of adoption of Zone or Standard time by the different countries varies considerably.

In case of doubt as to whether a birth-date was before or after such date of adoption, reference can be made to *Whitaker's Almanack* of the year in question, or inquiry can be made by letter to the overseas representative of the country.

Addresses of Embassies and Legations in England are given in *Whitaker's Almanack* and in the *London Telephone Directory*.

Example of Conversion of Zone Time to G.M.T.

Eastern Standard Time (E.S.T.) is −5.

Birth-time and date	10 p.m.	1st April
By addition	+ 5 hours	
G.M.T. ; time and date	3 a.m.	2nd April

	h m s		h m s
Aden	+03	Ascension Island	−00 57
Admiralty Islands	+10	Australian Capital Territory	+10
Alabama,* U.S.A.	−06	Austral Islands	−10
Alaska, south-east coast to		Austria	+01
and including Cross Sound,		Azores*	−02
Douglas, Juneau, Kimsham			
Cove and Petersburg ..	−08	Bahamas	−05
coast northward of Cross		Bahrein	+04
Sound to and including		Balearic Islands‡	+01
Prince William Sound ..	−09	Bali	+07 30
Anchorage, Fairbanks, Se-		Bangka	+07
ward, Valdez	−10	Barbados	−04
west coast (Nome) ..	−11	Basutoland	+02
Albania*	+01	Bechuanaland	+02
Alberta*	−07	Belgian Congo, western part,	
Aleutian Islands	−11	including Coquilhatville and	
Algeria..	00	Leopoldville	+01
Alor	+08	eastern part, including cos-	
Amirante Islands	+04	termansville, Elisabethville,	
Andaman Islands	+06 30	Lusambo, Stanleyville ..	+02
Anglo-Egyptian Sudan ..	+02	Belgium	+01
Angola (Port. W. Africa) ..	+01	Belitong	+07
Annobon Islands†	+01	Bermuda*	−04
Argentina‡	−03	Bolivia..	−04
Arkansas,* U.S.A.	−06	Borneo, Indonesian	+07 30
Arizona,*† U.S.A.	−07	North	+08
Aru Islands	+09	Brazil (Central)*	−04

* Summer time is kept in these countries.
† Standard time differs from this time. The time given is that in **normal use.**
‡ This applies to the greater portion of the state.

	h m s
Brazil (Eastern)*‖	−03
(Western)*	−05
British Columbia*	−08
British Guiana	−03 45
British Honduras†	−06
British New Guinea	+10
British North Borneo	+08
British Somaliland	+03
Broken Hill Area, N.S.W.	+09 30
Bulgaria	+02
Burma	+06 30
California,* U.S.A.	−08
Cameroons	+01
Canada	
Alberta*	−07
British Columbia*	−08
Labrador*	−03 30
Manitoba*	−06
New Brunswick*	−04
Newfoundland*	−03 30
Northwest Territories*	
(east of long. W. 68°)	−04
(W. 68° to W. 85°)	−05
(W. 85° to W. 102°)	−06
(W. 102° to W. 120°)	−07
(west of long. W. 120°)	−08
Nova Scotia*	−04
Ontario*	
(east of long. W. 90°)	−05
(west of long. W. 90°)	−06
Quebec*	
(east of long. W. 68°)	−04
(west of long. W. 68°)	−05
Saskatchewan*	
(except south-east)	−07
(south-eastern part)	−06
Yukon	−09
Canary Islands‡	00
Cape Verde Islands	−02
Caroline Islands	
(east of long E. 160°)	+12
(west of long. E. 160°)	+10
(Truk, Ponape)	+11
Cayman Islands	−05
Celebes	+08

	h m s
Ceylon	+05 30
Chagos Archipelago	+05
Channel Islands*	00
Chatham Islands‡	+12 15
Chile	−04
China*¶	+08
Christmas Island	
(Indian Ocean)	+07
(Pacific Ocean)	−10
Cocos Islands	+06 30
Colombia	−05
Colorado,* U.S.A.	−07
Comoro Islands	+03
Connecticut,* U.S.A.	−05
Cook Islands	
(except Niue)	−10 30
Corsica‡	+01
Costa Rica	−06
Crete	+02
Cuba	−05
Curaçao Island	−04 30
Cyprus	+02
Cyrenaica‡	+02
Czechoslovakia*	+01
Dahomey	00
Delaware,* U.S.A.	−05
Denmark	+01
Dominican Republic†	−05
Dutch Guiana (Surinam)	−03 30
Dutch New Guinea	+09 30
Ecuador	−05
Egypt	+02
Ellice Islands	+12
Eritrea	+03
Estonia	+03
Faeroes, The	00
Falkland Islands	−04
Fanning Island	−10
Fernando Noronha*	−02
Fernando Po‡	+01
Fiji	+12
Finland	+02
Flores	+08
Florida,*§ U.S.A.	−05

* Summer time is kept in these countries.
† Winter time is kept in these countries.
‡ Standard time differs from this time. The time given is that in normal use.
§ This applies to the greater portion of the state.
‖ Including all the coast.
¶ All the coast (except Hainan Island, Pakhoi and the Yangtze Kiang from Chungking to Shasze, which keep +07h), including Wuchau on the West River. Some areas may keep summer time.

	h m s		h m s
Formosa*	+08	Iraq	+03
France‡	+01	Ireland, Northern*	00
French Equatorial Africa	+01	Irish Republic*	00
French Guiana	−04	Israel*	+02
French Guinea	00	Italy	+01
French Somaliland	+03	Ivory Coast	00
Friendly Islands*	+12 20		
		Jamaica	−05
Gambia	00	Japan	+09
Georgia,* U.S.A.	−05	Jappen Islands	+09
Germany	+01	Java	+07 30
Gibraltar‡	+01	Johnston Island	−11
Gilbert and Ellice Is...	+12	Jordan	+02
Gold Coast Colony†	00		
Great Britain*	00	Kamchatka Peninsula	+12
Greece	+02	Kansas,*§ U.S.A.	−06
Greenland		Kei Islands	+09
Scoresby Sound	−02	Kentucky,*§ U.S.A.	−06
Angmagssalik, West Coast		Kenya	+03
(except Thule)	−03	Korea	+09
Thule	−04	Kuril Islands	+09
Guadeloupe	−04	Kuweit	+03
Guam	+10		
Guatemala	−06	Labrador*	−03 30
Guiana, British	−03 45	Labuan	+08
Guiana, Dutch	−03 30	Laccadive Islands	+05 30
Guiana, French	−04	Ladrones Islands	+10
Guinea, French	00	Latvia	+03
Guinea, Portuguese	−01	Lebanon	+02
Guinea, Spanish‡	+01	Leeward Islands	−04
		Liberia..	−00 44
Hainan Island, China	+07	Libya (Cyrenaica)‡	+02
Haiti	−05	(Tripolitania)*	+01
Hawaiian Islands (except Mid-		Lichtenstein	+01
way Island)	−10	Lithuania	+03
Holland	+01	Lomblem	+08
Honduras†	−06	Lombok	+07 30
Honduras, British†	−06	Lord Howe Island	+10
Hong Kong*	+08	Louisiana,* U.S.A.	−06
Hungary*	+01	Low Archipelago	−10
		Lower California	
Iceland*	−01	(see Mexico)	
Idaho,*1 U.S.A.	−07	Luxembourg‡	+01
Illinois,* U.S.A.	−06		
India	+05 30	Macao*	+08
Indiana,* U.S.A.	−06	Madagascar	+03
Indo-China	+08	Madeira*	−01
Iowa,* U.S.A.	−06	Madura	+07 30
Iran (Persia)	+03 30	Maine,* U.S.A.	−05

* Summer time is kept in these countries.
† Winter time is kept in these countries.
‡ Standard time differs from this time. The time given is that in normal use.
§ This applies to the greater portion of the state.

		h m s			h m s
Malaya, Federation of	..	+07 30	New York,* U.S.A. ..	..	−05
Maldive Islands	.. ..	+04 54	New Zealand	.. ..	+12
Malta	..	+01	Nicaragua*	..	−06
Manchuria	..	+09	Nicobar Islands	..	+06 30
Manitoba* ..	..	−06	Nigeria ..	..	+01
Marianas Islands	..	+10	Niue Island ..	..	−11 20
Marquesas Islands	..	−10	Norfolk Island	..	+11 30
Marshall Islands	..	+12	North Borneo ..	..	+08
Martinique ..	..	−04	North Carolina * U.S.A.	..	−05
Maryland,* U.S.A. ..	..	−05	North Dakota *§ U.S.A.	..	−06
Massachusetts,* U.S.A.		−05	Northern Ireland* ..	..	00
Mauritania		00	Northern Rhodesia ..	..	+02
Mauritius		+04	Northern Territory, Australia		+09 30
Mexico†	..	−06	Northwest Territories*		
Michigan,*§ U.S.A. ..	..	−05	(east of long. W. 68°)	..	−04
Midway Islands	..	−11	(W. 68° to W. 85°)	..	−05
Minnesota,* U.S.A. ..	..	−06	(W. 85° to W. 102°)	..	−06
Miquelon ..	..	−04	(W. 102° to W. 120°)	..	+07
Mississippi,* U.S.A. ..	..	−06	(west of long. W. 120°)	..	−08
Missouri,* U.S.A. ..	..	−06	Norway	..	+01
Molucca Islands	..	+08 30	Nova Scotia* ..	..	−04
Monaco‡ ..	..	+01	Novaya Zemlya	..	+05
Montana,* U.S.A. ..	..	−07	Nyasaland ..	..	+02
Morocco, French* ..	..	00			
Morocco, Spanish‡ ..	..	+01	Ocean Island	..	+11
Mozambique (Port E. Africa)		+02	Ohio,* U.S.A. ..	..	−05
Mukalla (Hadhramaut)	..	+03	Oklahoma,* U.S.A. ..	..	−06
			'Oman (Masira, Muscat,		
Nanyo-Gunto	..	+09	Salala)	..	+04
Natuna Islands	..	+07	Ontario*		
Nauru	..	+11 30	(east of long. W. 90°)	..	−05
Nayarit, Mexico	..	−07	(west of long. W. 90°)	..	−06
Nebraska,* U.S.A.			Oregon,* U.S.A. ..	..	−08
(eastern part)	..	−06			
(western part)	..	−07	Pakhoi, China	..	+07
Nevada,* U.S.A. ..	..	−08	Pakistan		
New Brunswick*	..	−04	(East)	..	+06
New Caledonia	..	+11	(West)	..	+04 30
Newfoundland* ..	..	−03 30	Panama Canal Zone ..	..	−05
New Guinea, British	..	+10	Panama (Republic of)	..	−05
New Guinea, Dutch	..	+09 30	Papua	..	+10
New Hampshire,* U.S.A.	..	−05	Paraguay	..	−04
New Hebrides ..	..	+11	Pennsylvania,* U.S.A.	..	−05
New Jersey,* U.S.A.	..	−05	Peru	..	−05
New Mexico,* U.S.A.	..	−07	Pescadores Islands ..	..	+09
New South Wales¶ ..	..	+10	Philippine Republic	..	+08

* Summer time is kept in these countries
‡ Standard time differs from this time. The time given is that in normal use
§ This applies to the greater portion of the state.
† Except the states of Sonora, Sinaloa, Nayarit and the Southern District of Lower California which keep −07h; and the Northern District of Lower California which keeps −08h in winter and −07h in summer.
¶ Except Broken Hill Area, which uses the time +09h 30m.

	h m s		h m s
Poland*	+01	Seychelles	+04
Ponape	+11	Siam (Thailand)	+07
Portugal*	00	Siberia	
Portuguese East Africa		(west of long. E. 67° 30')	+05
(Mozambique)	+02	(E. 67° 30' to E. 82° 30')	+06
Portuguese Guinea	−01	(E. 82° 30' to E. 97° 30')	+07
Portuguese India	+05 30	(E. 97° 30' to E. 112° 30')	+08
Portuguese West Africa		(E. 112° 30' to E. 127° 30')	+09
(Angola)	+01	(E. 127° 30' to E. 142° 30')	+10
Prince Edward Island* ..	−04	(E. 142° 30' to E. 157° 30')	+11
Principe	00	(E. 157° 30' to E. 172° 30')	+12
Puerto Rico	−04	(east of long. E. 172° 30')	+13
		Sicily	+01
Quebec*		Sierra Leone	00
(east of long. W. 68°) ..	−04	Sinaloa, Mexico	−07
(west of long. W. 68°) ..	−05	Singapore	+07 30
Queensland	+10	Society Islands	−10
		Socotra	+03
Rarotonga	−10 30	Solomon Islands	+11
Réunion	+04	Somalia	+03
Rhio Islands	+07	Somaliland, British	+03
Rhode Island,* U.S.A. ..	−05	Somaliland, French	+03
Rhodesia	+02	Sonora, Mexico	−07
Rio de Oro†	00	South Africa (Union of) ..	+02
Romania	+02	South Australia	+09 30
Russia		South Carolina,* U.S.A. ..	−05
(west of long. E. 40°) ..	+03	South Dakota,* U.S.A.	
(E. 40° to E. 52° 30') ..	+04	(eastern part)	−06
(east of long. E. 52° 30') ..	+05	(western part)	−07
		South Georgia	−01 30
St. Helena	00	Southern Rhodesia	+02
St. Pierre	−04	Spain†	+01
Sakhalin		Spanish Guinea†	+01
(south of lat. N. 50°) ..	+09	Spitzbergen	+01
(north of lat. N. 50°) ..	+10	Sudan, Anglo-Egyptian ..	+02
Salvador	−06	Sumatra, northern	+06 30
Samoa	−11	southern	+07
Santa Cruz Islands	+11	Sumba	+08
São Thomé	00	Sumbawa	+08
Sarawak	+08	Surinam	−03 30
Sardinia	+01	Swaziland	+02
Saskatchewan*		Sweden	+01
(south-eastern part) ..	−06	Switzerland	+01
(except south-eastern part)	−07	Syria	+02
Savage Island..	−11 20		
Savu	+08	Tanganyika Territory ..	+03
Schouten Islands	+09	Tangier*	00
Scoresby Sound, Greenland ..	−02	Tanimbar Islands	+09
Senegal	00	Tasmania	+10

* Summer time is kept in these countries.
† Standard time differs from this time. The time given is that in normal use.

		h	m	s
Tennessee,*† U.S.A.	..	−06		
Texas,*† U.S.A.	.. ..	−06		
Thailand (Siam)	.. ..	+07		
Timor	.. .. ..	+08		
Tobago	.. .. ..	−04		
Togoland	.. .. ..	00		
Tonga Islands	.. ..	+12	20	
Transjordan (Jordan)	..	+02		
Trinidad	.. .. ..	−04		
Trinidad Islands*				
(S. Atlantic)	.. ..	−02		
Tripolitania* ..	.. ..	+01		
Trucial 'Oman (Sharja)	..	+04		
Truk ..	.. ..	+11		
Tuamotu Archipelago	..	−10		
Tunisia	.. ..	+01		
Turkey*	.. ..	+02		
Uganda	.. ..	+03		
Union of South Africa	..	+02		
Uruguay (see Russia and				
Siberia)				
Utah,*† U.S.A.	.. ..	−07		
Venezuela	.. ..	−04	30	
Vermont,* U.S.A.	.. .	−05		
Victoria	.. ..	+10		
Viet Nam	.. ..	+08		
Virginia,* U.S.A.	.. ..	−05		
Washington, D.C.,* U.S.A.	..	−05		
Washington,* U.S.A.	..	−08		
West Virginia,* U.S.A.	..	−05		
Western Australia	..	+08		
Wetta	.. ..	+08	30	
Windward Islands‡	..	−04		

		h	m	s
Wisconsin,* U.S.A.	..	−06		
Wrangell Island	.. ..	+13		
Wyoming,* U.S.A.	.. ..	−07		
Yugoslavia	.. .. ..	+01		
Yukon	.. .. ..	−09		
Zanzibar	.. .. ..	+03		

DATE OR CALENDAR LINE

The date or Calendar Line is a modification of the line of the 180th meridian, which is drawn so as to include islands of any one group, etc., on the same side of the line.

It may be traced by joining up the following positions :

Lat. S. 60° 00′	Long. 180° 00′
Lat. 51° 00′	Long. 180° 00′
Lat. 45° 00′	Long. W. 172° 30′
Lat. 15° 00′	Long. W. 172° 30′
Lat. S. 5° 00′	Long. 180° 00′
Lat. N. 48° 00′	Long. 180° 00′
Lat. 53° 00′	Long. E. 170° 00′
Lat. N. 65° 30′	Long. W. 169° 00′

Thence through the centre of the Diomede Islands to :—

Lat. N. 68° 00′   Long. W. 169° 00′

Thence passing east of Herald Island to :—

Lat. N. 75° 00′   Long. 180° 00′

When crossing this line on a westerly course, the date must be advanced one day ; when crossing it on an easterly course, the date must be put back one day.

* Summer time is kept in these countries.
† This applies to the greater portion of the state.
‡ Grenada keeps summer time.

APPENDIX 3

ACCELERATION TABLE*

Example.—Acceleration on 4 hours 18 minutes = 0ᵐ 42·4ˢ

m.	0 h.	1 h.	2 h.	3 h.	4 h.	5 h.	6 h.	7 h.	8 h.	9 h.	10 h.	11 h.
	m. s.	m. s.	m. s.	m. s.	m. s.	m. s.	m. s.	m. s.	m. s.	m. s.	m. s.	m. s.
0	0 0·0	0 9·9	0 19·7	0 29·6	0 39·4	0 49·3	0 59·1	1 9·0	1 18·9	1 28·7	1 38·6	1 48·4
4	0 0·7	0 10·5	0 20·4	0 30·2	0 40·1	0 49·9	0 59·8	1 9·7	1 19·5	1 29·4	1 39·2	1 49·1
8	0 1·3	0 11·2	0 21·0	0 30·9	0 40·7	0 50·6	1 0·5	1 10·3	1 20·2	1 30·0	1 39·9	1 49·7
12	0 2·0	0 11·8	0 21·7	0 31·5	0 41·4	0 51·3	1 1·1	1 11·0	1 20·8	1 30·7	1 40·5	1 50·4
16	0 2·6	0 12·5	0 22·3	0 32·2	0 42·1	0 51·9	1 1·8	1 11·6	1 21·5	1 31·3	1 41·2	1 51·0
20	0 3·3	0 13·1	0 23·0	0 32·9	0 42·7	0 52·6	1 2·4	1 12·3	1 22·1	1 32·0	1 41·9	1 51·7
24	0 3·9	0 13·8	0 23·7	0 33·5	0 43·4	0 53·2	1 3·1	1 12·9	1 22·8	1 32·7	1 42·5	1 52·4
28	0 4·6	0 14·5	0 24·3	0 34·2	0 44·0	0 53·9	1 3·7	1 13·6	1 23·5	1 33·3	1 43·2	1 53·0
32	0 5·3	0 15·1	0 25·0	0 34·8	0 44·7	0 54·5	1 4·4	1 14·3	1 24·1	1 34·0	1 43·8	1 53·7
36	0 5·9	0 15·8	0 25·6	0 35·5	0 45·3	0 55·2	1 5·1	1 14·9	1 24·8	1 34·6	1 44·5	1 54·3
40	0 6·6	0 16·4	0 26·3	0 36·1	0 46·0	0 55·9	1 5·7	1 15·6	1 25·4	1 35·3	1 45·1	1 55·0
44	0 7·2	0 17·1	0 26·9	0 36·8	0 46·7	0 56·5	1 6·4	1 16·2	1 26·1	1 35·9	1 45·8	1 55·6
48	0 7·9	0 17·7	0 27·6	0 37·5	0 47·3	0 57·2	1 7·0	1 16·9	1 26·7	1 36·6	1 46·4	1 56·3
52	0 8·5	0 18·4	0 28·3	0 38·1	0 48·0	0 57·8	1 7·7	1 17·6	1 27·4	1 37·3	1 47·1	1 57·0
56	0 9·2	0 19·1	0 28·9	0 38·8	0 48·6	0 58·5	1 8·3	1 18·2	1 28·1	1 37·9	1 47·8	1 57·6

m.	12 h.	13 h.	14 h.	15 h.	16 h.	17 h.	18 h.	19 h.	20 h.	21 h.	22 h.	23 h.
	m. s.	m. s.	m. s.	m. s.	m. s.	m. s.	m. s.	m. s.	m. s.	m. s.	m. s.	m. s.
0	1 58·3	2 8·1	2 18·0	2 27·8	2 37·7	2 47·6	2 57·4	3 7·3	3 17·1	3 27·0	3 36·8	3 46·7
4	1 58·9	2 8·8	2 18·6	2 28·5	2 38·4	2 48·2	2 58·1	3 7·9	3 17·8	3 27·6	3 37·5	3 47·4
8	1 59·6	2 9·4	2 19·3	2 29·2	2 39·0	2 48·9	2 58·7	3 8·6	3 18·4	3 28·3	3 38·2	3 48·0
12	2 0·2	2 10·1	2 20·0	2 29·8	2 39·7	2 49·5	2 59·4	3 9·2	3 19·1	3 28·9	3 38·8	3 48·7
16	2 0·9	2 10·8	2 20·6	2 30·5	2 40·3	2 50·2	3 0·0	3 9·9	3 19·8	3 29·6	3 39·5	3 49·3
20	2 1·6	2 11·4	2 21·3	2 31·1	2 41·0	2 50·8	3 0·7	3 10·6	3 20·4	3 30·3	3 40·1	3 50·0
24	2 2·2	2 12·1	2 21·9	2 31·8	2 41·6	2 51·5	3 1·4	3 11·2	3 21·1	3 30·9	3 40·8	3 50·6
28	2 2·9	2 12·7	2 22·6	2 32·4	2 42·3	2 52·2	3 2·0	3 11·9	3 21·7	3 31·6	3 41·4	3 51·3
32	2 3·5	2 13·4	2 23·2	2 33·1	2 43·0	2 52·8	3 2·7	3 12·5	3 22·4	3 32·2	3 42·1	3 52·0
36	2 4·2	2 14·0	2 23·9	2 33·8	2 43·6	2 53·5	3 3·3	3 13·2	3 23·0	3 32·9	3 42·8	3 52·6
40	2 4·8	2 14·7	2 24·6	2 34·4	2 44·3	2 54·1	3 4·0	3 13·8	3 23·7	3 33·6	3 43·4	3 53·3
44	2 5·5	2 15·4	2 25·2	2 35·1	2 44·9	2 54·8	3 4·6	3 14·5	3 24·4	3 34·2	3 44·1	3 53·9
48	2 6·2	2 16·0	2 25·9	2 35·7	2 45·6	2 55·4	3 5·3	3 15·2	3 25·0	2 34·9	3 44·7	3 54·6
52	2 6·8	2 16·7	2 26·5	2 36·4	2 46·2	2 56·1	3 6·0	3 15·8	3 25·7	3 35·5	3 45·4	3 55·2
56	2 7·5	2 17·3	2 27·2	2 37·0	2 46·9	2 56·8	3 6·6	3 16·5	3 26·3	3 36·2	3 46·0	3 55·9

* Adapted from Brown's Nautical Almanac, by permission.

APPENDIX 4

TABLE FOR CONVERTING DEGREES AND MINUTES OF LONGITUDE INTO LONGITUDE EQUIVALENT IN TIME*

Example.—Rome, Long. 12° 29′ E

Required Longitude Equivalent in Time

$$12° \quad = \quad 0^h\ 48^m$$
$$29^m \quad = \quad 1^m\ 56^s$$
$$12°\ 29^m \quad = \quad 0^h\ 49^m\ 56^s$$

Round off to 0^h 50^m

H M	°	H M	°	H M	°	H M	°	H M	°	H M	°
M S	′	M S	′	M S	′	M S	′	M S	′	M S	′
4	1	2 4	31	4 4	61	6 4	91	8 4	121	10 4	151
8	2	2 8	32	4 8	62	6 8	92	8 8	122	10 8	152
12	3	2 12	33	4 12	63	6 12	93	8 12	123	10 12	153
16	4	2 16	34	4 16	64	6 16	94	8 16	124	10 16	154
0 20	5	2 20	35	4 20	65	6 20	95	8 20	125	10 20	155
24	6	2 24	36	4 24	66	6 24	96	8 24	126	10 24	156
28	7	2 28	37	4 28	67	6 28	97	8 28	127	10 28	157
32	8	2 32	38	4 32	68	6 32	98	8 32	128	10 32	158
36	9	2 36	39	4 36	69	6 36	99	8 36	129	10 36	159
0 40	10	2 40	40	4 40	70	6 40	100	8 40	130	10 40	160
44	11	2 44	41	4 44	71	6 44	101	8 44	131	10 44	161
48	12	2 48	42	4 48	72	6 48	102	8 48	132	10 48	162
52	13	2 52	43	4 52	73	6 52	103	8 52	133	10 52	163
56	14	2 56	44	4 56	74	6 56	104	8 56	134	10 56	164
1 0	15	3 0	45	5 0	75	7 0	105	9 0	135	11 0	165
1 4	16	3 4	46	5 4	76	7 4	106	9 4	136	11 4	166
1 8	17	3 8	47	5 8	77	7 8	107	9 8	137	11 8	167
1 12	18	3 12	48	5 12	78	7 12	108	9 12	138	11 12	168
1 16	19	3 16	49	5 16	79	7 16	109	9 16	139	11 16	169
1 20	20	3 20	50	5 20	80	7 20	110	9 20	140	11 20	170
1 24	21	3 24	51	5 24	81	7 24	111	9 24	141	11 24	171
1 28	22	3 28	52	5 28	82	7 28	112	9 28	142	11 28	172
1 32	23	3 32	53	5 32	83	7 32	113	9 32	143	11 32	173
1 36	24	3 36	54	5 36	84	7 36	114	9 36	144	11 36	174
1 40	25	3 40	55	5 40	85	7 40	115	9 40	145	11 40	175
1 44	26	3 44	56	5 44	86	7 44	116	9 44	146	11 44	176
1 48	27	3 48	57	5 48	87	7 48	117	9 48	147	11 48	177
1 52	28	3 52	58	5 52	88	7 52	118	9 52	148	11 52	178
1 56	29	3 56	59	5 56	89	7 56	119	9 56	149	11 56	179
2 0	30	4 0	60	6 0	90	8 0	120	10 0	150	12 0	180

* Adapted from Brown's Nautical Almanac, by permission.

REQUIREMENTS FOR ASTROLOGICAL WORK

Designed by

MARGARET E. HONE

Chart-Forms as examples in Chapter 11:—

With column for calculation by the " Direct Method "

No. 1. The " Ecliptic " Chart

No. 2. The " Houses " Chart

26p per dozen
£2·16 per 100

No. 3. The " Progressions " Chart. (Double page)

26p per dozen
£2·16 per dozen

Reference Card for finding noon-date 9½ × 11 in.

30p each

Enlarged Logarithm Cards—9½ × 12 in.

20p each

Calculation Forms—as examples in Chapter 11

Form A. Summarised instructions for calculation of Zodiacal positions of the planets for given time with spaces to enter working for a chart

26p per dozen

Form B. Summarised instructions for calculation for Local Sidereal Time for given time in order to obtain Ascendant and Midheaven with spaces to enter working for a chart

26p per dozen

Postage is extra on all the above items

COURSES OF TUITION AND YEARLY EXAMINATIONS FOR THE DIPLOMA
for
THE MAYO SCHOOL OF ASTROLOGY

These are conducted postally for External Students in England and in all countries abroad. For Prospectus of the Margaret Hone Course, write to:–

The Principal, The Mayo School of Astrology.   Dept B.

c/o L. N. Fowler & Co. Ltd., 1201/3 High Road, Chadwell Heath, Romford, Essex RM6 4DH

This house can also supply all requirements listed above; also all Ephemerides and Tables of Houses mentioned in this book. (See Jacket)

INDEX